THE UNBELIEVABLE

# GWENPOOL

## BELIEVE IT

GWENPOOL, THE UNBELIEVABLE VOL. 1: BELIEVE IT. Contains material originally published in magazine form as GWENPOOL, THE UNBELIEVABLE #0-4. First printing 2016. ISBN# 978-1-302-90176-9. Published by MARVEL WORLDWIDE, INC., a subsidiary of MARVEL ENTERTAINMENT, LLC. OFFICE OF PUBLICATION: 135 West 50th Street, New York, NY 10020. Copyright © 2016 MARVEL No similarity between any of the names, characters, persons, and/or institutions in this magazine with those of any living or dead person or institution is intended, and any such similarity which may exist is purely coincidental. **Printed in the U.S.A.** ALAN FINE, President, Marvel Entertainment; DAN BUCKLEY, President, TV, Publishing & Brand Management; JOE QUESADA, Chief Creative Officer; TOM BREVOORT, SVP of Publishing; DAVID BOGART, SVP of Business Affairs & Operations, Publishing & Partnership; C.B. CEBULSKI, VP of Brand Management & Development, Asia; DAVID GABRIEL, SVP of Sales & Marketing, Publishing; JEFF YOUNGQUIST, VP of Production & Special Projects; DAN CARR, Executive Director of Publishing Technology; ALEX MORALES, Director of Publishing Operations; SUSAN CRESPI, Production Manager; STAN LEE, Chairman Emeritus. For information regarding advertising in Marvel Comics or on Marvel.com, please contact Vit DeBellis, Integrated Sales Manager, at vdebellis@marvel.com. For Marvel subscription inquiries, please call 888-511-5480. **Manufactured between 9/16/2016 and 10/24/2016 by LSC COMMUNICATIONS INC., SALEM, VA, USA.**

10 9 8 7 6 5 4 3 2 1

# THE UNBELIEVABLE GWENPOOL
## BELIEVE IT

WRITER
CHRIS HASTINGS

*THE UNBELIEVABLE GWENPOOL #0*
ARTIST: DANILO BEYRUTH
COLOR ARTIST: TAMRA BONVILLAIN
LETTERER: VC's TRAVIS LANHAM
COVER ART: DANILO BEYRUTH & TAMRA BONVILLAIN

*GWENPOOL SPECIAL #1 & THE UNBELIEVABLE GWENPOOL #1-4*
ARTIST: GURIHIRU
PROLOGUE ART: DANILO BEYRUTH & TRAVIS BONVILLAIN
LETTERER: VC's CLAYTON COWLES
COVER ART: KRIS ANKA (SPECIAL #1), GURIHIRU (#1)
& STACEY LEE (#2-4)

ASSISTANT EDITOR: HEATHER ANTOS
EDITOR: JORDAN D. WHITE

COLLECTION EDITOR: JENNIFER GRÜNWALD
ASSOCIATE MANAGING EDITOR: KATERI WOODY
ASSOCIATE EDITOR: SARAH BRUNSTAD
EDITOR, SPECIAL PROJECTS: MARK D. BEAZLEY
VP PRODUCTION & SPECIAL PROJECTS: JEFF YOUNGQUIST
SVP PRINT, SALES & MARKETING: DAVID GABRIEL

EDITOR IN CHIEF: AXEL ALONSO
CHIEF CREATIVE OFFICER: JOE QUESADA
PUBLISHER: DAN BUCKLEY
EXECUTIVE PRODUCER: ALAN FINE

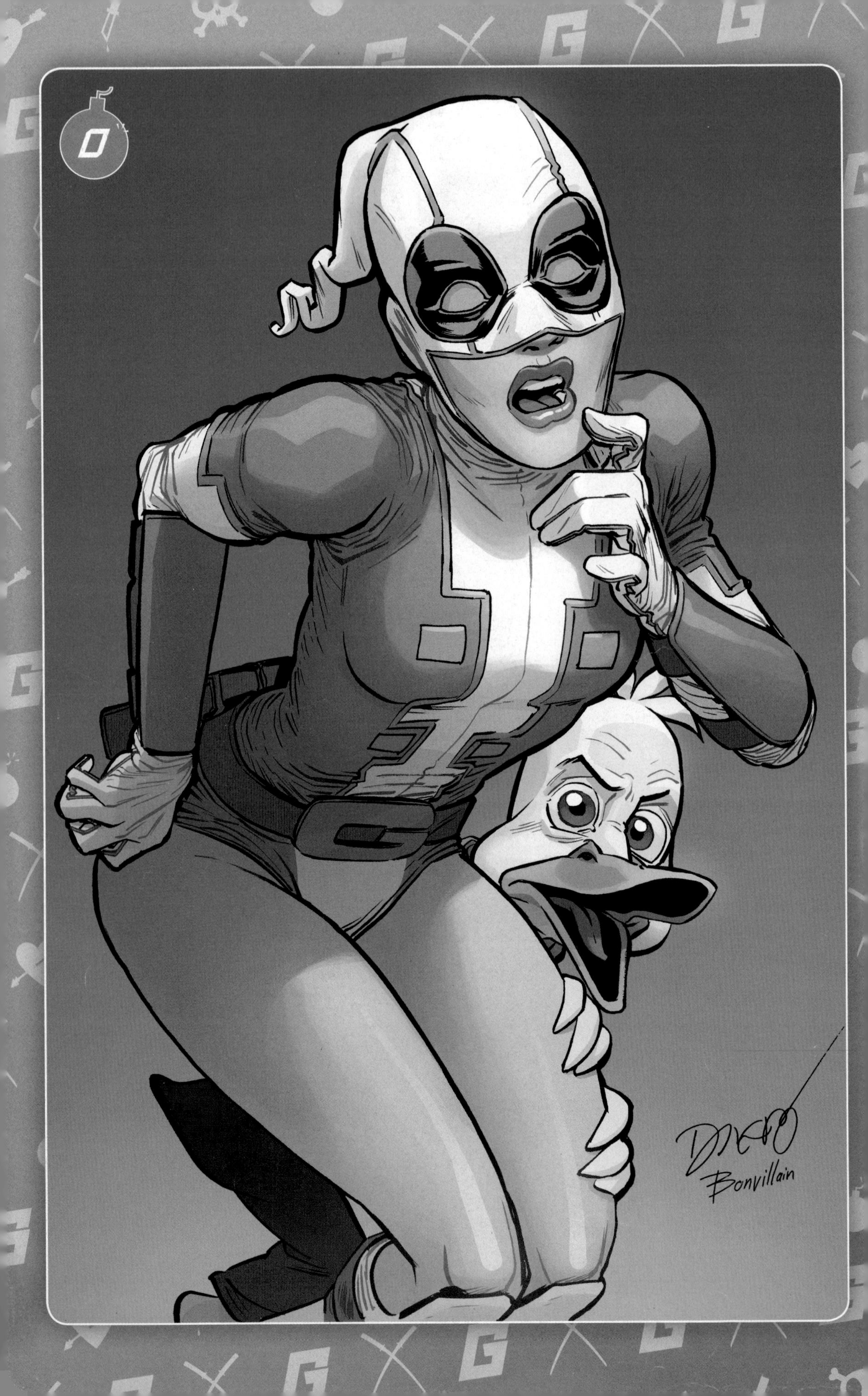
Bonvillain

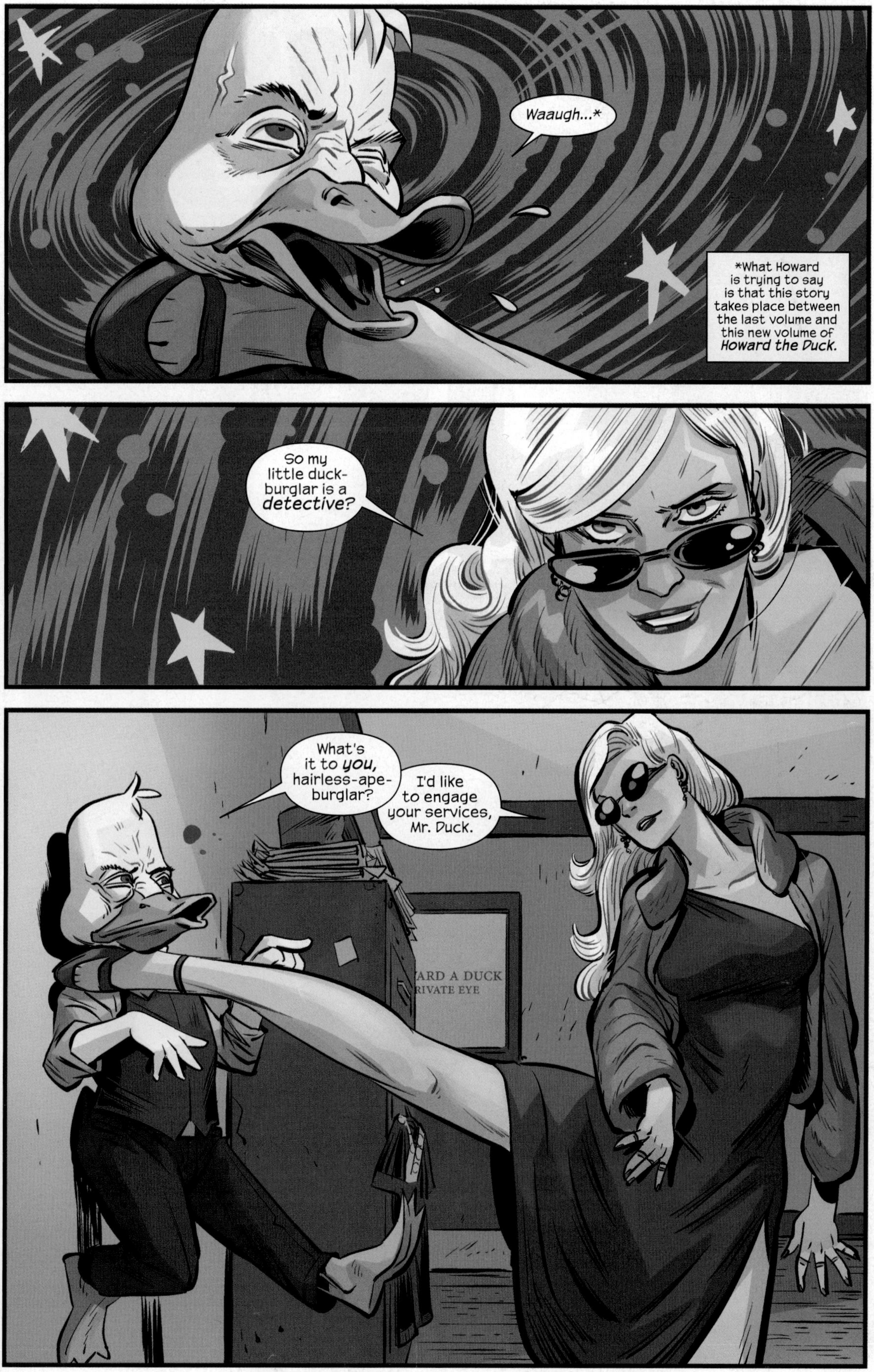
Waaugh...*
*What Howard is trying to say is that this story takes place between the last volume and this new volume of Howard the Duck.
So my little duck-burglar is a detective?
What's it to you, hairless-ape-burglar?
I'd like to engage your services, Mr. Duck.
ARD A DUCK
RIVATE EYE

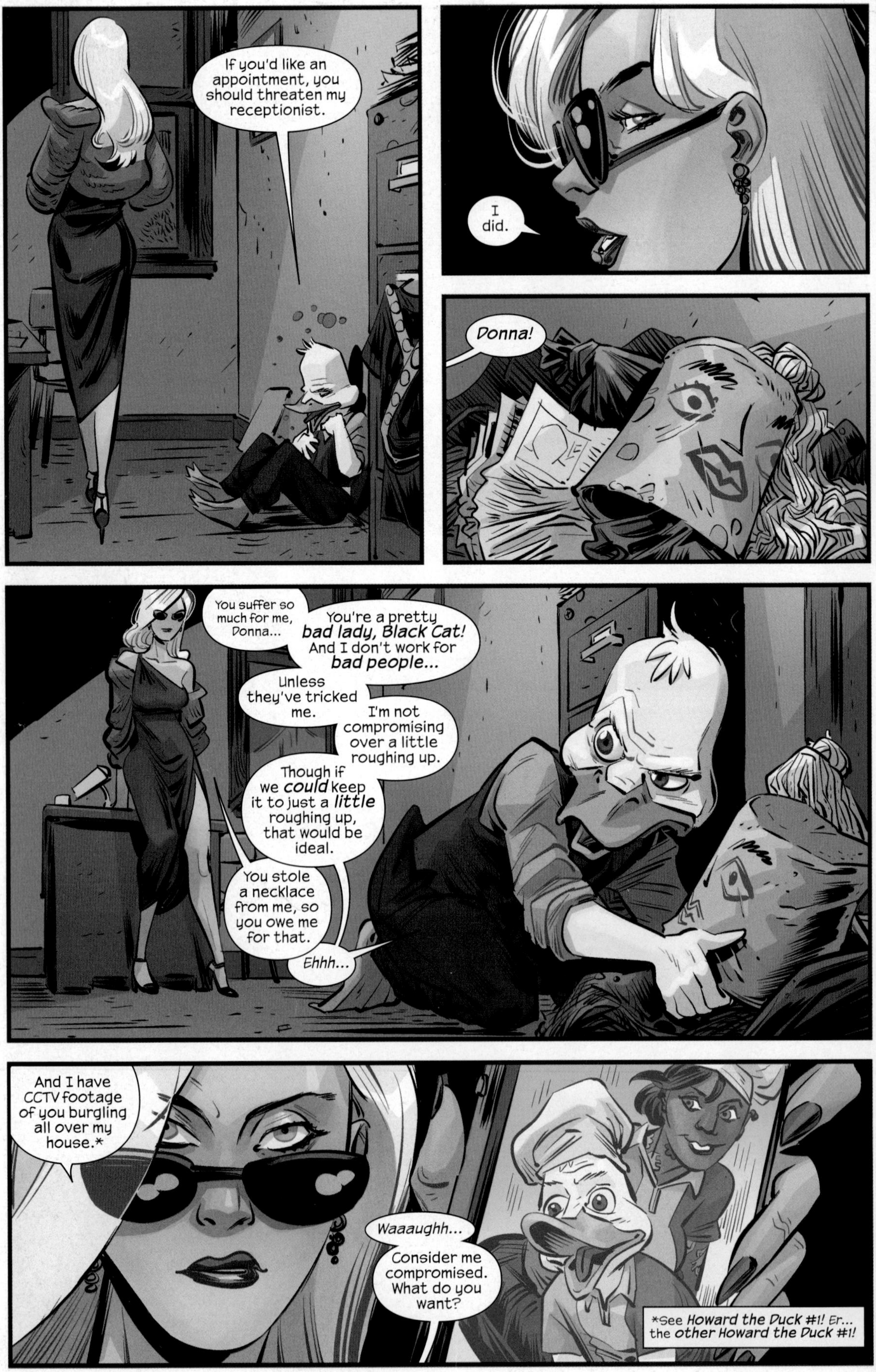
If you'd like an appointment, you should threaten my receptionist.
I did.
Donna!
You suffer so much for me, Donna...
You're a pretty bad lady, Black Cat! And I don't work for bad people...
Unless they've tricked me.
I'm not compromising over a little roughing up.
Though if we could keep it to just a little roughing up, that would be ideal.
You stole a necklace from me, so you owe me for that.
Ehhh...
And I have CCTV footage of you burgling all over my house.*
Waaaughh...
Consider me compromised. What do you want?
*See Howard the Duck #1! Er... the other Howard the Duck #1!

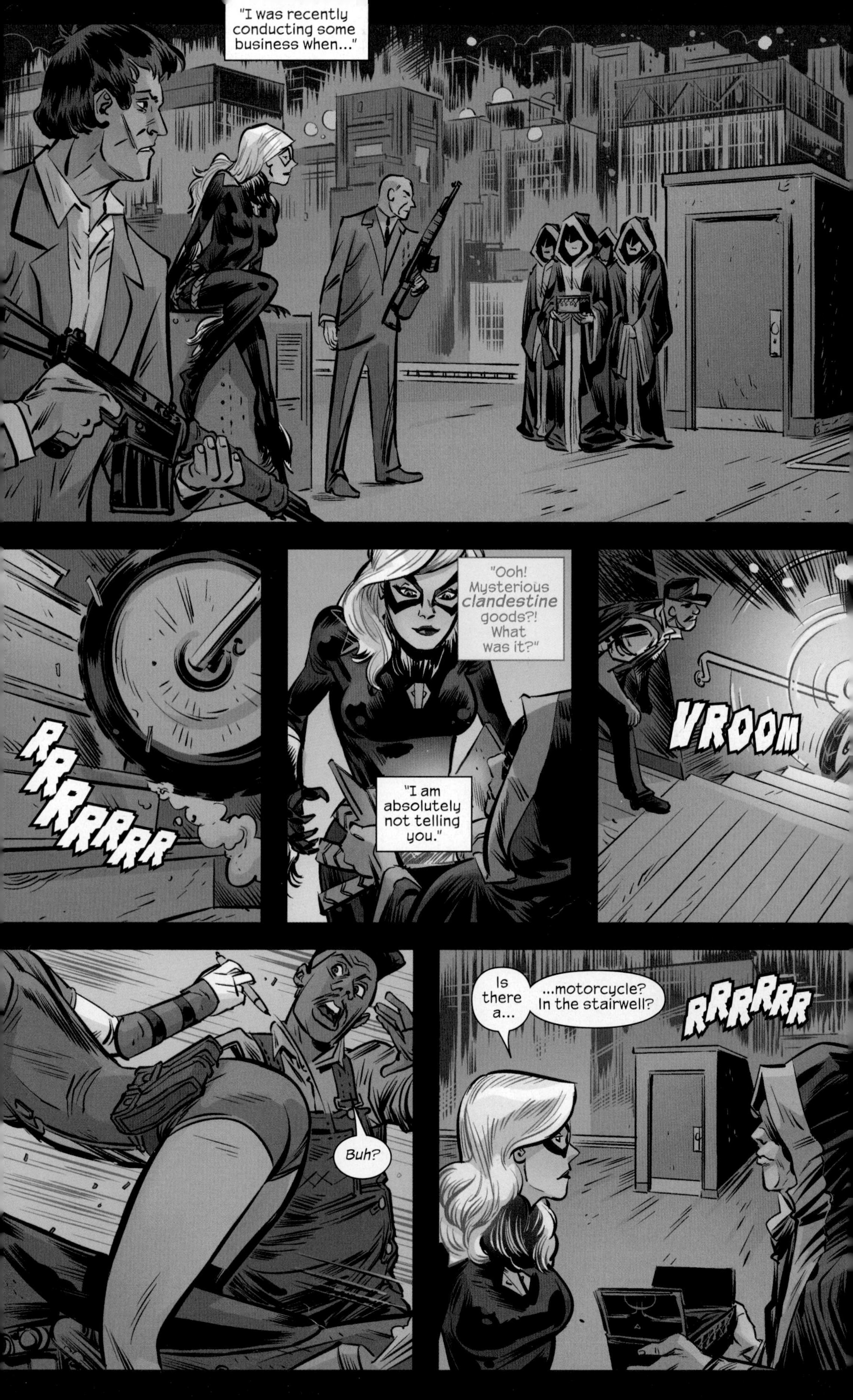
"I was recently conducting some business when..."
RRRRRRRR
"Ooh! Mysterious *clandestine* goods?! What was it?"
"I am absolutely not telling you."
VROOM
Buh?
Is there a...
...motorcycle? In the stairwell?
RRRRRR

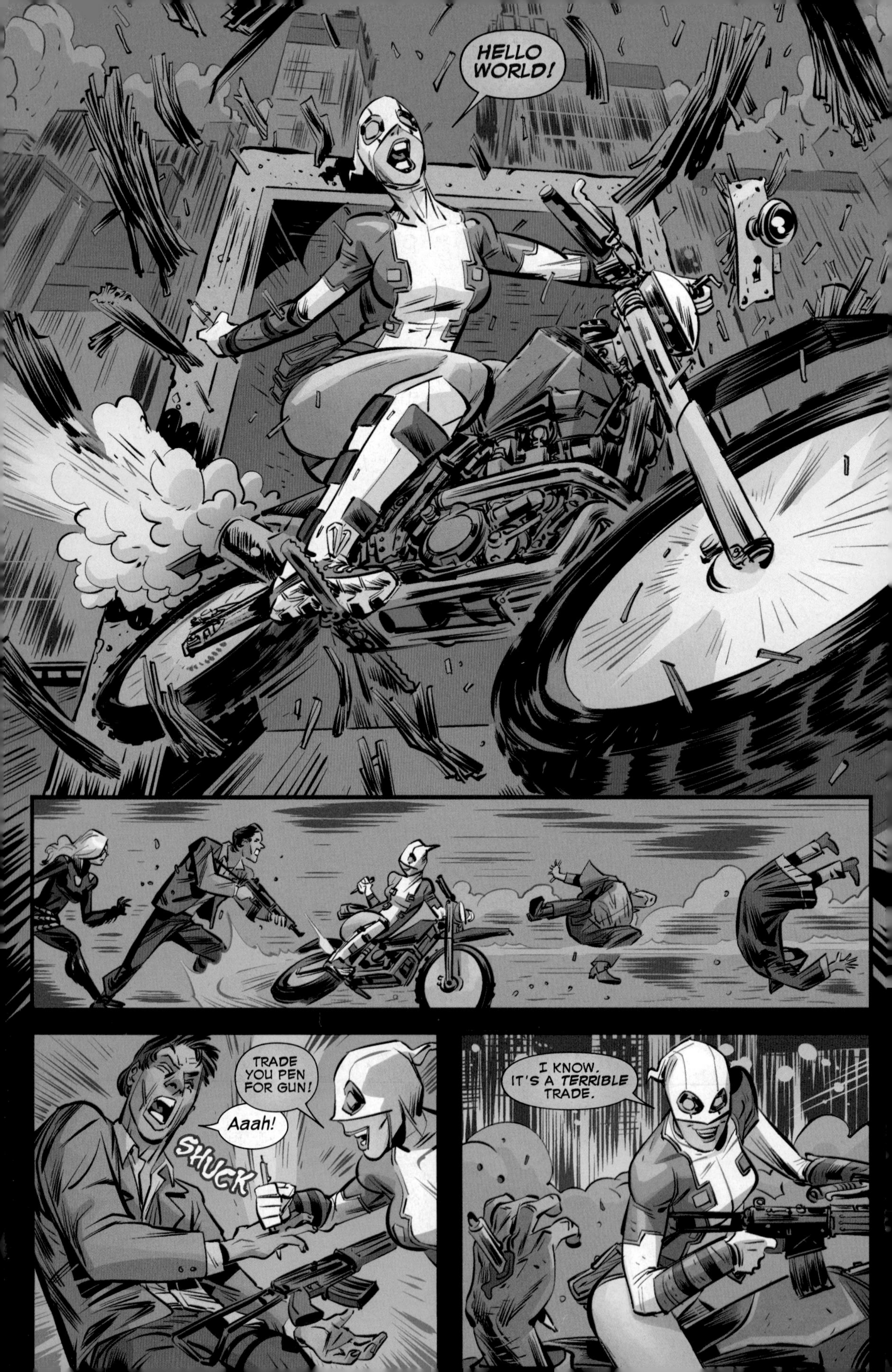
HELLO WORLD!
TRADE YOU PEN FOR GUN!
Aaah!
SHUCK
I KNOW. IT'S A *TERRIBLE* TRADE.

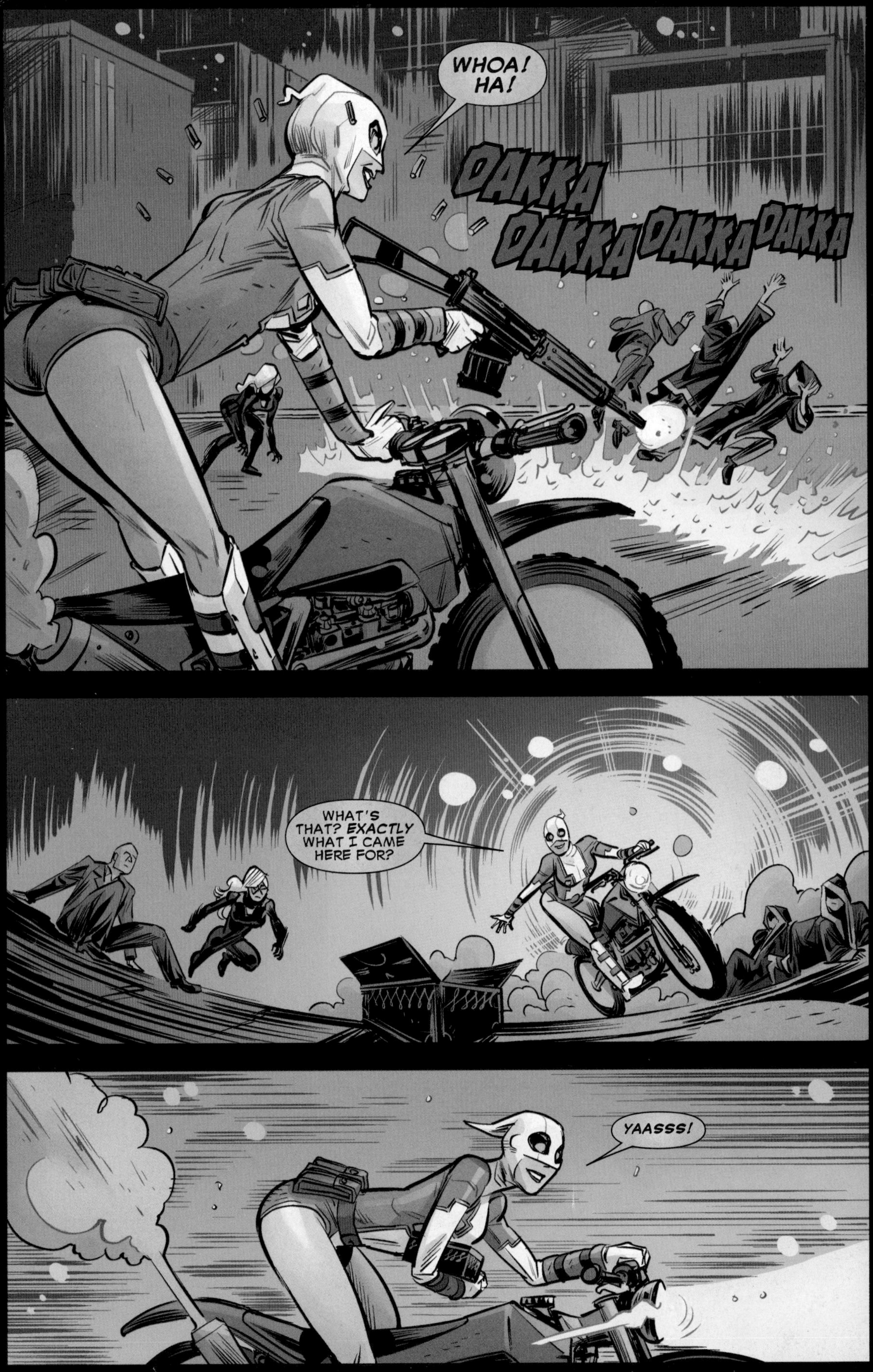
WHOA! HA!
DAKKA DAKKA DAKKA DAKKA
WHAT'S THAT? EXACTLY WHAT I CAME HERE FOR?
YAASSS!

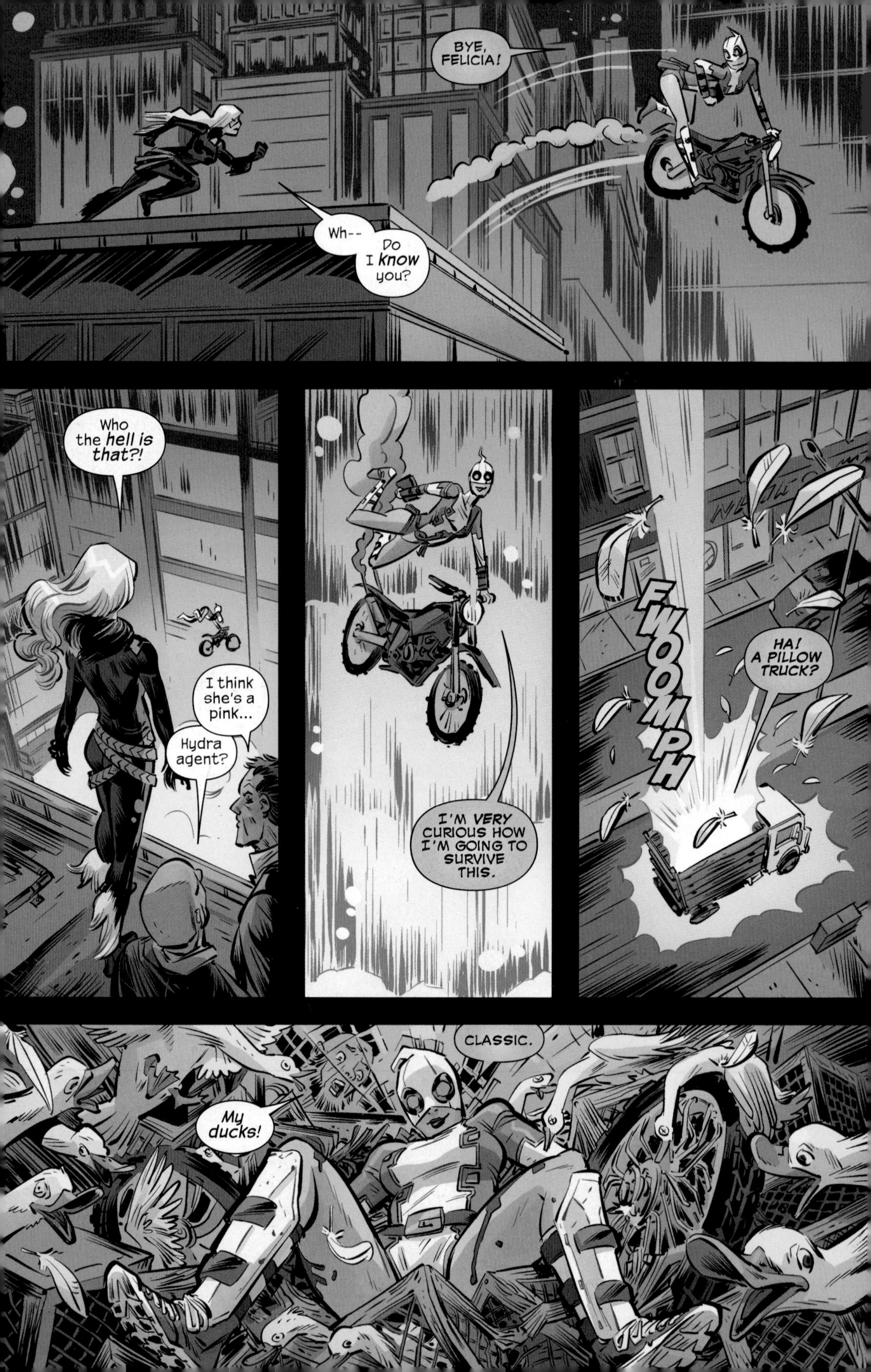
BYE, FELICIA!
Wh--
Do I know you?
Who the hell is that?!
I think she's a pink...
Hydra agent?
I'M VERY CURIOUS HOW I'M GOING TO SURVIVE THIS.
FWOOOMPH
HA! A PILLOW TRUCK?
CLASSIC.
My ducks!

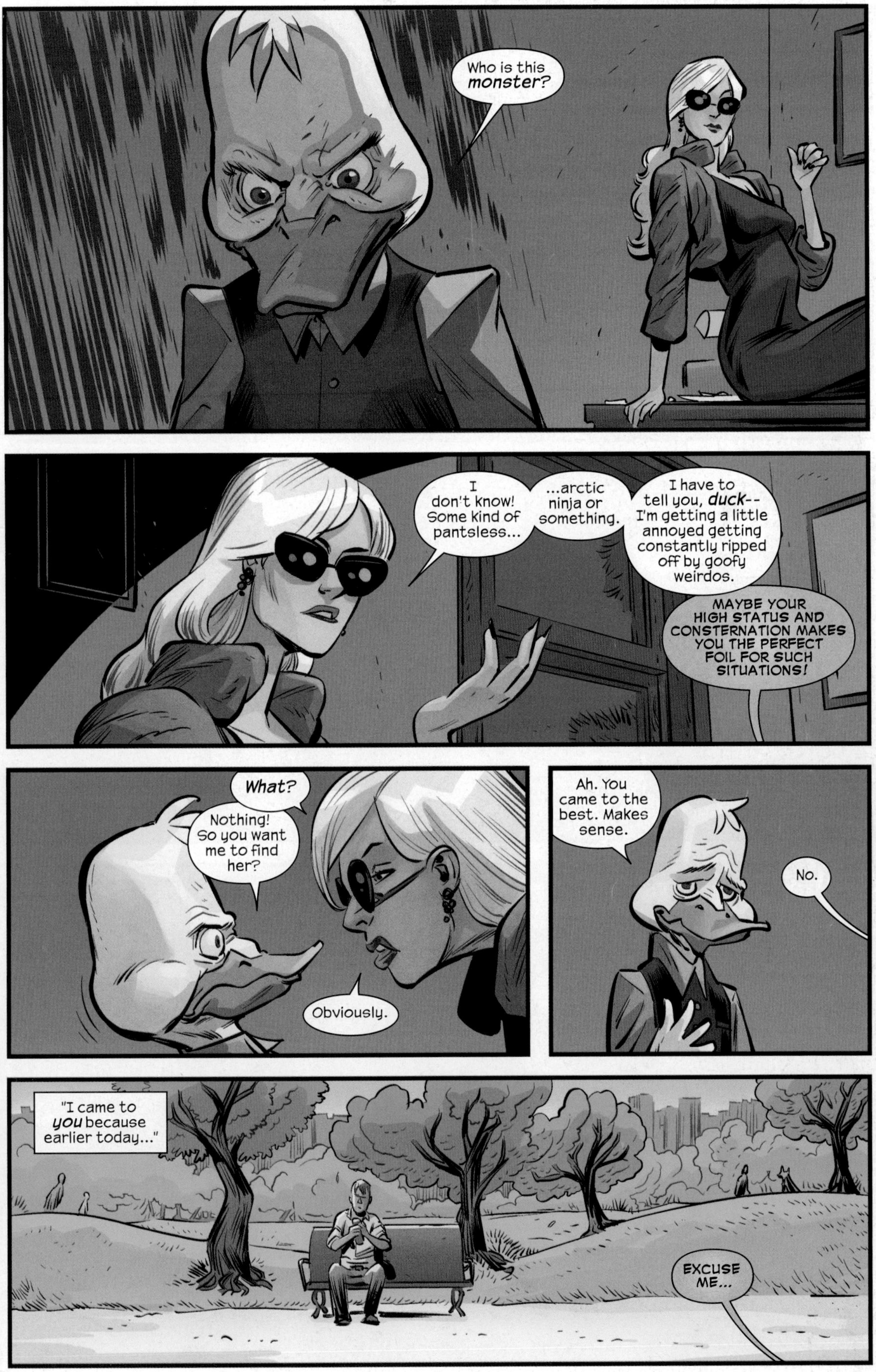
Who is this *monster*?
I don't know! Some kind of pantsless...
...arctic ninja or something.
I have to tell you, *duck*-- I'm getting a little annoyed getting constantly ripped off by goofy weirdos.
MAYBE YOUR HIGH STATUS AND CONSTERNATION MAKES YOU THE PERFECT FOIL FOR SUCH SITUATIONS!
*What?*
Nothing! So you want me to find her?
Obviously.
Ah. You came to the best. Makes sense.
No.
"I came to *you* because earlier today..."
EXCUSE ME...

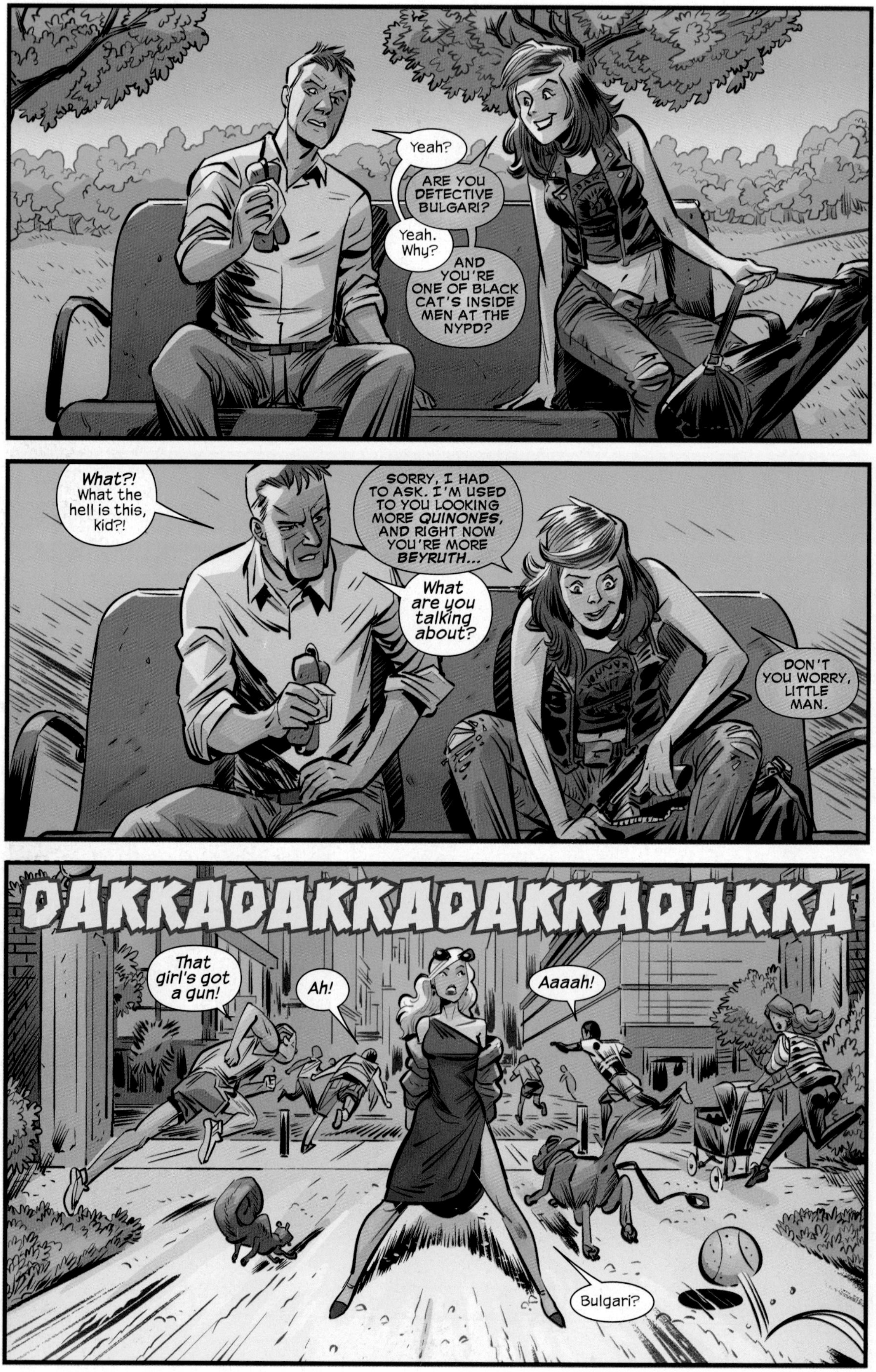

Yeah?
ARE YOU DETECTIVE BULGARI?
Yeah. Why?
AND YOU'RE ONE OF BLACK CAT'S INSIDE MEN AT THE NYPD?
What?! What the hell is this, kid?!
SORRY, I HAD TO ASK. I'M USED TO YOU LOOKING MORE QUINONES, AND RIGHT NOW YOU'RE MORE BEYRUTH...
What are you talking about?
DON'T YOU WORRY, LITTLE MAN.
DAKKADAKKADAKKADAKKA
That girl's got a gun!
Ah!
Aaaah!
Bulgari?

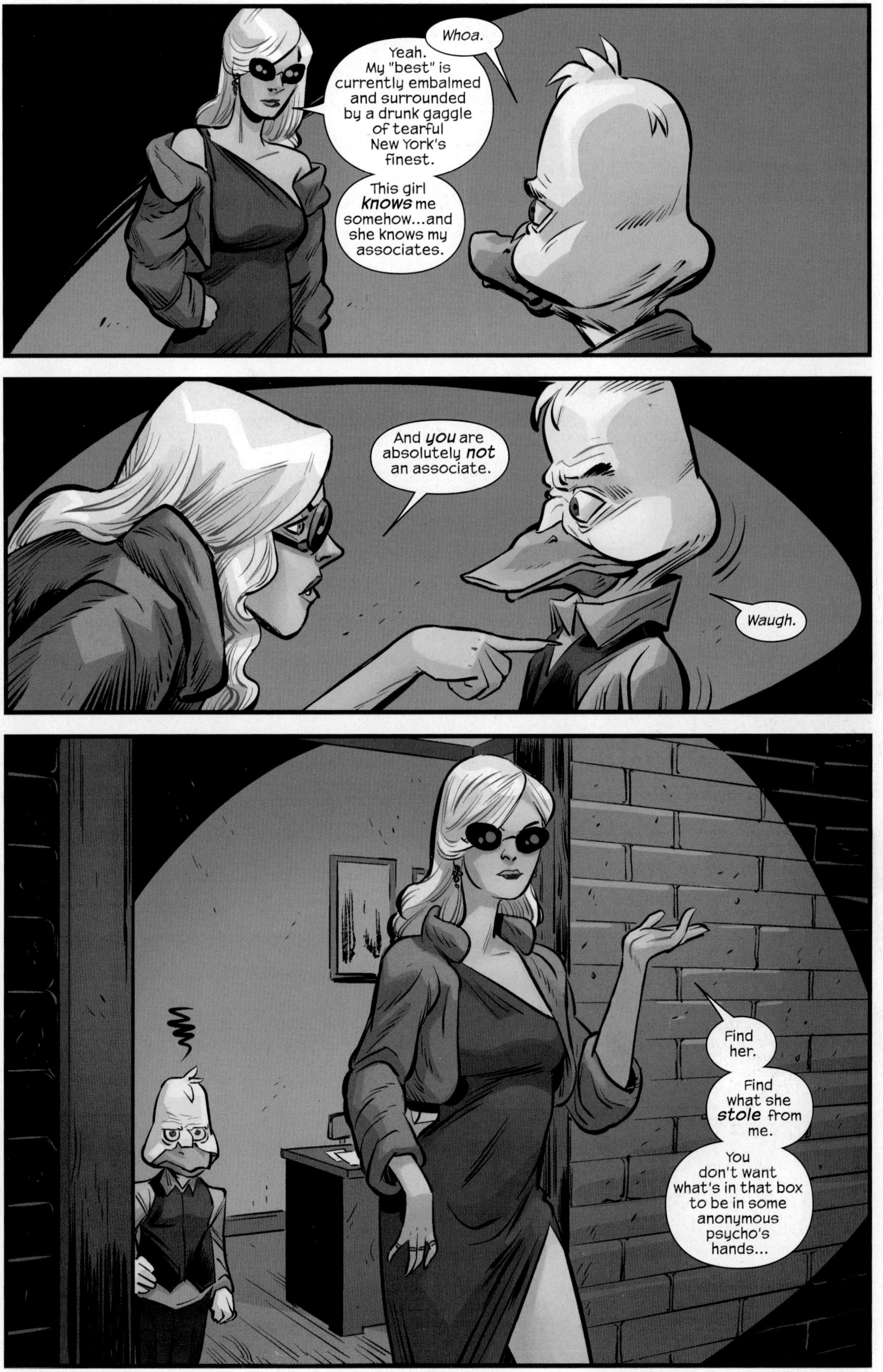
Whoa.
Yeah. My "best" is currently embalmed and surrounded by a drunk gaggle of tearful New York's finest.
This girl *knows* me somehow...and she knows my associates.
And *you* are absolutely *not* an associate.
Waugh.
Find her.
Find what she *stole* from me.
You don't want what's in that box to be in some anonymous psycho's hands...

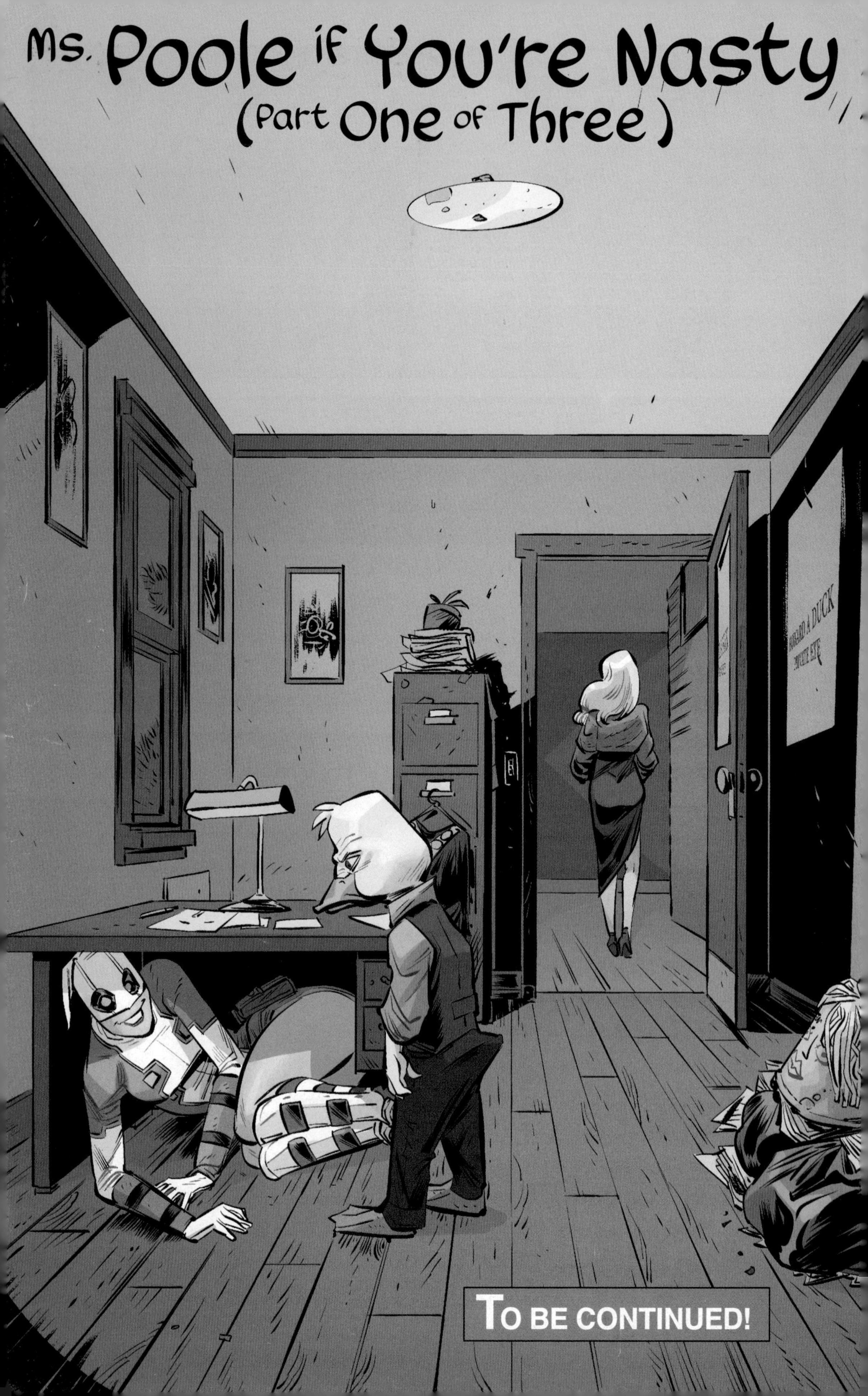

Ms. Poole if You're Nasty
(Part One of Three)
To be continued!

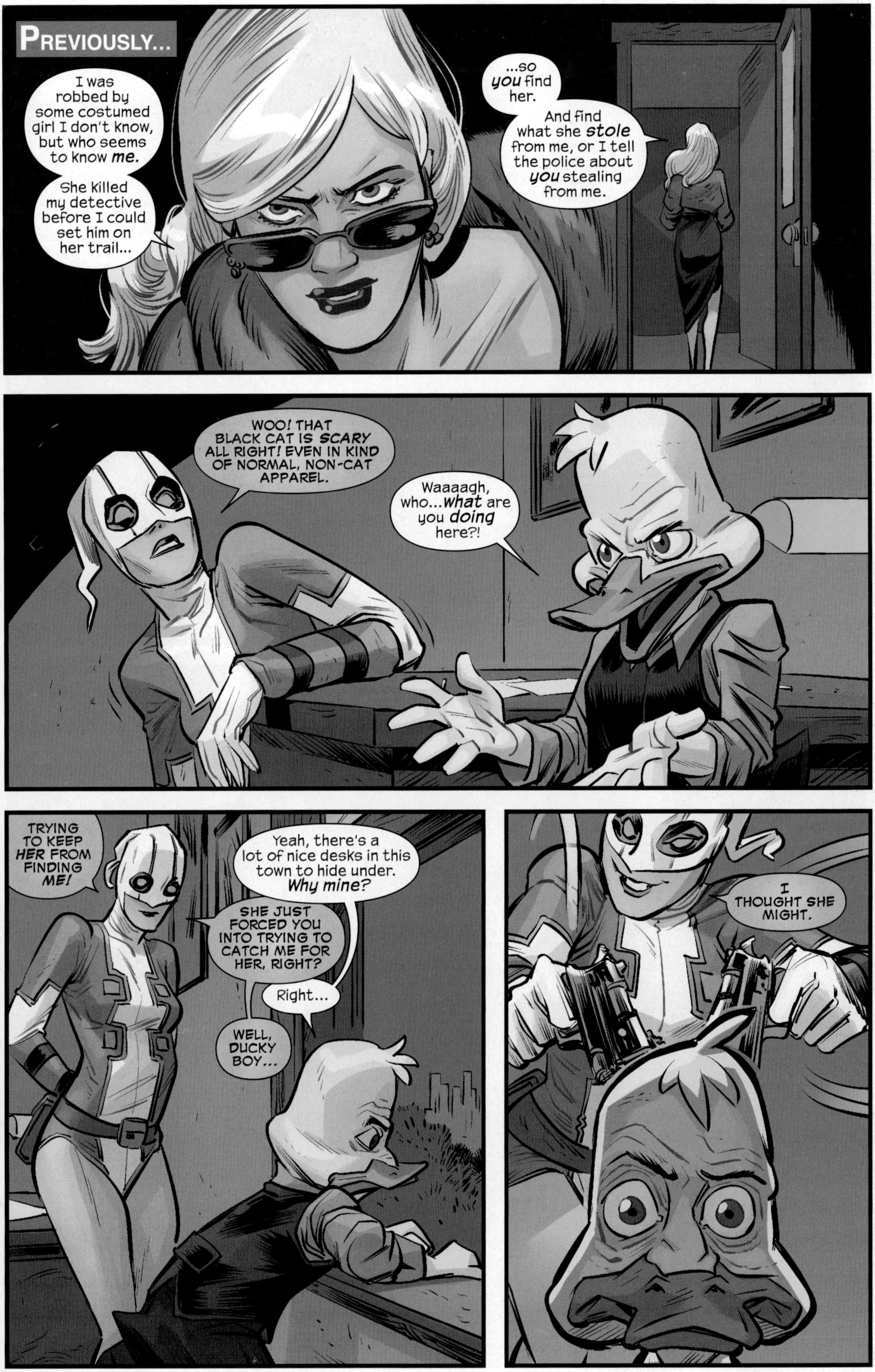
PREVIOUSLY...
I was robbed by some costumed girl I don't know, but who seems to know me.
She killed my detective before I could set him on her trail...
...so you find her.
And find what she stole from me, or I tell the police about you stealing from me.
WOO! THAT BLACK CAT IS SCARY ALL RIGHT! EVEN IN KIND OF NORMAL, NON-CAT APPAREL.
Waaaagh, who...what are you doing here?!
TRYING TO KEEP HER FROM FINDING ME!
Yeah, there's a lot of nice desks in this town to hide under. Why mine?
SHE JUST FORCED YOU INTO TRYING TO CATCH ME FOR HER, RIGHT?
Right...
WELL, DUCKY BOY...
I THOUGHT SHE MIGHT.

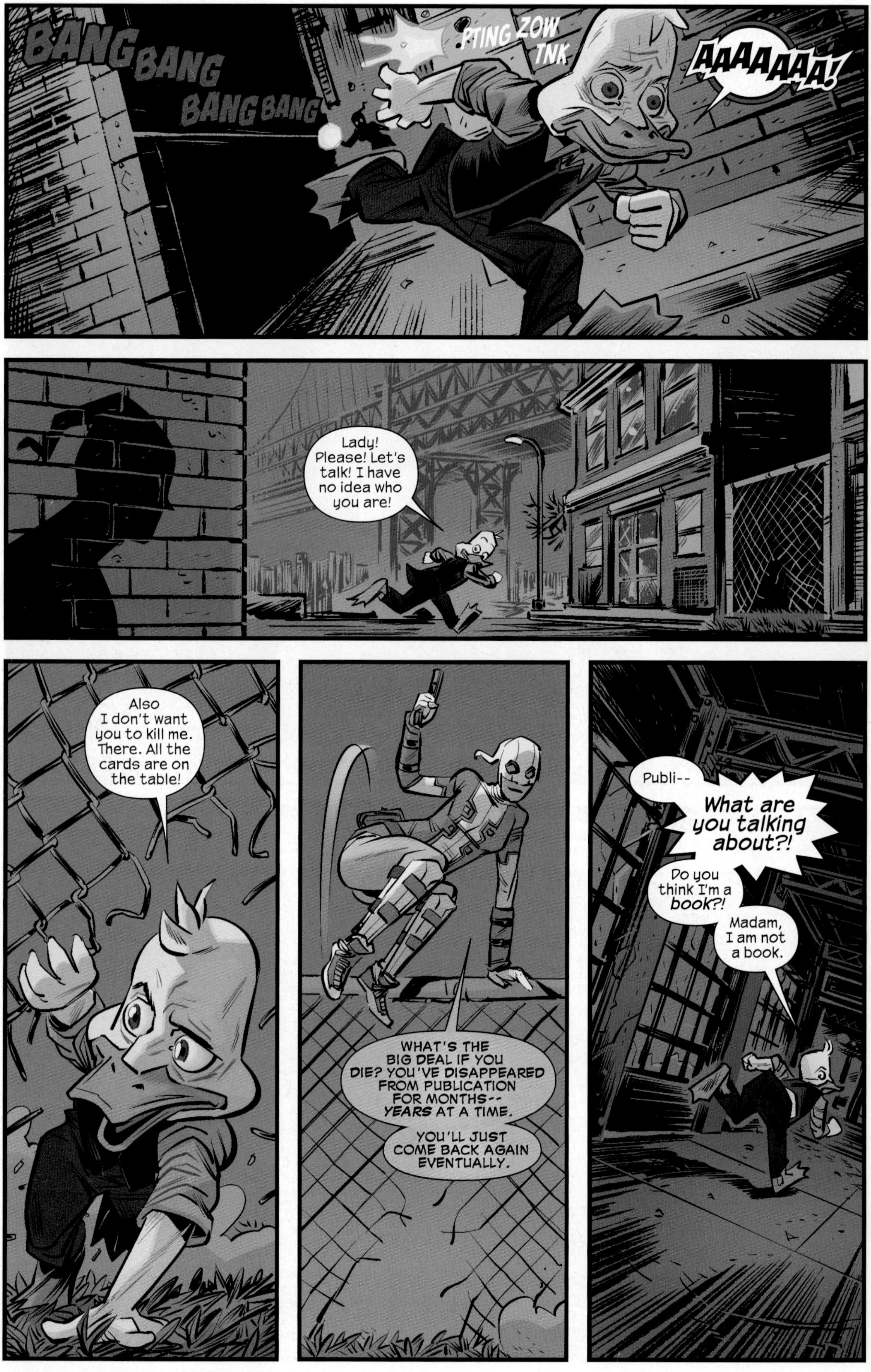

BANG BANG
BANG BANG
PTING ZOW
TNK
AAAAAAA!
Lady! Please! Let's talk! I have no idea who you are!
Also I don't want you to kill me. There. All the cards are on the table!
WHAT'S THE BIG DEAL IF YOU DIE? YOU'VE DISAPPEARED FROM PUBLICATION FOR MONTHS-- YEARS AT A TIME.
YOU'LL JUST COME BACK AGAIN EVENTUALLY.
Publi--
What are you talking about?!
Do you think I'm a book?!
Madam, I am not a book.

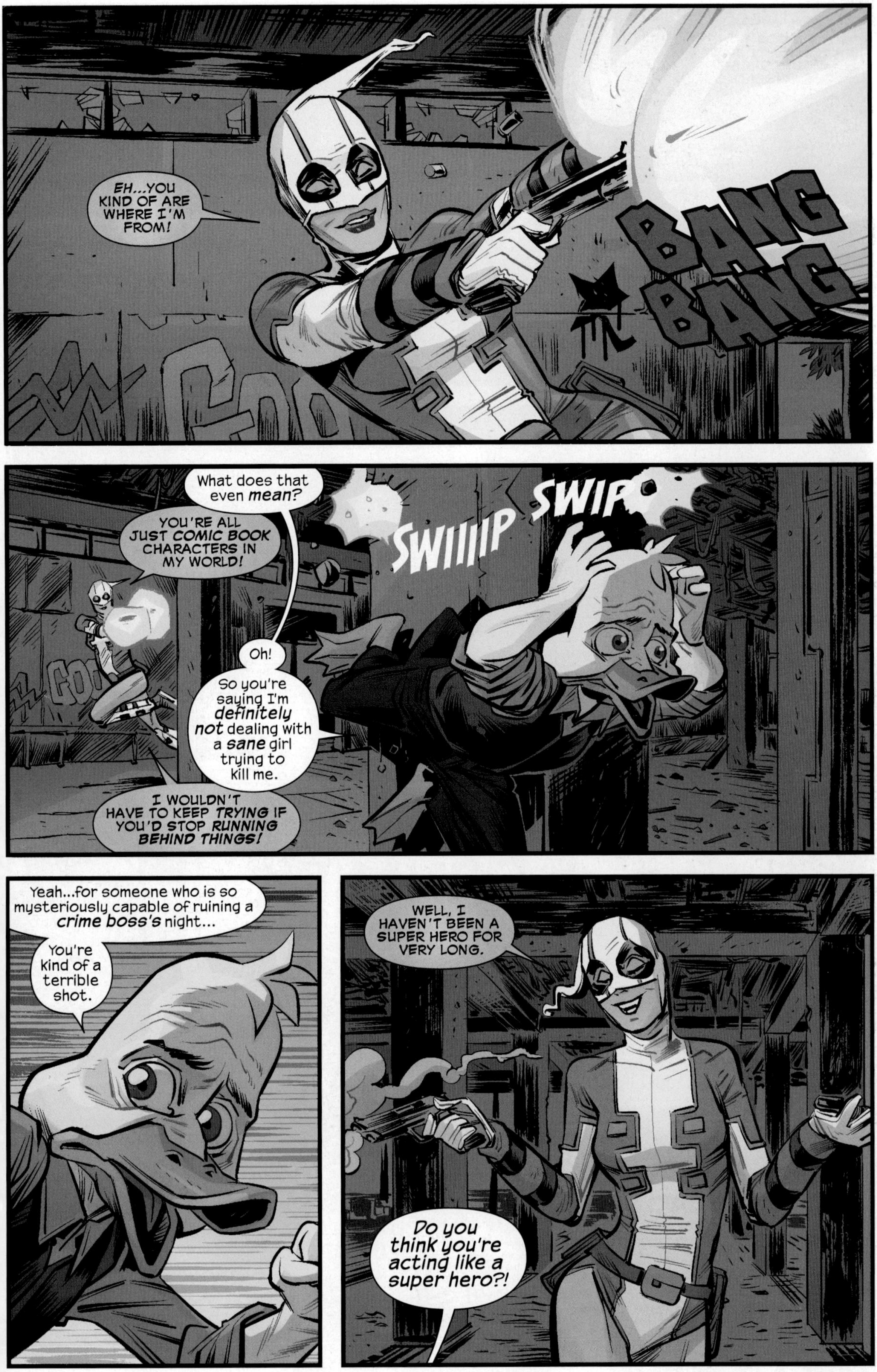

EH...YOU KIND OF ARE WHERE I'M FROM!
BANG BANG
What does that even mean?
YOU'RE ALL JUST COMIC BOOK CHARACTERS IN MY WORLD!
SWIIIIP SWIP
Oh!
So you're saying I'm definitely not dealing with a sane girl trying to kill me.
I WOULDN'T HAVE TO KEEP TRYING IF YOU'D STOP RUNNING BEHIND THINGS!
Yeah...for someone who is so mysteriously capable of ruining a crime boss's night...
You're kind of a terrible shot.
WELL, I HAVEN'T BEEN A SUPER HERO FOR VERY LONG.
Do you think you're acting like a super hero?!

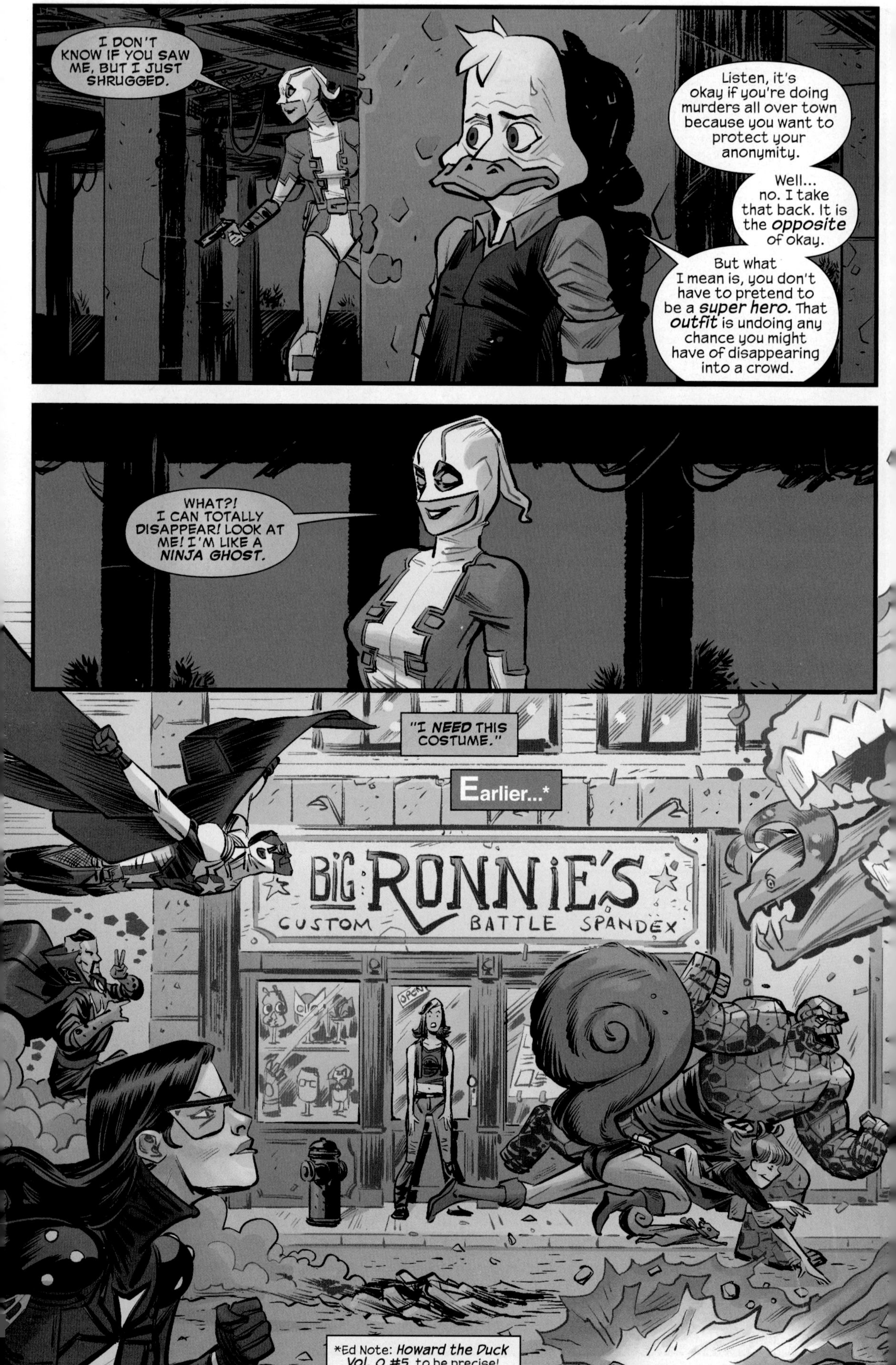
I DON'T KNOW IF YOU SAW ME, BUT I JUST SHRUGGED.
Listen, it's okay if you're doing murders all over town because you want to protect your anonymity.
Well... no. I take that back. It is the *opposite* of okay.
But what I mean is, you don't have to pretend to be a **super hero.** That **outfit** is undoing any chance you might have of disappearing into a crowd.
WHAT?! I CAN TOTALLY DISAPPEAR! LOOK AT ME! I'M LIKE A *NINJA GHOST.*
"I *NEED* THIS COSTUME."
Earlier...*
BIG RONNIE'S
CUSTOM BATTLE SPANDEX
OPEN
*Ed Note: *Howard the Duck Vol. 0 #5,* to be precise!

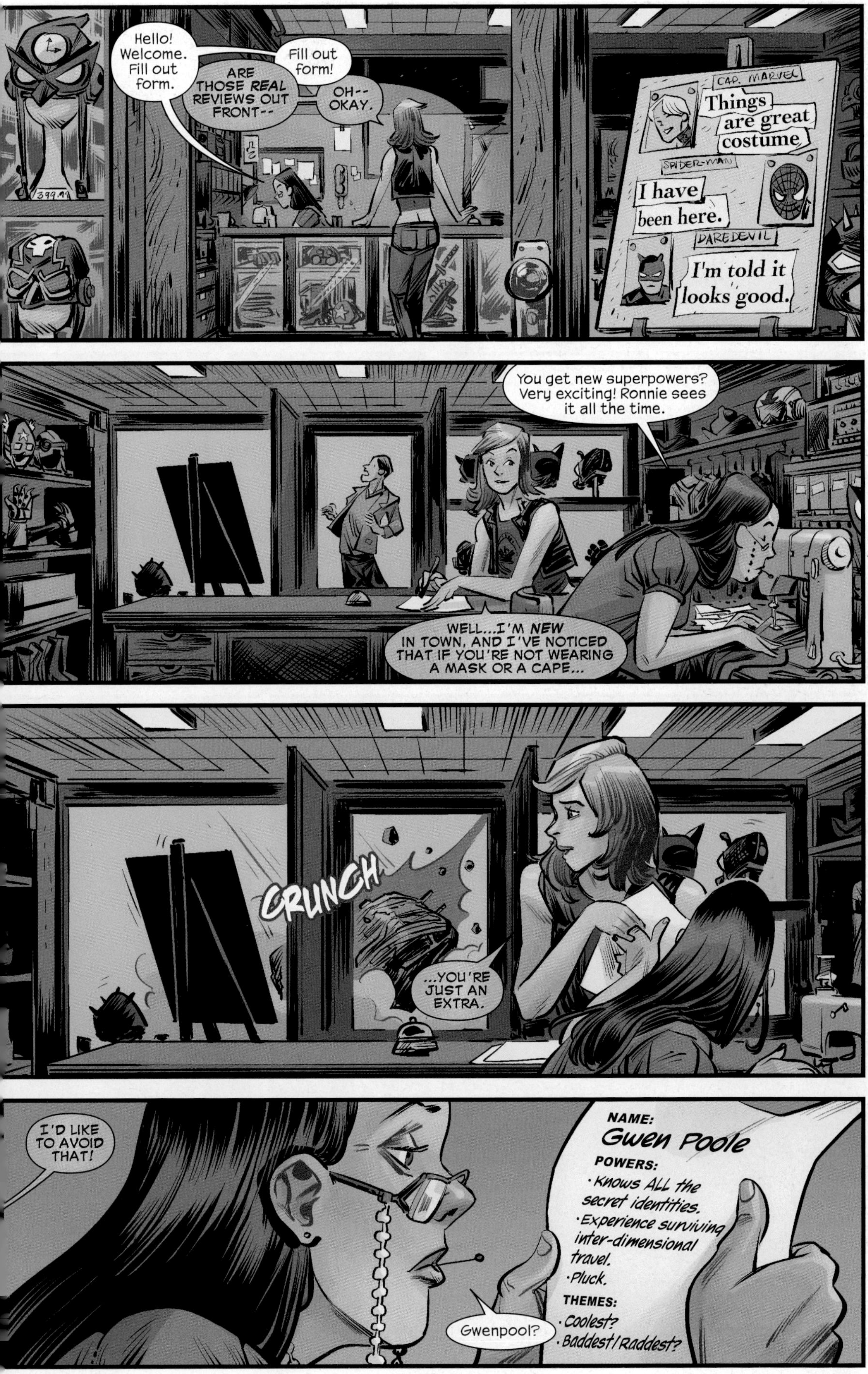

Hello! Welcome. Fill out form.
ARE THOSE REAL REVIEWS OUT FRONT--
Fill out form!
OH-- OKAY.
CAP. MARVEL
Things are great costume
SPIDER-MAN
I have been here.
DAREDEVIL
I'm told it looks good.
You get new superpowers? Very exciting! Ronnie sees it all the time.
WELL...I'M NEW IN TOWN, AND I'VE NOTICED THAT IF YOU'RE NOT WEARING A MASK OR A CAPE...
CRUNCH
...YOU'RE JUST AN EXTRA.
I'D LIKE TO AVOID THAT!
NAME:
Gwen Poole
POWERS:
·Knows ALL the secret identities.
·Experience surviving inter-dimensional travel.
·Pluck.
THEMES:
·Coolest?
·Baddest/Raddest?
Gwenpool?

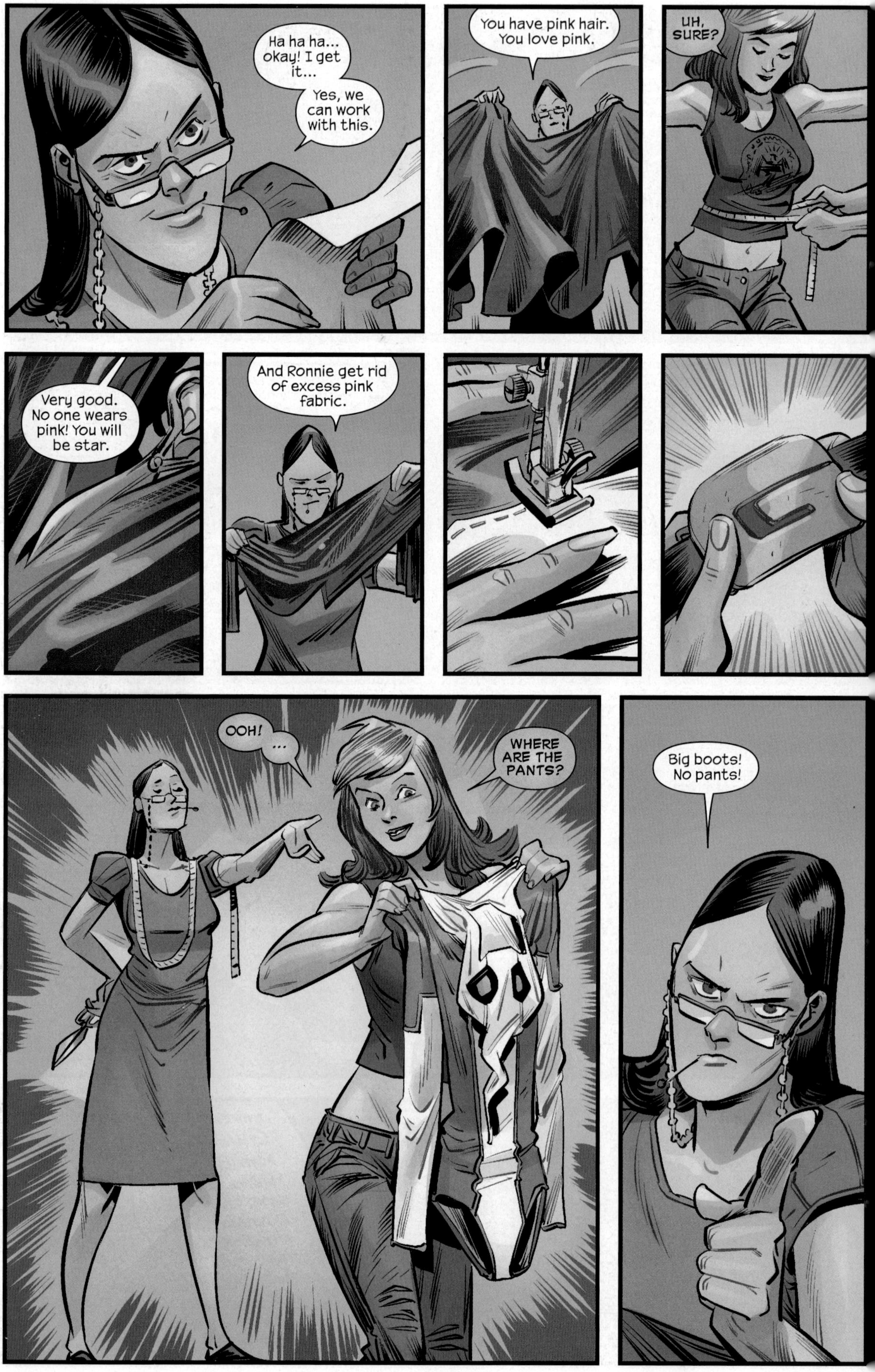
Ha ha ha... okay! I get it...
Yes, we can work with this.
You have pink hair. You love pink.
UH, SURE?
Very good. No one wears pink! You will be star.
And Ronnie get rid of excess pink fabric.
OOH! ...
WHERE ARE THE PANTS?
Big boots! No pants!

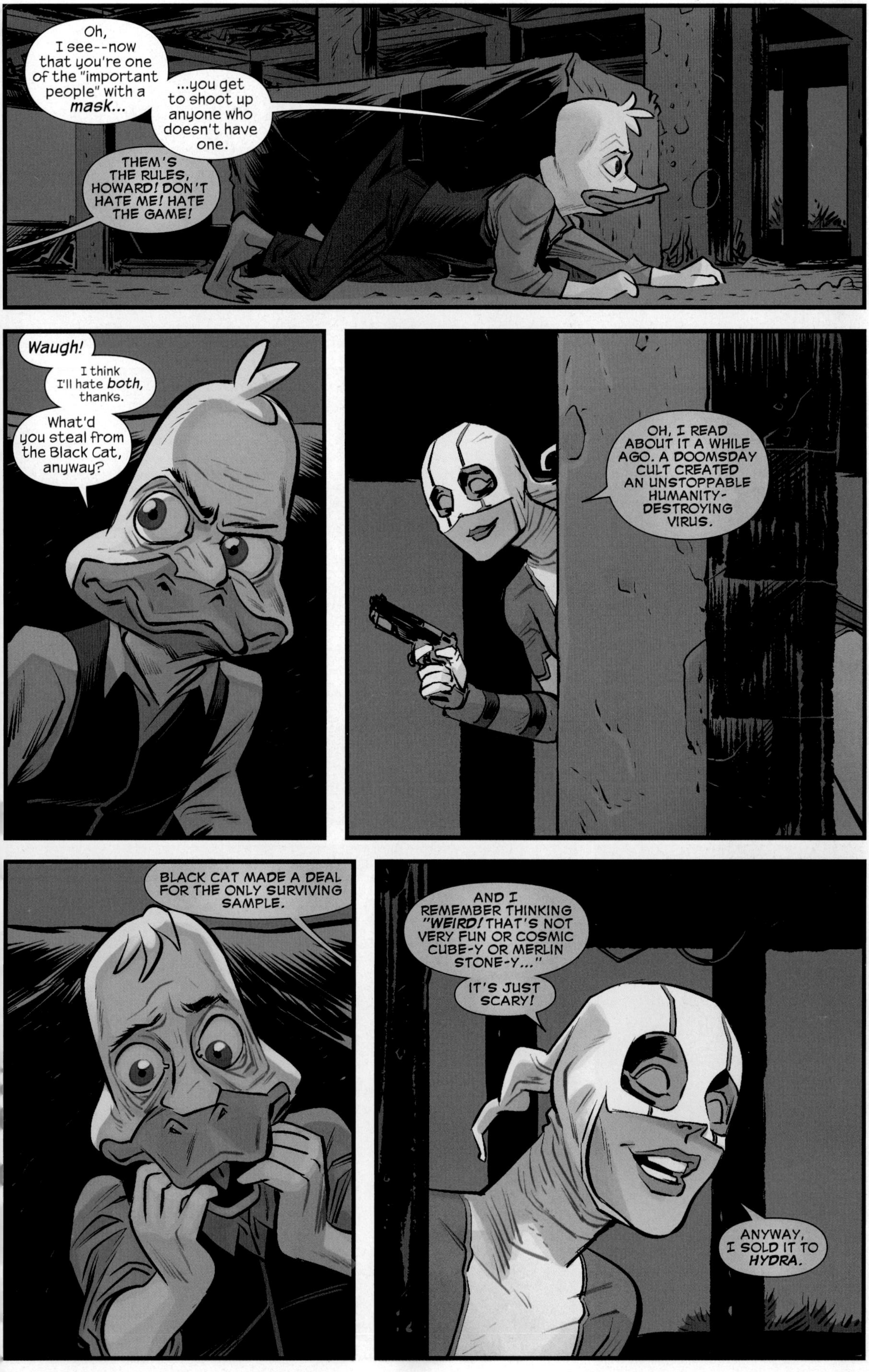
Oh, I see--now that you're one of the "important people" with a *mask*...
...you get to shoot up anyone who doesn't have one.
THEM'S THE RULES, HOWARD! DON'T HATE ME! HATE THE GAME!
*Waugh!*
I think I'll hate *both*, thanks.
What'd you steal from the Black Cat, anyway?
OH, I READ ABOUT IT A WHILE AGO. A DOOMSDAY CULT CREATED AN UNSTOPPABLE HUMANITY-DESTROYING VIRUS.
BLACK CAT MADE A DEAL FOR THE ONLY SURVIVING SAMPLE.
AND I REMEMBER THINKING "*WEIRD!* THAT'S NOT VERY FUN OR COSMIC CUBE-Y OR MERLIN STONE-Y..."
IT'S JUST SCARY!
ANYWAY, I SOLD IT TO *HYDRA*.

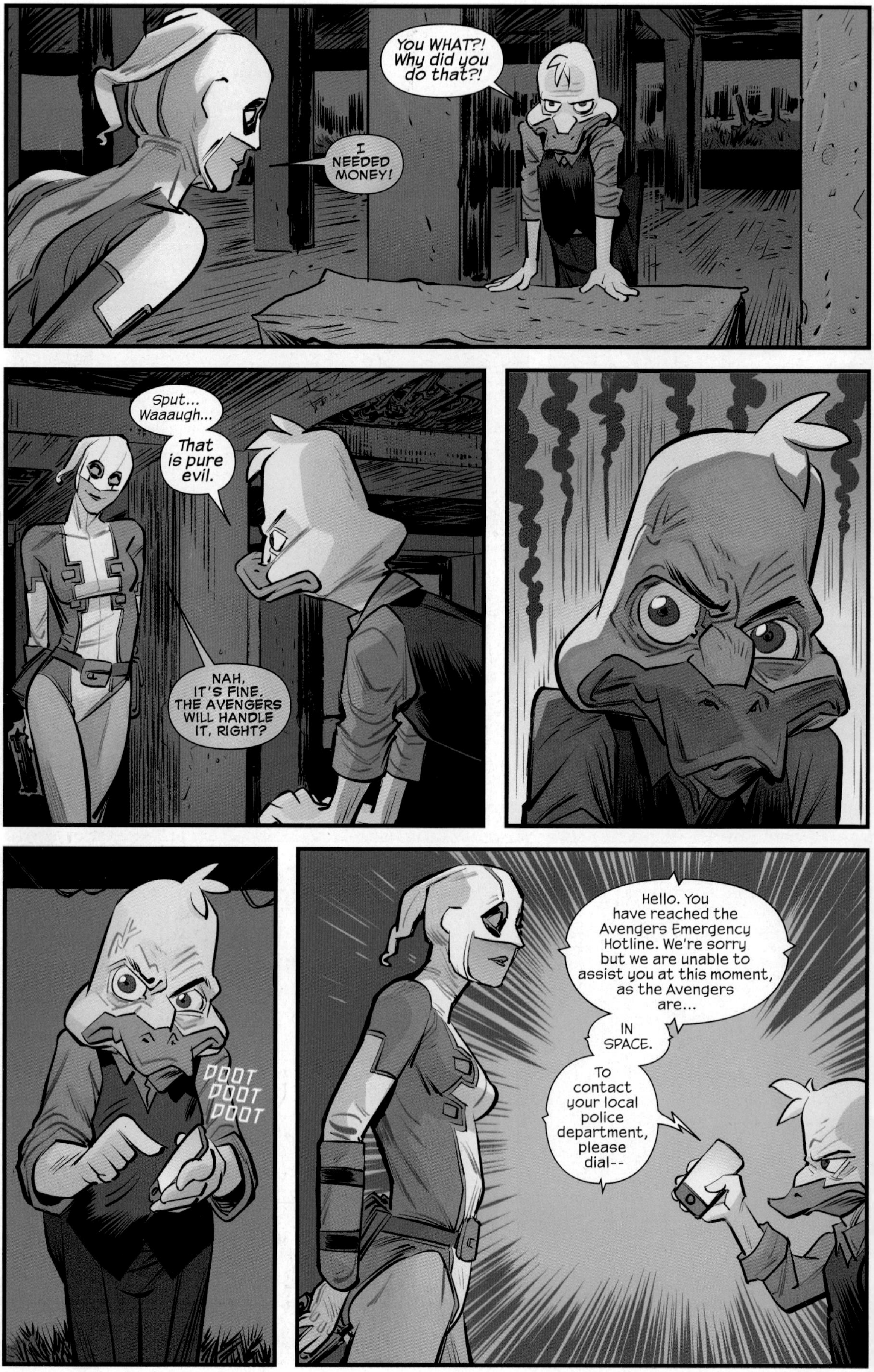
You WHAT?! Why did you do that?!
I NEEDED MONEY!
Sput... Waaaugh...
That is pure evil.
NAH, IT'S FINE. THE AVENGERS WILL HANDLE IT, RIGHT?
DOOT DOOT DOOT
Hello. You have reached the Avengers Emergency Hotline. We're sorry but we are unable to assist you at this moment, as the Avengers are...
IN SPACE.
To contact your local police department, please dial--

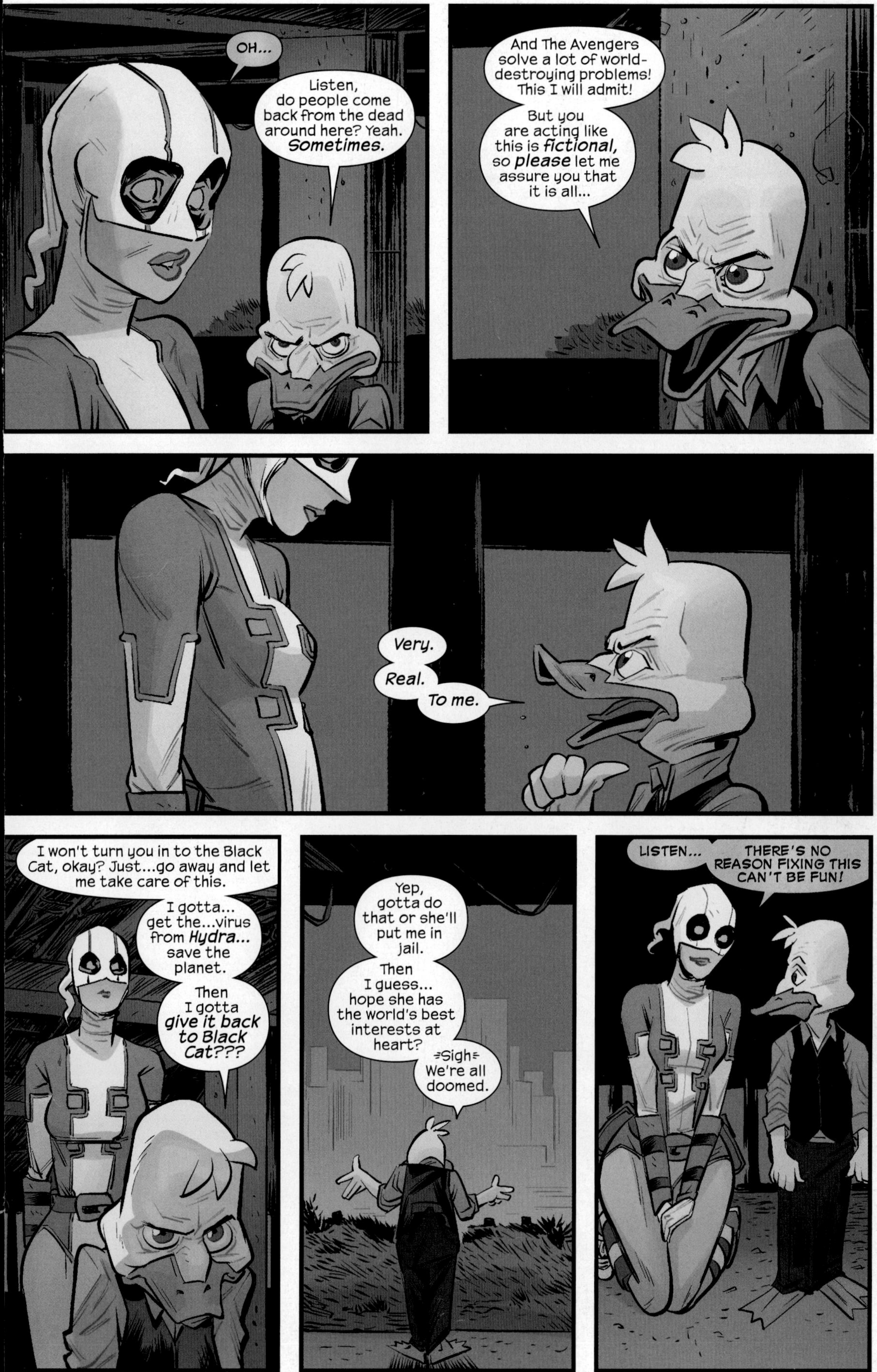
OH...
Listen, do people come back from the dead around here? Yeah. *Sometimes.*
And The Avengers solve a lot of world-destroying problems! This I will admit!
But you are acting like this is *fictional,* so *please* let me assure you that it is all...
*Very.*
*Real.*
*To me.*
I won't turn you in to the Black Cat, okay? Just...go away and let me take care of this.
I gotta... get the...virus from *Hydra...* save the planet.
Then I gotta *give it back to Black Cat???*
Yep, gotta do that or she'll put me in jail.
Then I guess... hope she has the world's best interests at heart?
=Sigh= We're all doomed.
LISTEN...
THERE'S NO REASON FIXING THIS CAN'T BE FUN!

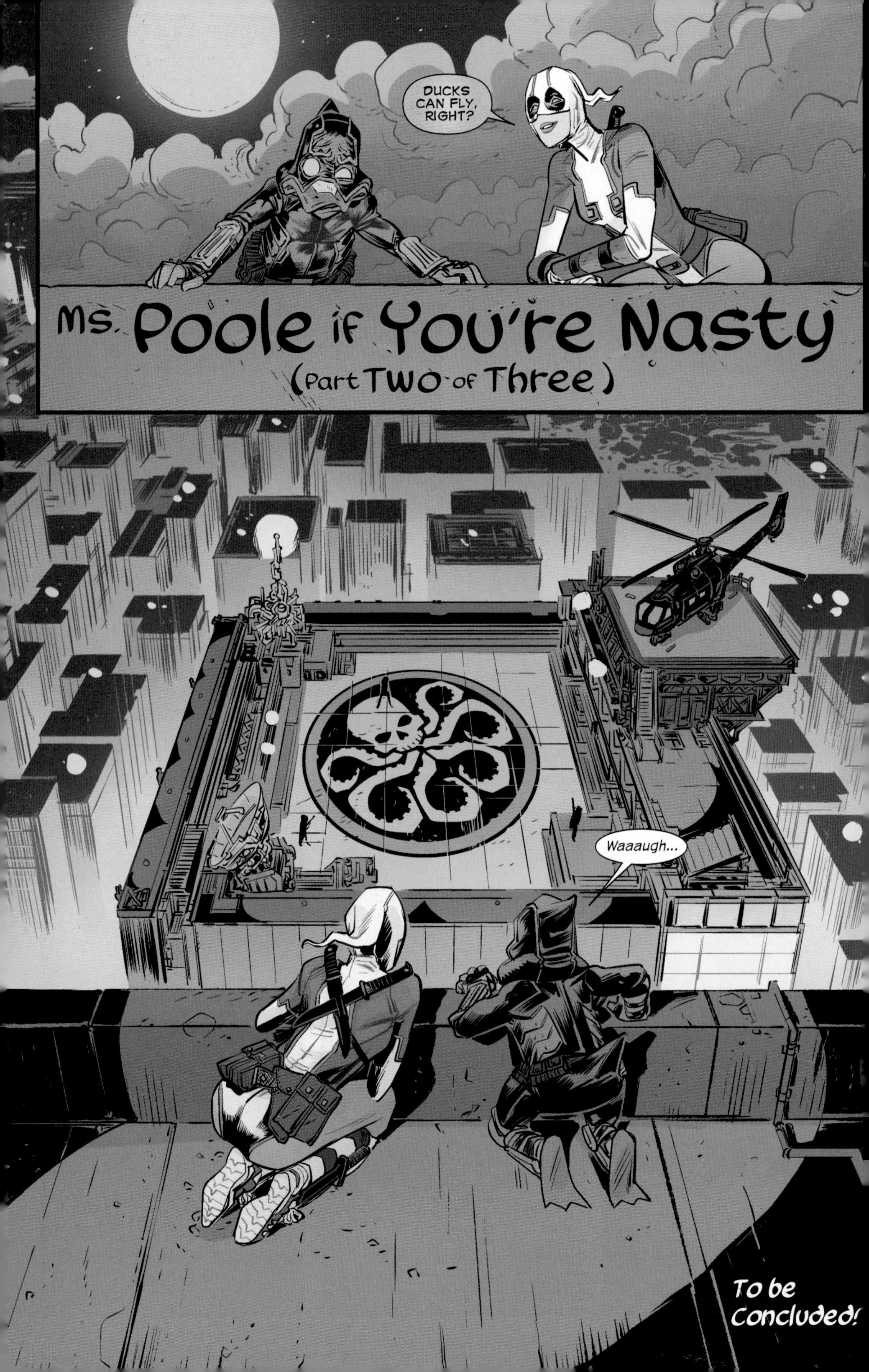
DUCKS CAN FLY, RIGHT?
Ms. Poole if You're Nasty
(Part TWO of Three)
Waaaugh...
To be Concluded!

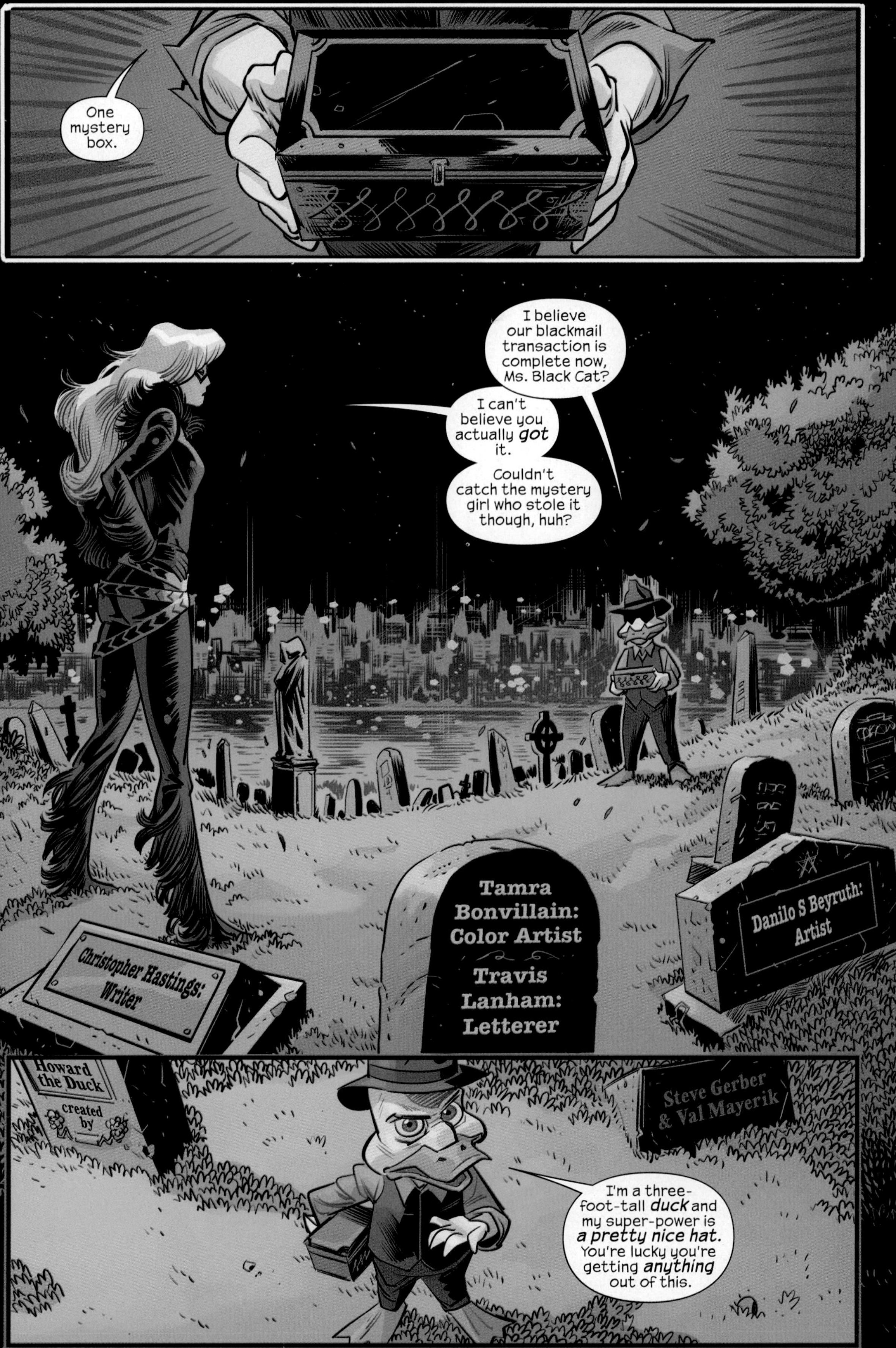
One mystery box.
I believe our blackmail transaction is complete now, Ms. Black Cat?
I can't believe you actually *got* it.
Couldn't catch the mystery girl who stole it though, huh?
Christopher Hastings: Writer
Tamra Bonvillain: Color Artist
Travis Lanham: Letterer
Danilo S Beyruth: Artist
Howard the Duck created by
Steve Gerber & Val Mayerik
I'm a three-foot-tall *duck* and my super-power is *a pretty nice hat.* You're lucky you're getting *anything* out of this.

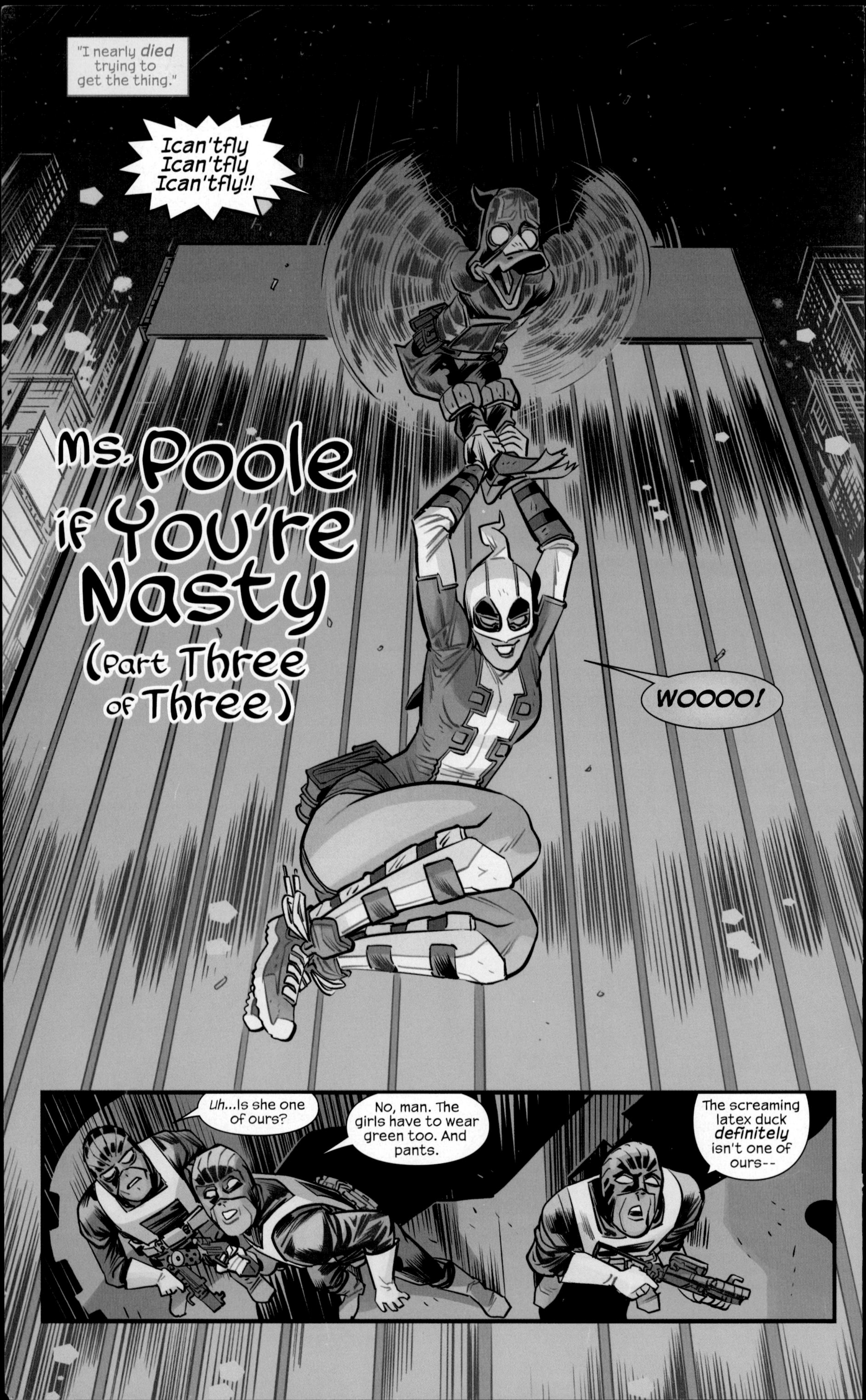
"I nearly died trying to get the thing."
Ican'tfly Ican'tfly Ican'tfly!!
Ms. Poole if You're Nasty
(Part Three of Three)
WOOOO!
Uh...Is she one of ours?
No, man. The girls have to wear green too. And pants.
The screaming latex duck definitely isn't one of ours--

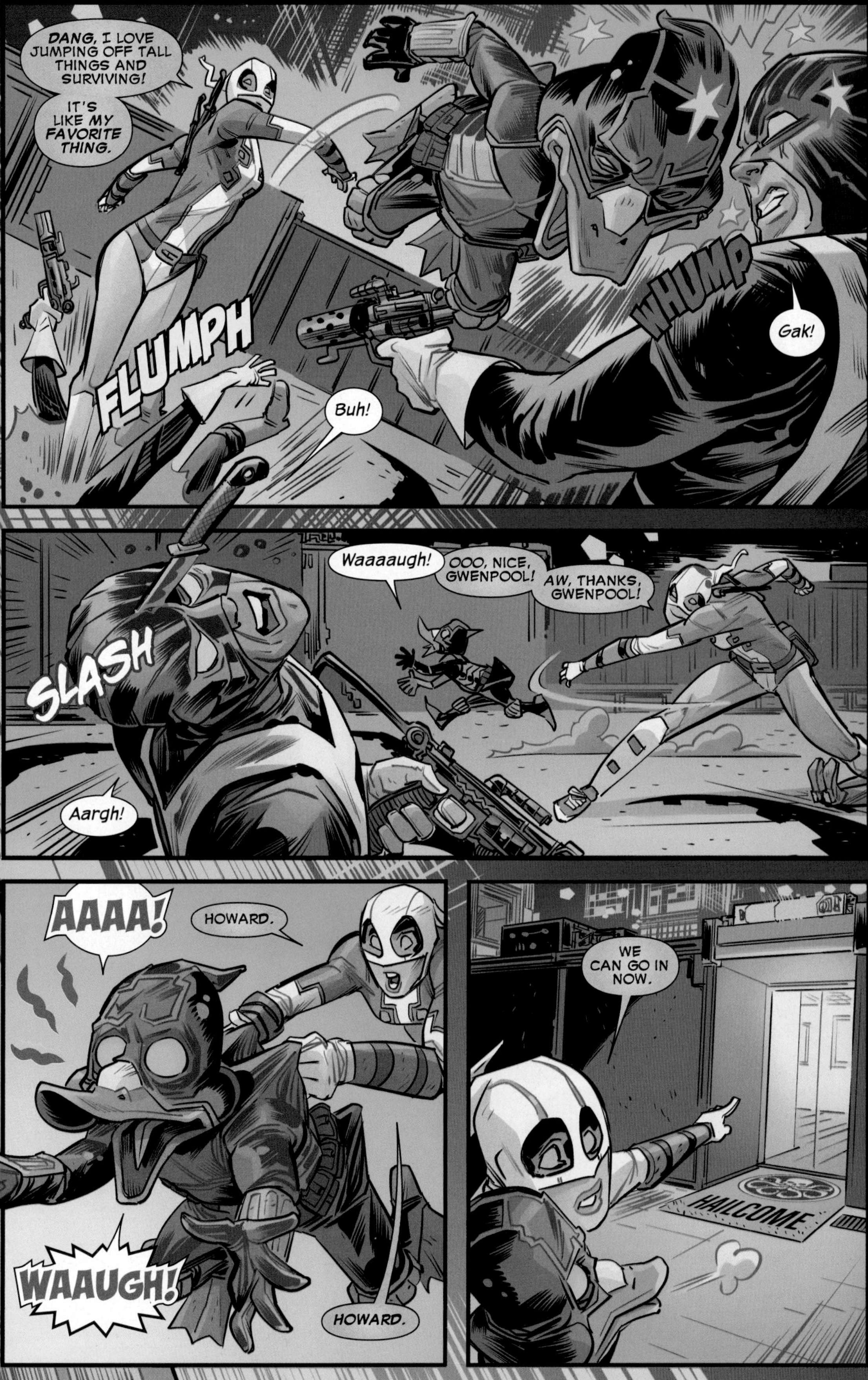
DANG, I LOVE JUMPING OFF TALL THINGS AND SURVIVING!
IT'S LIKE MY FAVORITE THING.
WHUMP
Gak!
FLUMPH
Buh!
Waaaaugh!
OOO, NICE, GWENPOOL!
AW, THANKS, GWENPOOL!
SLASH
Aargh!
AAAA!
HOWARD.
WAAUGH!
HOWARD.
WE CAN GO IN NOW.
HAILCOME

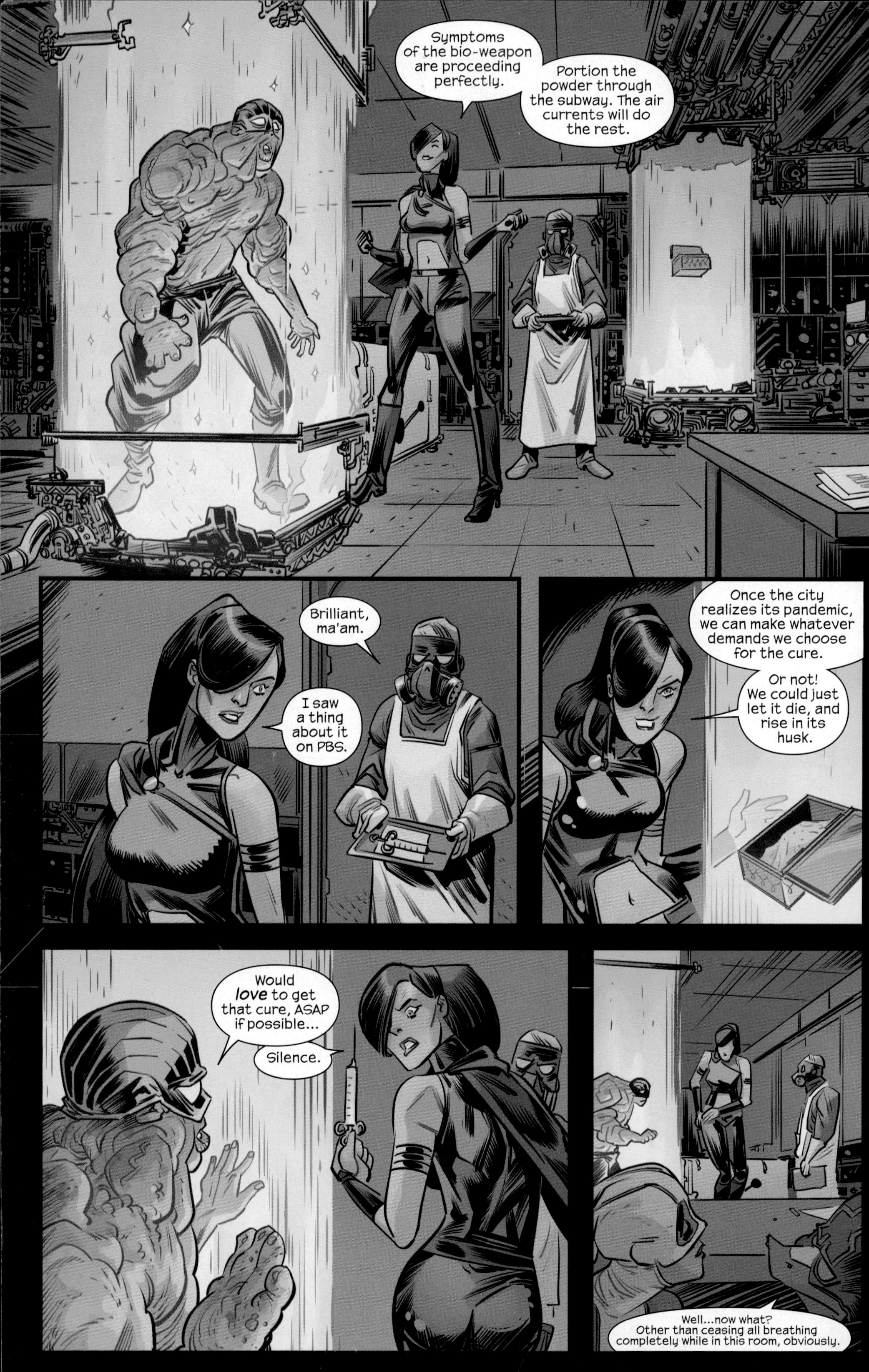

Symptoms of the bio-weapon are proceeding perfectly.
Portion the powder through the subway. The air currents will do the rest.
Brilliant, ma'am.
I saw a thing about it on PBS.
Once the city realizes its pandemic, we can make whatever demands we choose for the cure.
Or not! We could just let it die, and rise in its husk.
Would love to get that cure, ASAP if possible...
Silence.
Well...now what? Other than ceasing all breathing completely while in this room, obviously.

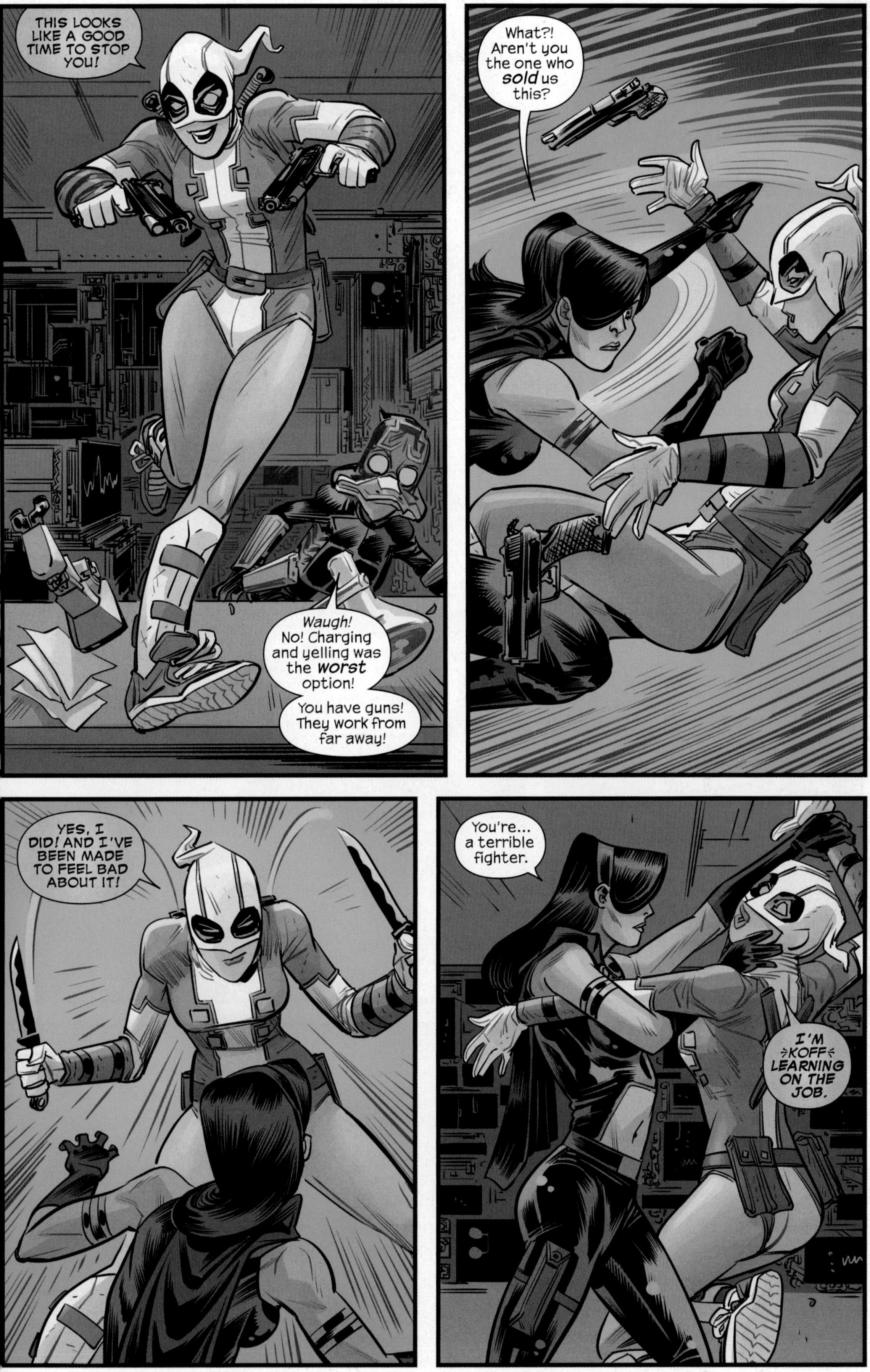
THIS LOOKS LIKE A GOOD TIME TO STOP YOU!
Waugh! No! Charging and yelling was the *worst* option!
You have guns! They work from far away!
What?! Aren't you the one who *sold* us this?
YES, I DID! AND I'VE BEEN MADE TO FEEL BAD ABOUT IT!
You're... a terrible fighter.
I'M KOFF LEARNING ON THE JOB.

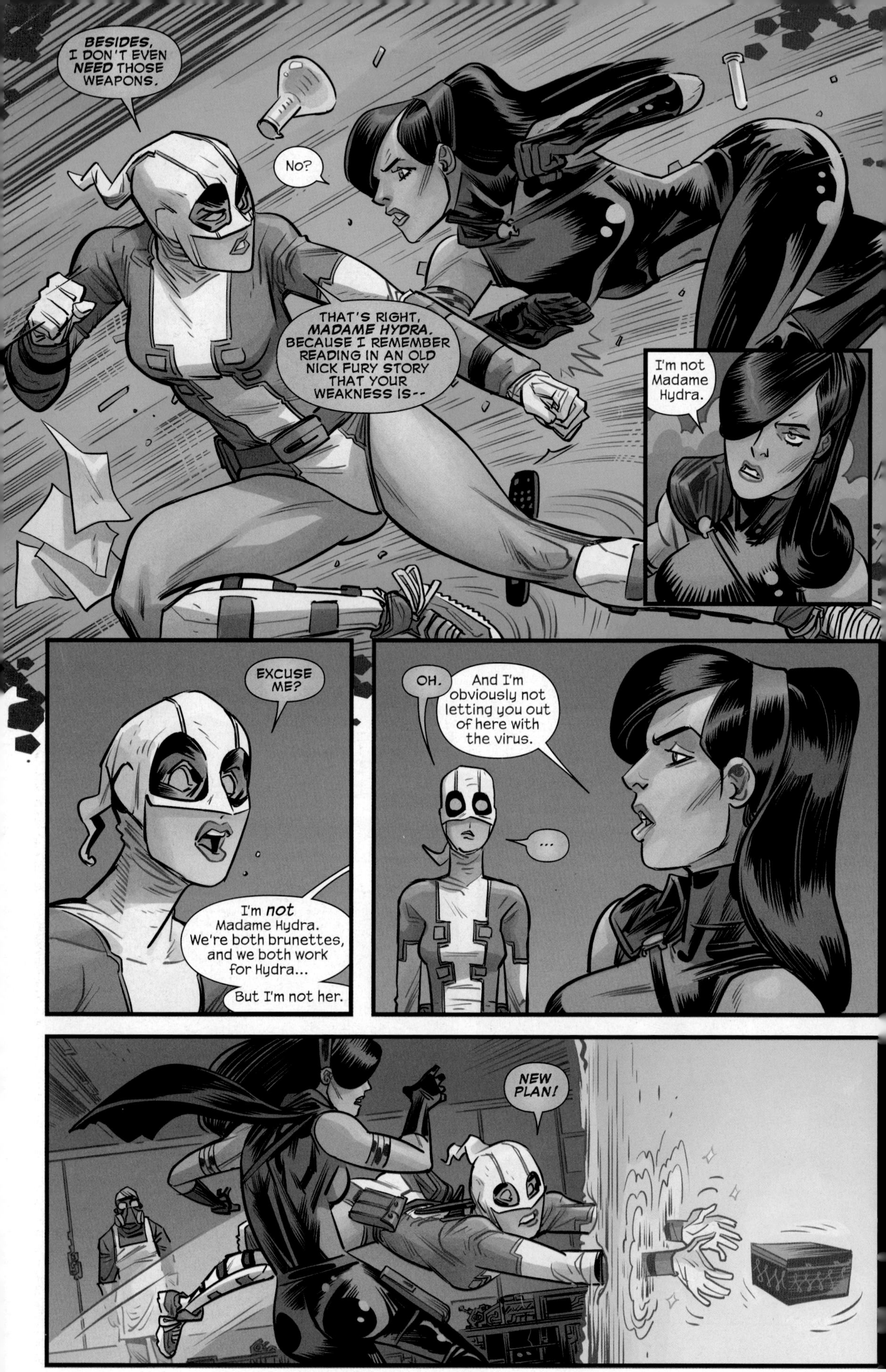
BESIDES, I DON'T EVEN NEED THOSE WEAPONS.
No?
THAT'S RIGHT, MADAME HYDRA. BECAUSE I REMEMBER READING IN AN OLD NICK FURY STORY THAT YOUR WEAKNESS IS--
I'm not Madame Hydra.
EXCUSE ME?
I'm not Madame Hydra. We're both brunettes, and we both work for Hydra...
But I'm not her.
OH.
And I'm obviously not letting you out of here with the virus.
...
NEW PLAN!

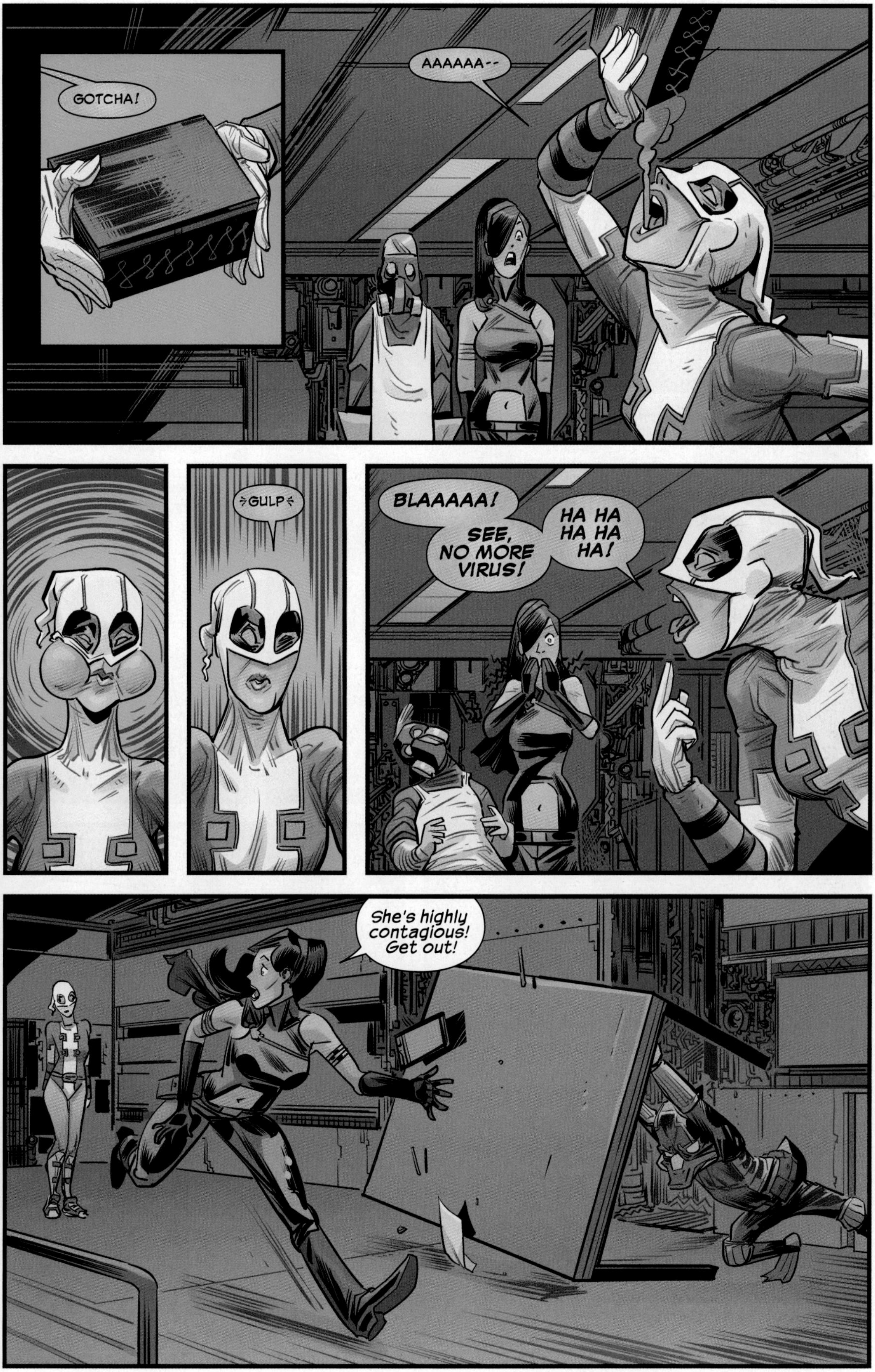

GOTCHA!
AAAAAA--
GULP
BLAAAAA!
SEE, NO MORE VIRUS!
HA HA HA HA HA!
She's highly contagious! Get out!

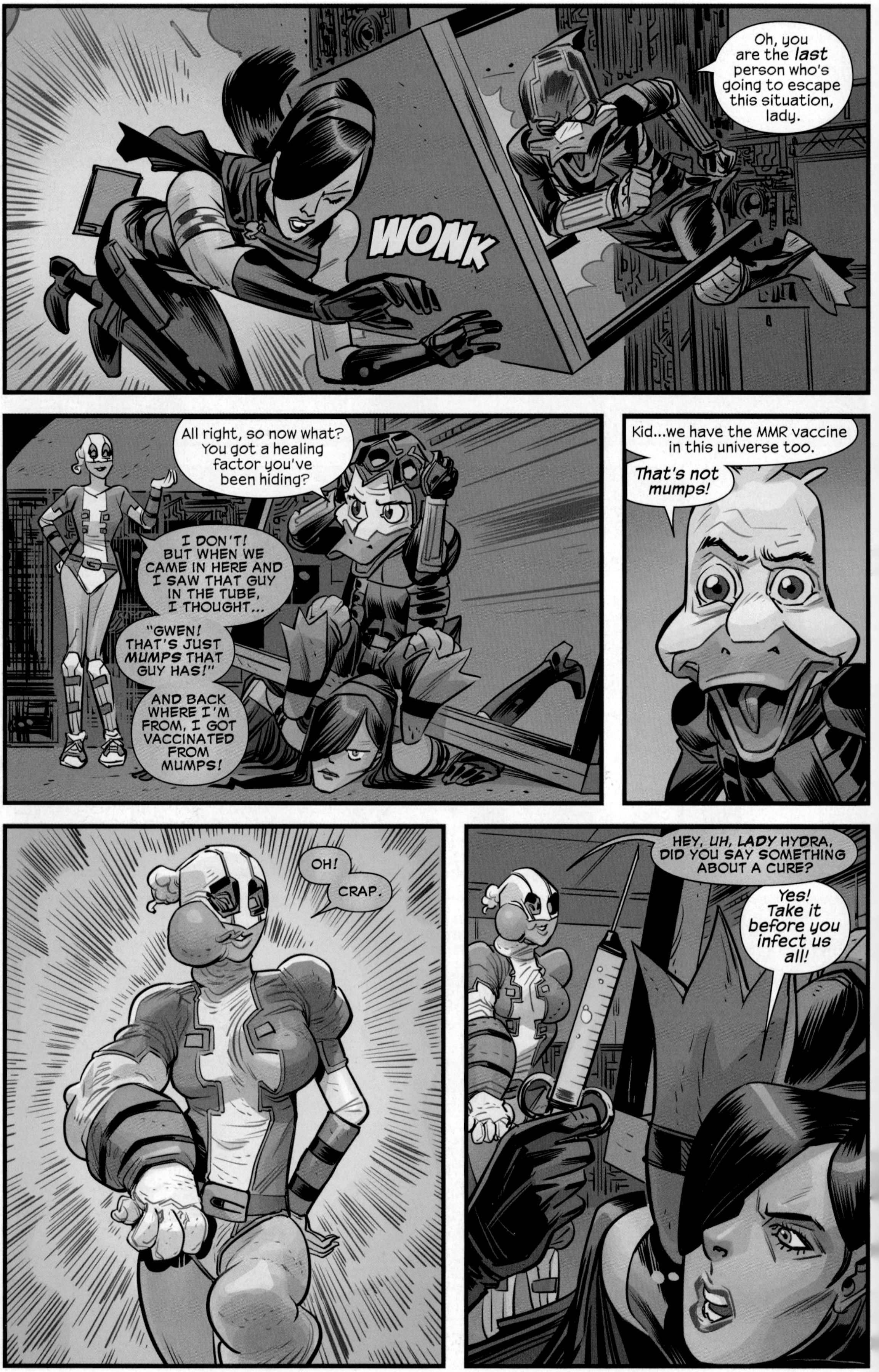
Oh, you are the *last* person who's going to escape this situation, lady.
WONK
All right, so now what? You got a healing factor you've been hiding?
I DON'T! BUT WHEN WE CAME IN HERE AND I SAW THAT GUY IN THE TUBE, I THOUGHT...
"GWEN! THAT'S JUST *MUMPS* THAT GUY HAS!"
AND BACK WHERE I'M FROM, I GOT VACCINATED FROM MUMPS!
Kid...we have the MMR vaccine in this universe too.
*That's not mumps!*
OH!
CRAP.
HEY, *UH, LADY* HYDRA, DID YOU SAY SOMETHING ABOUT A CURE?
*Yes! Take it before you infect us all!*

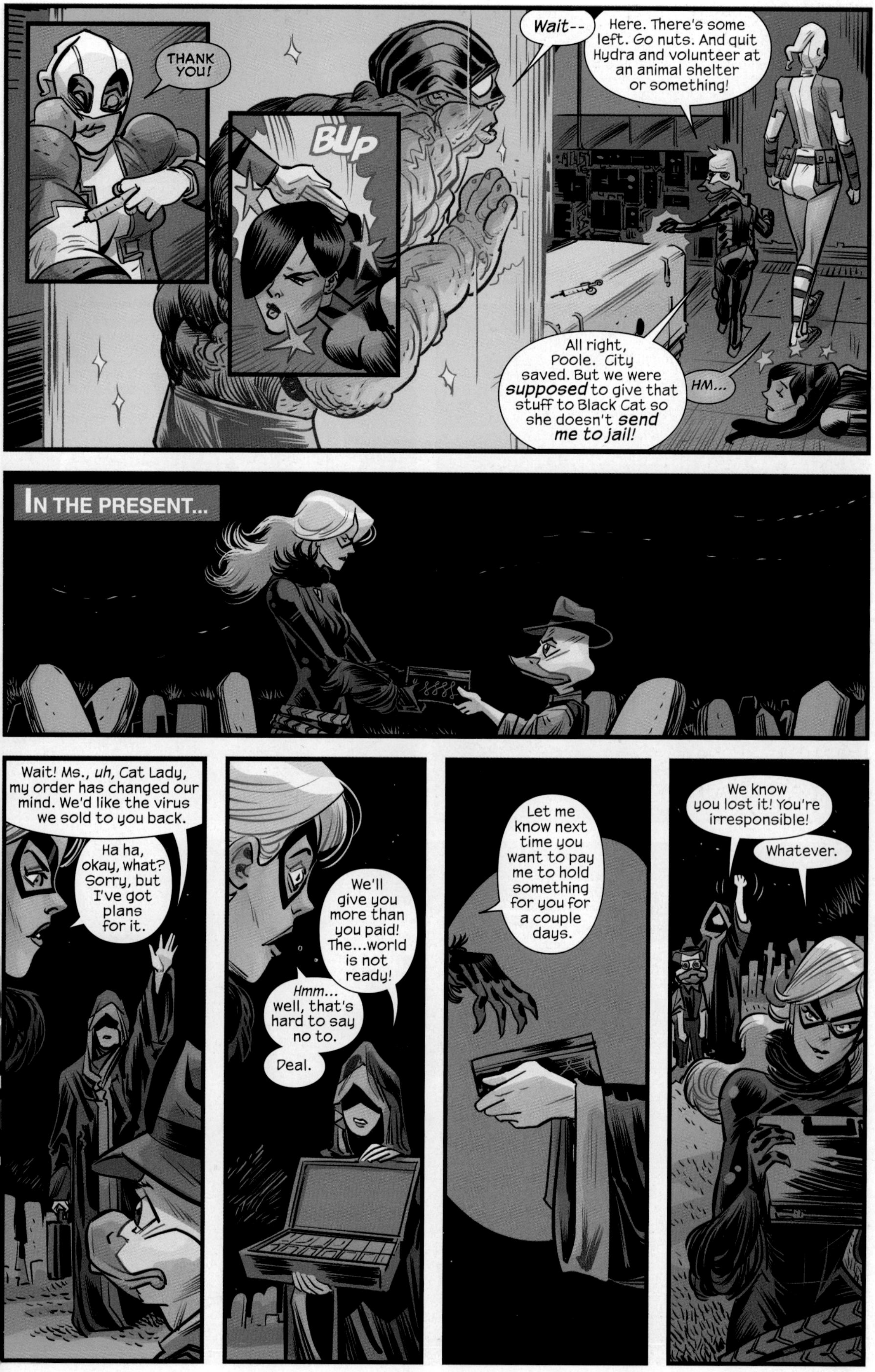
THANK YOU!
BUP
Wait--
Here. There's some left. Go nuts. And quit Hydra and volunteer at an animal shelter or something!
All right, Poole. City saved. But we were *supposed* to give that stuff to Black Cat so she doesn't *send me to jail!*
HM...
IN THE PRESENT...
Wait! Ms., *uh,* Cat Lady, my order has changed our mind. We'd like the virus we sold to you back.
Ha ha, okay, what? Sorry, but I've got plans for it.
We'll give you more than you paid! The...world is not ready!
*Hmm...* well, that's hard to say no to.
Deal.
Let me know next time you want to pay me to hold something for you for a couple days.
We know you lost it! You're irresponsible!
Whatever.

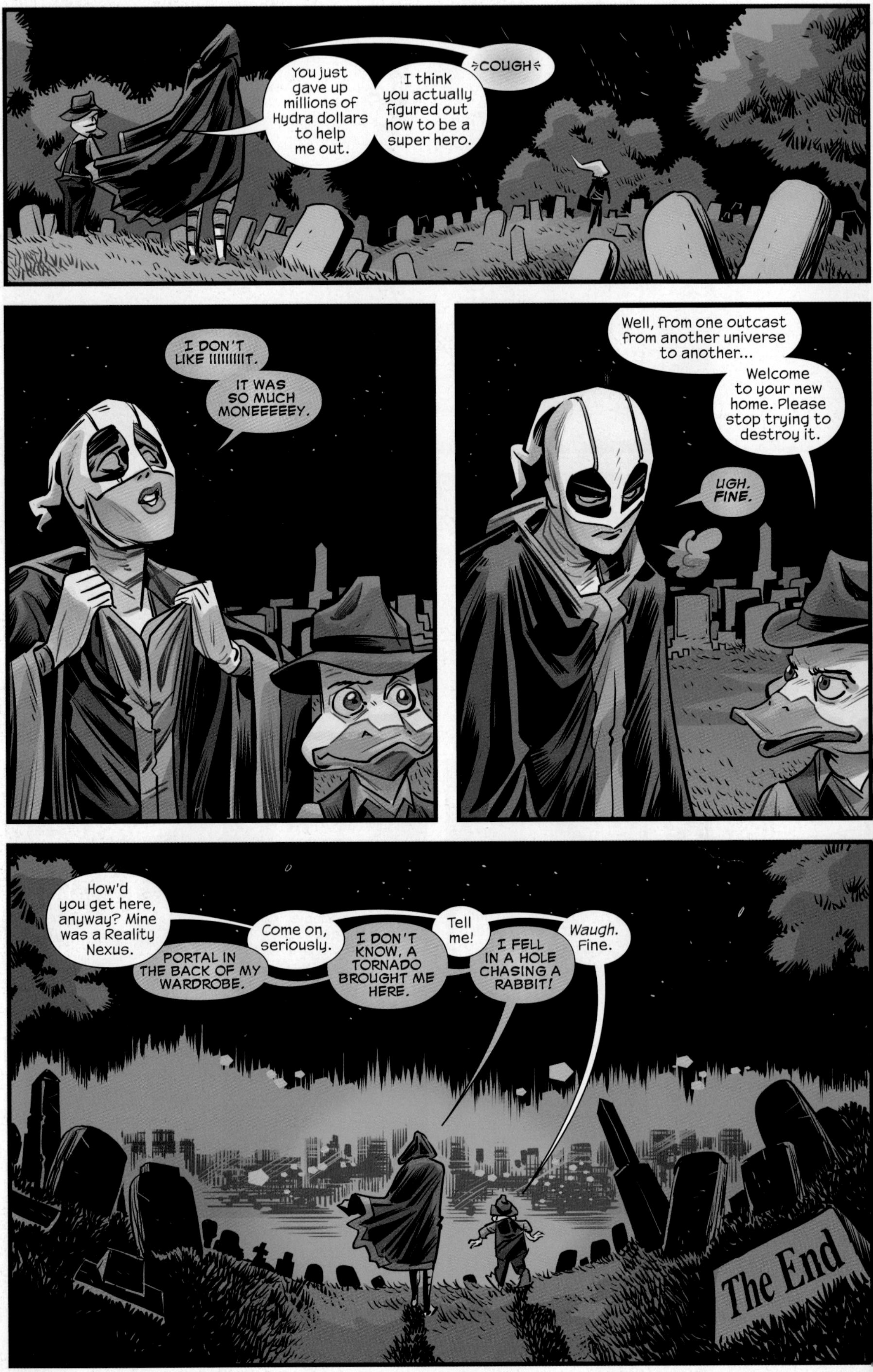
You just gave up millions of Hydra dollars to help me out.
COUGH
I think you actually figured out how to be a super hero.
I DON'T LIKE IIIIIIIIT.
IT WAS SO MUCH MONEEEEEY.
Well, from one outcast from another universe to another...
Welcome to your new home. Please stop trying to destroy it.
UGH. FINE.
How'd you get here, anyway? Mine was a Reality Nexus.
PORTAL IN THE BACK OF MY WARDROBE.
Come on, seriously.
I DON'T KNOW, A TORNADO BROUGHT ME HERE.
Tell me!
I FELL IN A HOLE CHASING A RABBIT!
Waugh. Fine.
The End

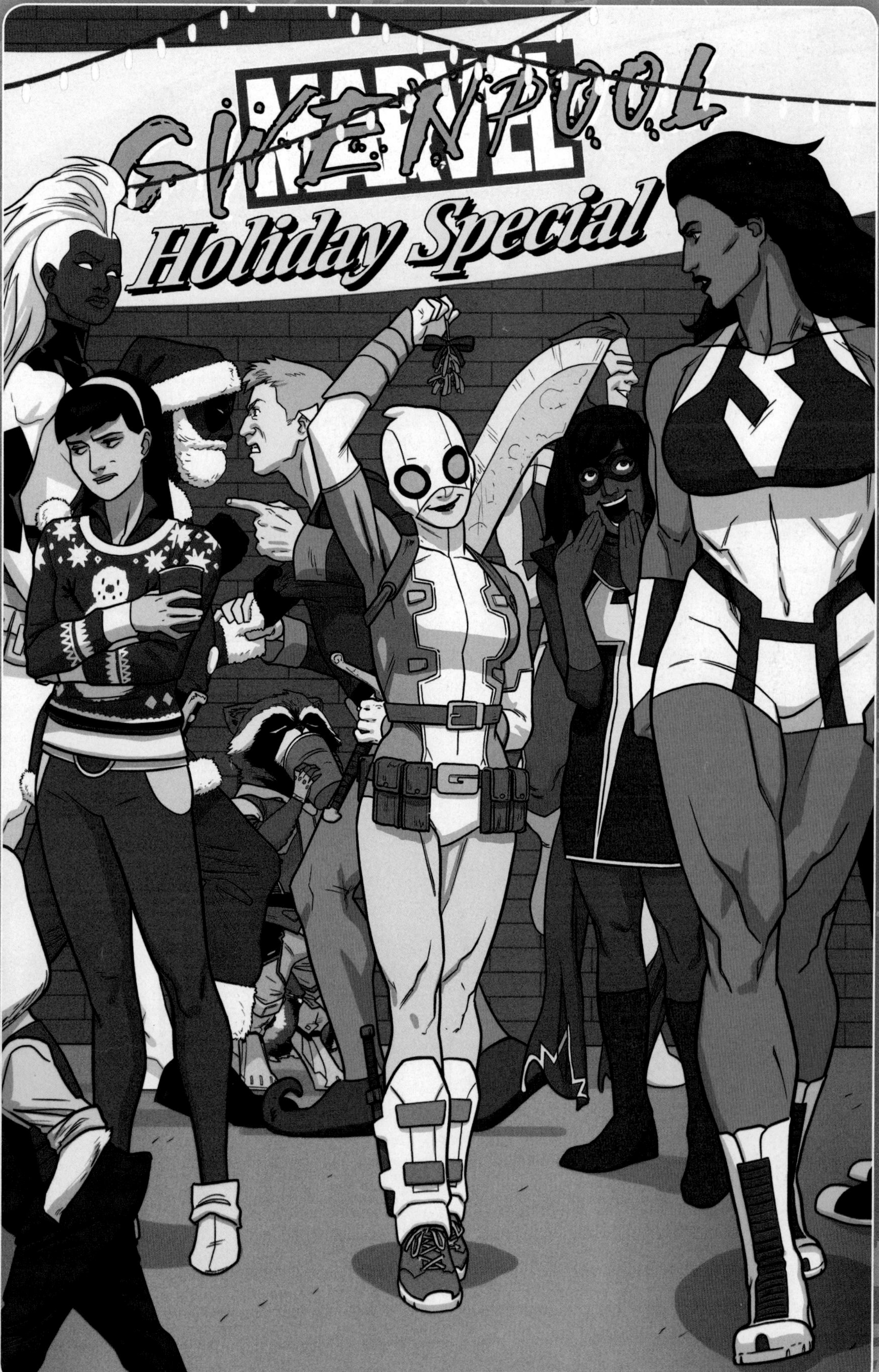
MARVEL
GWENPOOL
Holiday Special

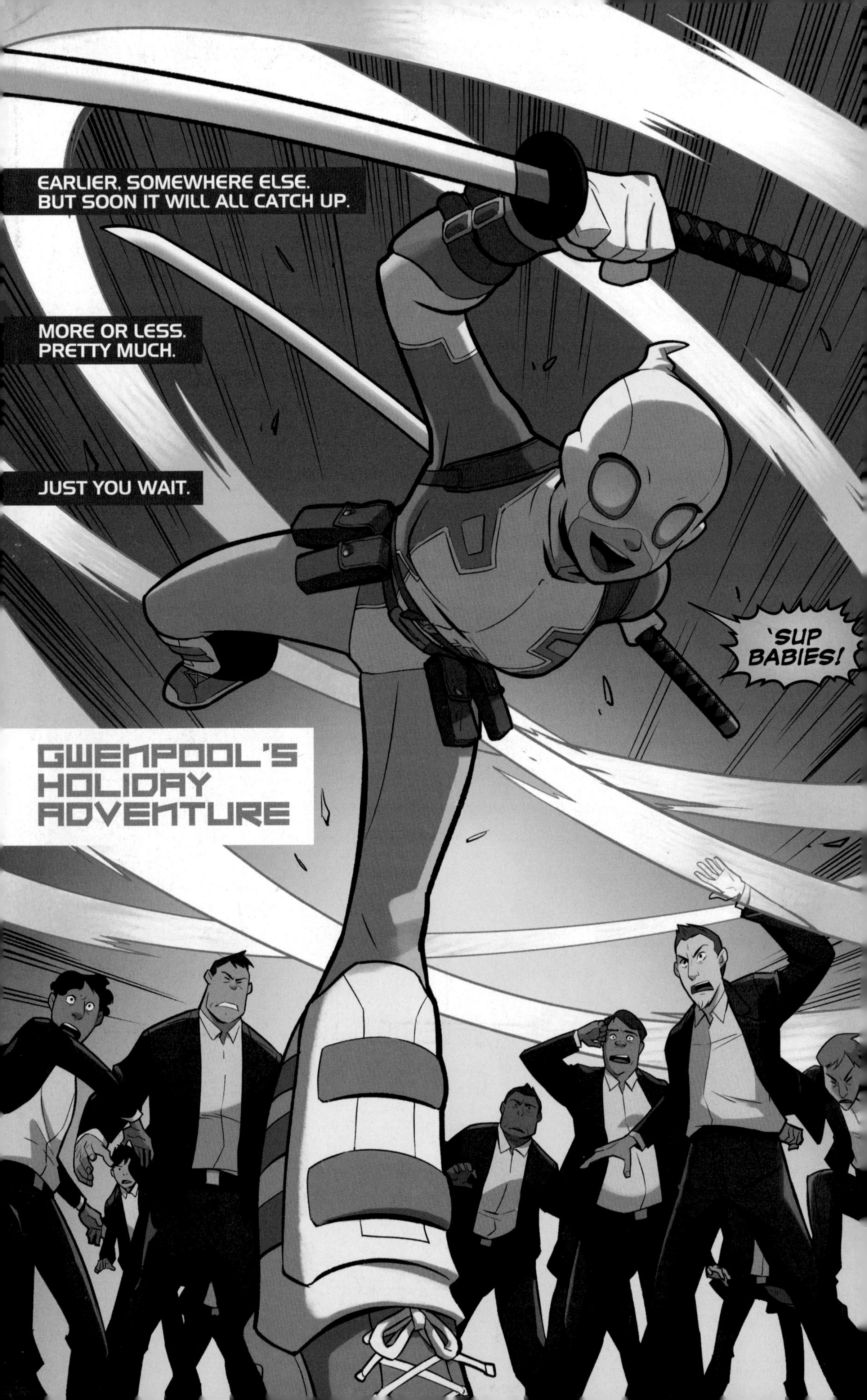
EARLIER, SOMEWHERE ELSE.
BUT SOON IT WILL ALL CATCH UP.
MORE OR LESS.
PRETTY MUCH.
JUST YOU WAIT.
'SUP BABIES!
GWENPOOL'S HOLIDAY ADVENTURE

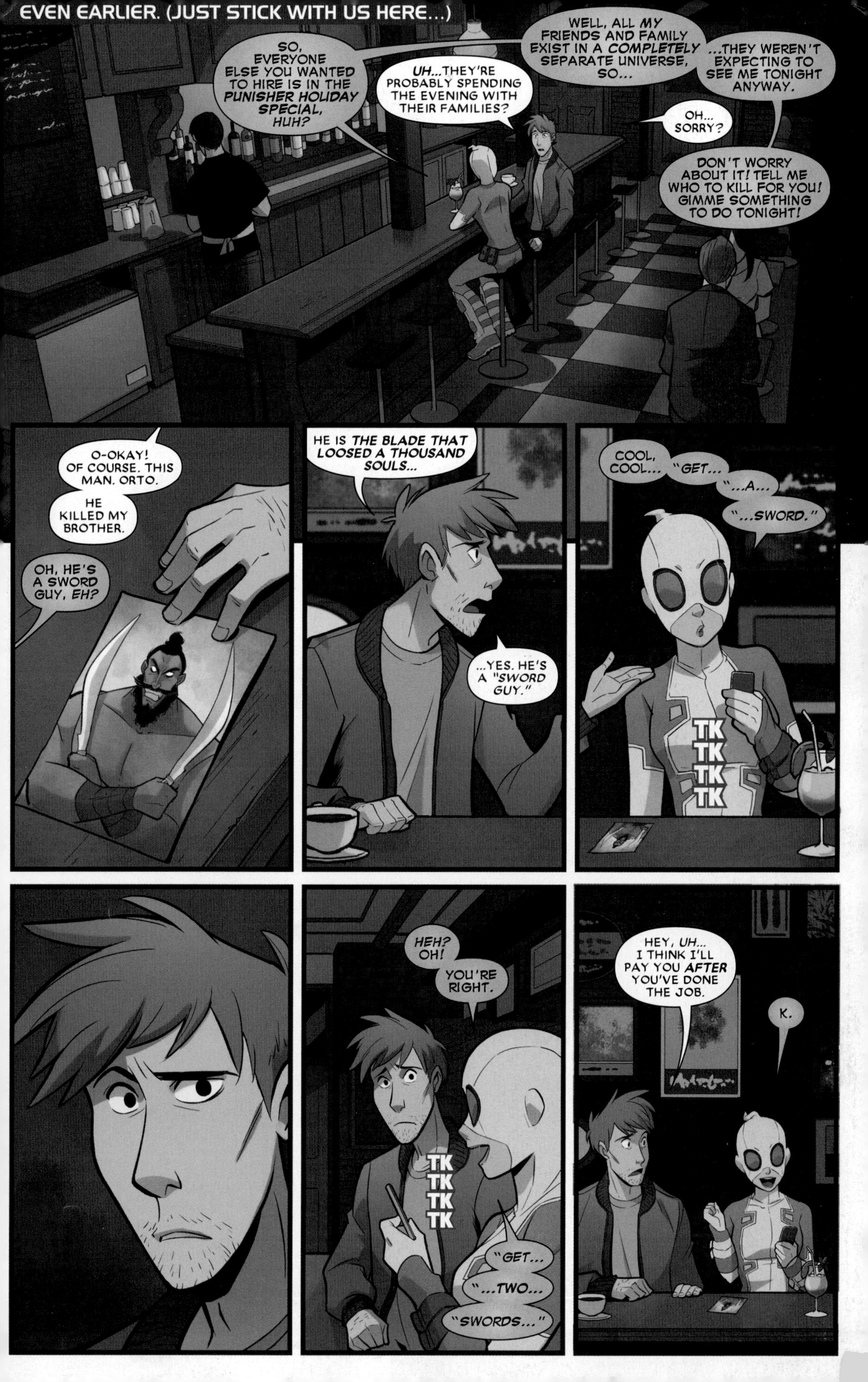
EVEN EARLIER. (JUST STICK WITH US HERE...)
SO, EVERYONE ELSE YOU WANTED TO HIRE IS IN THE PUNISHER HOLIDAY SPECIAL, HUH?
UH... THEY'RE PROBABLY SPENDING THE EVENING WITH THEIR FAMILIES?
WELL, ALL MY FRIENDS AND FAMILY EXIST IN A COMPLETELY SEPARATE UNIVERSE, SO...
...THEY WEREN'T EXPECTING TO SEE ME TONIGHT ANYWAY.
OH... SORRY?
DON'T WORRY ABOUT IT! TELL ME WHO TO KILL FOR YOU! GIMME SOMETHING TO DO TONIGHT!
O-OKAY! OF COURSE. THIS MAN. ORTO.
HE KILLED MY BROTHER.
OH, HE'S A SWORD GUY, EH?
HE IS THE BLADE THAT LOOSED A THOUSAND SOULS...
...YES. HE'S A "SWORD GUY."
COOL, COOL... "GET...
"...A...
"...SWORD."
TK TK TK TK
HEH? OH!
YOU'RE RIGHT.
TK TK TK TK
"GET...
"...TWO...
"SWORDS..."
HEY, UH... I THINK I'LL PAY YOU AFTER YOU'VE DONE THE JOB.
K.

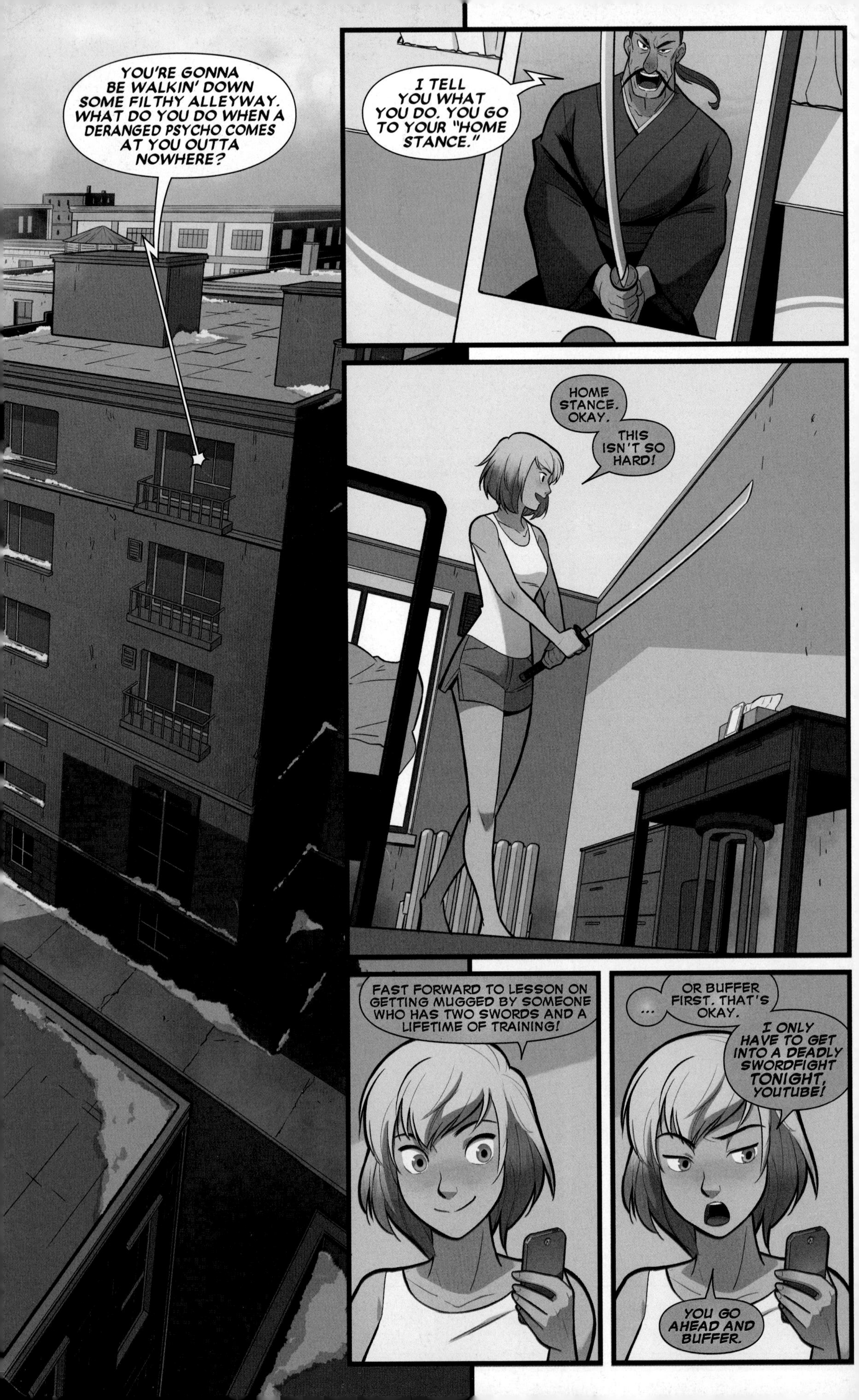
YOU'RE GONNA BE WALKIN' DOWN SOME FILTHY ALLEYWAY. WHAT DO YOU DO WHEN A DERANGED PSYCHO COMES AT YOU OUTTA NOWHERE?
I TELL YOU WHAT YOU DO. YOU GO TO YOUR "HOME STANCE."
HOME STANCE. OKAY.
THIS ISN'T SO HARD!
FAST FORWARD TO LESSON ON GETTING MUGGED BY SOMEONE WHO HAS TWO SWORDS AND A LIFETIME OF TRAINING!
...
OR BUFFER FIRST. THAT'S OKAY.
I ONLY HAVE TO GET INTO A DEADLY SWORDFIGHT TONIGHT, YOUTUBE!
YOU GO AHEAD AND BUFFER.

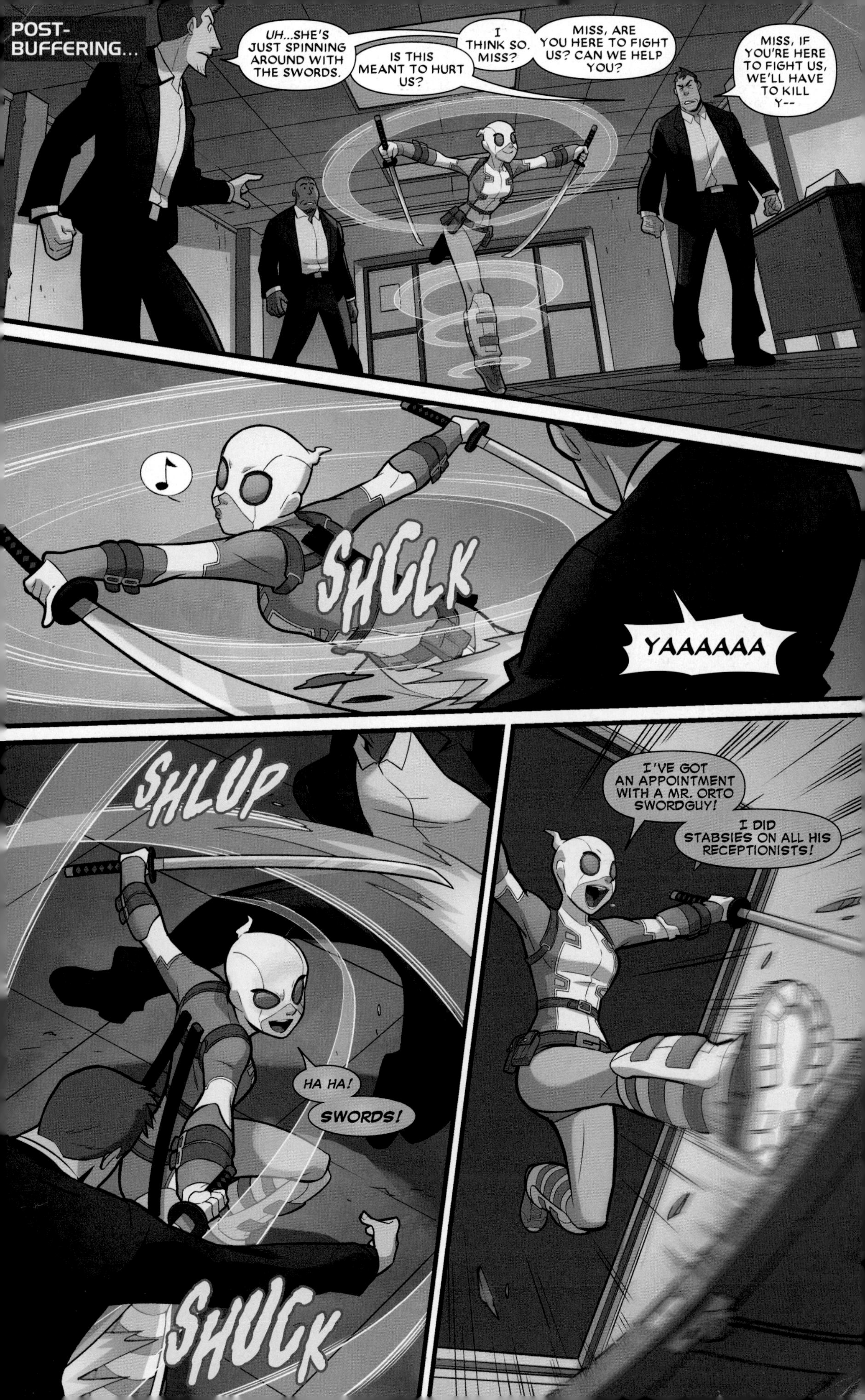
POST-BUFFERING...
UH...SHE'S JUST SPINNING AROUND WITH THE SWORDS.
IS THIS MEANT TO HURT US?
I THINK SO. MISS?
MISS, ARE YOU HERE TO FIGHT US? CAN WE HELP YOU?
MISS, IF YOU'RE HERE TO FIGHT US, WE'LL HAVE TO KILL Y--
SHCLK
YAAAAAA
SHLUP
HA HA!
SWORDS!
SHUCK
I'VE GOT AN APPOINTMENT WITH A MR. ORTO SWORDGUY!
I DID STABSIES ON ALL HIS RECEPTIONISTS!

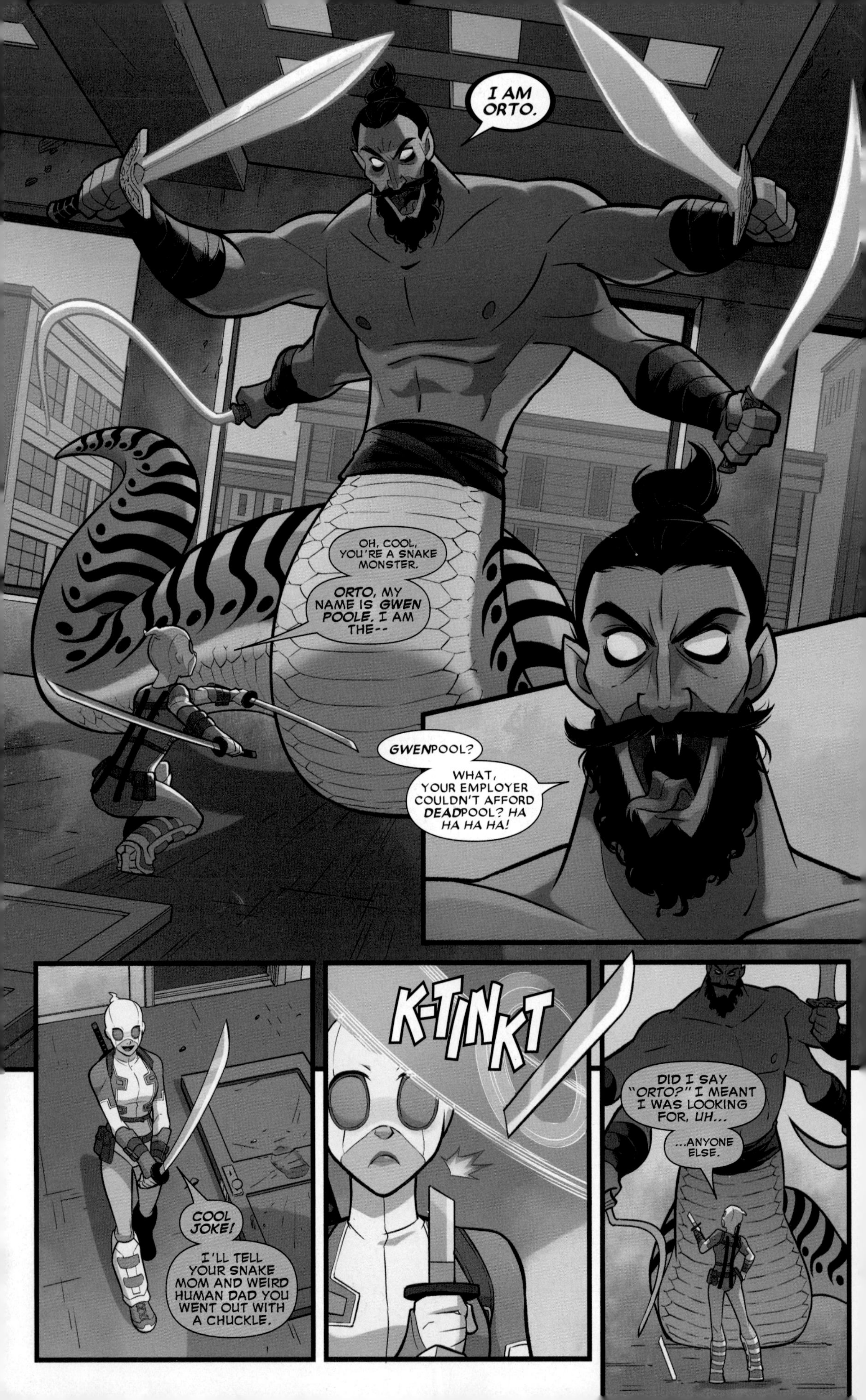
I AM ORTO.
OH, COOL, YOU'RE A SNAKE MONSTER.
ORTO, MY NAME IS GWEN POOLE. I AM THE--
GWENPOOL?
WHAT, YOUR EMPLOYER COULDN'T AFFORD DEADPOOL? HA HA HA HA!
COOL JOKE!
I'LL TELL YOUR SNAKE MOM AND WEIRD HUMAN DAD YOU WENT OUT WITH A CHUCKLE.
K-TINKT
DID I SAY "ORTO?" I MEANT I WAS LOOKING FOR, UH...
...ANYONE ELSE.

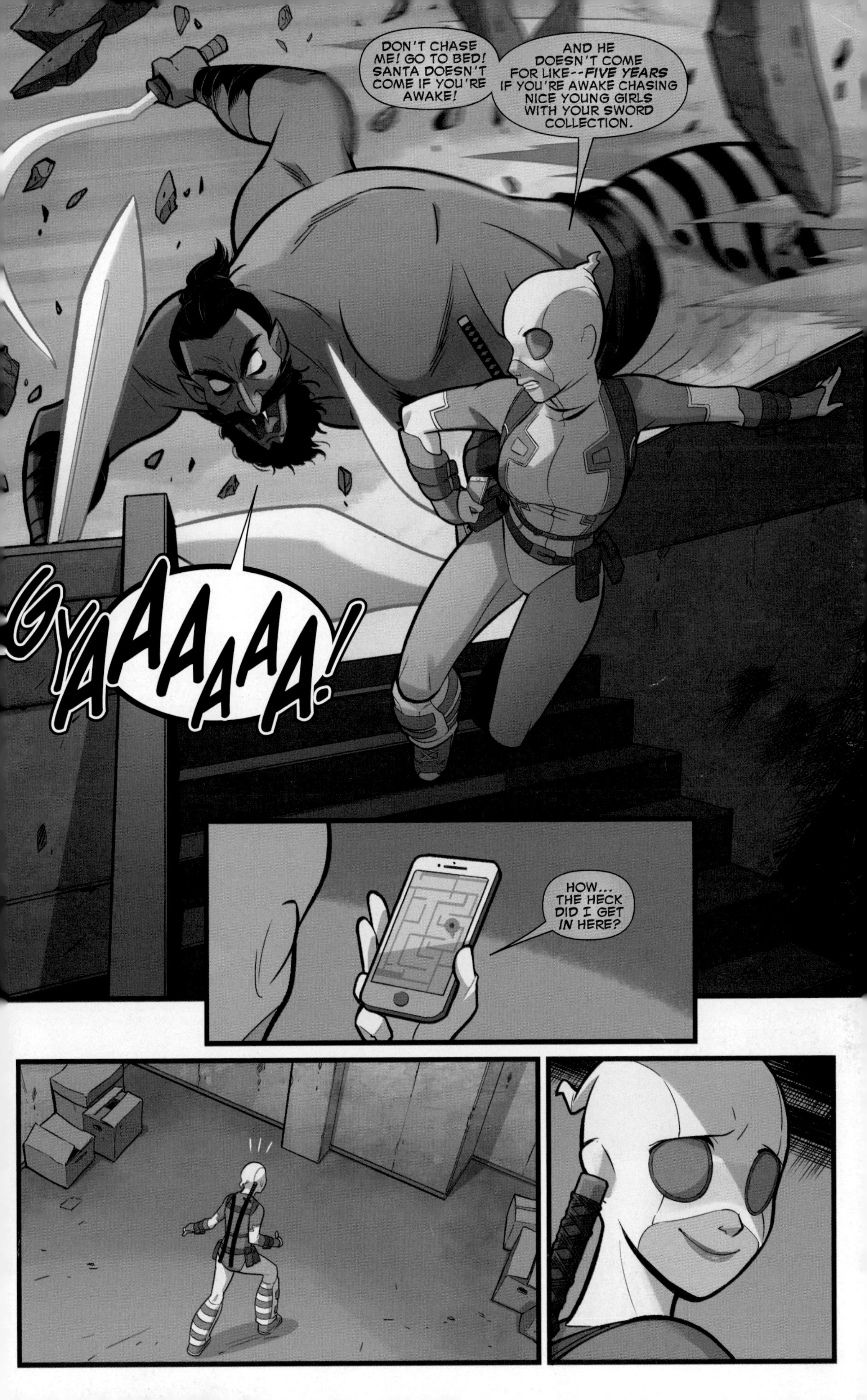
DON'T CHASE ME! GO TO BED! SANTA DOESN'T COME IF YOU'RE AWAKE!
AND HE DOESN'T COME FOR LIKE--*FIVE YEARS* IF YOU'RE AWAKE CHASING NICE YOUNG GIRLS WITH YOUR SWORD COLLECTION.
GYAAAAAAA!
HOW... THE HECK DID I GET IN HERE?

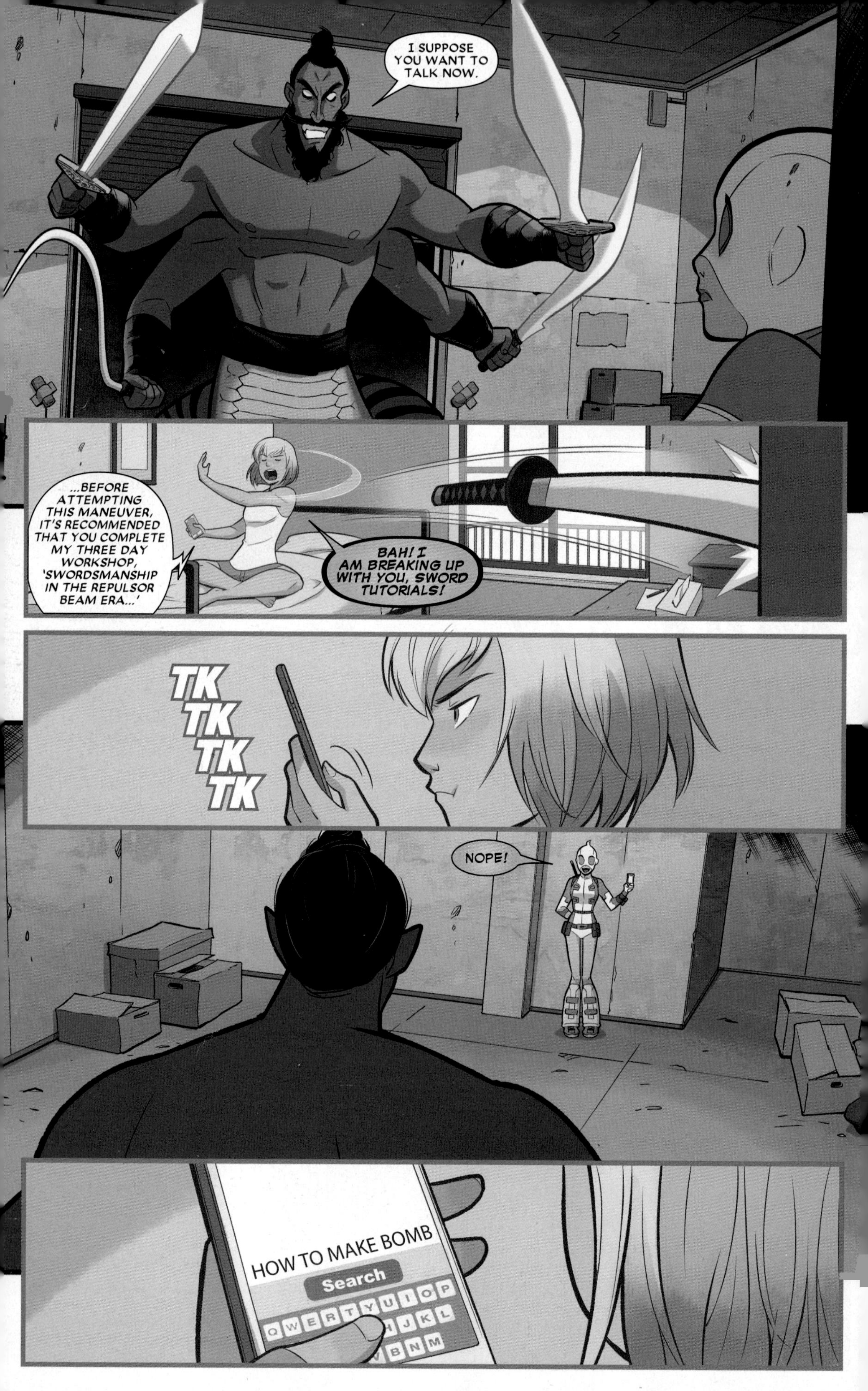
I SUPPOSE YOU WANT TO TALK NOW.
...BEFORE ATTEMPTING THIS MANEUVER, IT'S RECOMMENDED THAT YOU COMPLETE MY THREE DAY WORKSHOP, 'SWORDSMANSHIP IN THE REPULSOR BEAM ERA...'
BAH! I AM BREAKING UP WITH YOU, SWORD TUTORIALS!
TK TK TK TK
NOPE!
HOW TO MAKE BOMB
Search

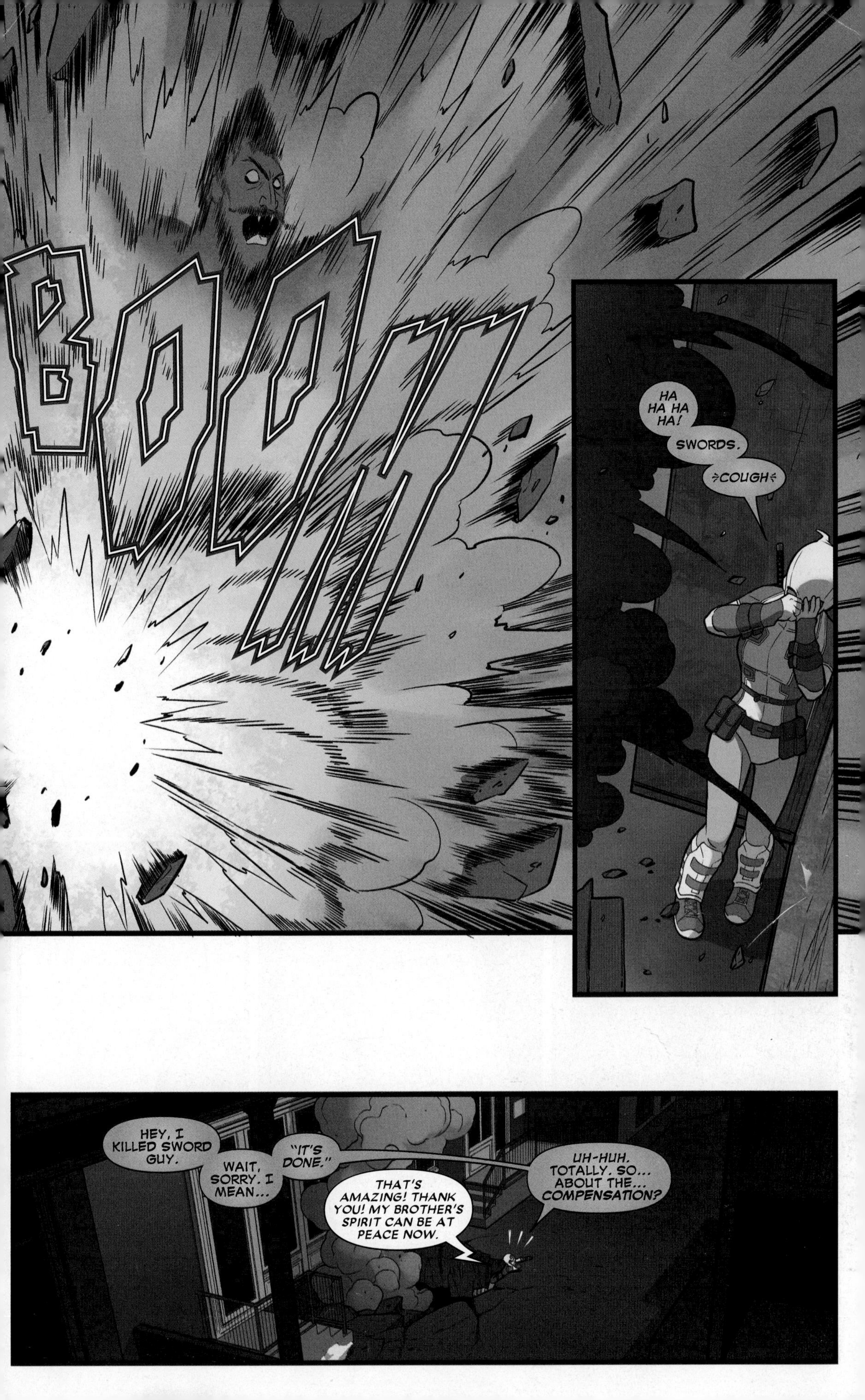
BOOM
HA HA HA HA!
SWORDS.
COUGH
HEY, I KILLED SWORD GUY.
WAIT, SORRY. I MEAN...
"IT'S DONE."
THAT'S AMAZING! THANK YOU! MY BROTHER'S SPIRIT CAN BE AT PEACE NOW.
UH-HUH. TOTALLY. SO... ABOUT THE... COMPENSATION?

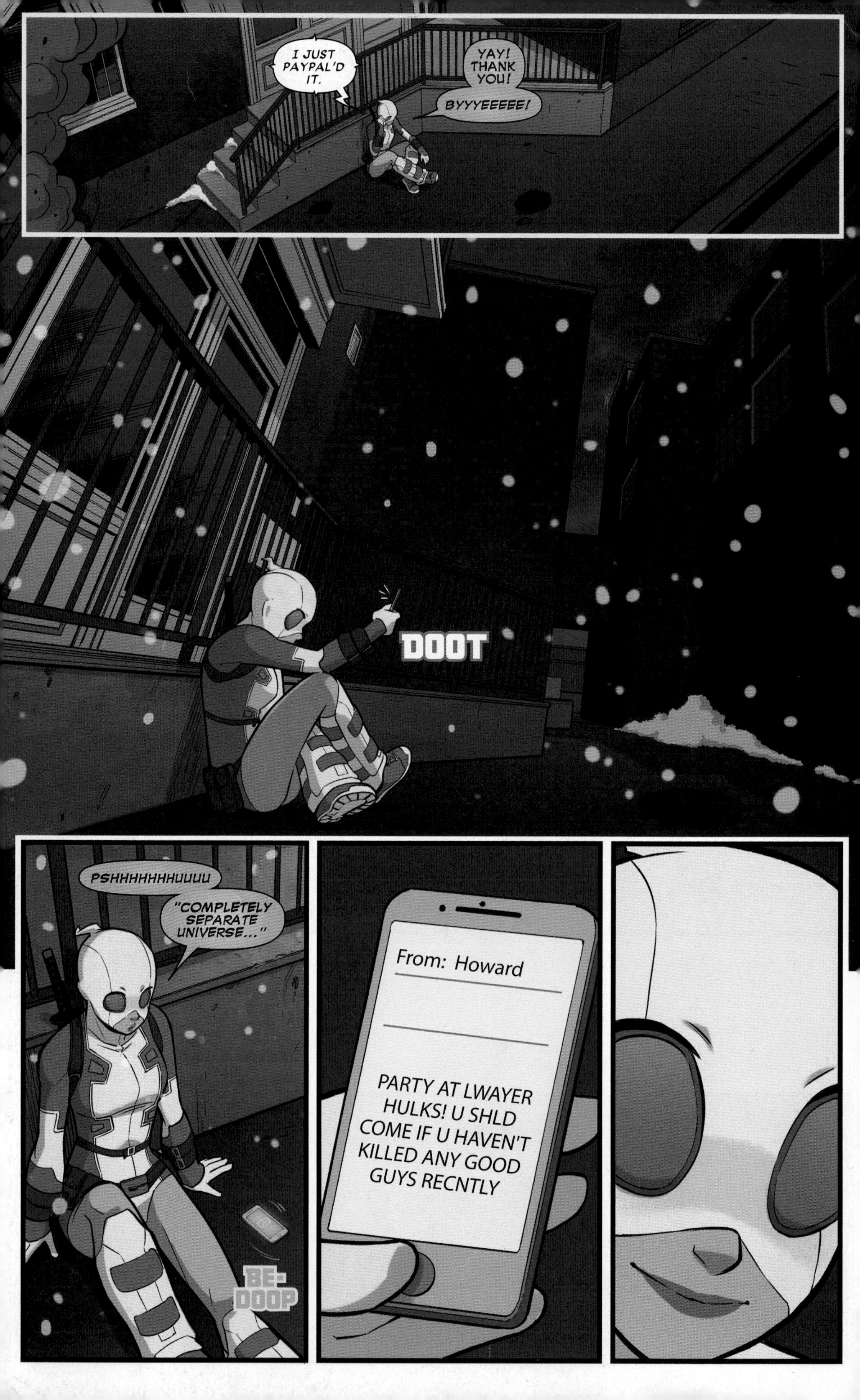
I JUST PAYPAL'D IT.
YAY! THANK YOU!
BYYYEEEEE!
DOOT
PSHHHHHHHHUUUU
"COMPLETELY SEPARATE UNIVERSE..."
BE-DOOP
From: Howard
PARTY AT LWAYER HULKS! U SHLD COME IF U HAVEN'T KILLED ANY GOOD GUYS RECNTLY

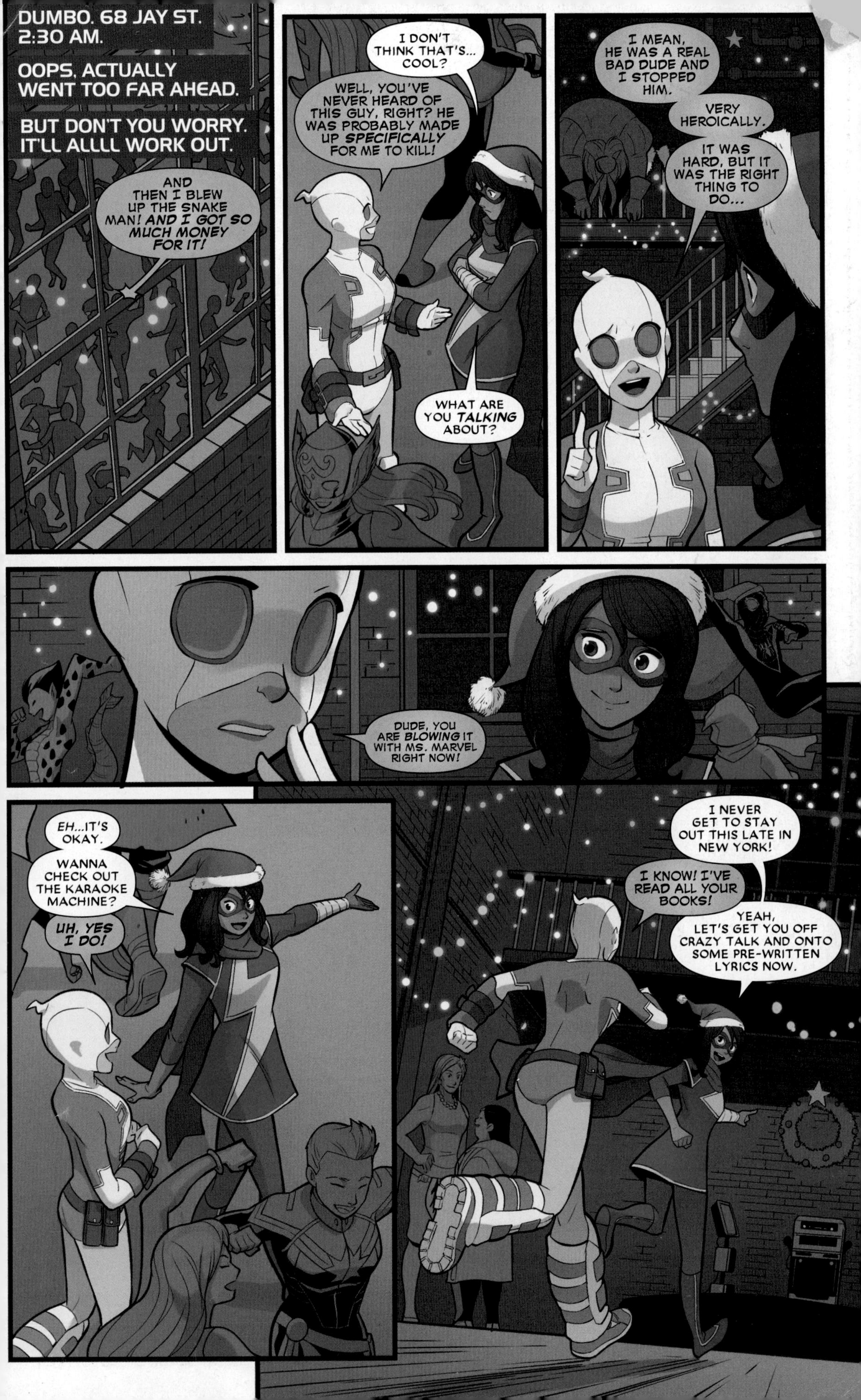
DUMBO. 68 JAY ST. 2:30 AM.
OOPS, ACTUALLY WENT TOO FAR AHEAD.
BUT DON'T YOU WORRY. IT'LL ALLLL WORK OUT.
AND THEN I BLEW UP THE SNAKE MAN! AND I GOT SO MUCH MONEY FOR IT!
I DON'T THINK THAT'S... COOL?
WELL, YOU'VE NEVER HEARD OF THIS GUY, RIGHT? HE WAS PROBABLY MADE UP SPECIFICALLY FOR ME TO KILL!
WHAT ARE YOU TALKING ABOUT?
I MEAN, HE WAS A REAL BAD DUDE AND I STOPPED HIM.
VERY HEROICALLY.
IT WAS HARD, BUT IT WAS THE RIGHT THING TO DO...
DUDE, YOU ARE BLOWING IT WITH MS. MARVEL RIGHT NOW!
EH...IT'S OKAY.
WANNA CHECK OUT THE KARAOKE MACHINE?
UH, YES I DO!
I NEVER GET TO STAY OUT THIS LATE IN NEW YORK!
I KNOW! I'VE READ ALL YOUR BOOKS!
YEAH, LET'S GET YOU OFF CRAZY TALK AND ONTO SOME PRE-WRITTEN LYRICS NOW.

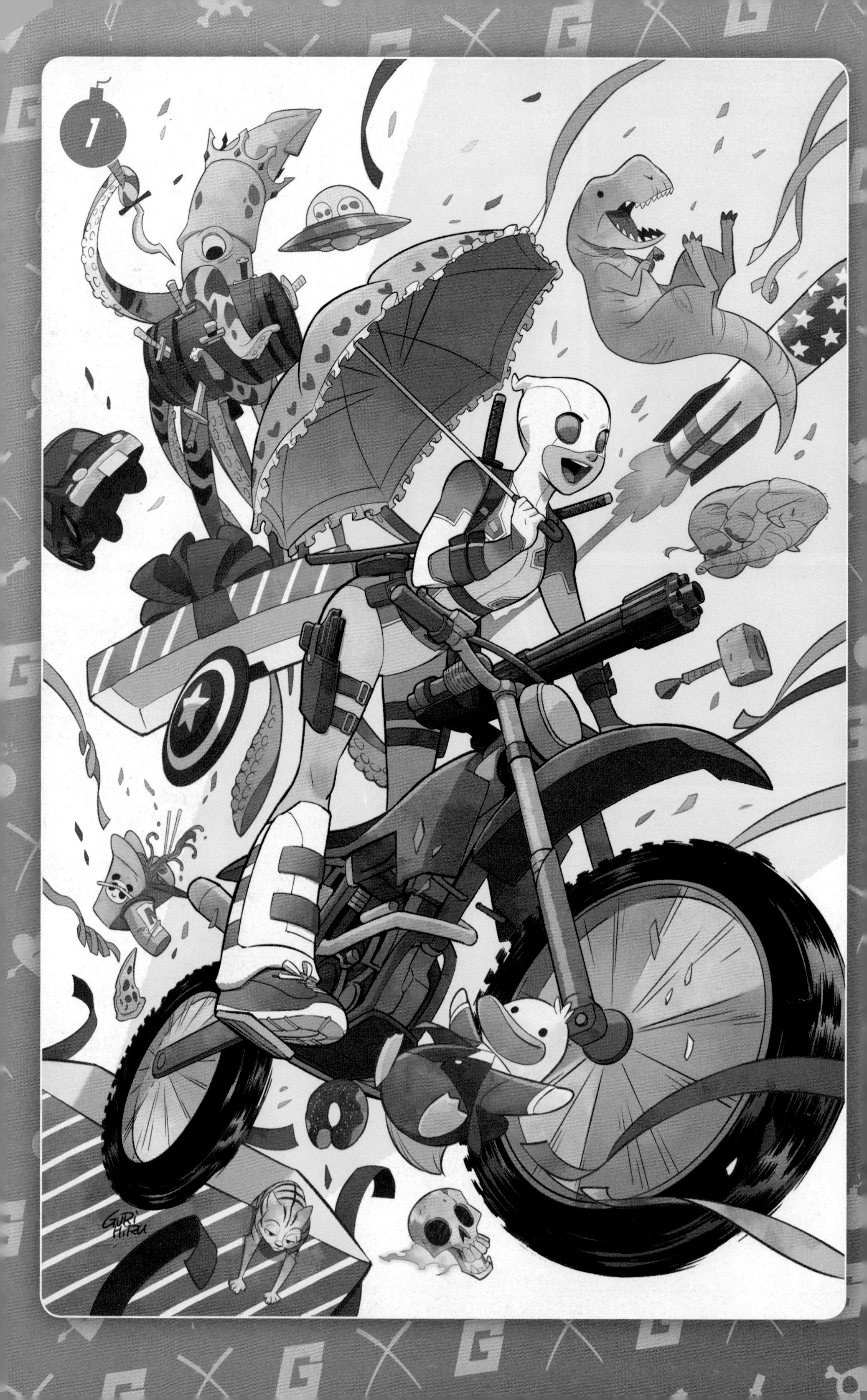
1
GURI HIRU

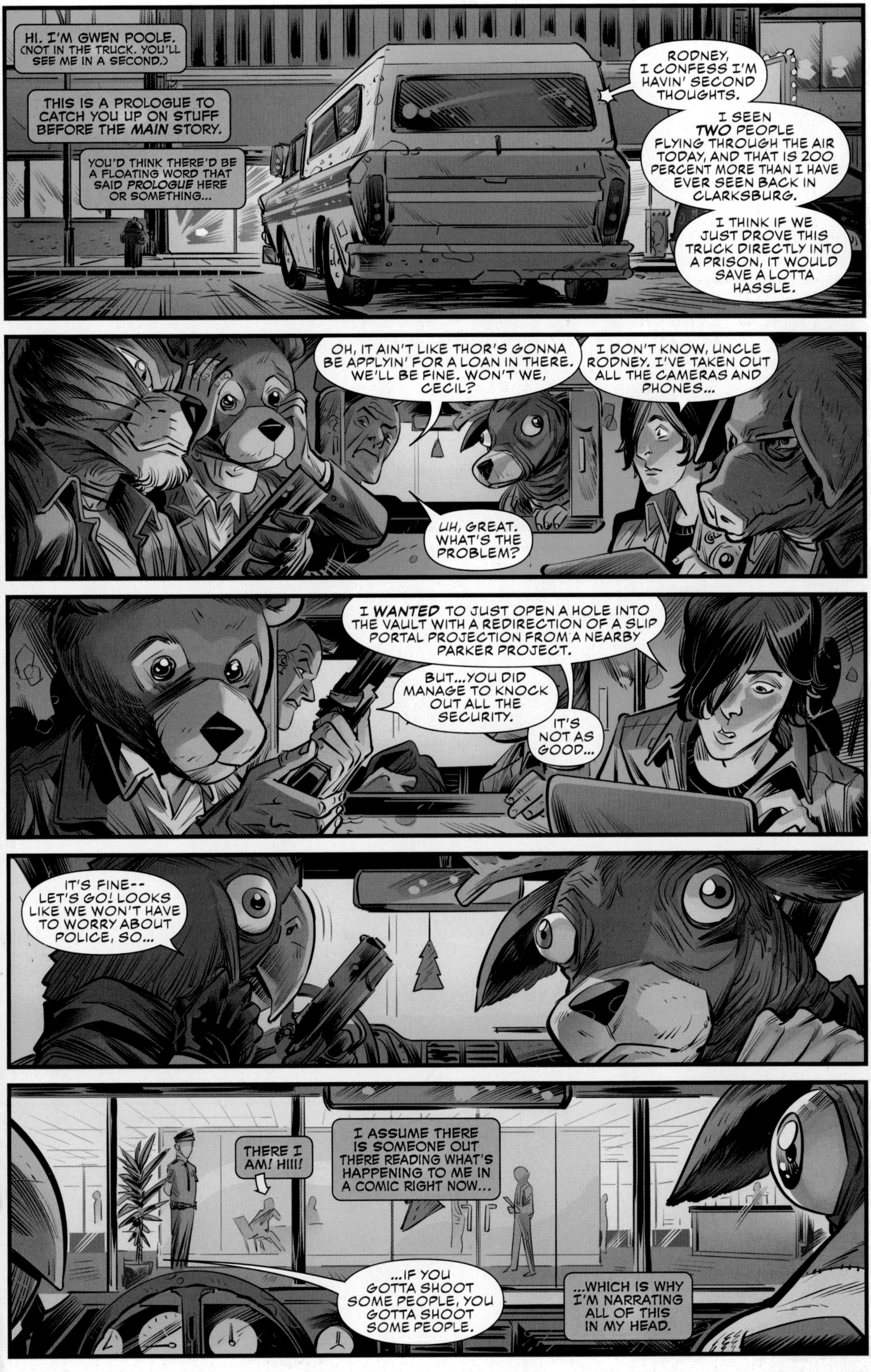

HI. I'M GWEN POOLE. (NOT IN THE TRUCK. YOU'LL SEE ME IN A SECOND.)
THIS IS A PROLOGUE TO CATCH YOU UP ON STUFF BEFORE THE MAIN STORY.
YOU'D THINK THERE'D BE A FLOATING WORD THAT SAID PROLOGUE HERE OR SOMETHING...
RODNEY, I CONFESS I'M HAVIN' SECOND THOUGHTS.
I SEEN TWO PEOPLE FLYING THROUGH THE AIR TODAY, AND THAT IS 200 PERCENT MORE THAN I HAVE EVER SEEN BACK IN CLARKSBURG.
I THINK IF WE JUST DROVE THIS TRUCK DIRECTLY INTO A PRISON, IT WOULD SAVE A LOTTA HASSLE.
OH, IT AIN'T LIKE THOR'S GONNA BE APPLYIN' FOR A LOAN IN THERE. WE'LL BE FINE. WON'T WE, CECIL?
I DON'T KNOW, UNCLE RODNEY. I'VE TAKEN OUT ALL THE CAMERAS AND PHONES...
UH, GREAT. WHAT'S THE PROBLEM?
I WANTED TO JUST OPEN A HOLE INTO THE VAULT WITH A REDIRECTION OF A SLIP PORTAL PROJECTION FROM A NEARBY PARKER PROJECT.
BUT...YOU DID MANAGE TO KNOCK OUT ALL THE SECURITY.
IT'S NOT AS GOOD...
IT'S FINE-- LET'S GO! LOOKS LIKE WE WON'T HAVE TO WORRY ABOUT POLICE, SO...
THERE I AM! HIII!
I ASSUME THERE IS SOMEONE OUT THERE READING WHAT'S HAPPENING TO ME IN A COMIC RIGHT NOW...
...IF YOU GOTTA SHOOT SOME PEOPLE, YOU GOTTA SHOOT SOME PEOPLE.
...WHICH IS WHY I'M NARRATING ALL OF THIS IN MY HEAD.

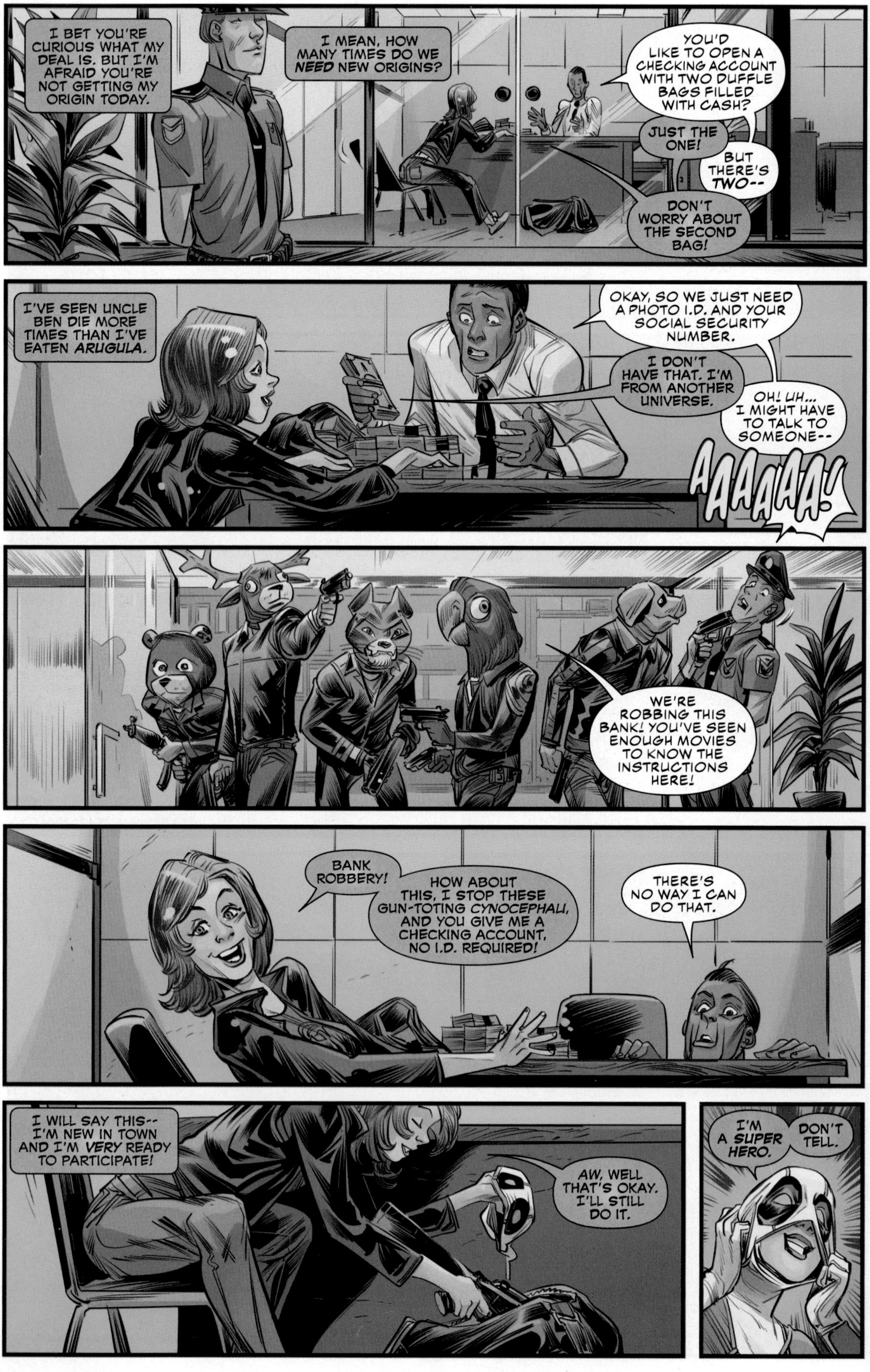

I BET YOU'RE CURIOUS WHAT MY DEAL IS. BUT I'M AFRAID YOU'RE NOT GETTING MY ORIGIN TODAY.
I MEAN, HOW MANY TIMES DO WE NEED NEW ORIGINS?
YOU'D LIKE TO OPEN A CHECKING ACCOUNT WITH TWO DUFFLE BAGS FILLED WITH CASH?
JUST THE ONE!
BUT THERE'S TWO--
DON'T WORRY ABOUT THE SECOND BAG!
I'VE SEEN UNCLE BEN DIE MORE TIMES THAN I'VE EATEN ARUGULA.
OKAY, SO WE JUST NEED A PHOTO I.D. AND YOUR SOCIAL SECURITY NUMBER.
I DON'T HAVE THAT. I'M FROM ANOTHER UNIVERSE.
OH! UH... I MIGHT HAVE TO TALK TO SOMEONE--
AAAAAA!
WE'RE ROBBING THIS BANK! YOU'VE SEEN ENOUGH MOVIES TO KNOW THE INSTRUCTIONS HERE!
BANK ROBBERY!
HOW ABOUT THIS, I STOP THESE GUN-TOTING CYNOCEPHALI, AND YOU GIVE ME A CHECKING ACCOUNT, NO I.D. REQUIRED!
THERE'S NO WAY I CAN DO THAT.
I WILL SAY THIS-- I'M NEW IN TOWN AND I'M VERY READY TO PARTICIPATE!
AW, WELL THAT'S OKAY. I'LL STILL DO IT.
I'M A SUPER HERO.
DON'T TELL.

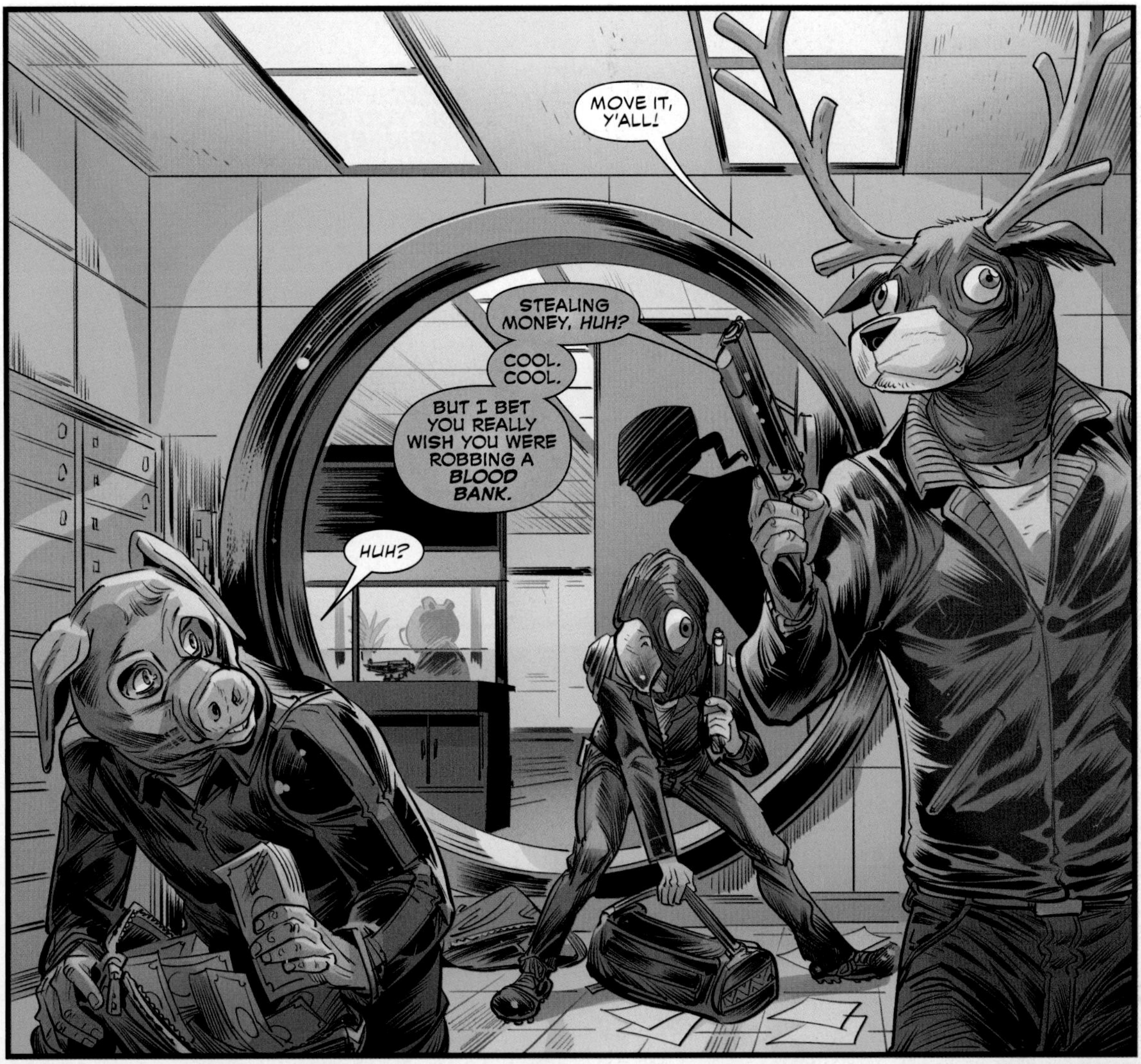
MOVE IT, Y'ALL!
STEALING MONEY, HUH?
COOL. COOL.
BUT I BET YOU REALLY WISH YOU WERE ROBBING A BLOOD BANK.
HUH?

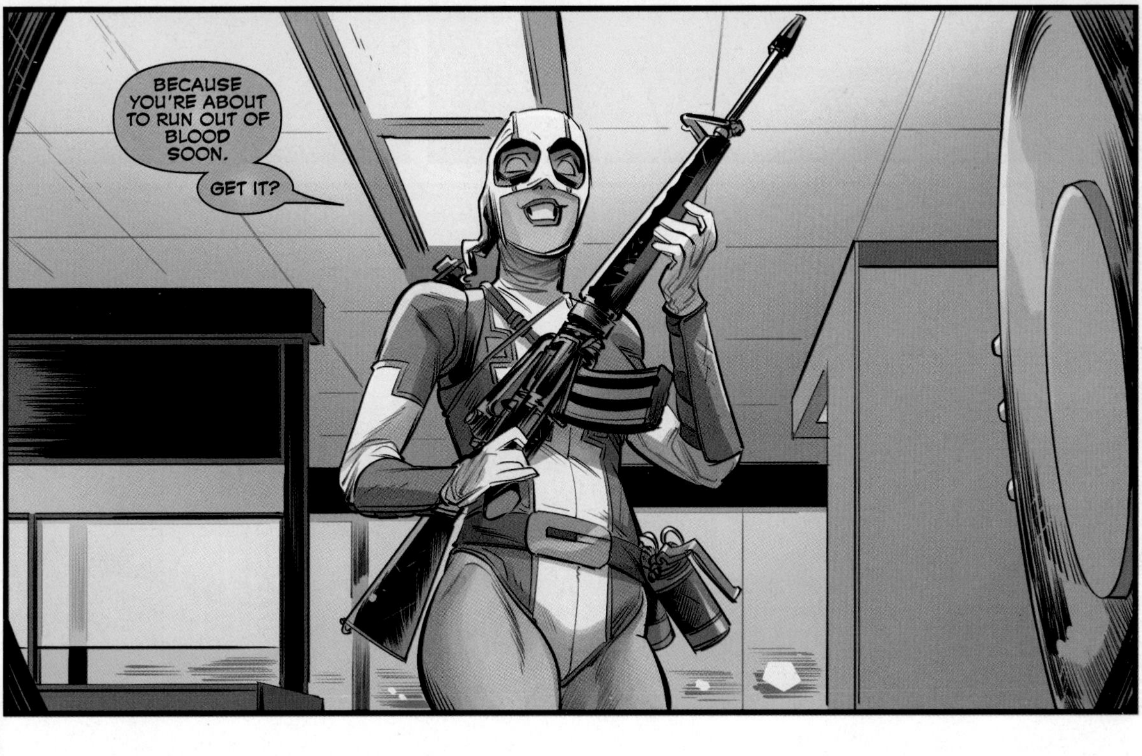
BECAUSE YOU'RE ABOUT TO RUN OUT OF BLOOD SOON.
GET IT?

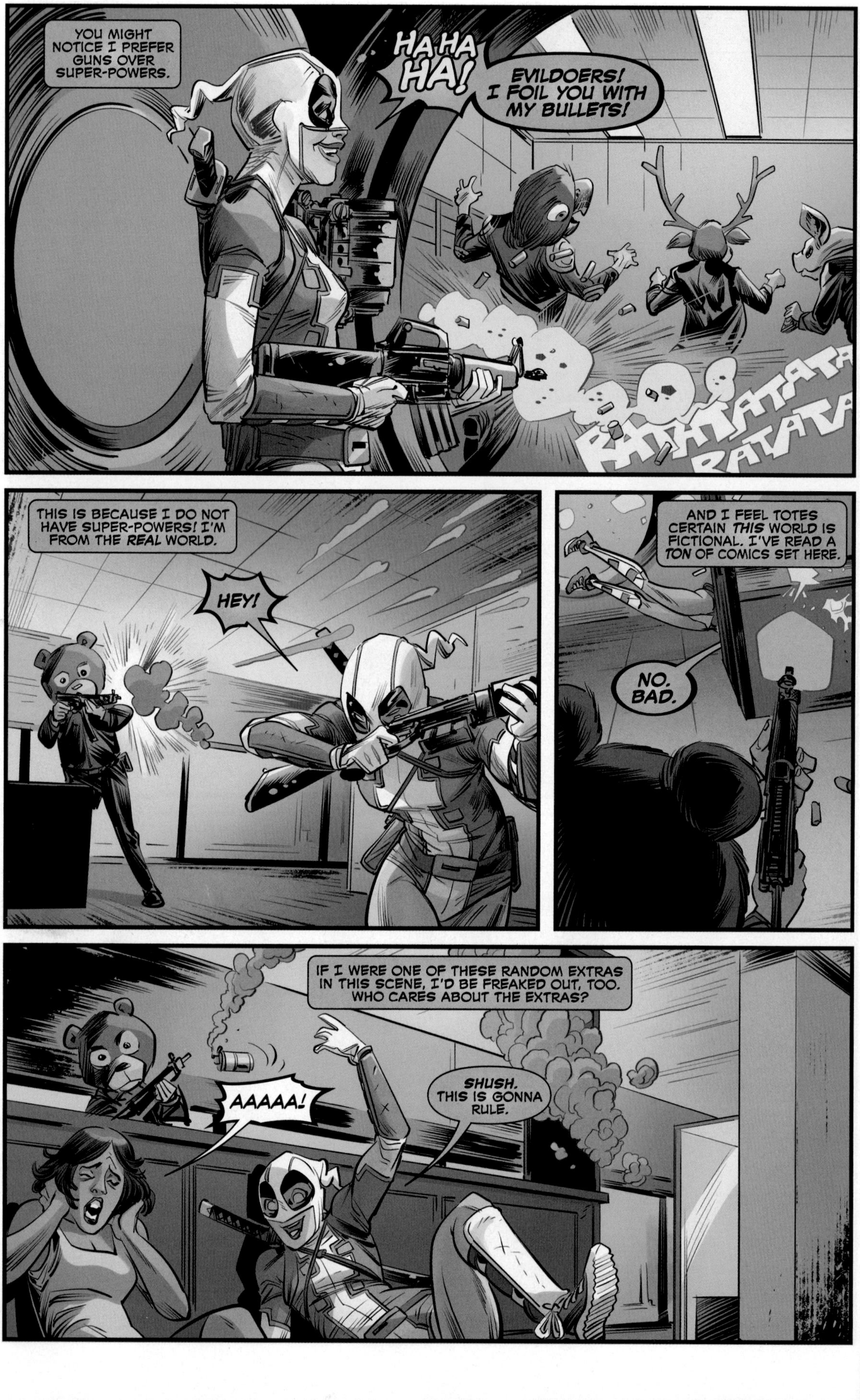
YOU MIGHT NOTICE I PREFER GUNS OVER SUPER-POWERS.
HA HA HA!
EVILDOERS! I FOIL YOU WITH MY BULLETS!
RATATATATA RATATATA
THIS IS BECAUSE I DO NOT HAVE SUPER-POWERS! I'M FROM THE *REAL* WORLD.
HEY!
AND I FEEL TOTES CERTAIN *THIS* WORLD IS FICTIONAL. I'VE READ A *TON* OF COMICS SET HERE.
NO. BAD.
IF I WERE ONE OF THESE RANDOM EXTRAS IN THIS SCENE, I'D BE FREAKED OUT, TOO. WHO CARES ABOUT THE EXTRAS?
AAAAA!
*SHUSH.* THIS IS GONNA RULE.

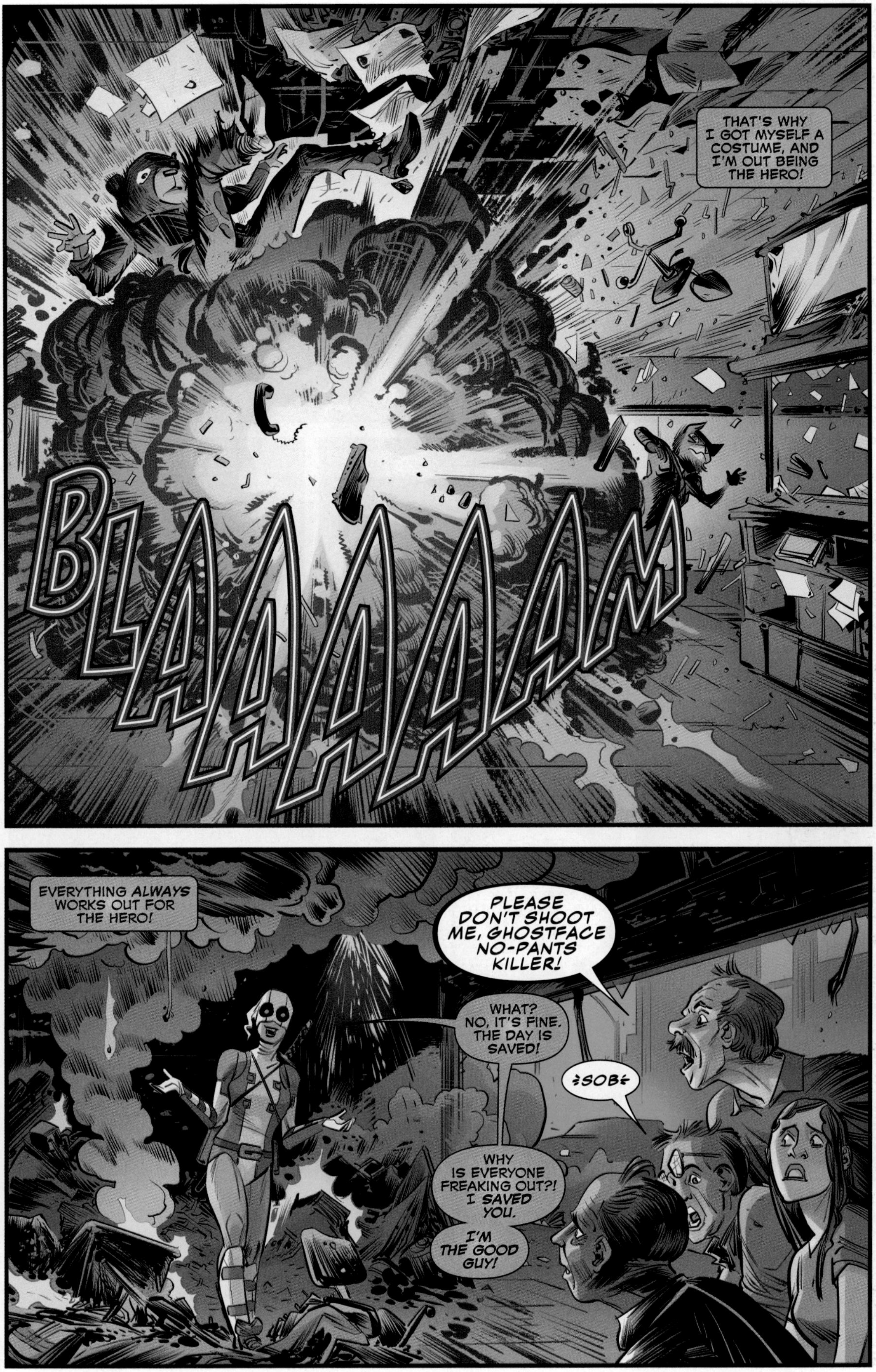
THAT'S WHY I GOT MYSELF A COSTUME, AND I'M OUT BEING THE HERO!
BLAAAAAAM
EVERYTHING ALWAYS WORKS OUT FOR THE HERO!
PLEASE DON'T SHOOT ME, GHOSTFACE NO-PANTS KILLER!
WHAT? NO, IT'S FINE. THE DAY IS SAVED!
SOB
WHY IS EVERYONE FREAKING OUT?! I SAVED YOU.
I'M THE GOOD GUY!

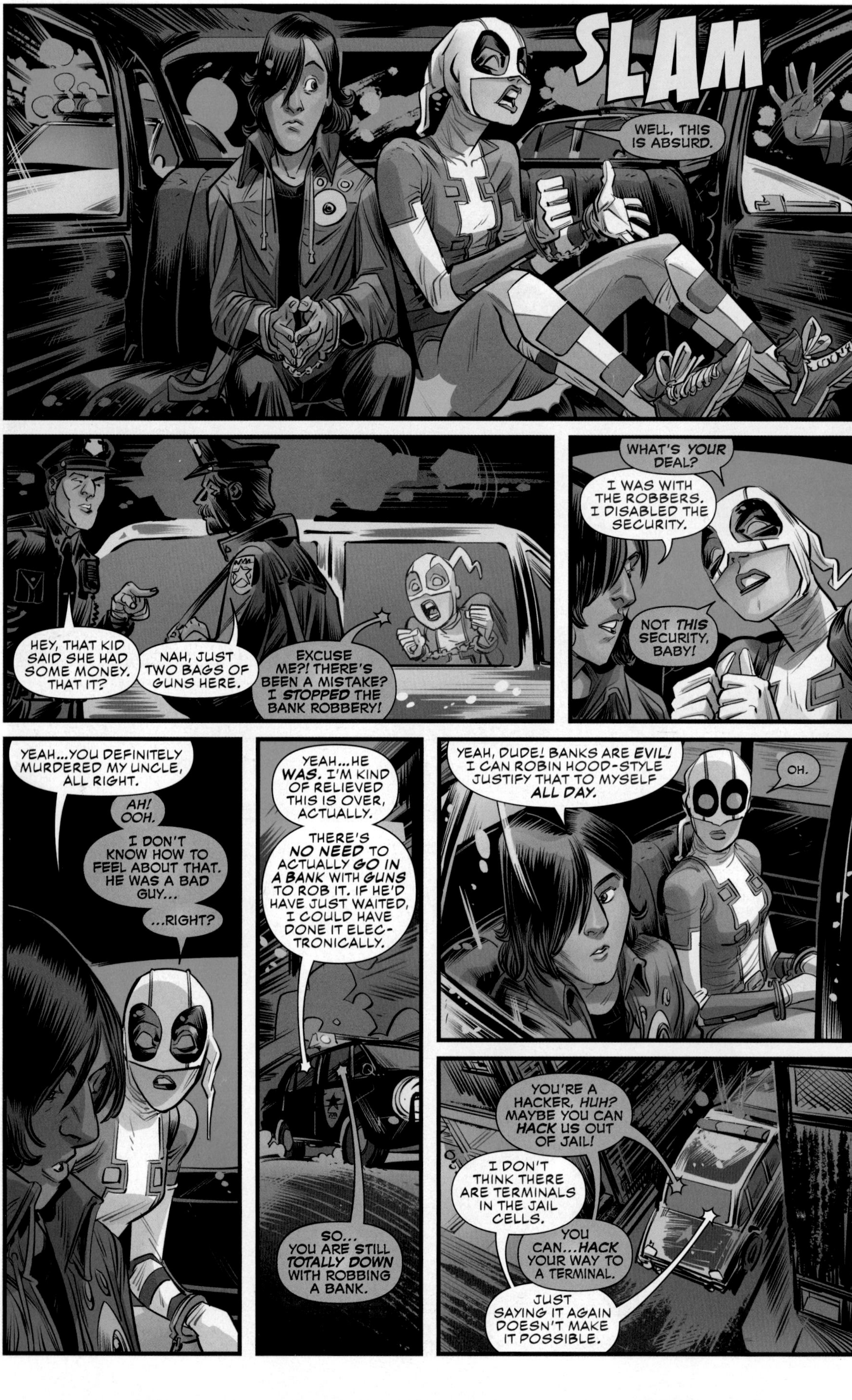
SLAM
WELL, THIS IS ABSURD.
HEY, THAT KID SAID SHE HAD SOME MONEY. THAT IT?
NAH, JUST TWO BAGS OF GUNS HERE.
EXCUSE ME?! THERE'S BEEN A MISTAKE? I STOPPED THE BANK ROBBERY!
WHAT'S YOUR DEAL?
I WAS WITH THE ROBBERS. I DISABLED THE SECURITY.
NOT THIS SECURITY, BABY!
YEAH...YOU DEFINITELY MURDERED MY UNCLE, ALL RIGHT.
AH! OOH.
I DON'T KNOW HOW TO FEEL ABOUT THAT. HE WAS A BAD GUY...
...RIGHT?
YEAH...HE WAS. I'M KIND OF RELIEVED THIS IS OVER, ACTUALLY.
THERE'S NO NEED TO ACTUALLY GO IN A BANK WITH GUNS TO ROB IT. IF HE'D HAVE JUST WAITED, I COULD HAVE DONE IT ELECTRONICALLY.
SO... YOU ARE STILL TOTALLY DOWN WITH ROBBING A BANK.
YEAH, DUDE! BANKS ARE EVIL! I CAN ROBIN HOOD-STYLE JUSTIFY THAT TO MYSELF ALL DAY.
OH.
YOU'RE A HACKER, HUH? MAYBE YOU CAN HACK US OUT OF JAIL!
I DON'T THINK THERE ARE TERMINALS IN THE JAIL CELLS.
YOU CAN...HACK YOUR WAY TO A TERMINAL.
JUST SAYING IT AGAIN DOESN'T MAKE IT POSSIBLE.

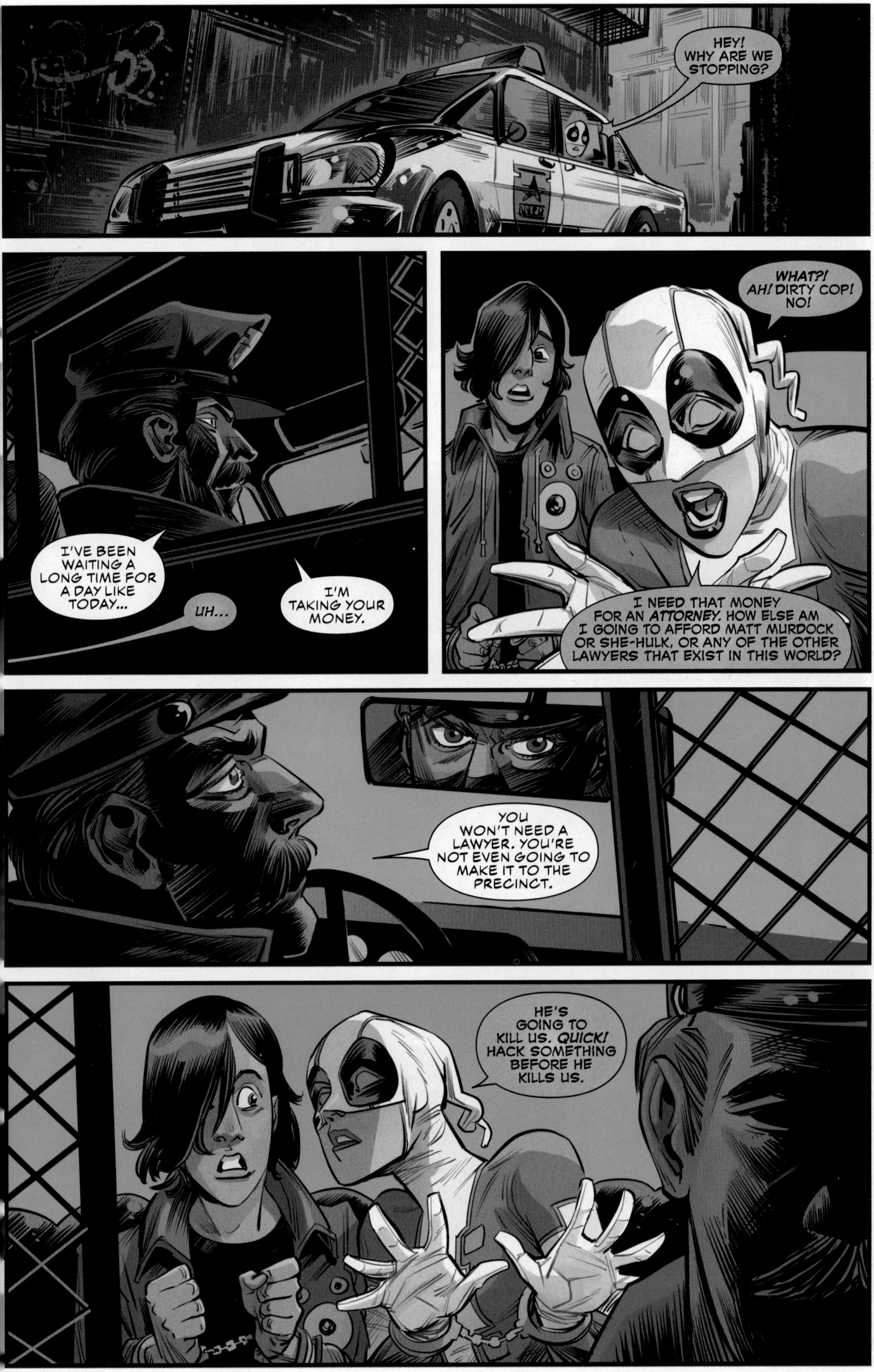
HEY! WHY ARE WE STOPPING?
I'VE BEEN WAITING A LONG TIME FOR A DAY LIKE TODAY...
UH...
I'M TAKING YOUR MONEY.
WHAT?! AH! DIRTY COP! NO!
I NEED THAT MONEY FOR AN ATTORNEY. HOW ELSE AM I GOING TO AFFORD MATT MURDOCK OR SHE-HULK, OR ANY OF THE OTHER LAWYERS THAT EXIST IN THIS WORLD?
YOU WON'T NEED A LAWYER. YOU'RE NOT EVEN GOING TO MAKE IT TO THE PRECINCT.
HE'S GOING TO KILL US. QUICK! HACK SOMETHING BEFORE HE KILLS US.

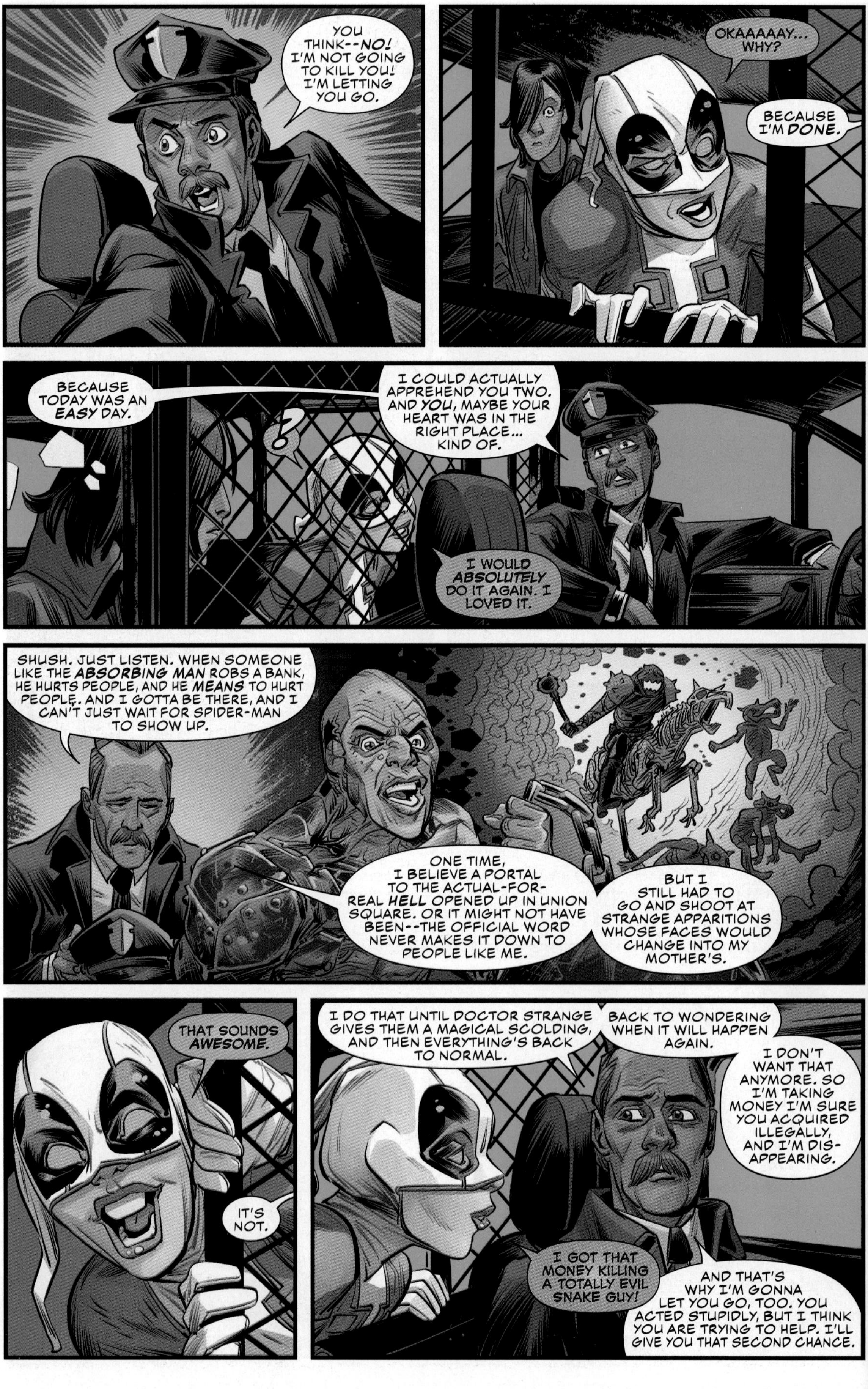
YOU THINK--NO! I'M NOT GOING TO KILL YOU! I'M LETTING YOU GO.
OKAAAAAY... WHY?
BECAUSE I'M DONE.
BECAUSE TODAY WAS AN EASY DAY.
I COULD ACTUALLY APPREHEND YOU TWO. AND YOU, MAYBE YOUR HEART WAS IN THE RIGHT PLACE... KIND OF.
I WOULD ABSOLUTELY DO IT AGAIN. I LOVED IT.
SHUSH. JUST LISTEN. WHEN SOMEONE LIKE THE ABSORBING MAN ROBS A BANK, HE HURTS PEOPLE, AND HE MEANS TO HURT PEOPLE. AND I GOTTA BE THERE, AND I CAN'T JUST WAIT FOR SPIDER-MAN TO SHOW UP.
ONE TIME, I BELIEVE A PORTAL TO THE ACTUAL-FOR-REAL HELL OPENED UP IN UNION SQUARE. OR IT MIGHT NOT HAVE BEEN--THE OFFICIAL WORD NEVER MAKES IT DOWN TO PEOPLE LIKE ME.
BUT I STILL HAD TO GO AND SHOOT AT STRANGE APPARITIONS WHOSE FACES WOULD CHANGE INTO MY MOTHER'S.
THAT SOUNDS AWESOME.
IT'S NOT.
I DO THAT UNTIL DOCTOR STRANGE GIVES THEM A MAGICAL SCOLDING, AND THEN EVERYTHING'S BACK TO NORMAL.
BACK TO WONDERING WHEN IT WILL HAPPEN AGAIN.
I DON'T WANT THAT ANYMORE. SO I'M TAKING MONEY I'M SURE YOU ACQUIRED ILLEGALLY, AND I'M DIS-APPEARING.
I GOT THAT MONEY KILLING A TOTALLY EVIL SNAKE GUY!
AND THAT'S WHY I'M GONNA LET YOU GO, TOO. YOU ACTED STUPIDLY, BUT I THINK YOU ARE TRYING TO HELP. I'LL GIVE YOU THAT SECOND CHANCE.

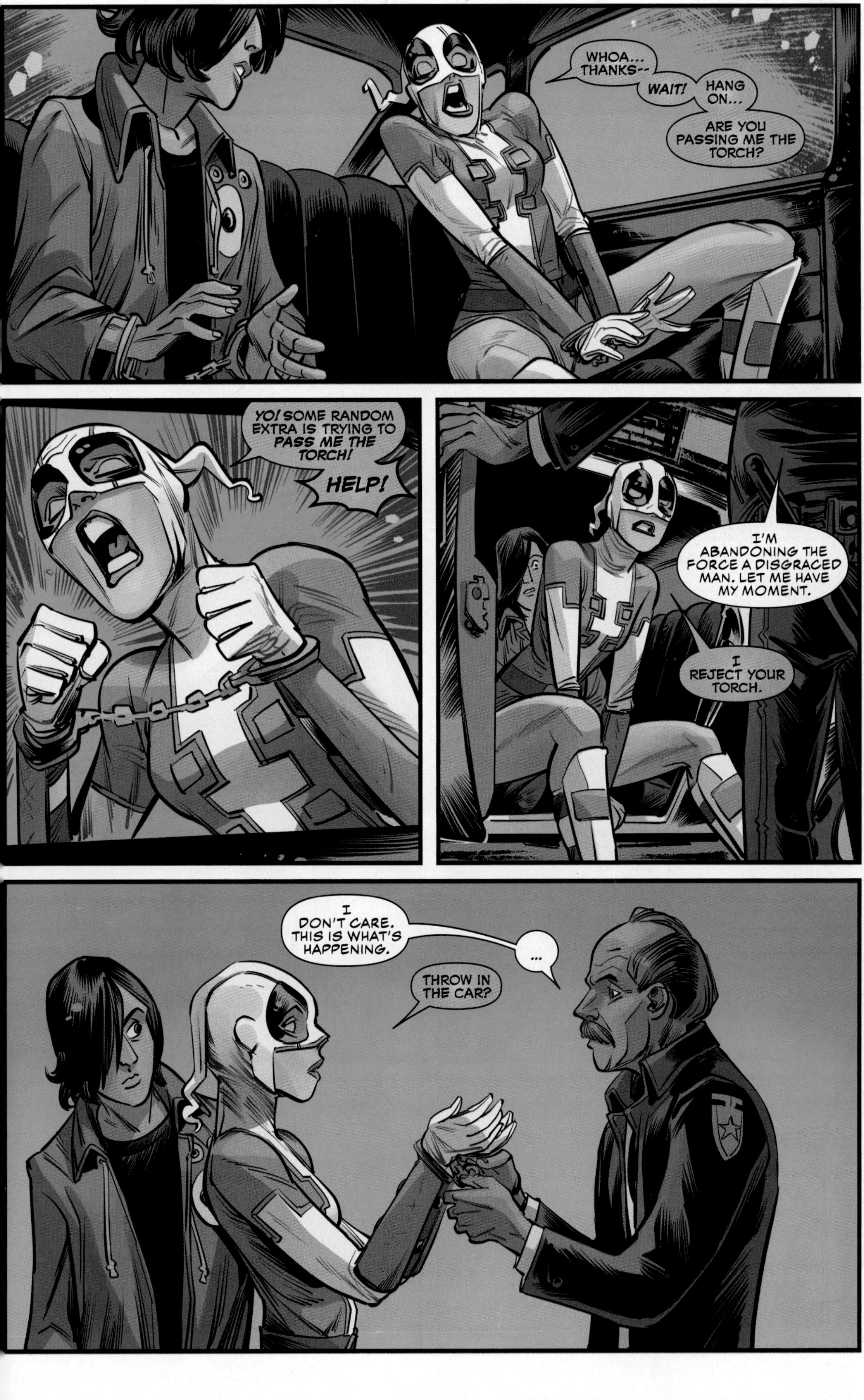
WHOA... THANKS--
WAIT!
HANG ON...
ARE YOU PASSING ME THE TORCH?
YO! SOME RANDOM EXTRA IS TRYING TO PASS ME THE TORCH!
HELP!
I'M ABANDONING THE FORCE A DISGRACED MAN. LET ME HAVE MY MOMENT.
I REJECT YOUR TORCH.
I DON'T CARE. THIS IS WHAT'S HAPPENING.
...
THROW IN THE CAR?

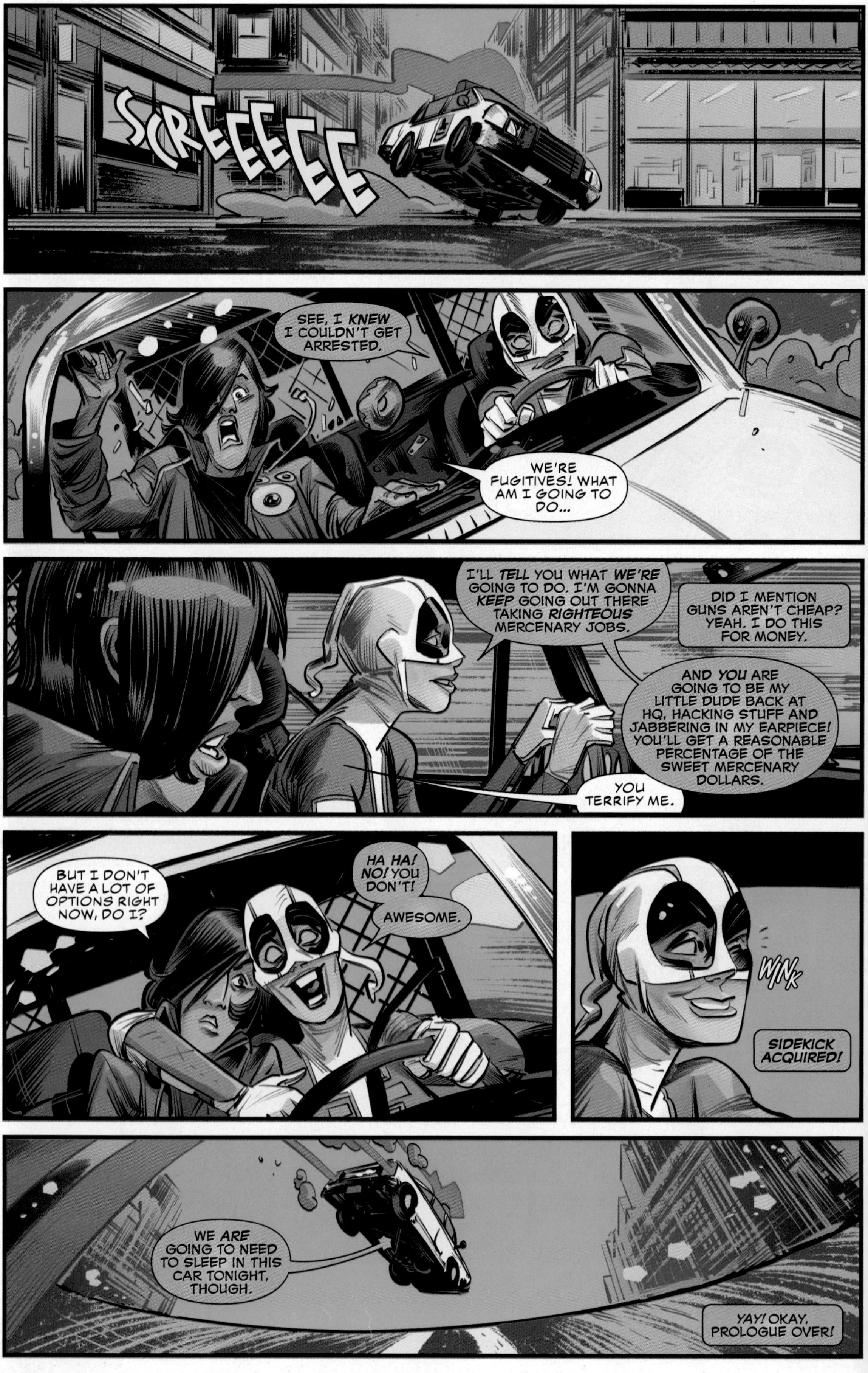
SCREEEEEEE
SEE, I KNEW I COULDN'T GET ARRESTED.
WE'RE FUGITIVES! WHAT AM I GOING TO DO...
I'LL TELL YOU WHAT WE'RE GOING TO DO. I'M GONNA KEEP GOING OUT THERE TAKING RIGHTEOUS MERCENARY JOBS.
DID I MENTION GUNS AREN'T CHEAP? YEAH. I DO THIS FOR MONEY.
AND YOU ARE GOING TO BE MY LITTLE DUDE BACK AT HQ, HACKING STUFF AND JABBERING IN MY EARPIECE! YOU'LL GET A REASONABLE PERCENTAGE OF THE SWEET MERCENARY DOLLARS.
YOU TERRIFY ME.
BUT I DON'T HAVE A LOT OF OPTIONS RIGHT NOW, DO I?
HA HA! NO! YOU DON'T!
AWESOME.
WINK
SIDEKICK ACQUIRED!
WE ARE GOING TO NEED TO SLEEP IN THIS CAR TONIGHT, THOUGH.
YAY! OKAY, PROLOGUE OVER!

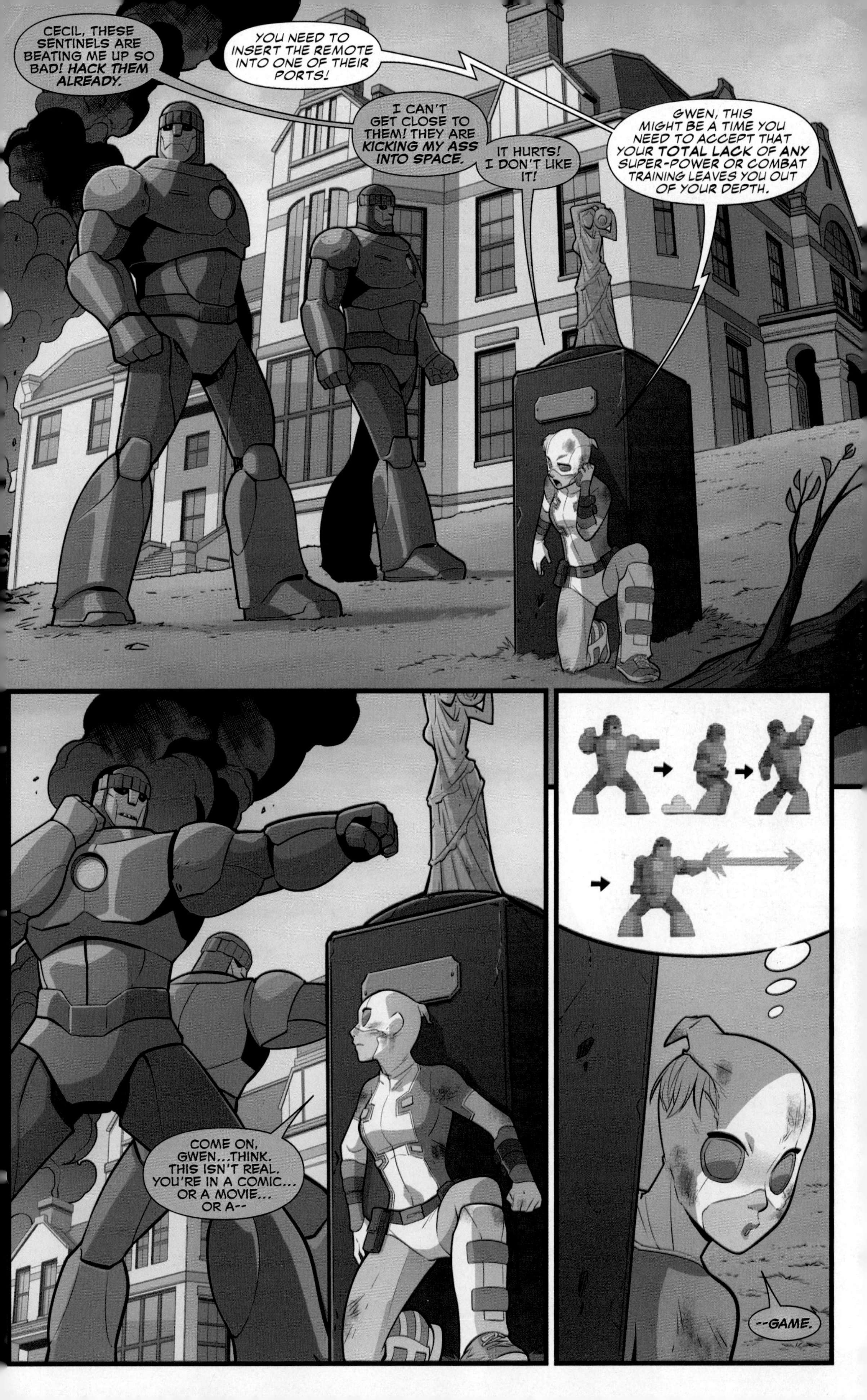
CECIL, THESE SENTINELS ARE BEATING ME UP SO BAD! HACK THEM ALREADY.
YOU NEED TO INSERT THE REMOTE INTO ONE OF THEIR PORTS!
I CAN'T GET CLOSE TO THEM! THEY ARE KICKING MY ASS INTO SPACE.
IT HURTS! I DON'T LIKE IT!
GWEN, THIS MIGHT BE A TIME YOU NEED TO ACCEPT THAT YOUR TOTAL LACK OF ANY SUPER-POWER OR COMBAT TRAINING LEAVES YOU OUT OF YOUR DEPTH.
COME ON, GWEN...THINK. THIS ISN'T REAL. YOU'RE IN A COMIC... OR A MOVIE... OR A--
--GAME.

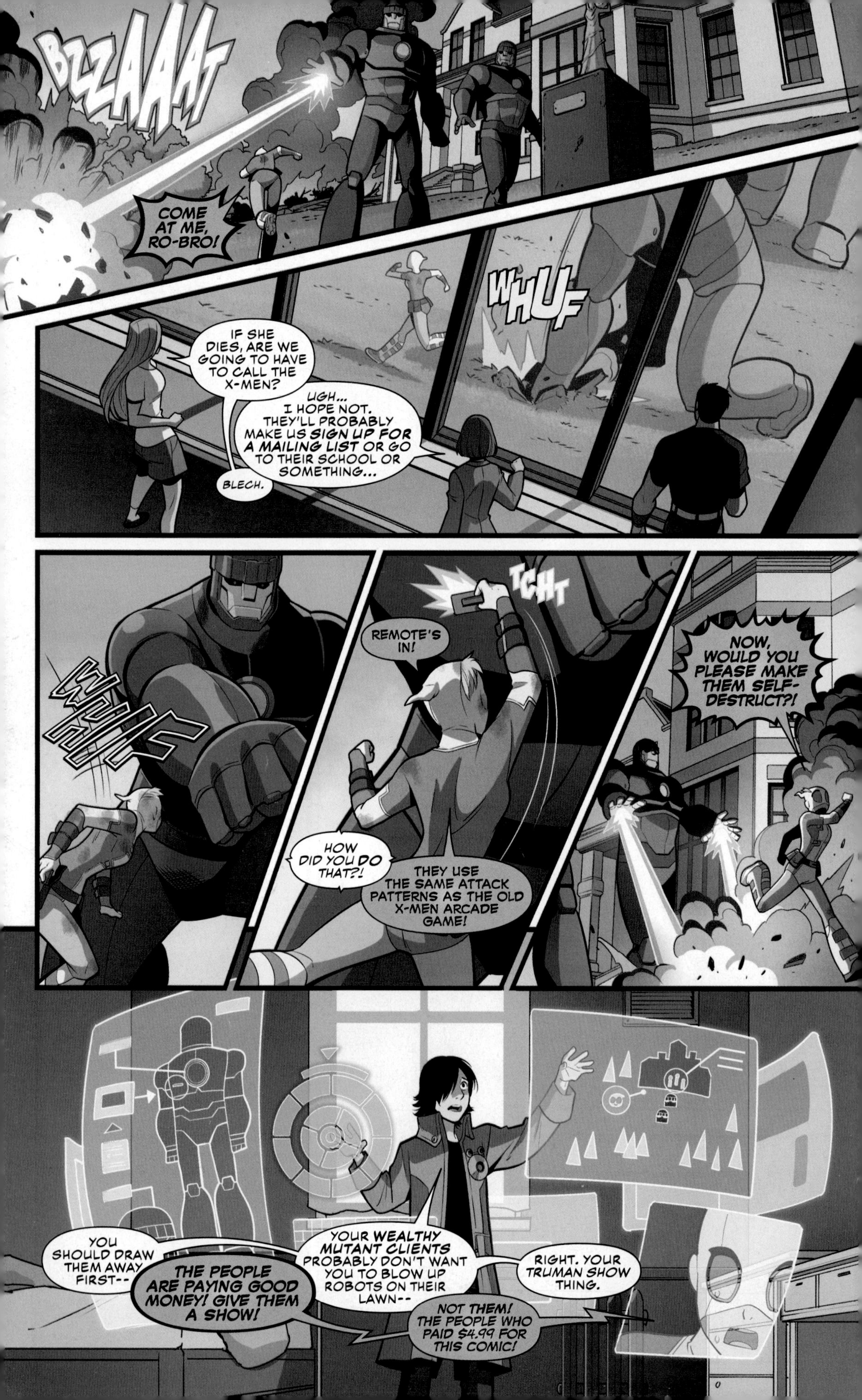
BZZAAAT
COME AT ME, RO-BRO!
WHUF
IF SHE DIES, ARE WE GOING TO HAVE TO CALL THE X-MEN?
UGH... I HOPE NOT. THEY'LL PROBABLY MAKE US SIGN UP FOR A MAILING LIST OR GO TO THEIR SCHOOL OR SOMETHING...
BLECH.
REMOTE'S IN!
TCHT
HOW DID YOU DO THAT?!
THEY USE THE SAME ATTACK PATTERNS AS THE OLD X-MEN ARCADE GAME!
NOW, WOULD YOU PLEASE MAKE THEM SELF-DESTRUCT?!
YOU SHOULD DRAW THEM AWAY FIRST--
THE PEOPLE ARE PAYING GOOD MONEY! GIVE THEM A SHOW!
YOUR WEALTHY MUTANT CLIENTS PROBABLY DON'T WANT YOU TO BLOW UP ROBOTS ON THEIR LAWN--
RIGHT. YOUR TRUMAN SHOW THING.
NOT THEM! THE PEOPLE WHO PAID $4.99 FOR THIS COMIC!

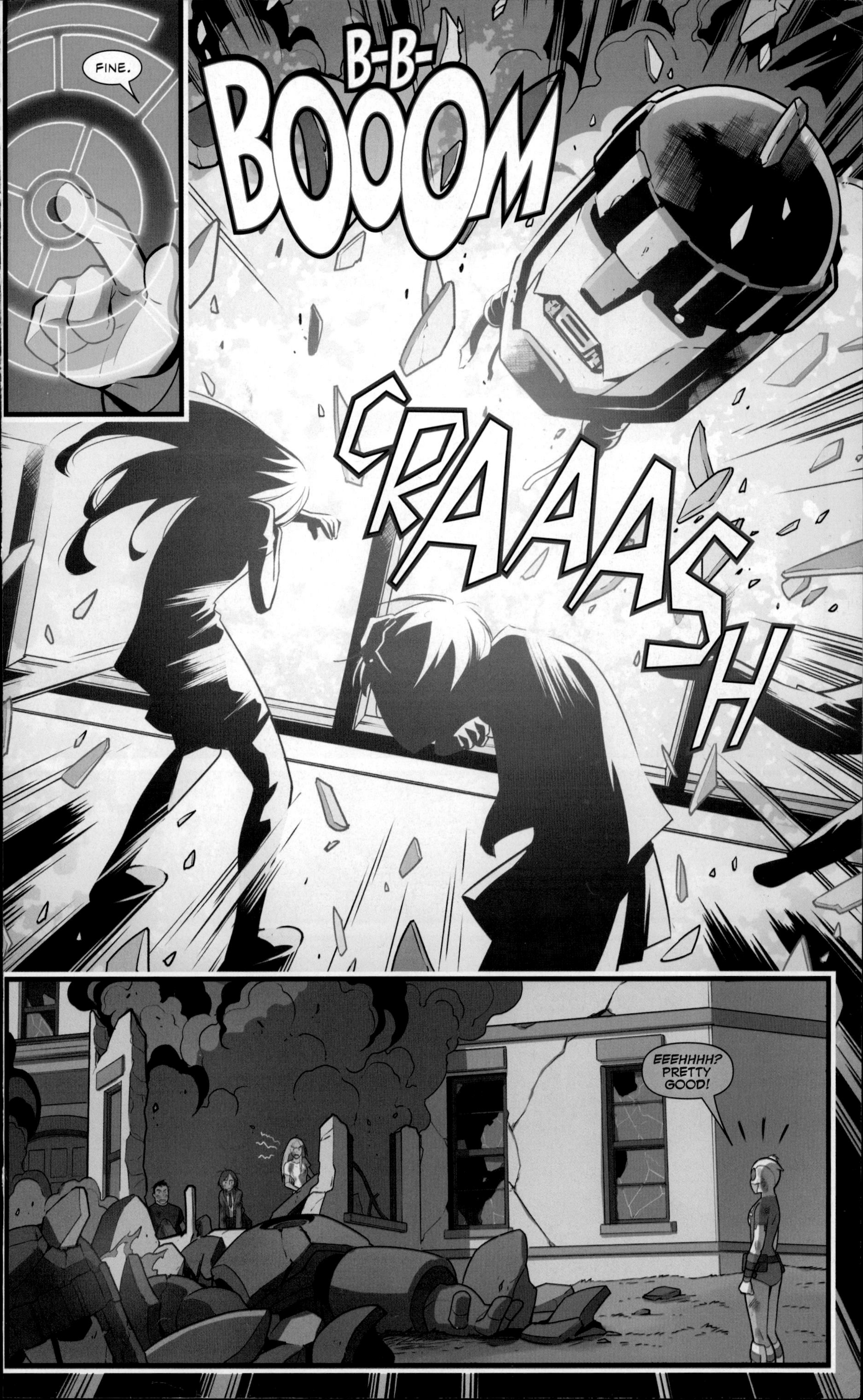
FINE.
B-B-BOOOM
CRAAAASH
EEEHHHH? PRETTY GOOD!

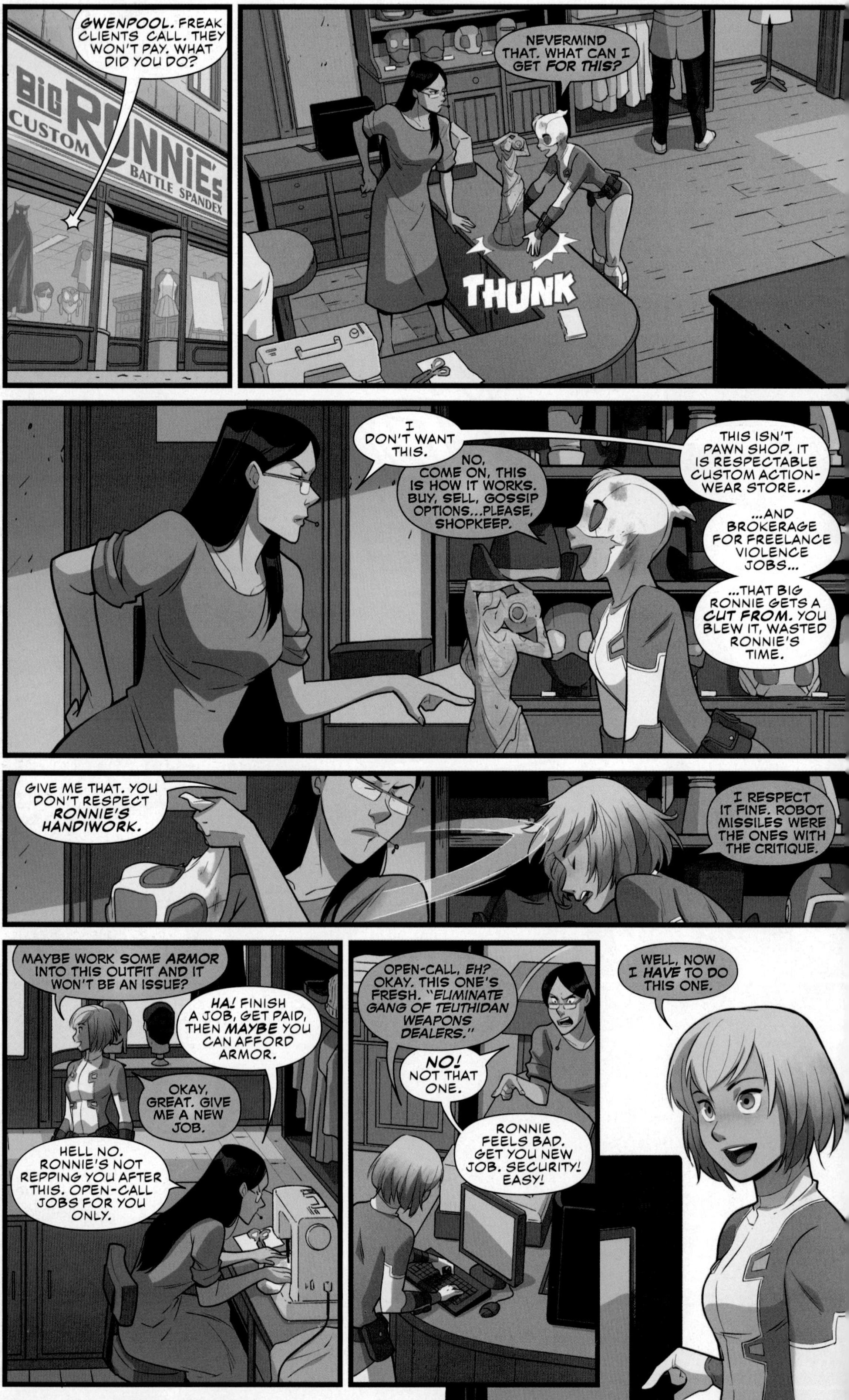
GWENPOOL. FREAK CLIENTS CALL. THEY WON'T PAY. WHAT DID YOU DO?
BIG RONNIE'S CUSTOM BATTLE SPANDEX
NEVERMIND THAT. WHAT CAN I GET FOR THIS?
THUNK
I DON'T WANT THIS.
NO, COME ON, THIS IS HOW IT WORKS. BUY, SELL, GOSSIP OPTIONS...PLEASE, SHOPKEEP.
THIS ISN'T PAWN SHOP. IT IS RESPECTABLE CUSTOM ACTION-WEAR STORE...
...AND BROKERAGE FOR FREELANCE VIOLENCE JOBS...
...THAT BIG RONNIE GETS A CUT FROM. YOU BLEW IT, WASTED RONNIE'S TIME.
GIVE ME THAT. YOU DON'T RESPECT RONNIE'S HANDIWORK.
I RESPECT IT FINE. ROBOT MISSILES WERE THE ONES WITH THE CRITIQUE.
MAYBE WORK SOME ARMOR INTO THIS OUTFIT AND IT WON'T BE AN ISSUE?
HA! FINISH A JOB, GET PAID, THEN MAYBE YOU CAN AFFORD ARMOR.
OKAY, GREAT. GIVE ME A NEW JOB.
HELL NO. RONNIE'S NOT REPPING YOU AFTER THIS. OPEN-CALL JOBS FOR YOU ONLY.
OPEN-CALL, EH? OKAY. THIS ONE'S FRESH. "ELIMINATE GANG OF TEUTHIDAN WEAPONS DEALERS."
NO! NOT THAT ONE.
RONNIE FEELS BAD. GET YOU NEW JOB. SECURITY! EASY!
WELL, NOW I HAVE TO DO THIS ONE.

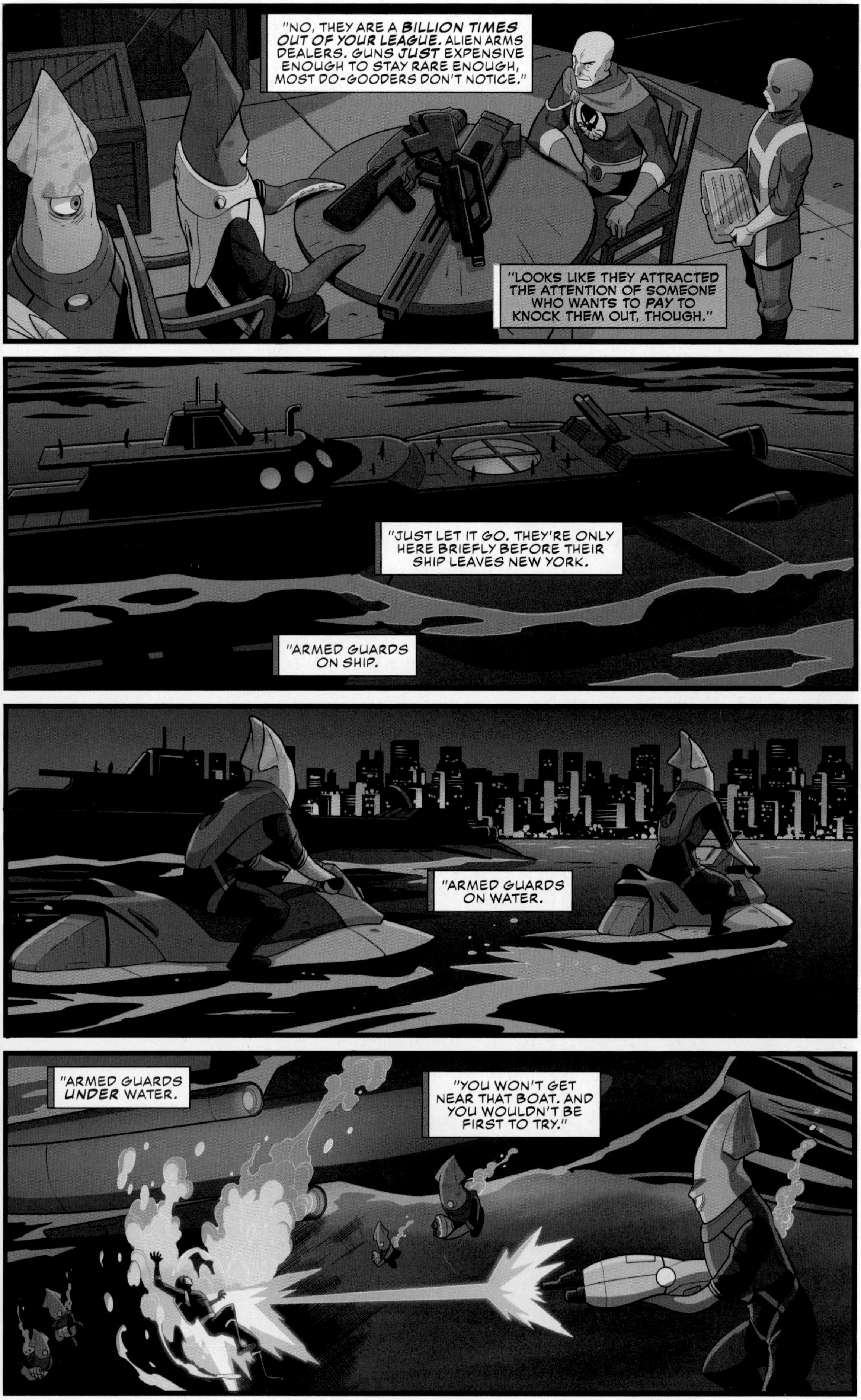
"NO, THEY ARE A BILLION TIMES OUT OF YOUR LEAGUE. ALIEN ARMS DEALERS. GUNS JUST EXPENSIVE ENOUGH TO STAY RARE ENOUGH, MOST DO-GOODERS DON'T NOTICE."
"LOOKS LIKE THEY ATTRACTED THE ATTENTION OF SOMEONE WHO WANTS TO PAY TO KNOCK THEM OUT, THOUGH."
"JUST LET IT GO. THEY'RE ONLY HERE BRIEFLY BEFORE THEIR SHIP LEAVES NEW YORK.
"ARMED GUARDS ON SHIP.
"ARMED GUARDS ON WATER.
"ARMED GUARDS UNDER WATER.
"YOU WON'T GET NEAR THAT BOAT. AND YOU WOULDN'T BE FIRST TO TRY."

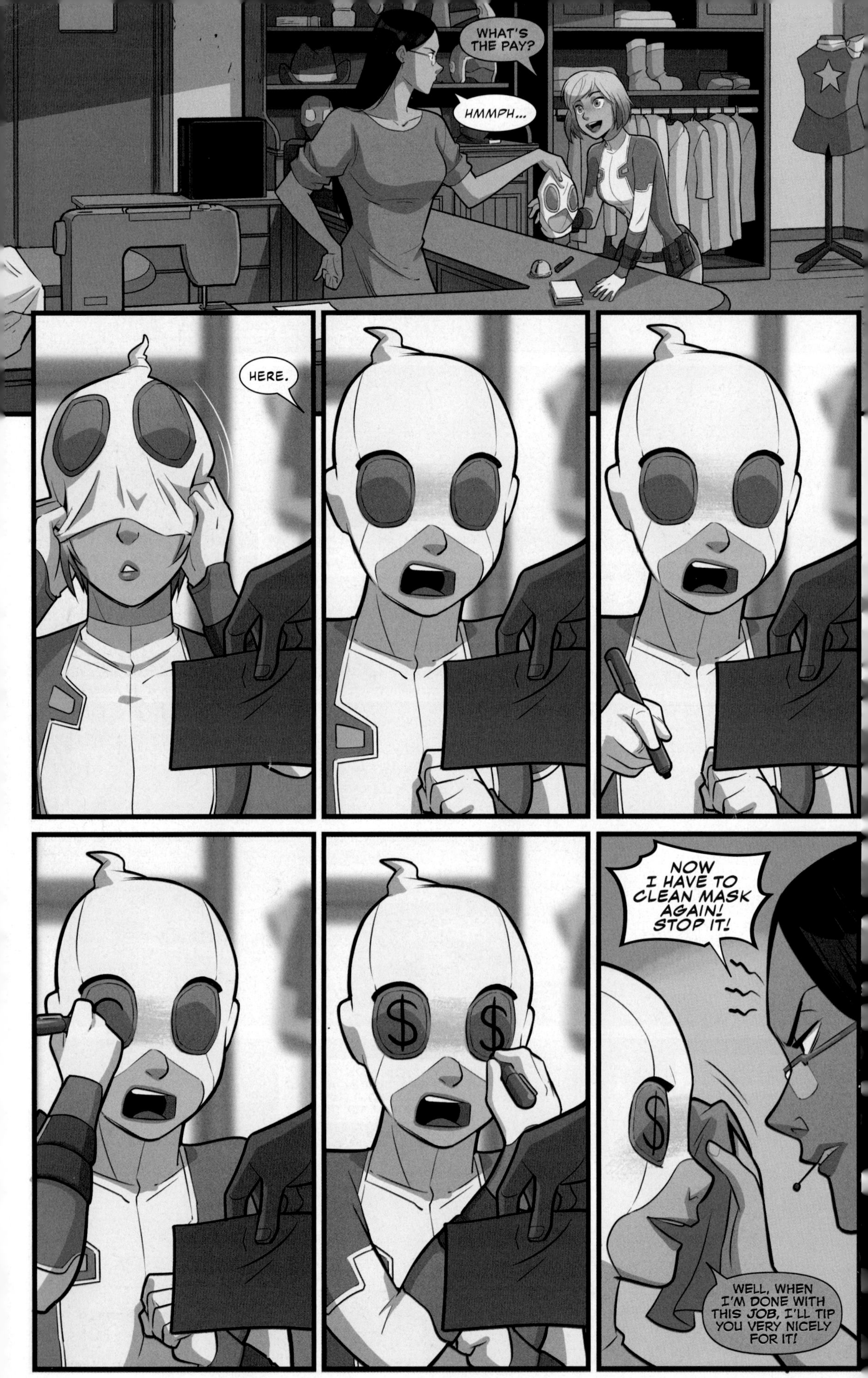
WHAT'S THE PAY?
HMMPH...
HERE.
NOW I HAVE TO CLEAN MASK AGAIN! STOP IT!
WELL, WHEN I'M DONE WITH THIS JOB, I'LL TIP YOU VERY NICELY FOR IT!

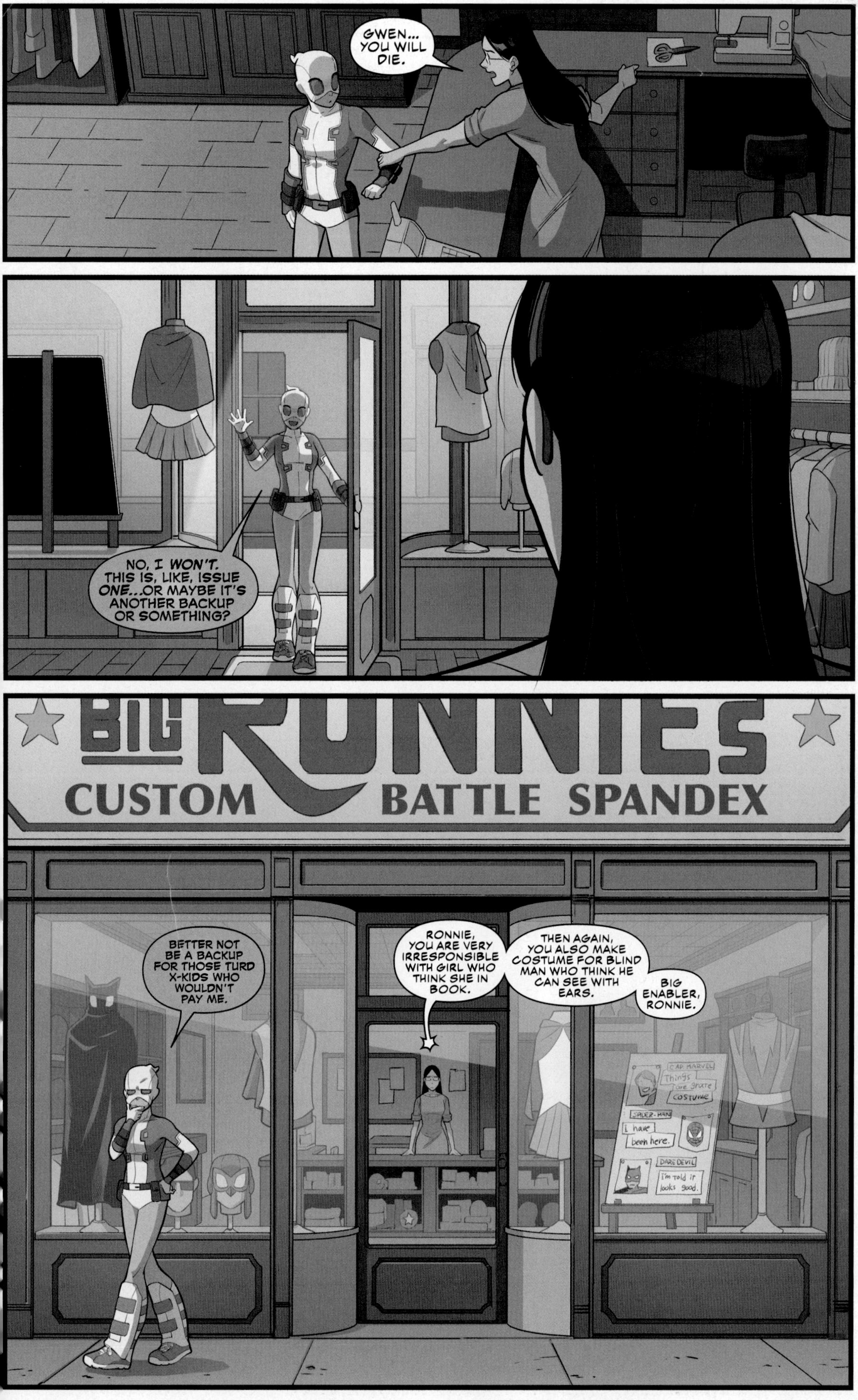
GWEN... YOU WILL DIE.
NO, I WON'T. THIS IS, LIKE, ISSUE ONE...OR MAYBE IT'S ANOTHER BACKUP OR SOMETHING?
BIG RONNIES
CUSTOM BATTLE SPANDEX
BETTER NOT BE A BACKUP FOR THOSE TURD X-KIDS WHO WOULDN'T PAY ME.
RONNIE, YOU ARE VERY IRRESPONSIBLE WITH GIRL WHO THINK SHE IN BOOK.
THEN AGAIN, YOU ALSO MAKE COSTUME FOR BLIND MAN WHO THINK HE CAN SEE WITH EARS.
BIG ENABLER, RONNIE.
CAP MARVEL
Things are grate costume
SPIDER-MAN
I have been here.
DARE DEVIL
I'm told it looks good.

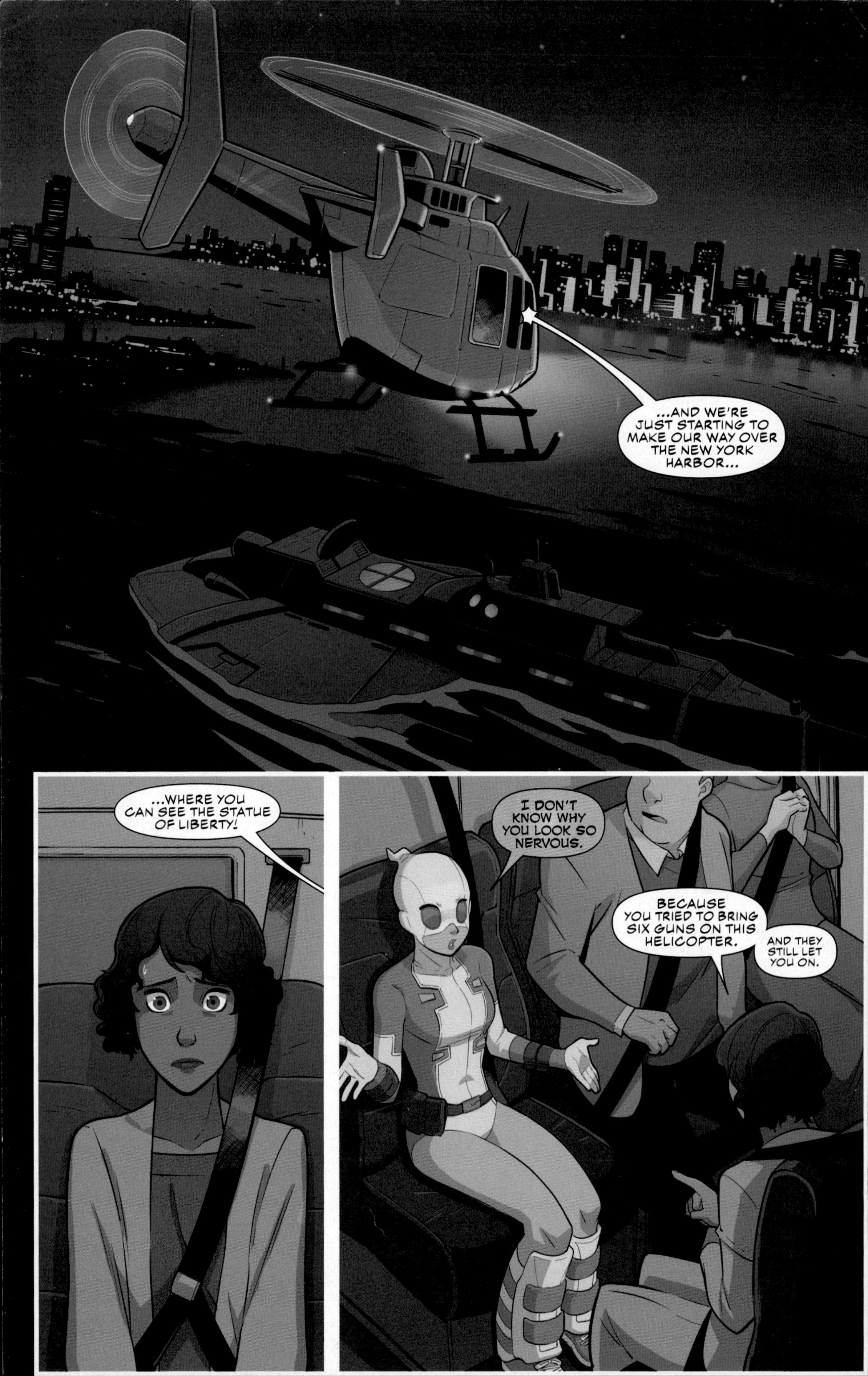

...AND WE'RE JUST STARTING TO MAKE OUR WAY OVER THE NEW YORK HARBOR...
...WHERE YOU CAN SEE THE STATUE OF LIBERTY!
I DON'T KNOW WHY YOU LOOK SO NERVOUS.
BECAUSE YOU TRIED TO BRING SIX GUNS ON THIS HELICOPTER.
AND THEY STILL LET YOU ON.

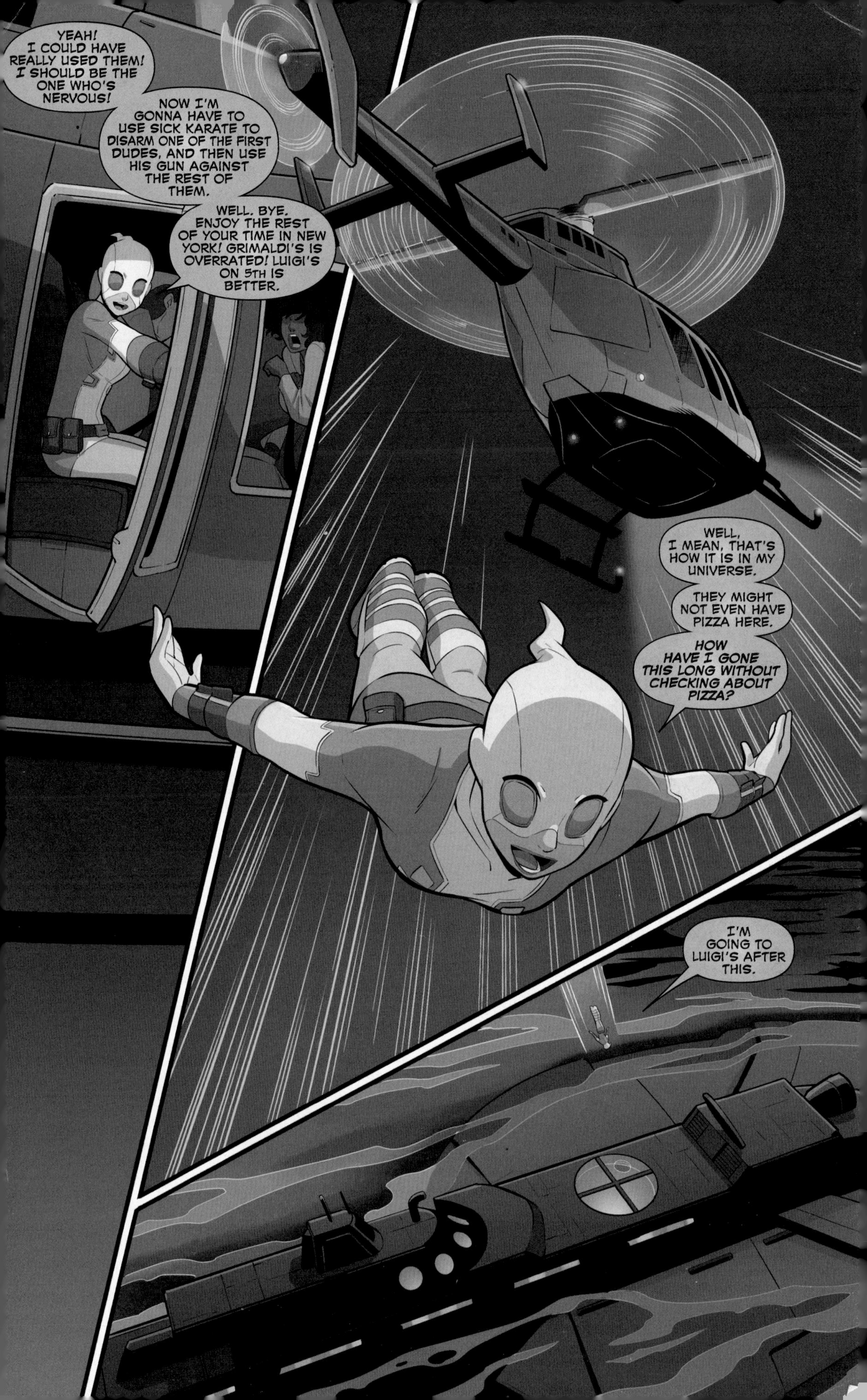
YEAH! I COULD HAVE REALLY USED THEM! I SHOULD BE THE ONE WHO'S NERVOUS!
NOW I'M GONNA HAVE TO USE SICK KARATE TO DISARM ONE OF THE FIRST DUDES, AND THEN USE HIS GUN AGAINST THE REST OF THEM.
WELL. BYE. ENJOY THE REST OF YOUR TIME IN NEW YORK! GRIMALDI'S IS OVERRATED! LUIGI'S ON 5TH IS BETTER.
WELL, I MEAN, THAT'S HOW IT IS IN MY UNIVERSE.
THEY MIGHT NOT EVEN HAVE PIZZA HERE.
HOW HAVE I GONE THIS LONG WITHOUT CHECKING ABOUT PIZZA?
I'M GOING TO LUIGI'S AFTER THIS.

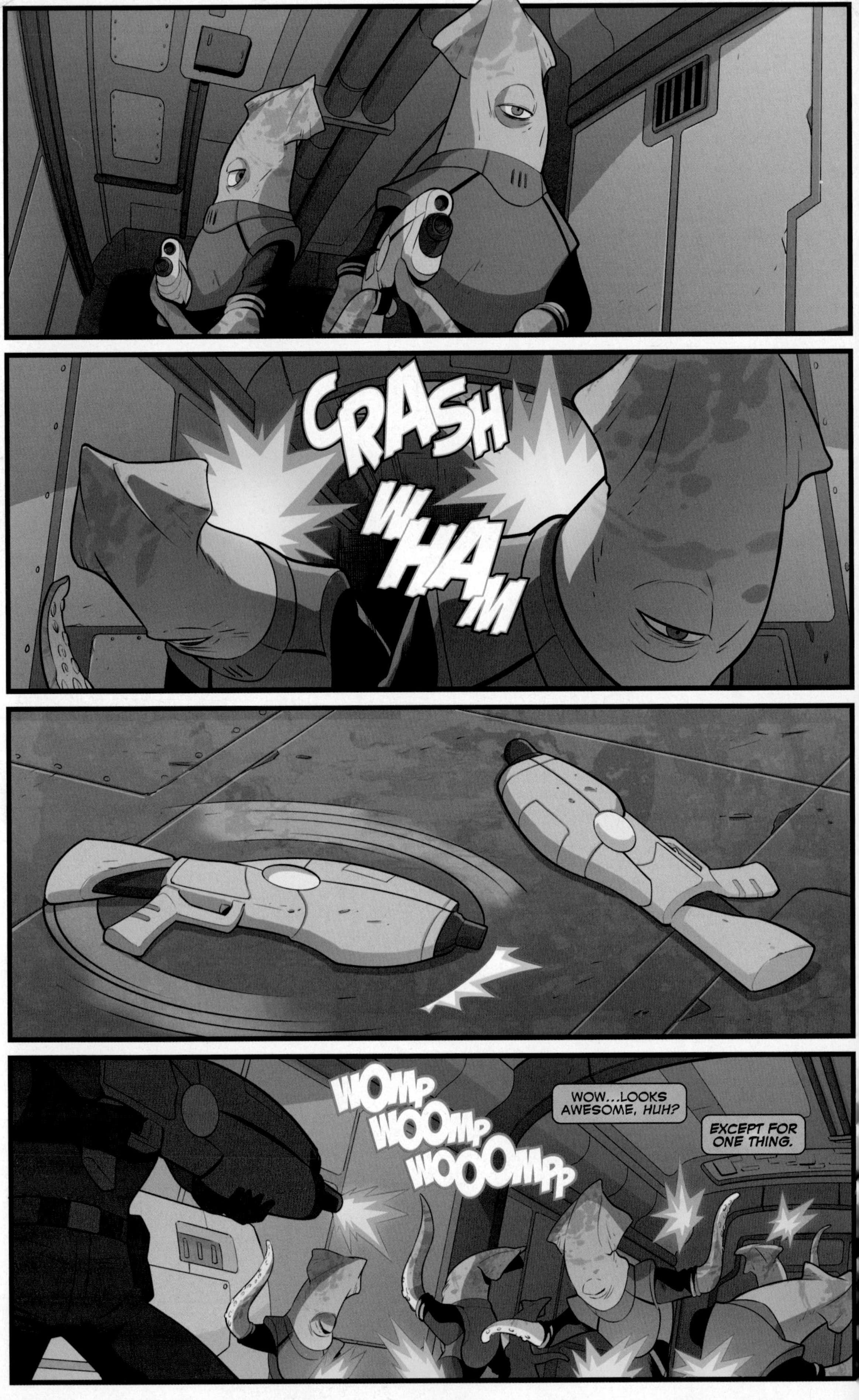
CRASH
WHAM
WOMP
WOOMP
WOOOMPP
WOW...LOOKS AWESOME, HUH?
EXCEPT FOR ONE THING.

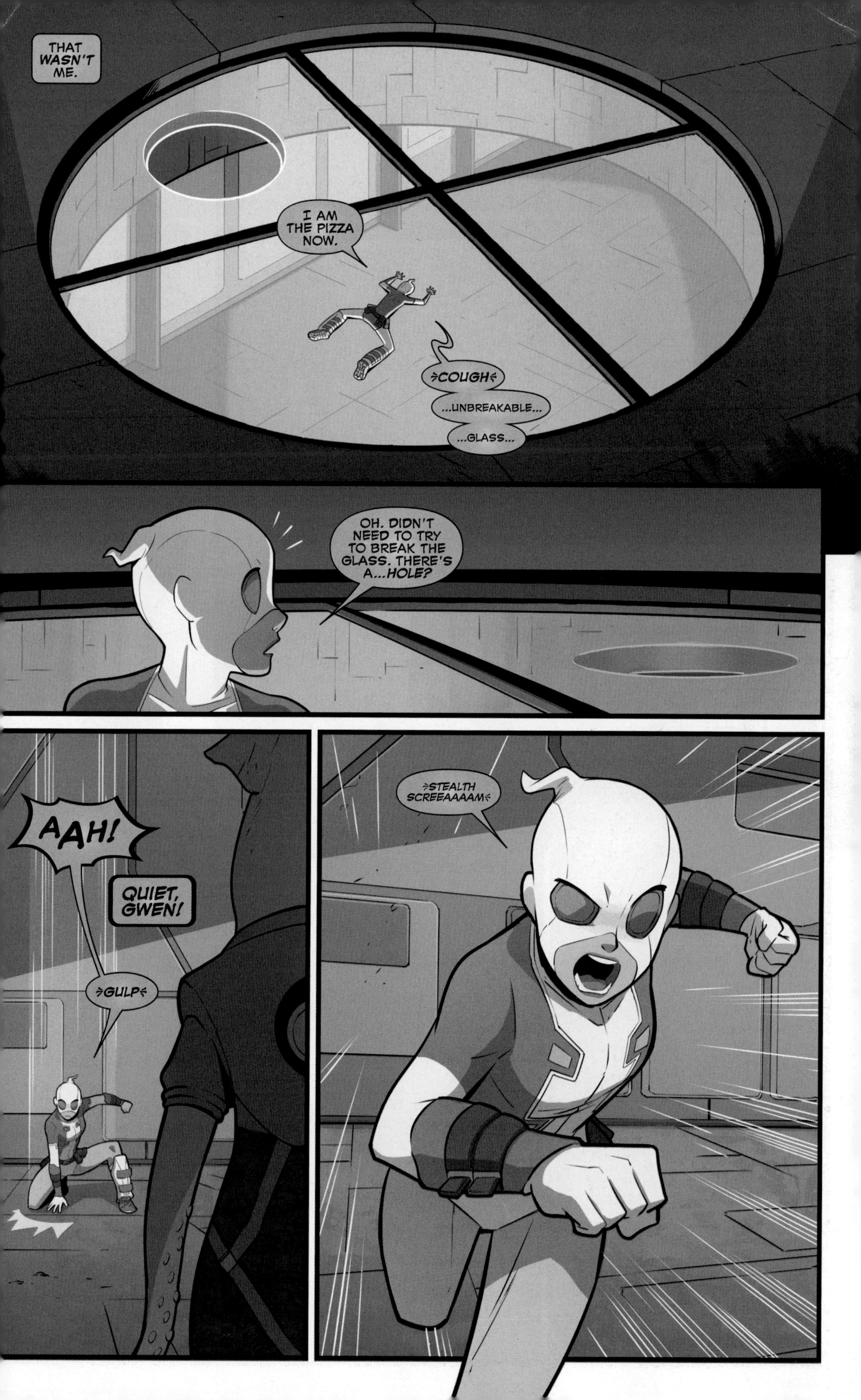
THAT WASN'T ME.
I AM THE PIZZA NOW.
⋟COUGH⋞
...UNBREAKABLE...
...GLASS...
OH. DIDN'T NEED TO TRY TO BREAK THE GLASS. THERE'S A...HOLE?
AAH!
QUIET, GWEN!
⋟GULP⋞
⋟STEALTH SCREEAAAAM⋞

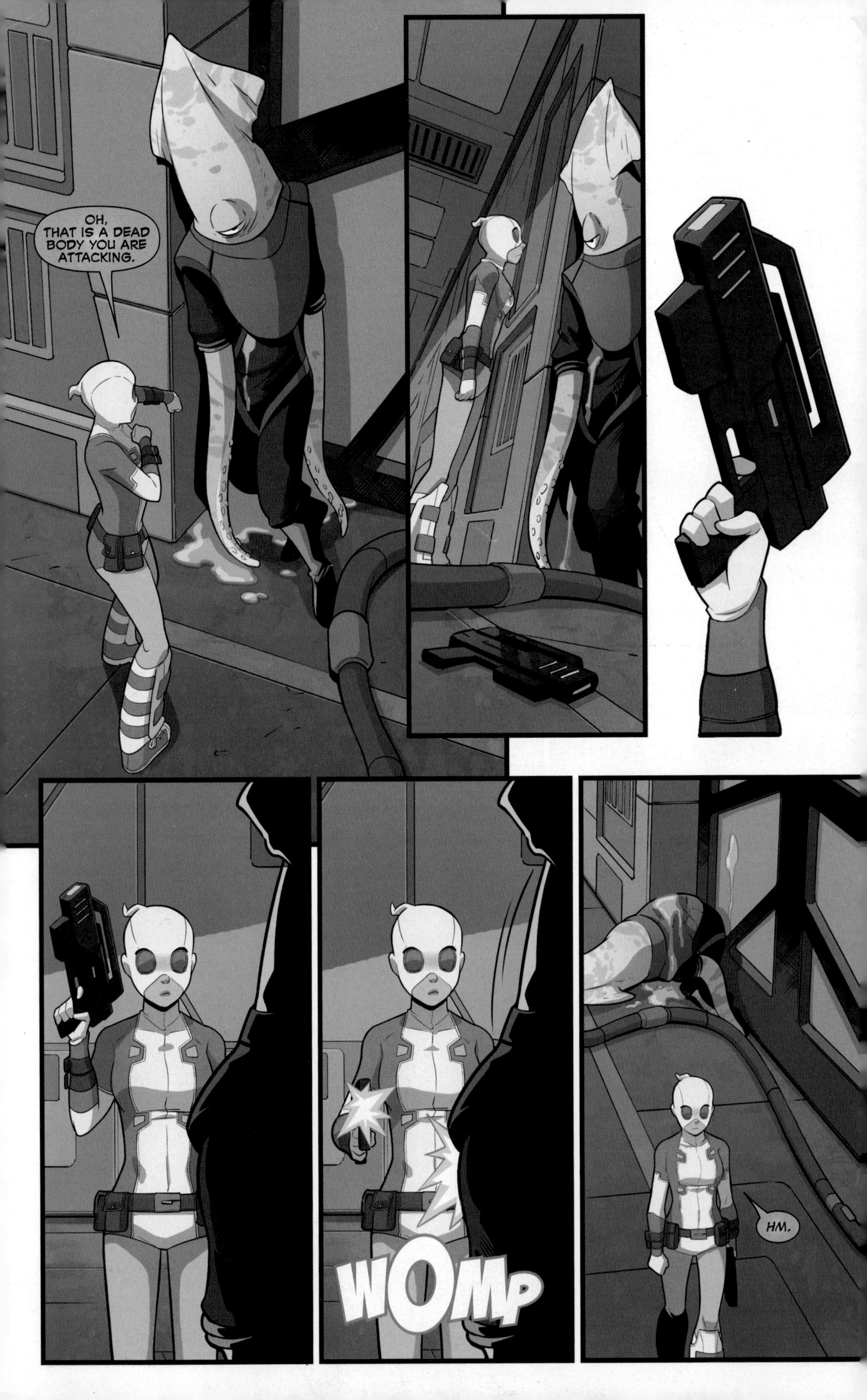
OH, THAT IS A DEAD BODY YOU ARE ATTACKING.
WOMP
HM.

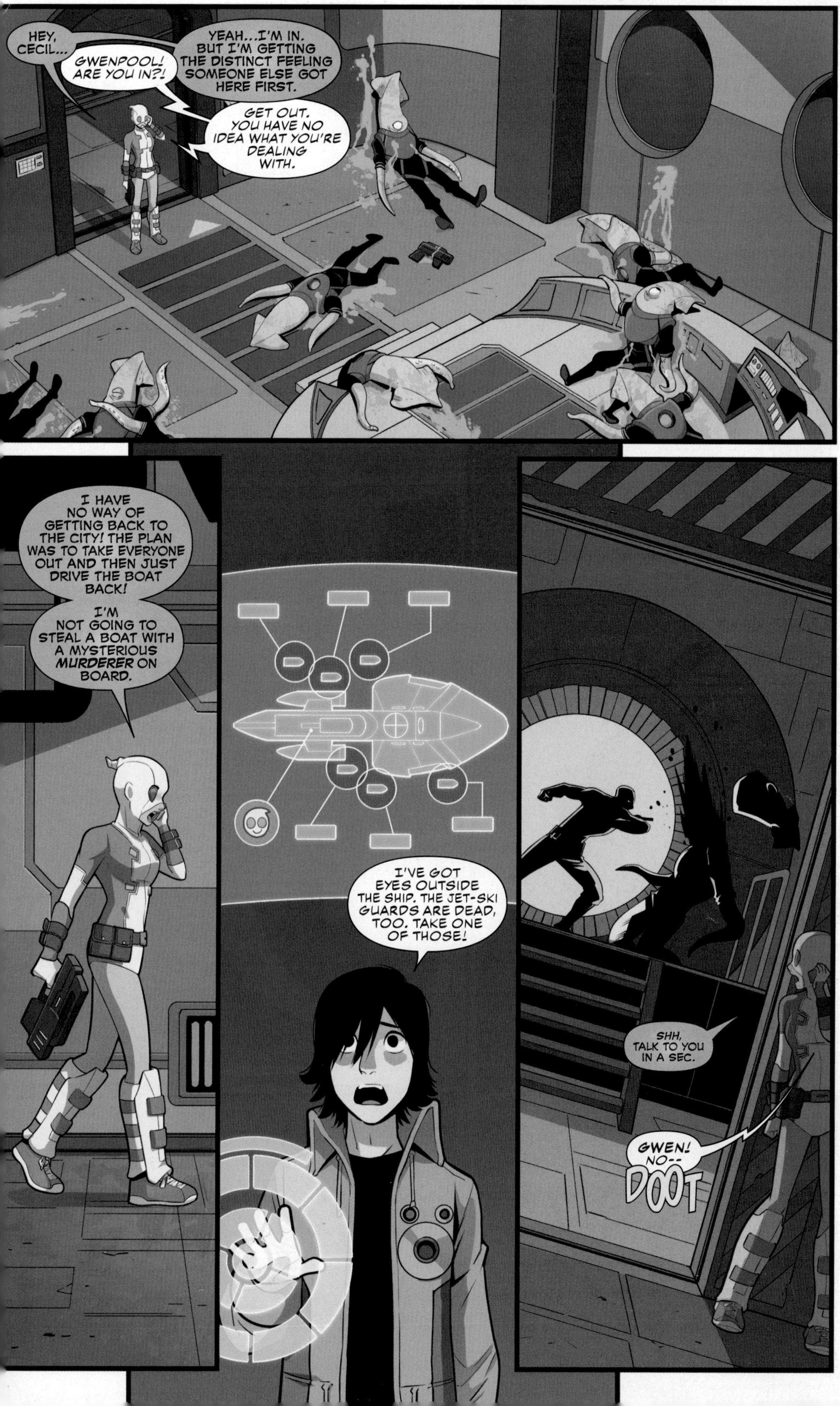
HEY, CECIL...
GWENPOOL! ARE YOU IN?!
YEAH...I'M IN. BUT I'M GETTING THE DISTINCT FEELING SOMEONE ELSE GOT HERE FIRST.
GET OUT. YOU HAVE NO IDEA WHAT YOU'RE DEALING WITH.
I HAVE NO WAY OF GETTING BACK TO THE CITY! THE PLAN WAS TO TAKE EVERYONE OUT AND THEN JUST DRIVE THE BOAT BACK!
I'M NOT GOING TO STEAL A BOAT WITH A MYSTERIOUS MURDERER ON BOARD.
I'VE GOT EYES OUTSIDE THE SHIP. THE JET-SKI GUARDS ARE DEAD, TOO. TAKE ONE OF THOSE!
SHH, TALK TO YOU IN A SEC.
GWEN! NO--
DOOT

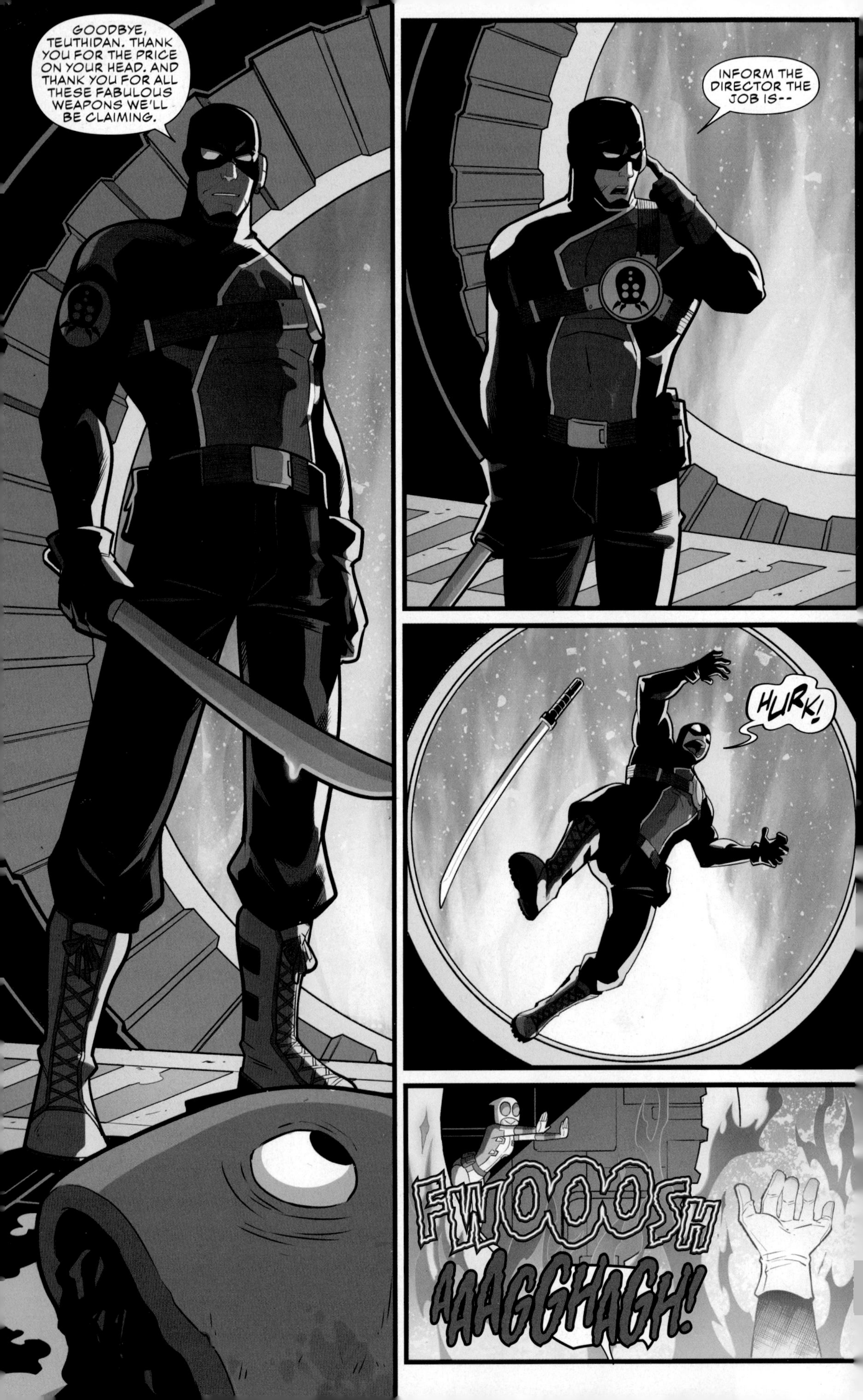
GOODBYE, TEUTHIDAN. THANK YOU FOR THE PRICE ON YOUR HEAD. AND THANK YOU FOR ALL THESE FABULOUS WEAPONS WE'LL BE CLAIMING.
INFORM THE DIRECTOR THE JOB IS--
HURK!
FWOOOSH
AAAGGHAGH!

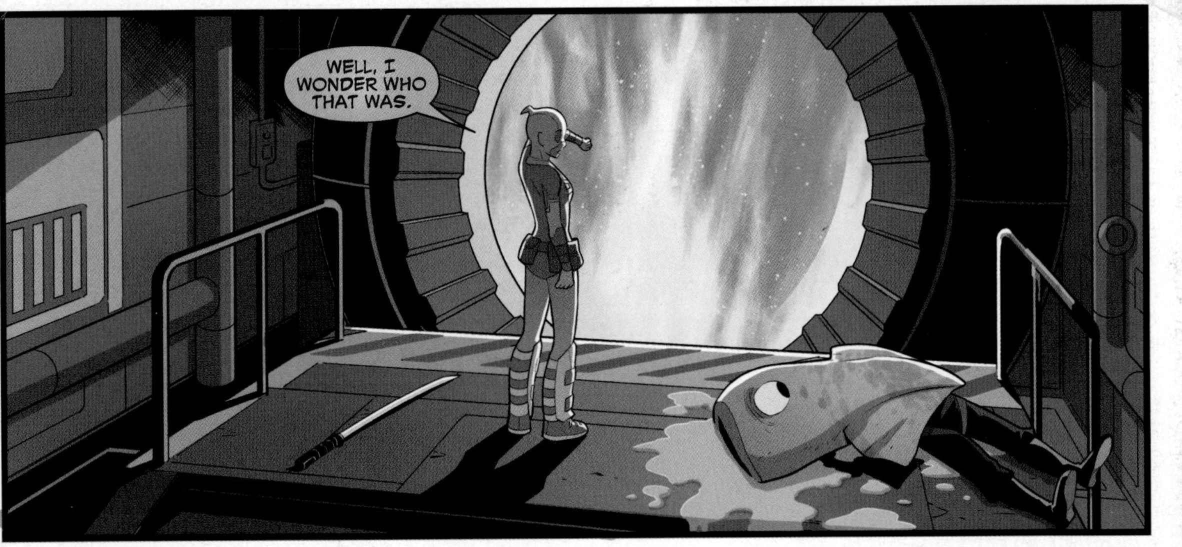
WELL, I WONDER WHO THAT WAS.

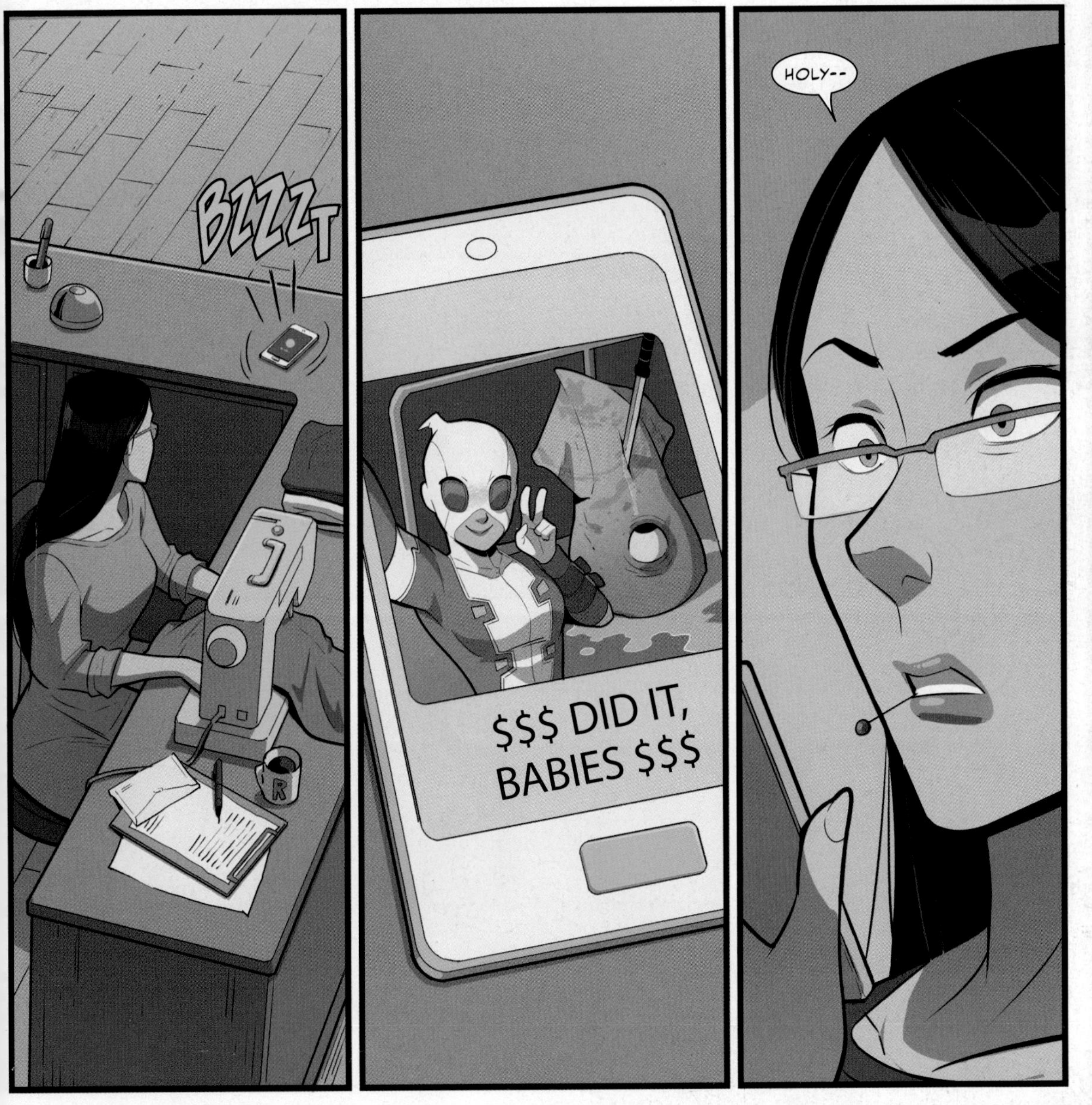
BZZZT
$$$ DID IT, BABIES $$$
HOLY--

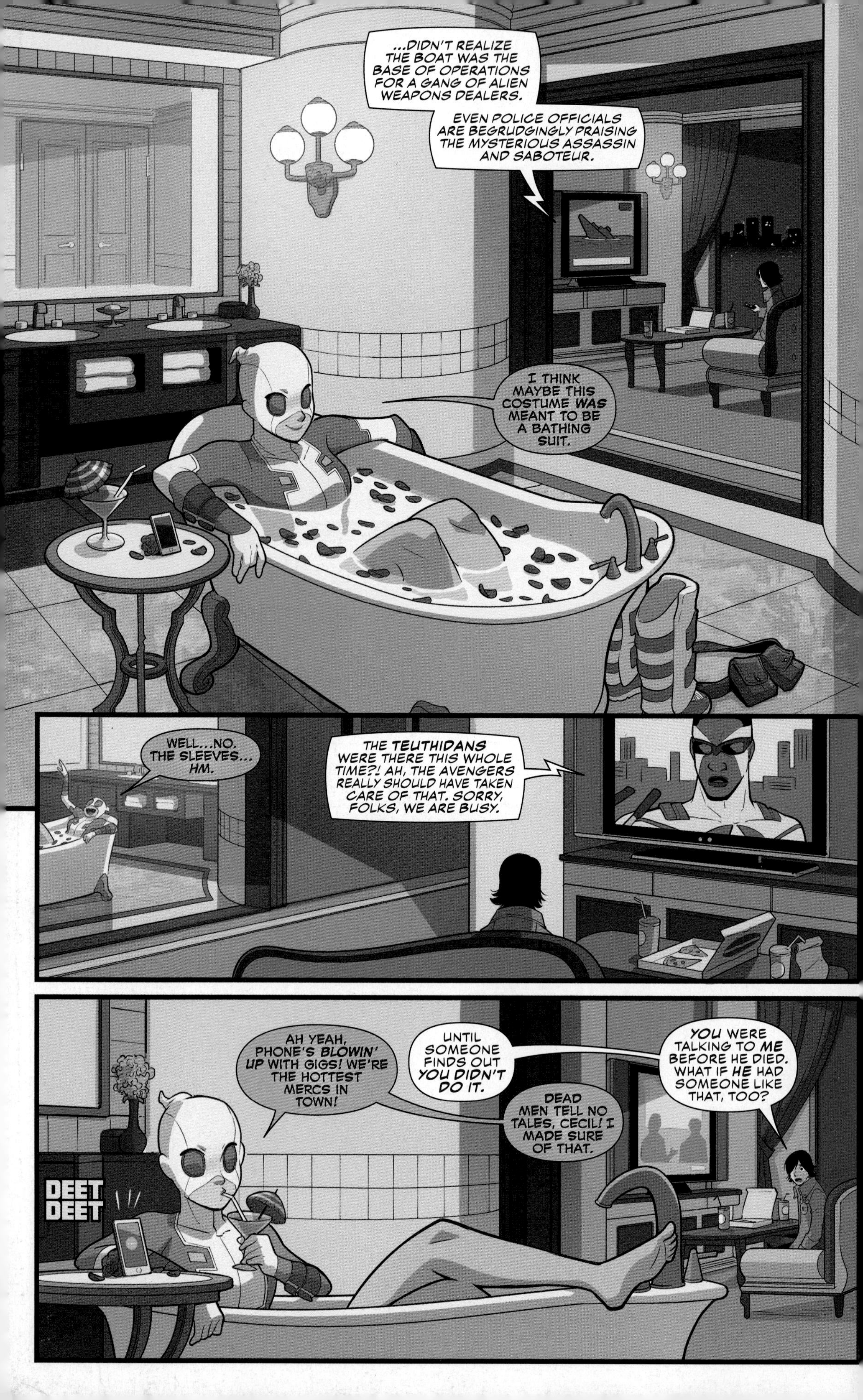

...DIDN'T REALIZE THE BOAT WAS THE BASE OF OPERATIONS FOR A GANG OF ALIEN WEAPONS DEALERS.
EVEN POLICE OFFICIALS ARE BEGRUDGINGLY PRAISING THE MYSTERIOUS ASSASSIN AND SABOTEUR.
I THINK MAYBE THIS COSTUME *WAS* MEANT TO BE A BATHING SUIT.
WELL...NO. THE SLEEVES... HM.
THE **TEUTHIDANS** WERE THERE THIS WHOLE TIME?! AH, THE AVENGERS REALLY SHOULD HAVE TAKEN CARE OF THAT. SORRY, FOLKS, WE ARE BUSY.
DEET DEET
AH YEAH, PHONE'S *BLOWIN' UP* WITH GIGS! WE'RE THE HOTTEST MERCS IN TOWN!
UNTIL SOMEONE FINDS OUT *YOU DIDN'T DO IT.*
DEAD MEN TELL NO TALES, CECIL! I MADE SURE OF THAT.
*YOU* WERE TALKING TO *ME* BEFORE HE DIED. WHAT IF *HE* HAD SOMEONE LIKE THAT, TOO?

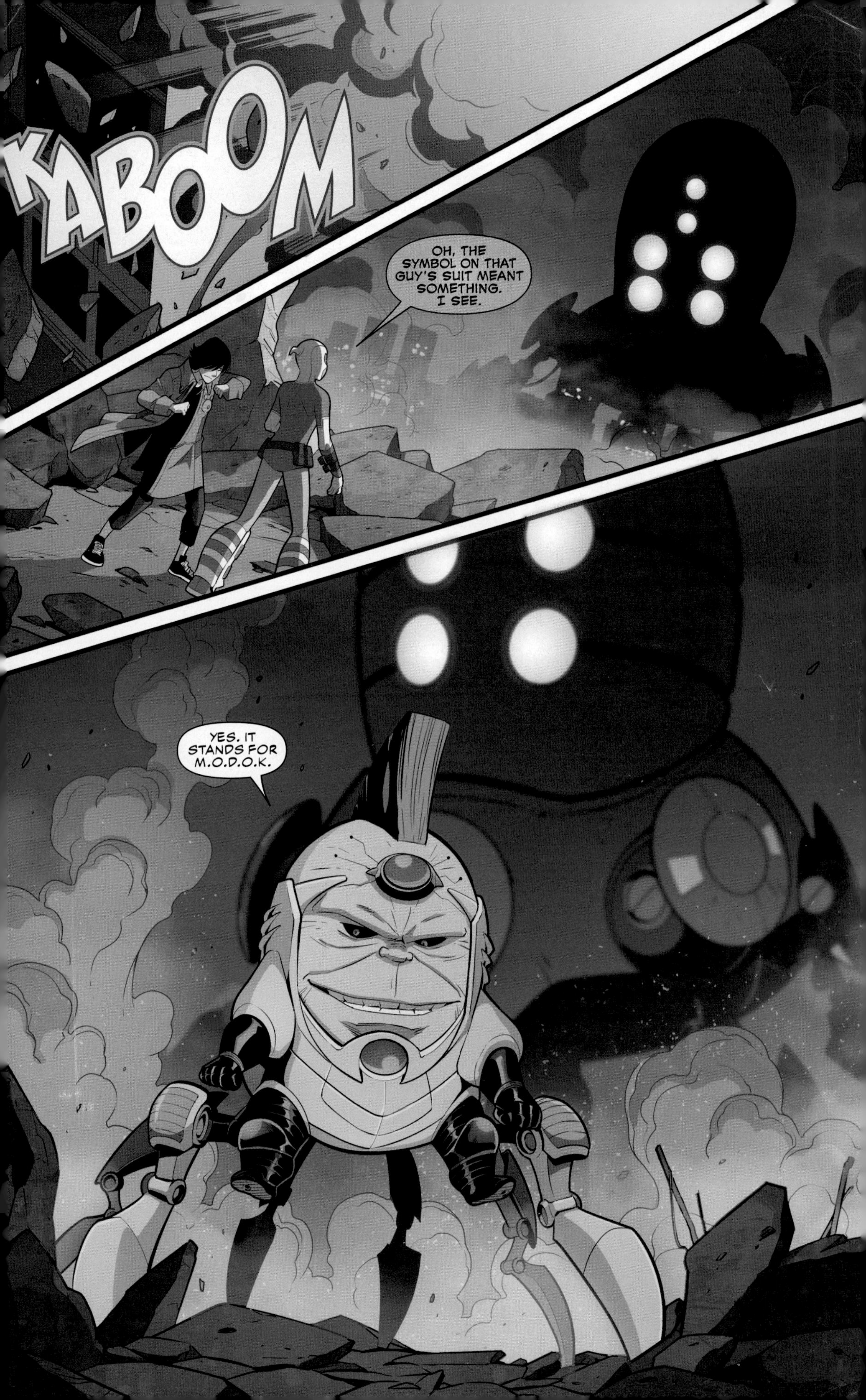
KABOOM
OH, THE SYMBOL ON THAT GUY'S SUIT MEANT SOMETHING. I SEE.
YES. IT STANDS FOR M.O.D.O.K.

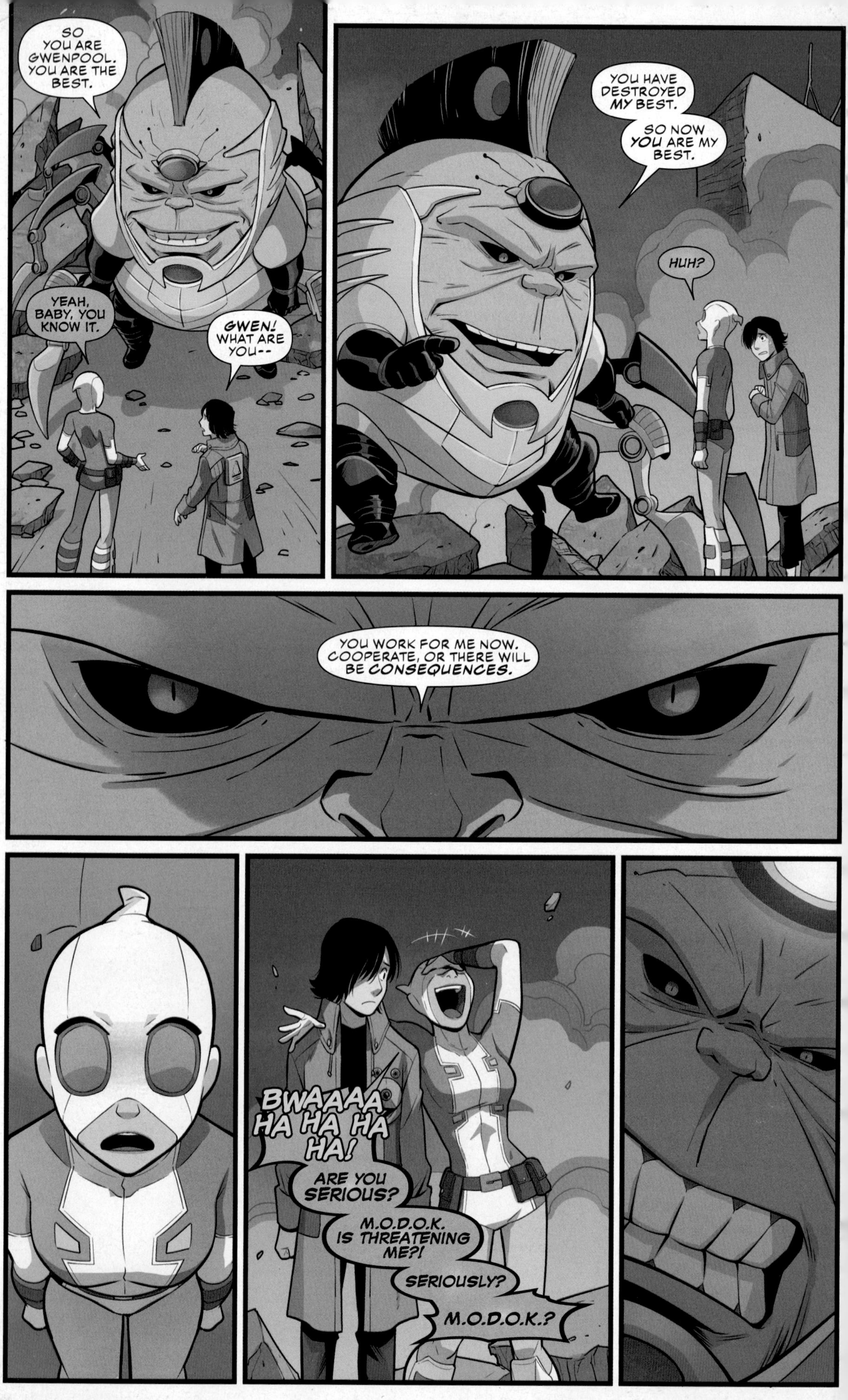
SO YOU ARE GWENPOOL. YOU ARE THE BEST.
YEAH, BABY, YOU KNOW IT.
GWEN! WHAT ARE YOU--
YOU HAVE DESTROYED MY BEST.
SO NOW YOU ARE MY BEST.
HUH?
YOU WORK FOR ME NOW. COOPERATE, OR THERE WILL BE CONSEQUENCES.
BWAAAA HA HA HA HA!
ARE YOU SERIOUS?
M.O.D.O.K. IS THREATENING ME?!
SERIOUSLY?
M.O.D.O.K.?

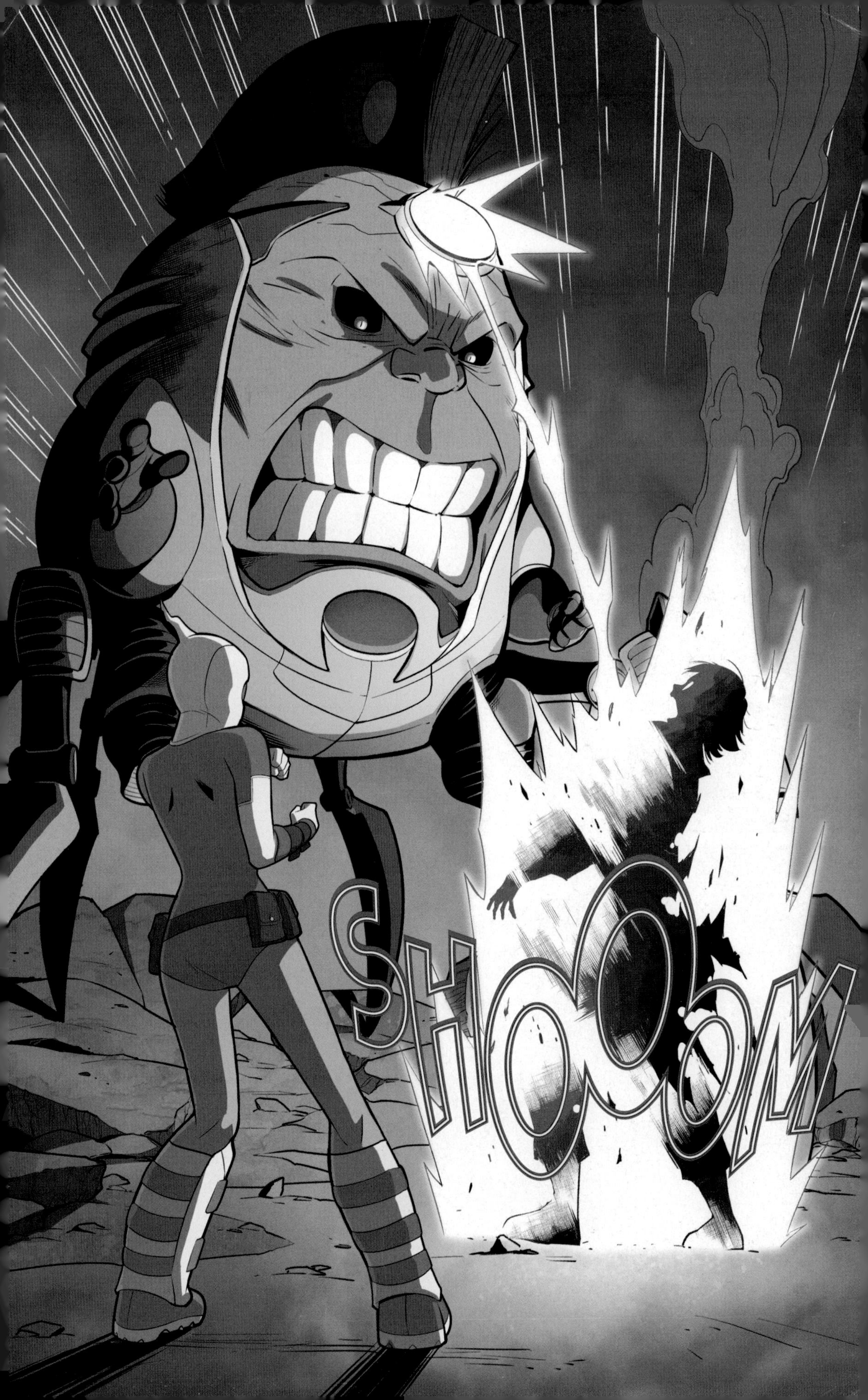
SHOOOM

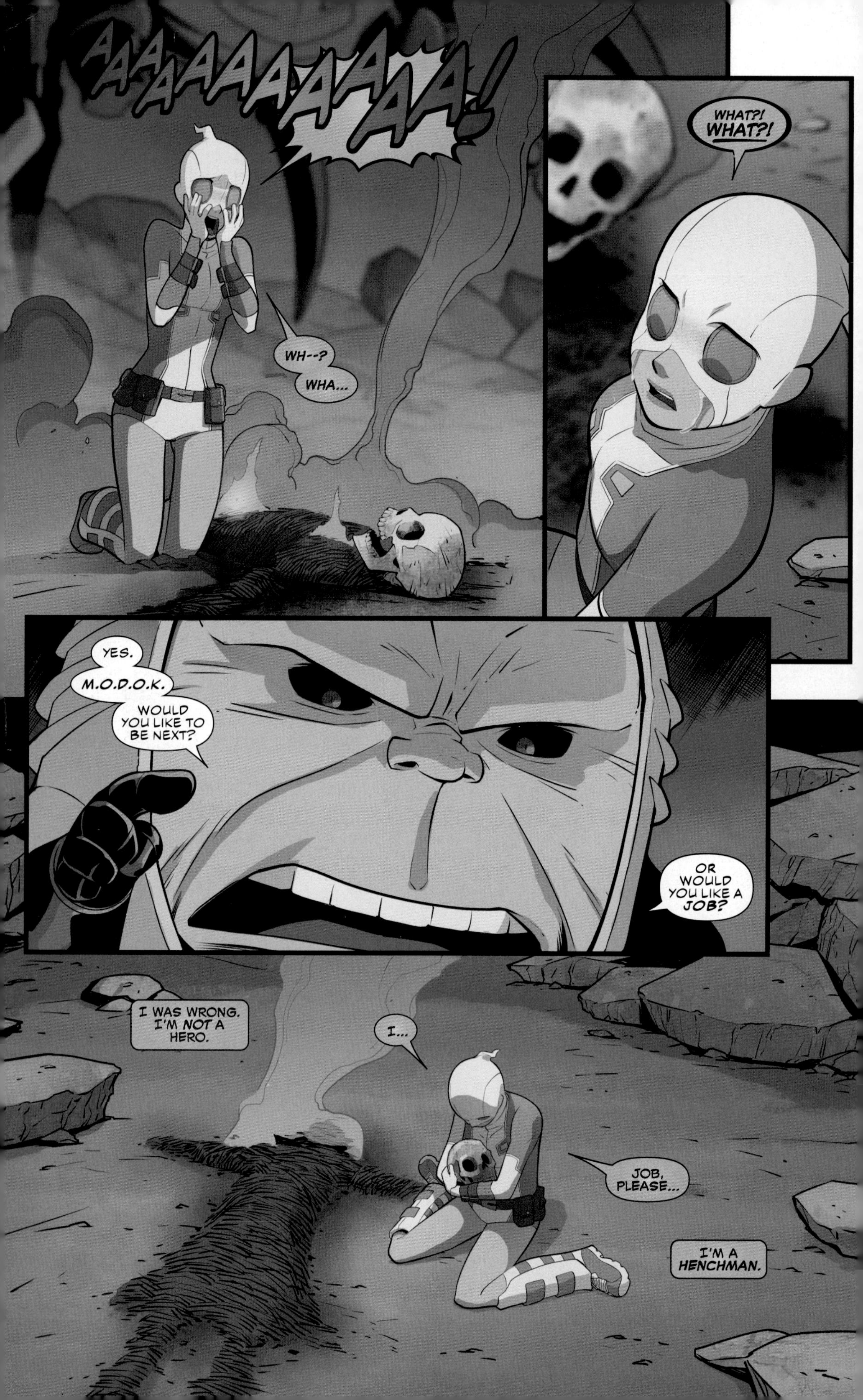
AAAAAAAAAAAA!
WH--?
WHA...
WHAT?!
WHAT?!
YES.
M.O.D.O.K.
WOULD YOU LIKE TO BE NEXT?
OR WOULD YOU LIKE A JOB?
I WAS WRONG. I'M NOT A HERO.
I...
JOB, PLEASE...
I'M A HENCHMAN.

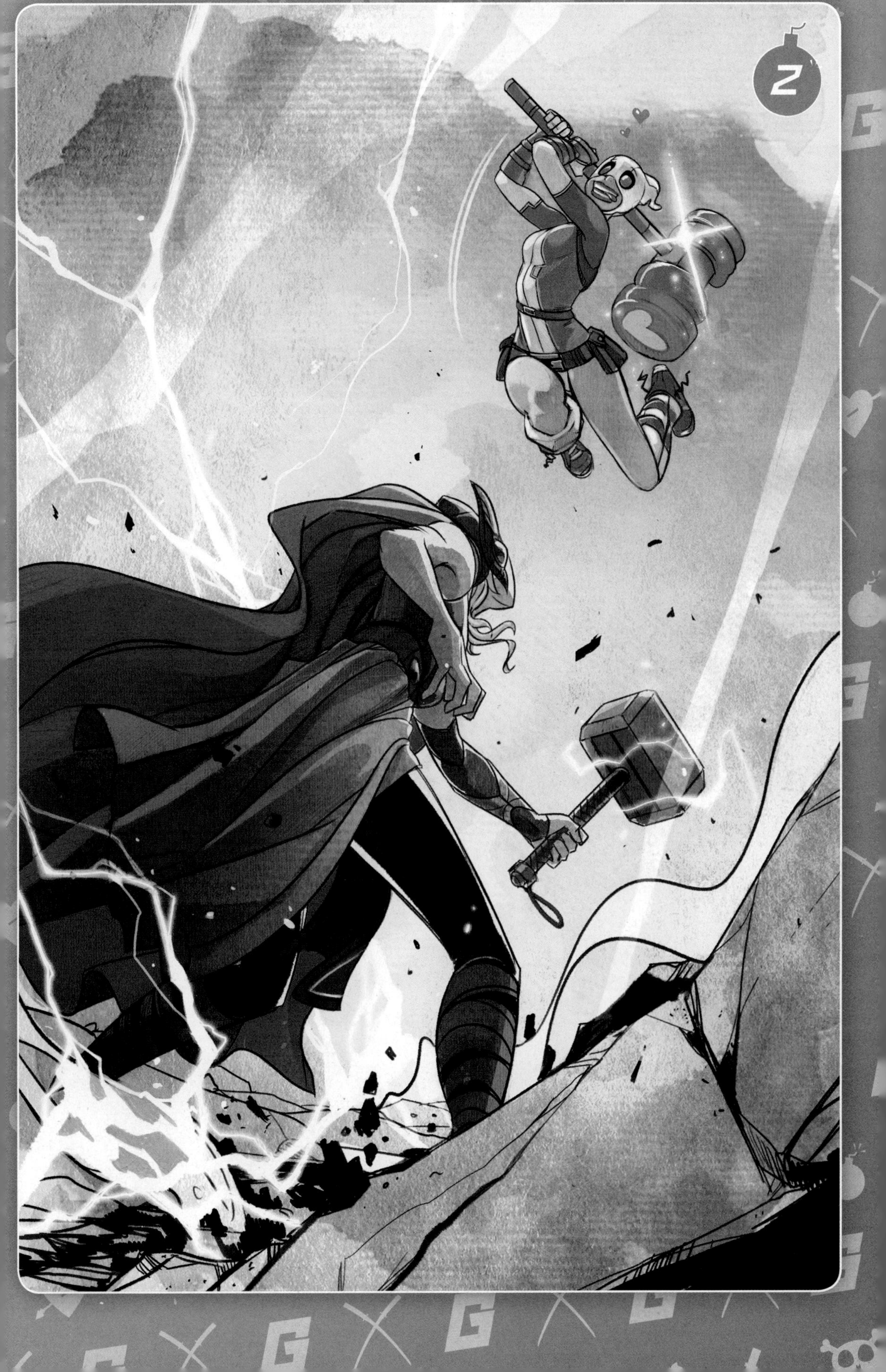
2

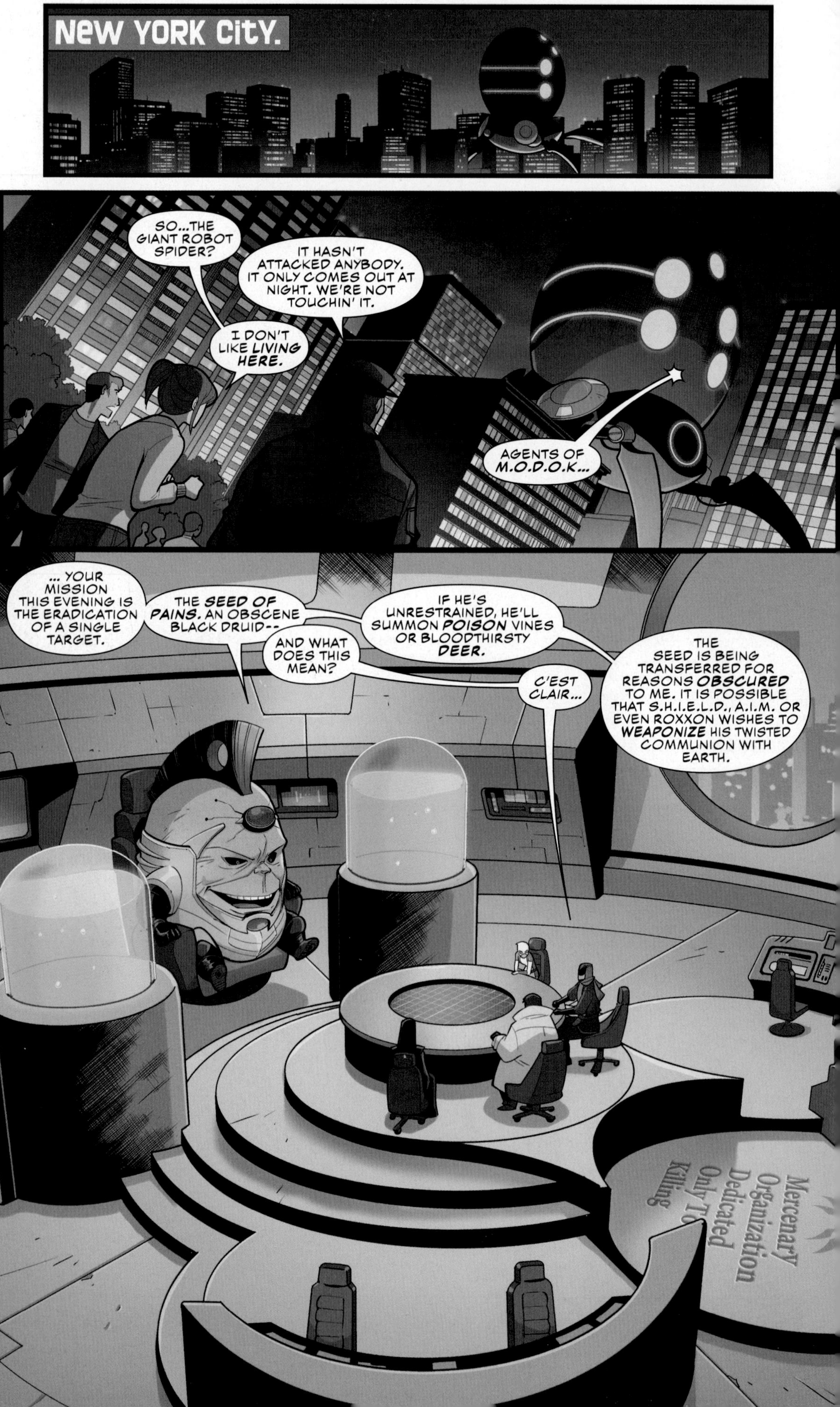
NEW YORK CITY.
SO...THE GIANT ROBOT SPIDER?
IT HASN'T ATTACKED ANYBODY. IT ONLY COMES OUT AT NIGHT. WE'RE NOT TOUCHIN' IT.
I DON'T LIKE LIVING HERE.
AGENTS OF M.O.D.O.K...
... YOUR MISSION THIS EVENING IS THE ERADICATION OF A SINGLE TARGET.
THE SEED OF PAINS. AN OBSCENE BLACK DRUID--
AND WHAT DOES THIS MEAN?
IF HE'S UNRESTRAINED, HE'LL SUMMON POISON VINES OR BLOODTHIRSTY DEER.
C'EST CLAIR...
THE SEED IS BEING TRANSFERRED FOR REASONS OBSCURED TO ME. IT IS POSSIBLE THAT S.H.I.E.L.D., A.I.M. OR EVEN ROXXON WISHES TO WEAPONIZE HIS TWISTED COMMUNION WITH EARTH.
Mercenary Organization Dedicated Only To Killing

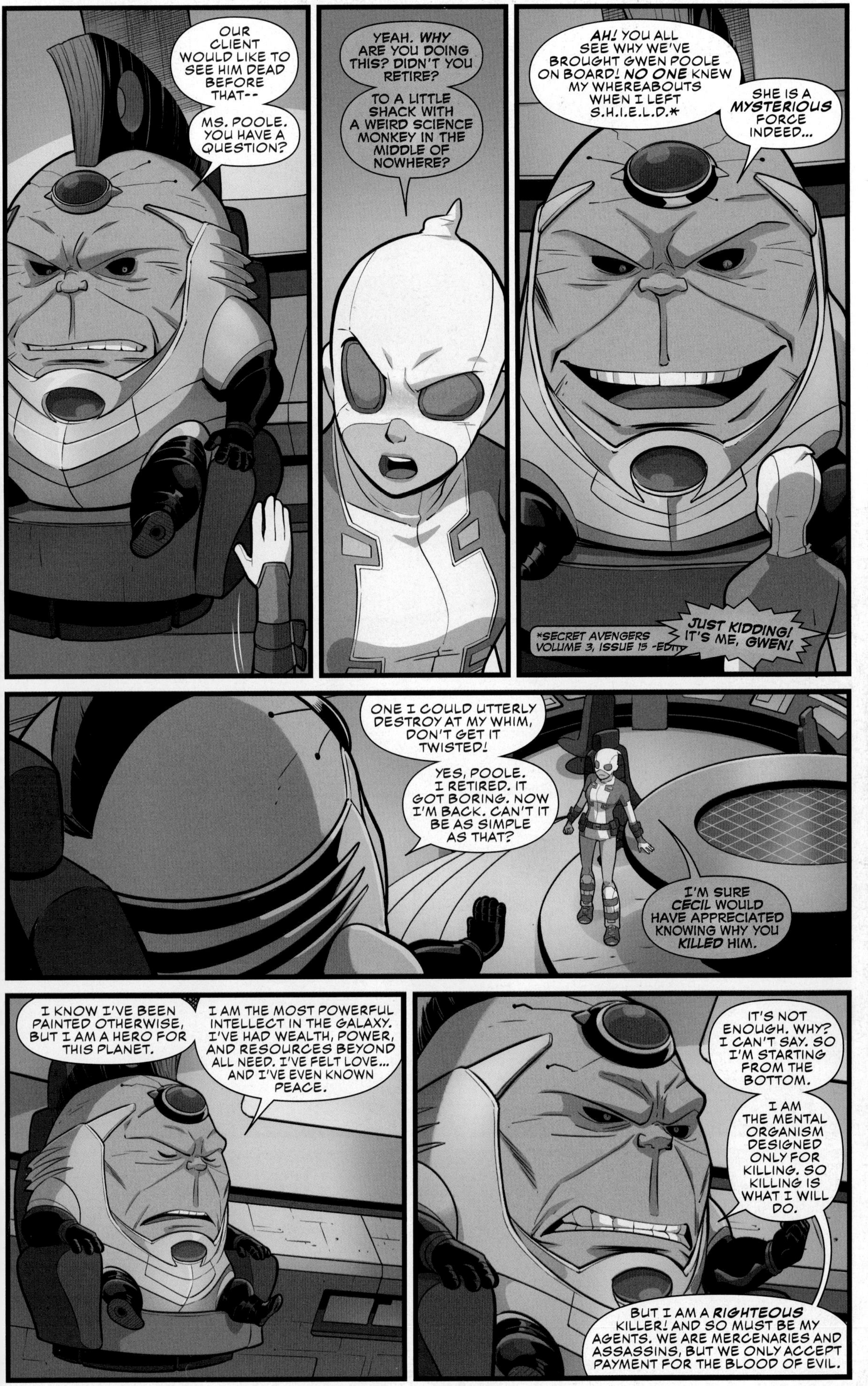
OUR CLIENT WOULD LIKE TO SEE HIM DEAD BEFORE THAT--
MS. POOLE. YOU HAVE A QUESTION?
YEAH. WHY ARE YOU DOING THIS? DIDN'T YOU RETIRE?
TO A LITTLE SHACK WITH A WEIRD SCIENCE MONKEY IN THE MIDDLE OF NOWHERE?
AH! YOU ALL SEE WHY WE'VE BROUGHT GWEN POOLE ON BOARD! NO ONE KNEW MY WHEREABOUTS WHEN I LEFT S.H.I.E.L.D.*
SHE IS A MYSTERIOUS FORCE INDEED...
*SECRET AVENGERS VOLUME 3, ISSUE 15 -EDITOR
JUST KIDDING! IT'S ME, GWEN!
ONE I COULD UTTERLY DESTROY AT MY WHIM, DON'T GET IT TWISTED!
YES, POOLE. I RETIRED. IT GOT BORING. NOW I'M BACK. CAN'T IT BE AS SIMPLE AS THAT?
I'M SURE CECIL WOULD HAVE APPRECIATED KNOWING WHY YOU KILLED HIM.
I KNOW I'VE BEEN PAINTED OTHERWISE, BUT I AM A HERO FOR THIS PLANET.
I AM THE MOST POWERFUL INTELLECT IN THE GALAXY. I'VE HAD WEALTH, POWER, AND RESOURCES BEYOND ALL NEED. I'VE FELT LOVE... AND I'VE EVEN KNOWN PEACE.
IT'S NOT ENOUGH. WHY? I CAN'T SAY. SO I'M STARTING FROM THE BOTTOM.
I AM THE MENTAL ORGANISM DESIGNED ONLY FOR KILLING. SO KILLING IS WHAT I WILL DO.
BUT I AM A RIGHTEOUS KILLER! AND SO MUST BE MY AGENTS. WE ARE MERCENARIES AND ASSASSINS, BUT WE ONLY ACCEPT PAYMENT FOR THE BLOOD OF EVIL.

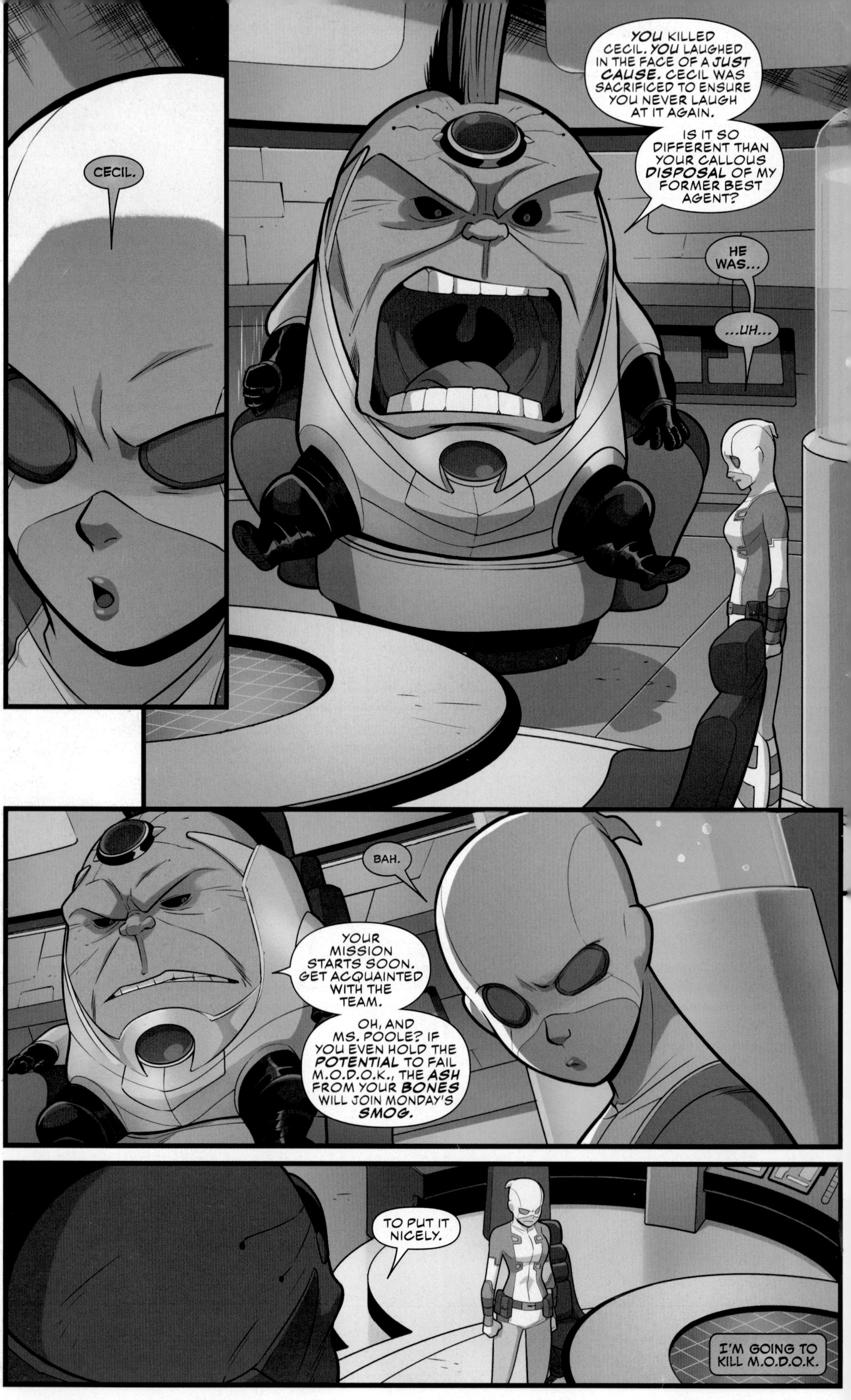
CECIL.
YOU KILLED CECIL. YOU LAUGHED IN THE FACE OF A JUST CAUSE. CECIL WAS SACRIFICED TO ENSURE YOU NEVER LAUGH AT IT AGAIN.
IS IT SO DIFFERENT THAN YOUR CALLOUS DISPOSAL OF MY FORMER BEST AGENT?
HE WAS...
...UH...
BAH.
YOUR MISSION STARTS SOON. GET ACQUAINTED WITH THE TEAM.
OH, AND MS. POOLE? IF YOU EVEN HOLD THE POTENTIAL TO FAIL M.O.D.O.K., THE ASH FROM YOUR BONES WILL JOIN MONDAY'S SMOG.
TO PUT IT NICELY.
I'M GOING TO KILL M.O.D.O.K.

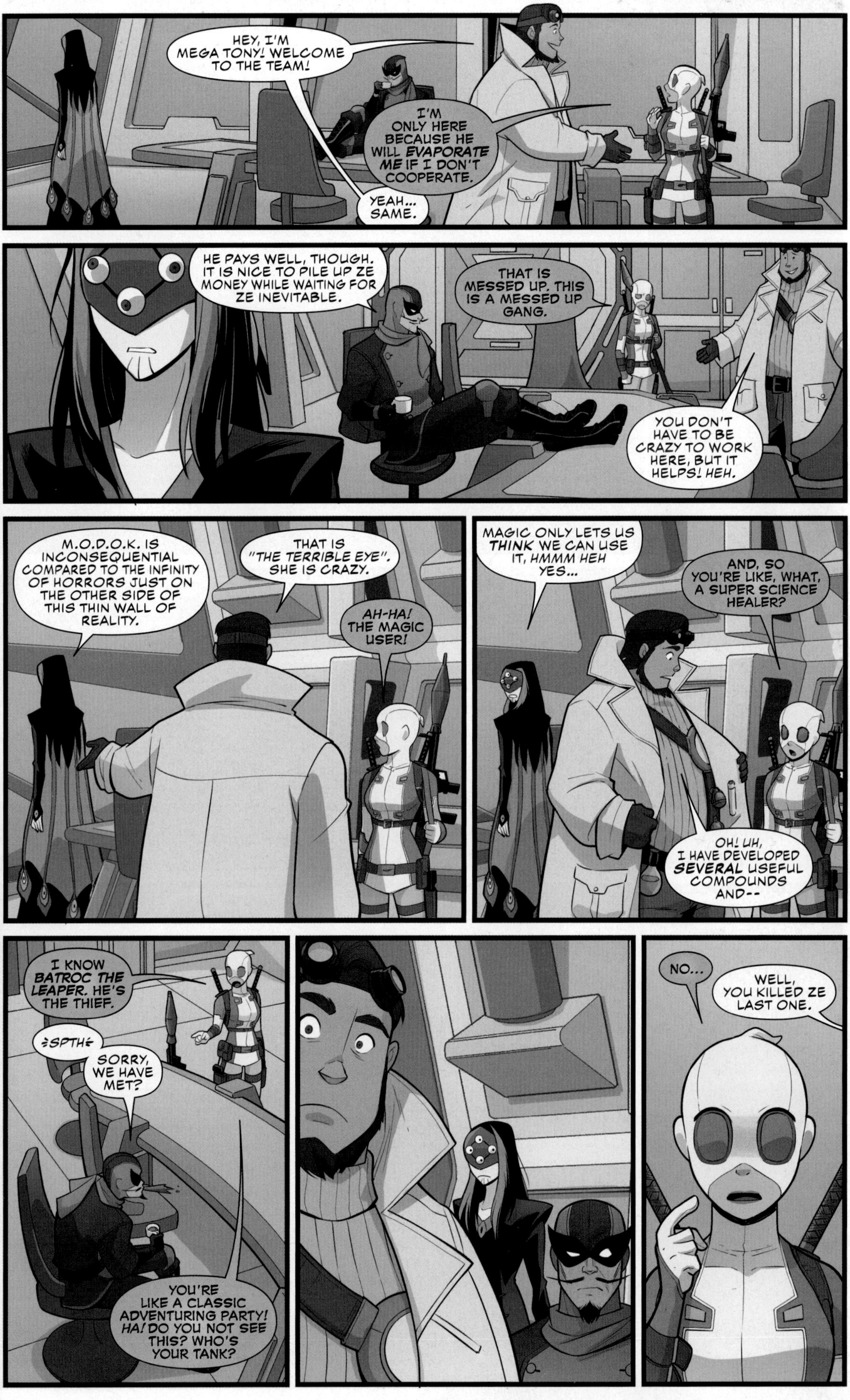
HEY, I'M MEGA TONY! WELCOME TO THE TEAM!
I'M ONLY HERE BECAUSE HE WILL EVAPORATE ME IF I DON'T COOPERATE.
YEAH... SAME.
HE PAYS WELL, THOUGH. IT IS NICE TO PILE UP ZE MONEY WHILE WAITING FOR ZE INEVITABLE.
THAT IS MESSED UP. THIS IS A MESSED UP GANG.
YOU DON'T HAVE TO BE CRAZY TO WORK HERE, BUT IT HELPS! HEH.
M.O.D.O.K. IS INCONSEQUENTIAL COMPARED TO THE INFINITY OF HORRORS JUST ON THE OTHER SIDE OF THIS THIN WALL OF REALITY.
THAT IS "THE TERRIBLE EYE". SHE IS CRAZY.
AH-HA! THE MAGIC USER!
MAGIC ONLY LETS US THINK WE CAN USE IT, HMMM HEH YES...
AND, SO YOU'RE LIKE, WHAT, A SUPER SCIENCE HEALER?
OH! UH, I HAVE DEVELOPED SEVERAL USEFUL COMPOUNDS AND--
I KNOW BATROC THE LEAPER. HE'S THE THIEF.
SPTH
SORRY, WE HAVE MET?
YOU'RE LIKE A CLASSIC ADVENTURING PARTY! HA! DO YOU NOT SEE THIS? WHO'S YOUR TANK?
NO...
WELL, YOU KILLED ZE LAST ONE.

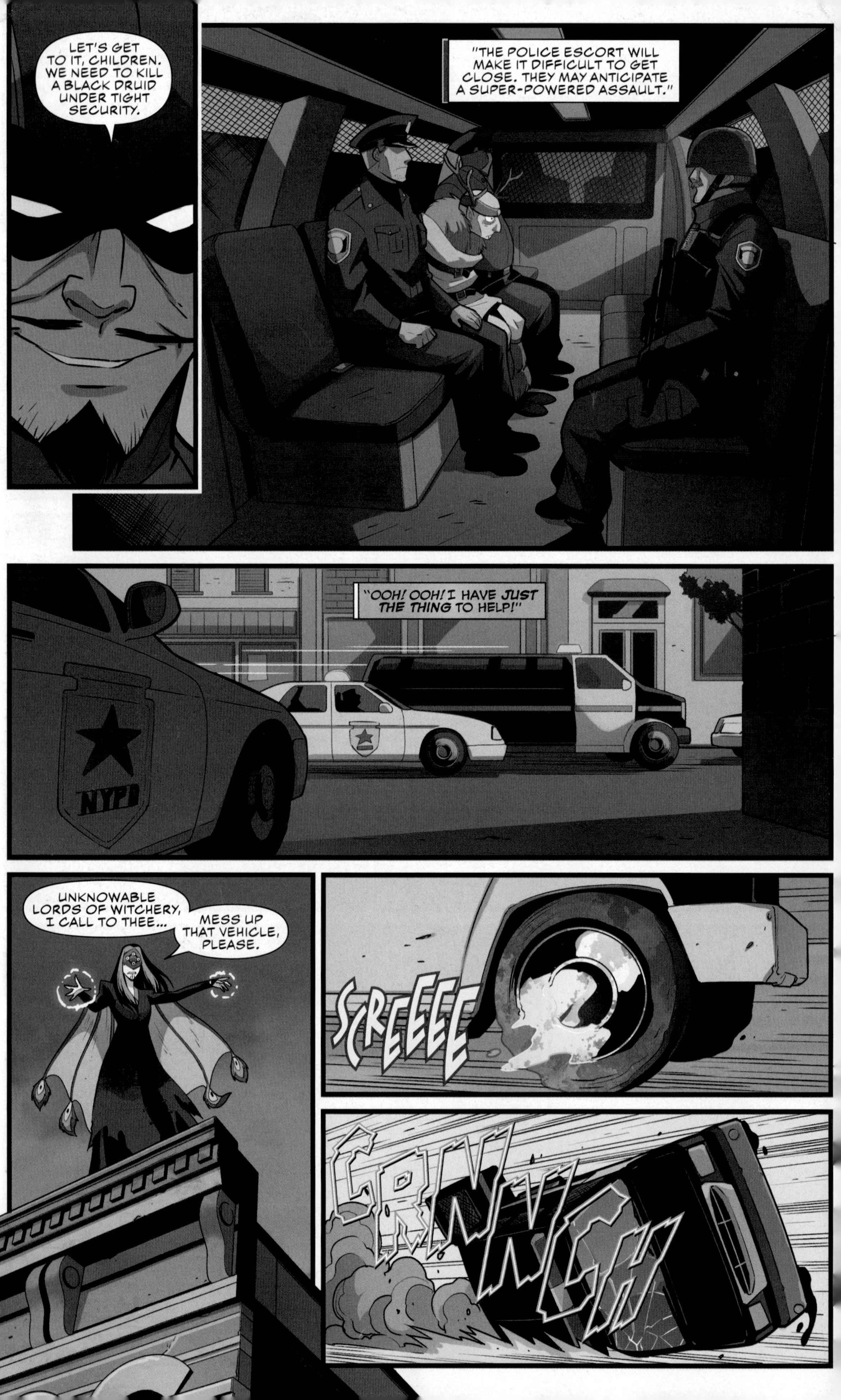
LET'S GET TO IT, CHILDREN. WE NEED TO KILL A BLACK DRUID UNDER TIGHT SECURITY.
"THE POLICE ESCORT WILL MAKE IT DIFFICULT TO GET CLOSE. THEY MAY ANTICIPATE A SUPER-POWERED ASSAULT."
"OOH! OOH! I HAVE JUST THE THING TO HELP!"
NYPD
UNKNOWABLE LORDS OF WITCHERY, I CALL TO THEE...
MESS UP THAT VEHICLE, PLEASE.
SCREEEE
GRNNCH

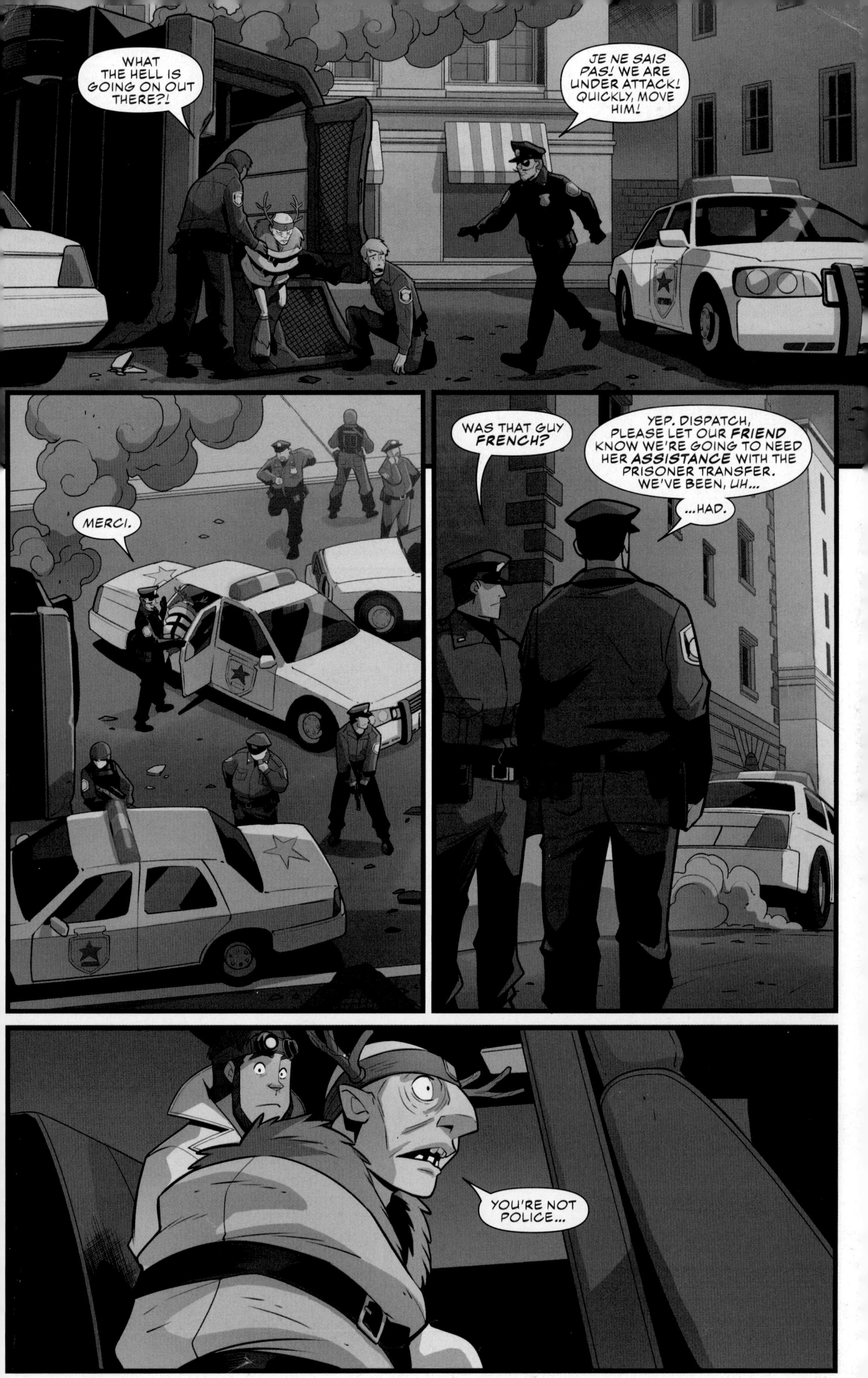
WHAT THE HELL IS GOING ON OUT THERE?!
JE NE SAIS PAS! WE ARE UNDER ATTACK! QUICKLY, MOVE HIM!
MERCI.
WAS THAT GUY FRENCH?
YEP. DISPATCH, PLEASE LET OUR FRIEND KNOW WE'RE GOING TO NEED HER ASSISTANCE WITH THE PRISONER TRANSFER. WE'VE BEEN, UH...
...HAD.
YOU'RE NOT POLICE...

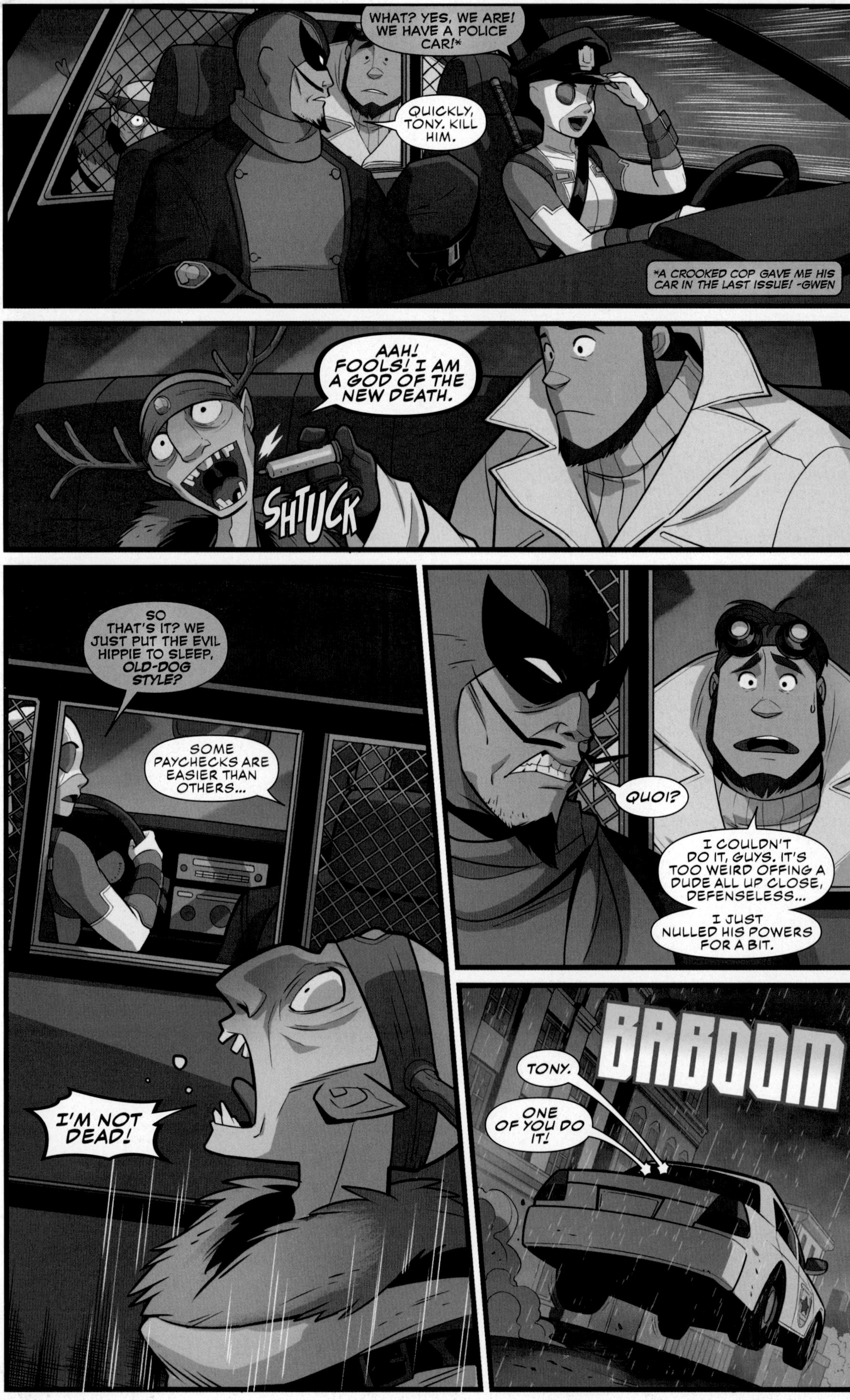
WHAT? YES, WE ARE! WE HAVE A POLICE CAR!*
QUICKLY, TONY. KILL HIM.
*A CROOKED COP GAVE ME HIS CAR IN THE LAST ISSUE! -GWEN
AAH! FOOLS! I AM A GOD OF THE NEW DEATH.
SHTUCK
SO THAT'S IT? WE JUST PUT THE EVIL HIPPIE TO SLEEP, OLD-DOG STYLE?
SOME PAYCHECKS ARE EASIER THAN OTHERS...
QUOI?
I COULDN'T DO IT, GUYS. IT'S TOO WEIRD OFFING A DUDE ALL UP CLOSE, DEFENSELESS...
I JUST NULLED HIS POWERS FOR A BIT.
I'M NOT DEAD!
BABOOM
TONY.
ONE OF YOU DO IT!

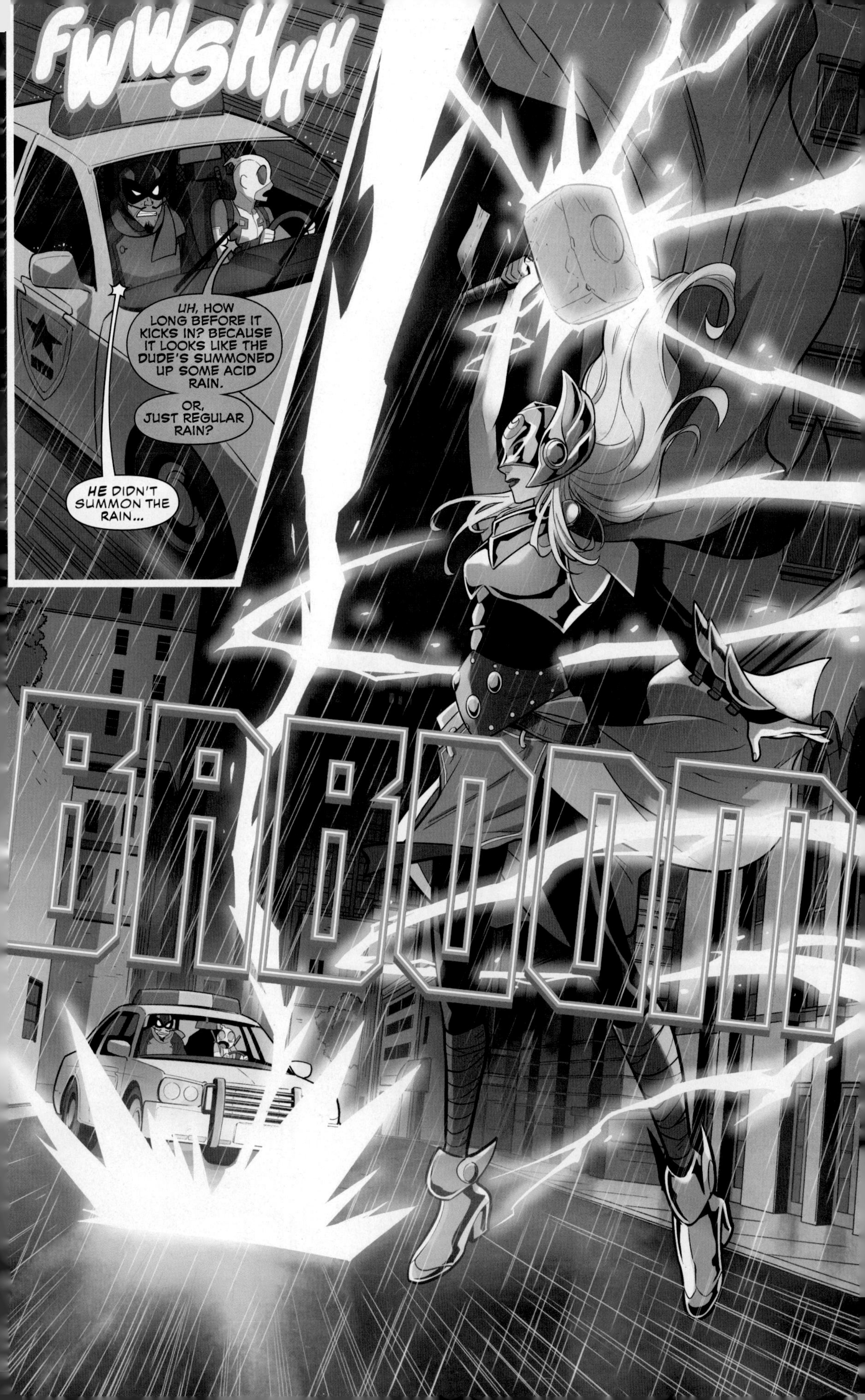
FWWSHHH
UH, HOW LONG BEFORE IT KICKS IN? BECAUSE IT LOOKS LIKE THE DUDE'S SUMMONED UP SOME ACID RAIN.
OR, JUST REGULAR RAIN?
HE DIDN'T SUMMON THE RAIN...
BRROOM

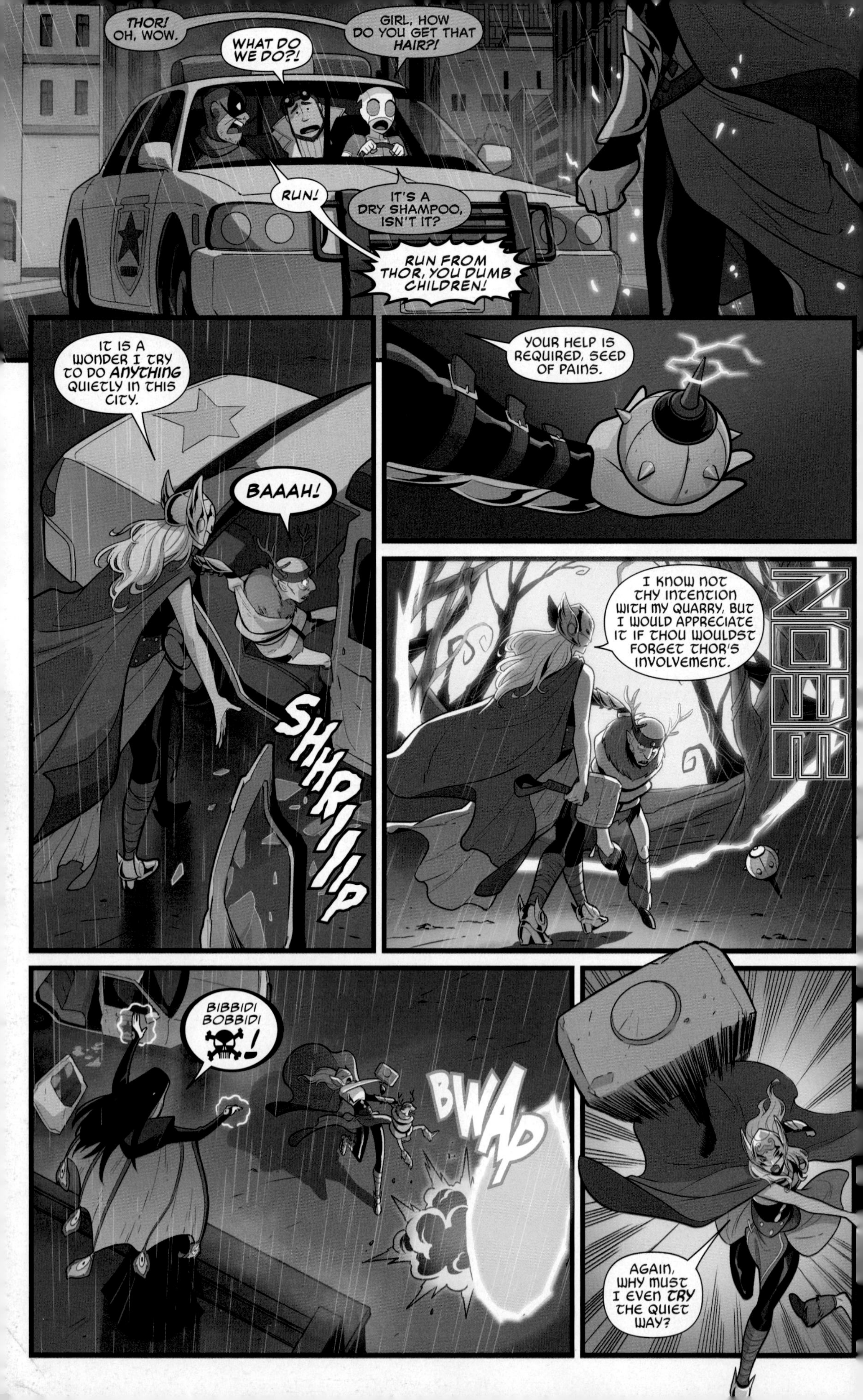
THOR! OH, WOW.
GIRL, HOW DO YOU GET THAT HAIR?!
WHAT DO WE DO?!
RUN!
IT'S A DRY SHAMPOO, ISN'T IT?
RUN FROM THOR, YOU DUMB CHILDREN!
IT IS A WONDER I TRY TO DO ANYTHING QUIETLY IN THIS CITY.
BAAAH!
SHHRIIIIP
YOUR HELP IS REQUIRED, SEED OF PAINS.
I KNOW NOT THY INTENTION WITH MY QUARRY, BUT I WOULD APPRECIATE IT IF THOU WOULDST FORGET THOR'S INVOLVEMENT.
BIBBIDI BOBBIDI !
BWAP
AGAIN, WHY MUST I EVEN TRY THE QUIET WAY?

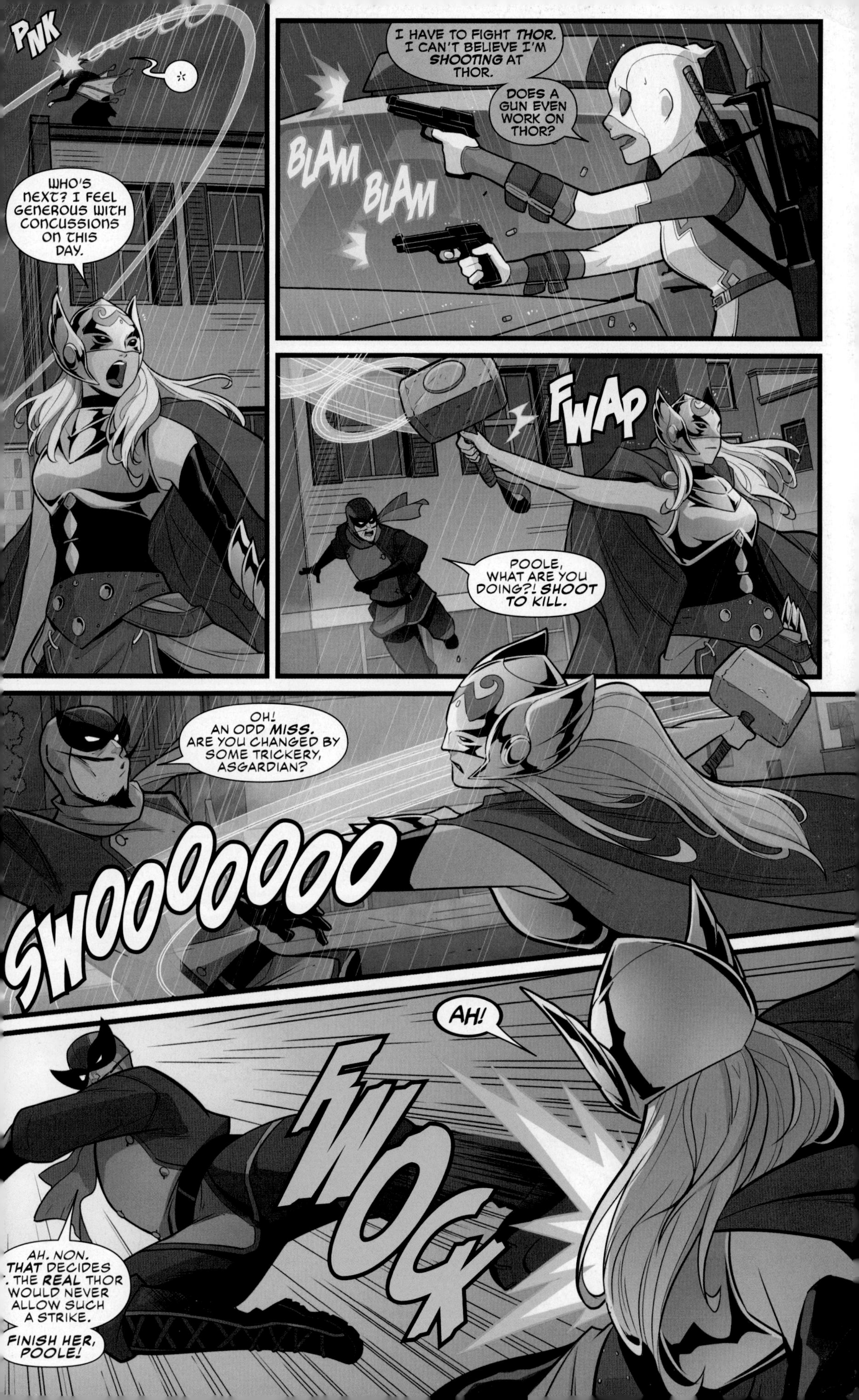
PNK
WHO'S NEXT? I FEEL GENEROUS WITH CONCUSSIONS ON THIS DAY.
I HAVE TO FIGHT THOR. I CAN'T BELIEVE I'M SHOOTING AT THOR.
DOES A GUN EVEN WORK ON THOR?
BLAM
BLAM
FWAP
POOLE, WHAT ARE YOU DOING?! SHOOT TO KILL.
OH! AN ODD MISS. ARE YOU CHANGED BY SOME TRICKERY, ASGARDIAN?
SWOOOOOOOO
AH!
FWOCK
AH. NON. THAT DECIDES IT. THE REAL THOR WOULD NEVER ALLOW SUCH A STRIKE.
FINISH HER, POOLE!

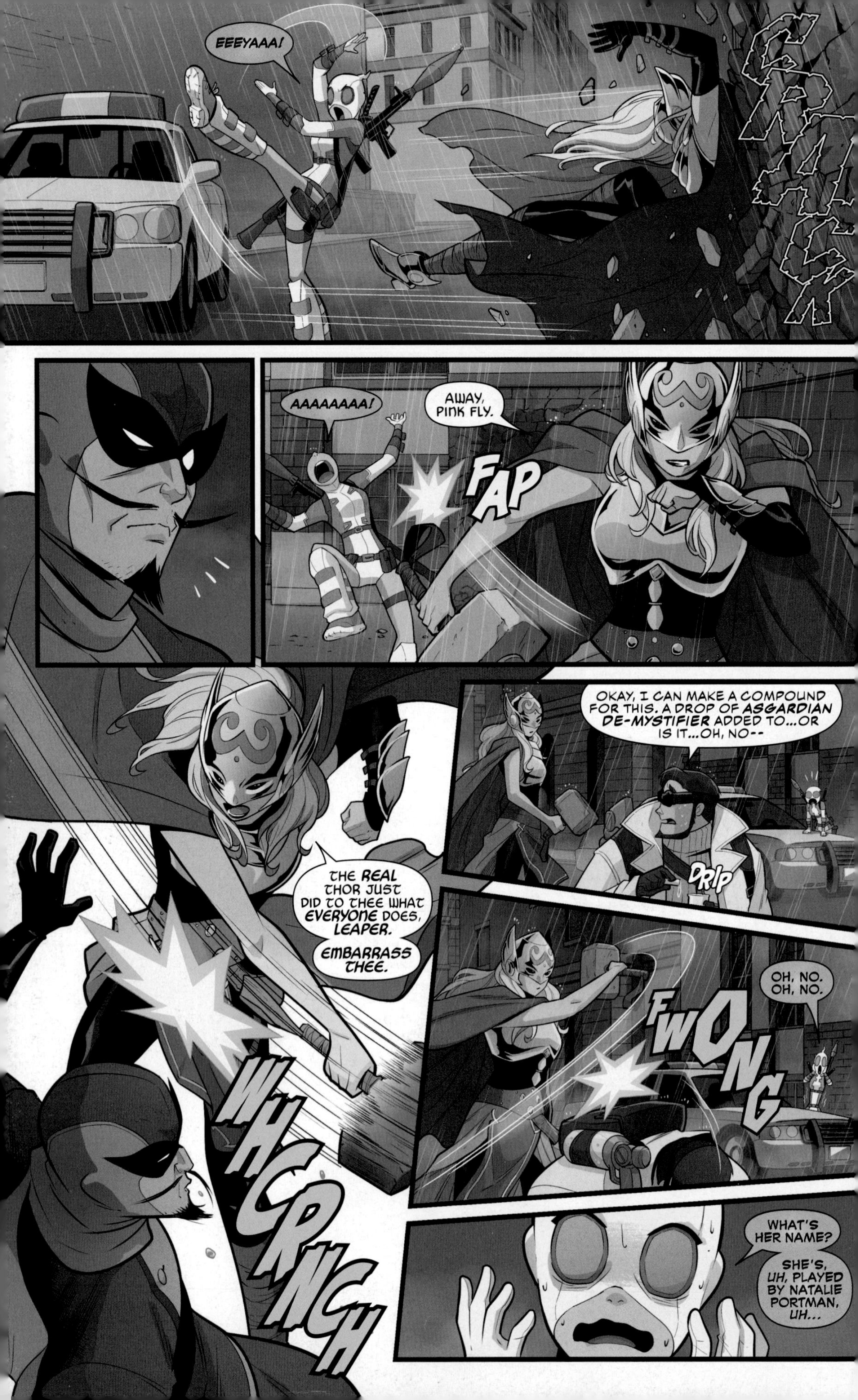
EEEYAAA!
CRACK
AAAAAAAA!
AWAY, PINK FLY.
FAP
THE REAL THOR JUST DID TO THEE WHAT EVERYONE DOES, LEAPER.
EMBARRASS THEE.
WHCRNCH
OKAY, I CAN MAKE A COMPOUND FOR THIS. A DROP OF ASGARDIAN DE-MYSTIFIER ADDED TO...OR IS IT...OH, NO--
DRIP
OH, NO. OH, NO.
FWONG
WHAT'S HER NAME?
SHE'S, UH, PLAYED BY NATALIE PORTMAN, UH...

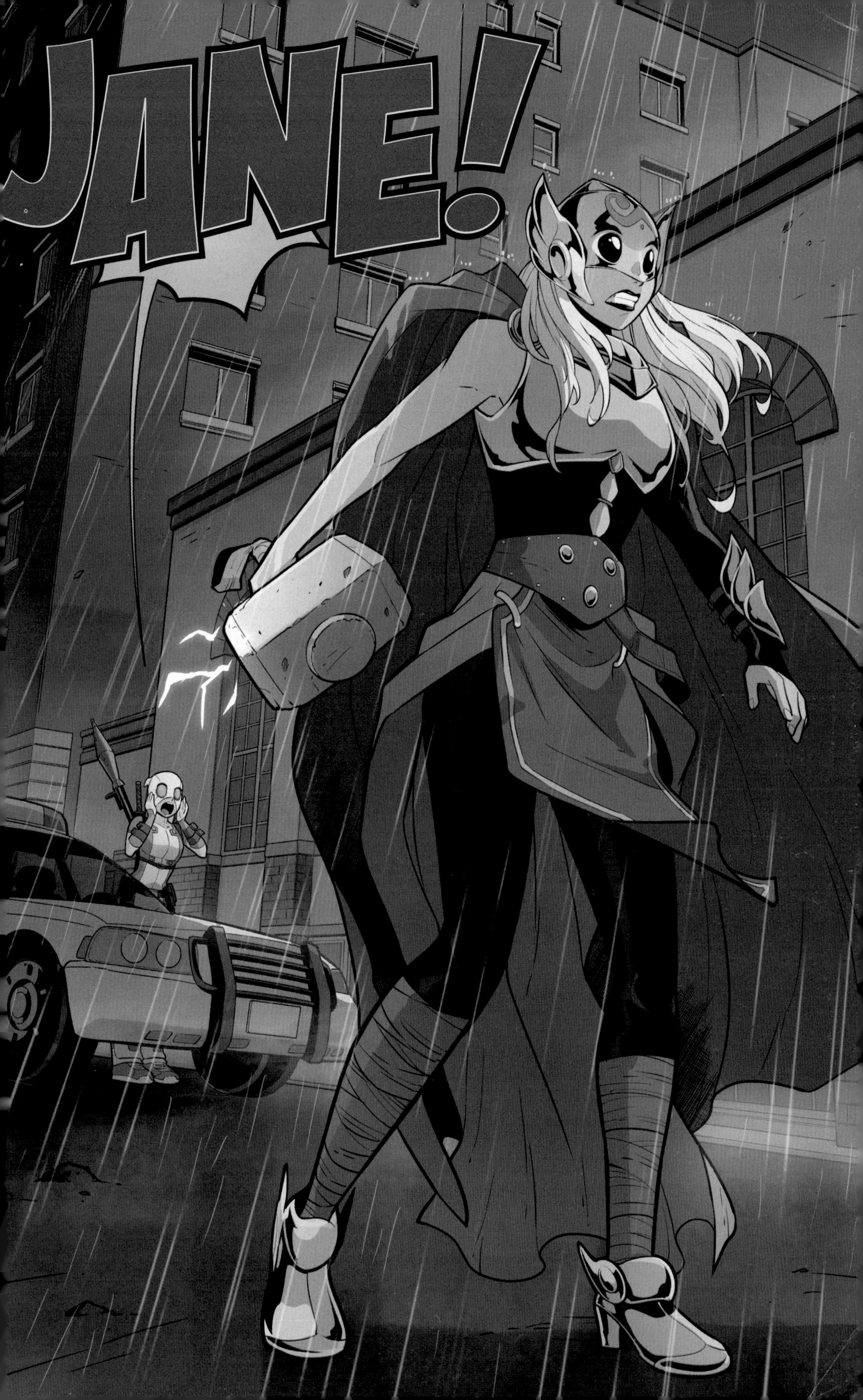
JANE!

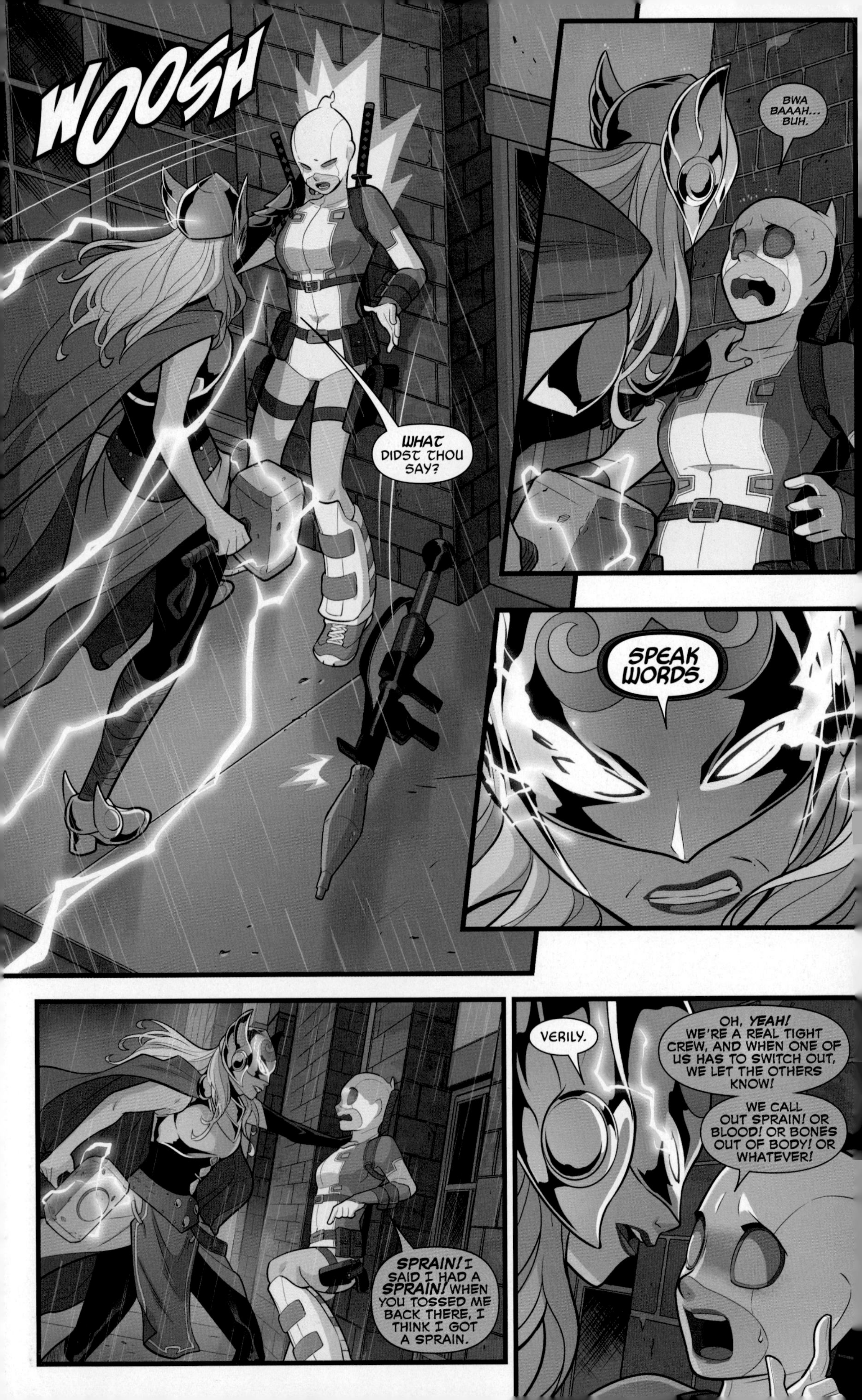
WOOSH
WHAT DIDST THOU SAY?
BWA BAAAH... BUH.
SPEAK WORDS.
SPRAIN! I SAID I HAD A SPRAIN! WHEN YOU TOSSED ME BACK THERE, I THINK I GOT A SPRAIN.
VERILY.
OH, YEAH! WE'RE A REAL TIGHT CREW, AND WHEN ONE OF US HAS TO SWITCH OUT, WE LET THE OTHERS KNOW!
WE CALL OUT SPRAIN! OR BLOOD! OR BONES OUT OF BODY! OR WHATEVER!

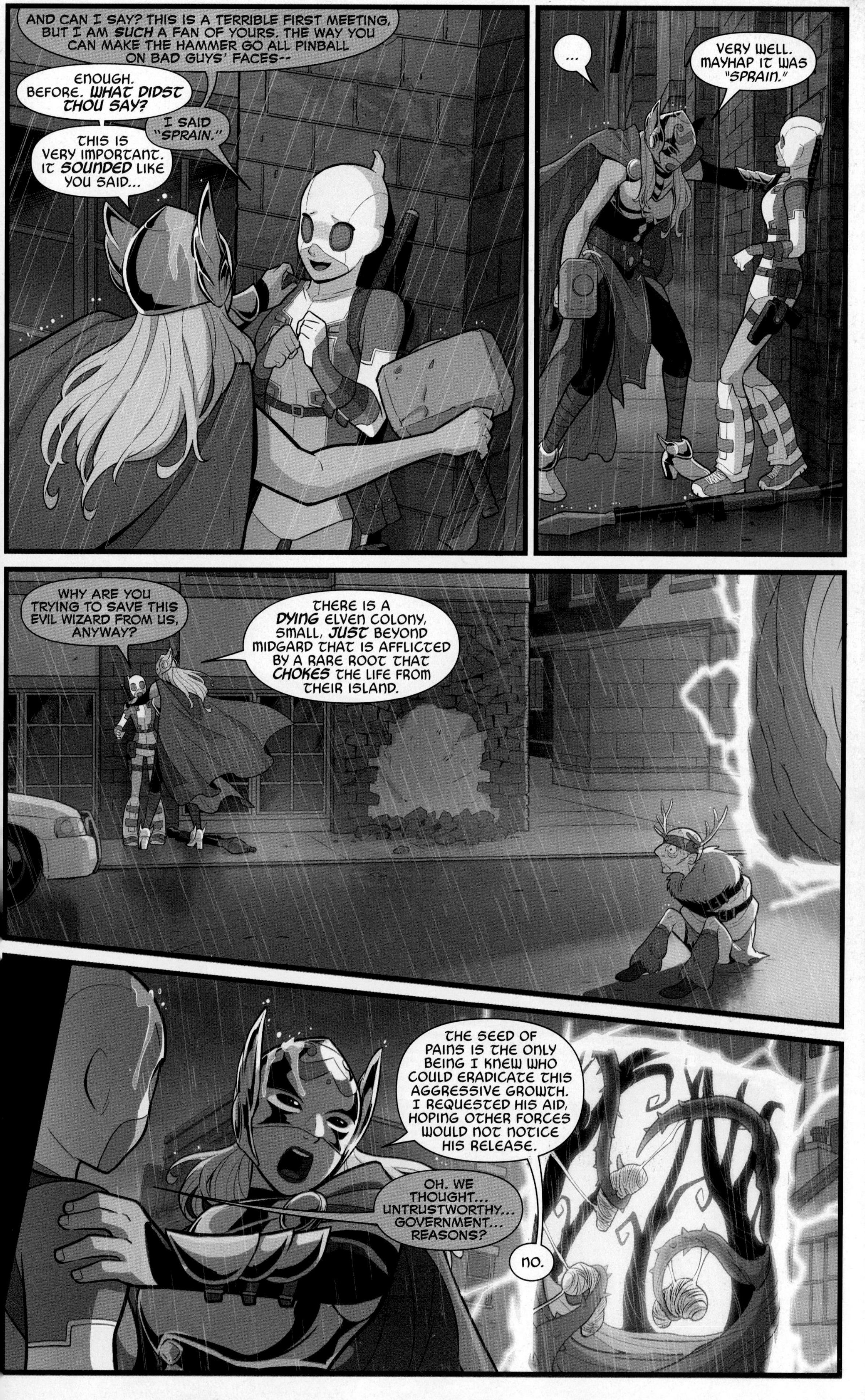
AND CAN I SAY? THIS IS A TERRIBLE FIRST MEETING, BUT I AM SUCH A FAN OF YOURS. THE WAY YOU CAN MAKE THE HAMMER GO ALL PINBALL ON BAD GUYS' FACES--
ENOUGH. BEFORE. WHAT DIDST THOU SAY?
I SAID "SPRAIN."
THIS IS VERY IMPORTANT. IT SOUNDED LIKE YOU SAID...
...
VERY WELL. MAYHAP IT WAS "SPRAIN."
WHY ARE YOU TRYING TO SAVE THIS EVIL WIZARD FROM US, ANYWAY?
THERE IS A DYING ELVEN COLONY, SMALL, JUST BEYOND MIDGARD THAT IS AFFLICTED BY A RARE ROOT THAT CHOKES THE LIFE FROM THEIR ISLAND.
THE SEED OF PAINS IS THE ONLY BEING I KNEW WHO COULD ERADICATE THIS AGGRESSIVE GROWTH. I REQUESTED HIS AID, HOPING OTHER FORCES WOULD NOT NOTICE HIS RELEASE.
OH. WE THOUGHT... UNTRUSTWORTHY... GOVERNMENT... REASONS?
no.

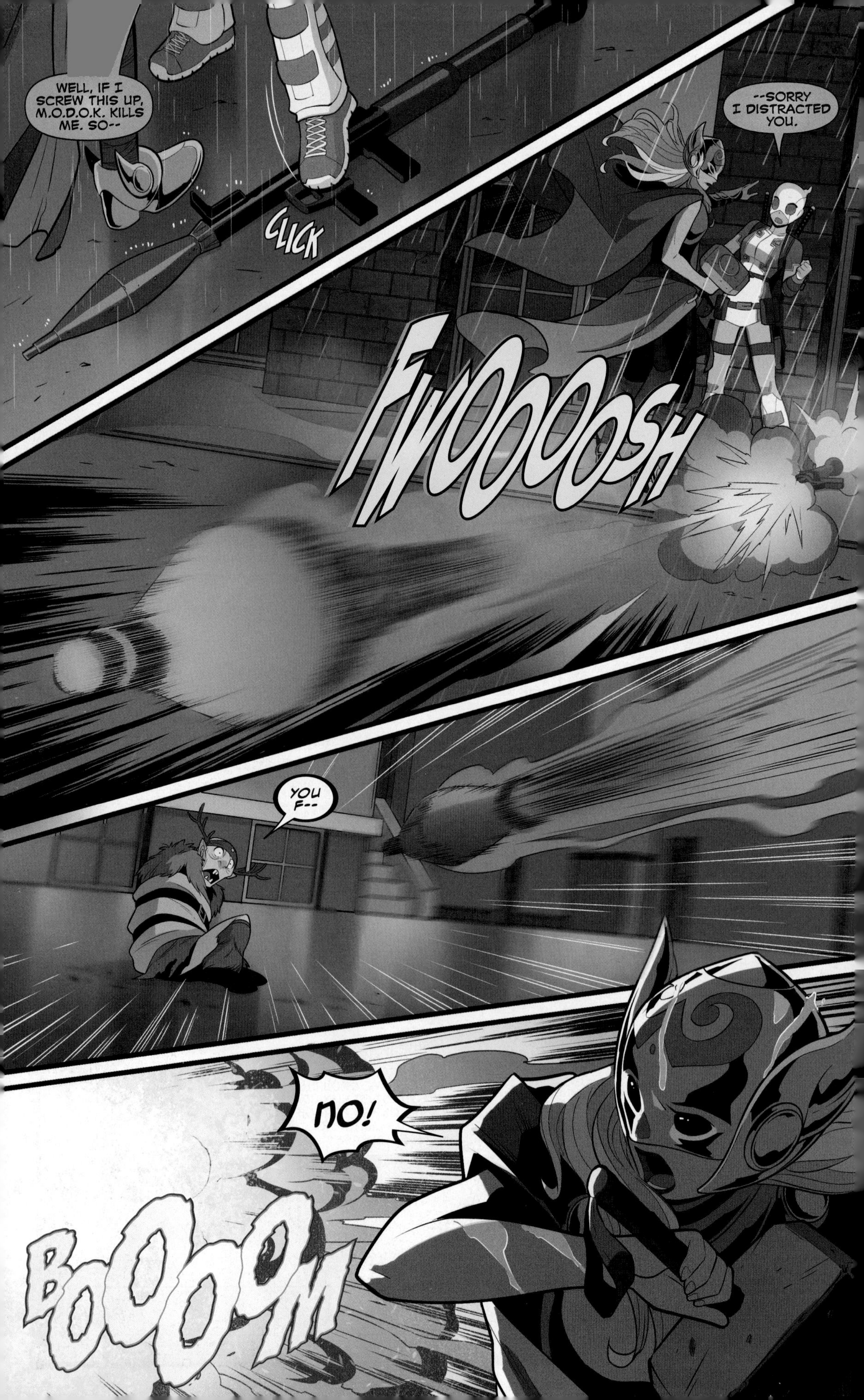

WELL, IF I SCREW THIS UP, M.O.D.O.K. KILLS ME. SO--
CLICK
--SORRY I DISTRACTED YOU.
FWOOOOOSH
YOU F--
NO!
BOOOOM

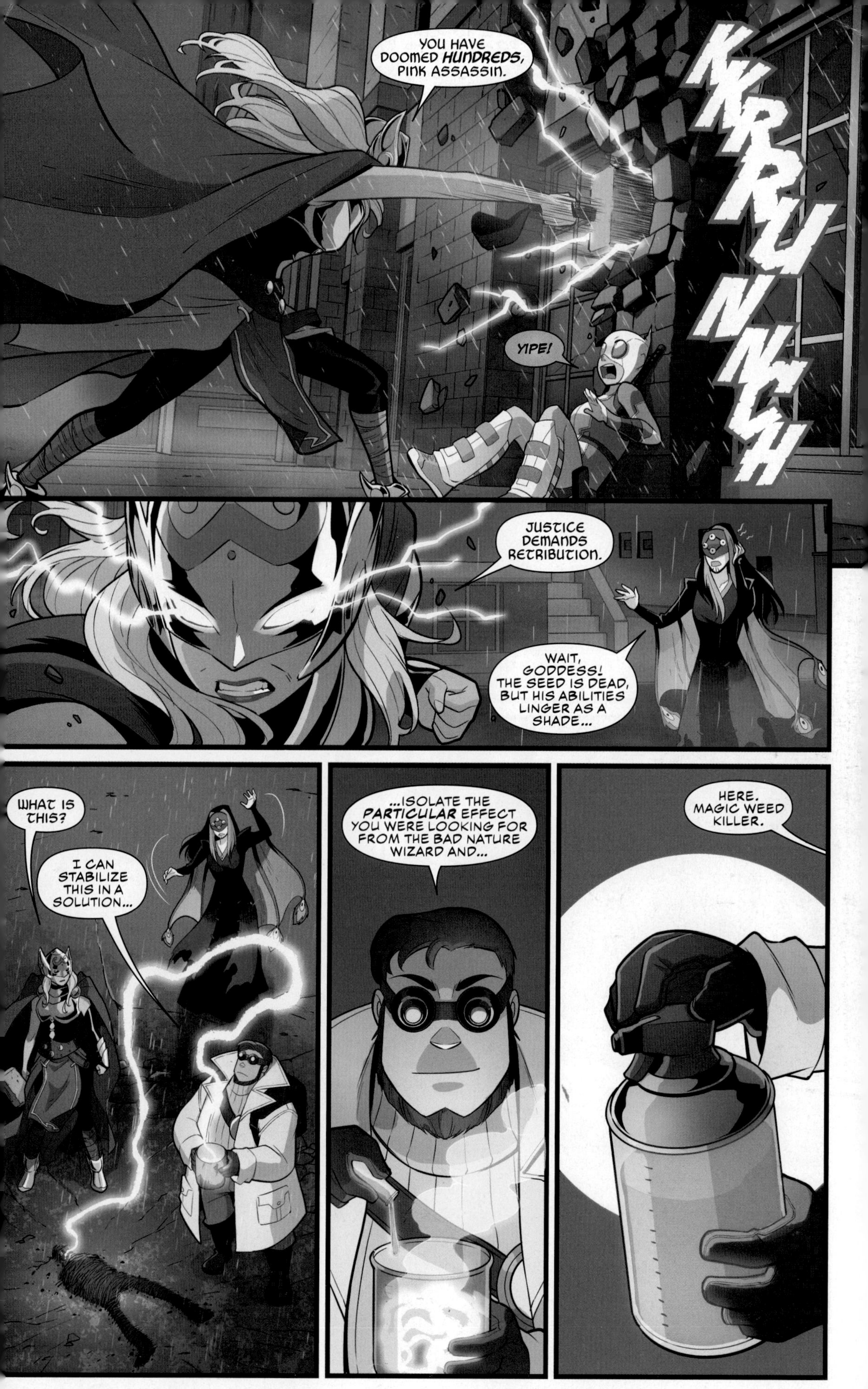
YOU HAVE DOOMED HUNDREDS, PINK ASSASSIN.
KKRUNNNCH
YIPE!
JUSTICE DEMANDS RETRIBUTION.
WAIT, GODDESS! THE SEED IS DEAD, BUT HIS ABILITIES LINGER AS A SHADE...
WHAT IS THIS?
I CAN STABILIZE THIS IN A SOLUTION...
...ISOLATE THE PARTICULAR EFFECT YOU WERE LOOKING FOR FROM THE BAD NATURE WIZARD AND...
HERE. MAGIC WEED KILLER.

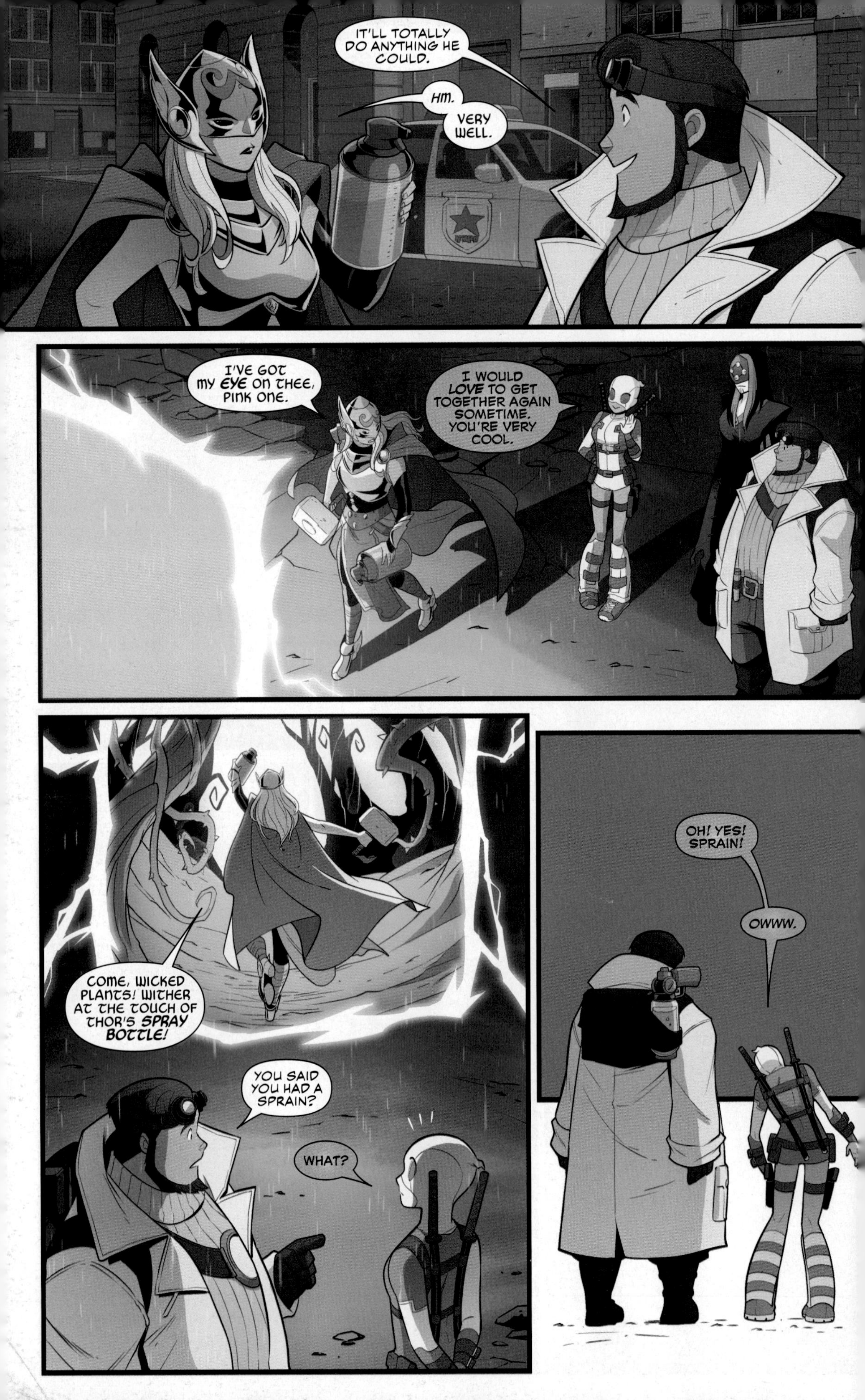
IT'LL TOTALLY DO ANYTHING HE COULD.
HM.
VERY WELL.
I'VE GOT MY EYE ON THEE, PINK ONE.
I WOULD LOVE TO GET TOGETHER AGAIN SOMETIME. YOU'RE VERY COOL.
COME, WICKED PLANTS! WITHER AT THE TOUCH OF THOR'S SPRAY BOTTLE!
YOU SAID YOU HAD A SPRAIN?
WHAT?
OH! YES! SPRAIN!
OWWW.

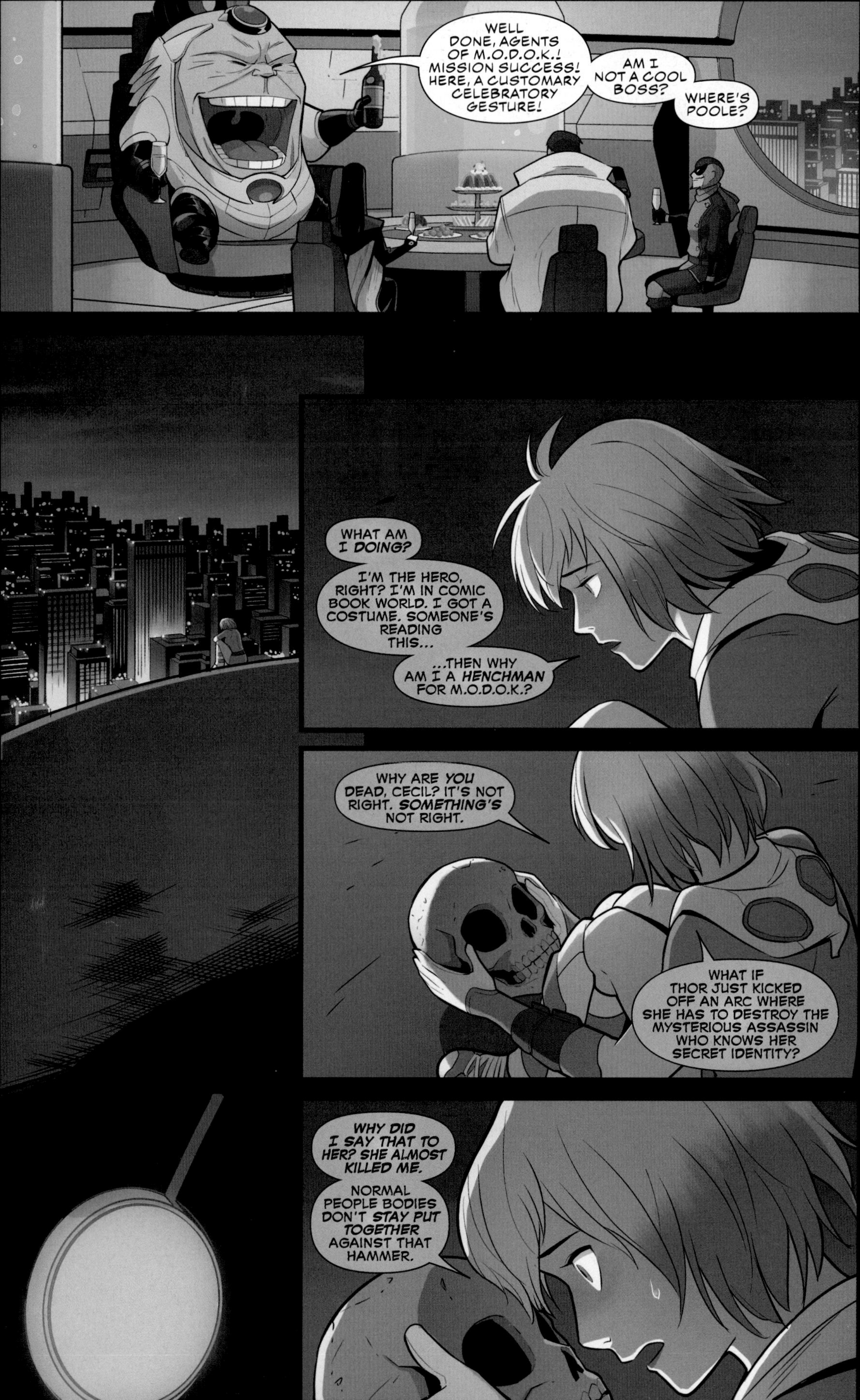
WELL DONE, AGENTS OF M.O.D.O.K.! MISSION SUCCESS! HERE, A CUSTOMARY CELEBRATORY GESTURE!
AM I NOT A COOL BOSS?
WHERE'S POOLE?
WHAT AM I *DOING?*
I'M THE HERO, RIGHT? I'M IN COMIC BOOK WORLD. I GOT A COSTUME. SOMEONE'S READING THIS...
...THEN WHY AM I A *HENCHMAN* FOR M.O.D.O.K.?
WHY ARE *YOU* DEAD, CECIL? IT'S NOT RIGHT. *SOMETHING'S* NOT RIGHT.
WHAT IF THOR JUST KICKED OFF AN ARC WHERE SHE HAS TO DESTROY THE MYSTERIOUS ASSASSIN WHO KNOWS HER SECRET IDENTITY?
*WHY DID I SAY THAT TO HER? SHE ALMOST KILLED ME.*
NORMAL PEOPLE BODIES DON'T *STAY PUT TOGETHER* AGAINST THAT HAMMER.

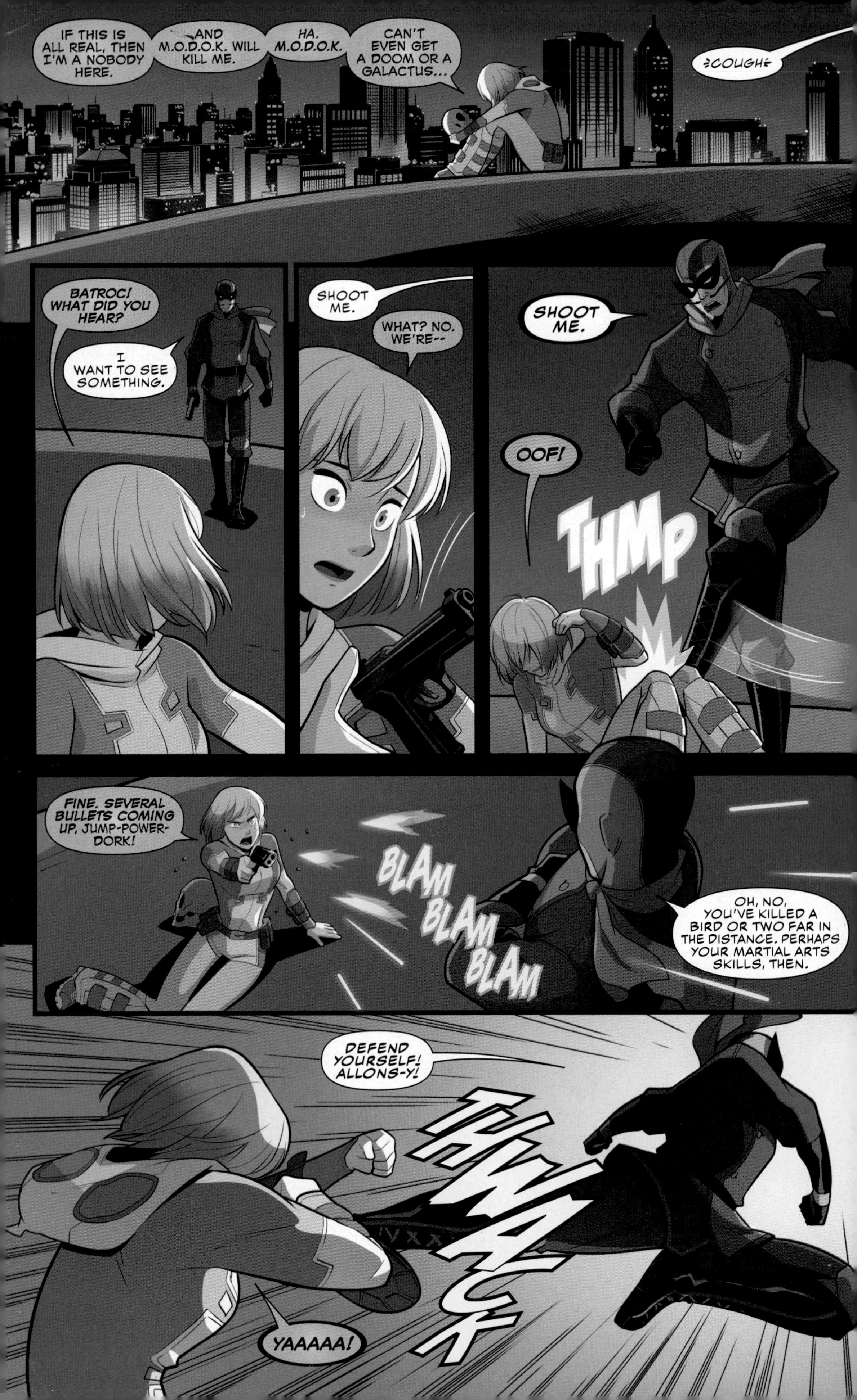
IF THIS IS ALL REAL, THEN I'M A NOBODY HERE.
AND M.O.D.O.K. WILL KILL ME.
HA. M.O.D.O.K.
CAN'T EVEN GET A DOOM OR A GALACTUS...
COUGH
BATROC! WHAT DID YOU HEAR?
I WANT TO SEE SOMETHING.
SHOOT ME.
WHAT? NO. WE'RE--
SHOOT ME.
OOF!
THMP
FINE. SEVERAL BULLETS COMING UP, JUMP-POWER-DORK!
BLAM
BLAM
BLAM
OH, NO, YOU'VE KILLED A BIRD OR TWO FAR IN THE DISTANCE. PERHAPS YOUR MARTIAL ARTS SKILLS, THEN.
DEFEND YOURSELF! ALLONS-Y!
THWACK
YAAAAA!

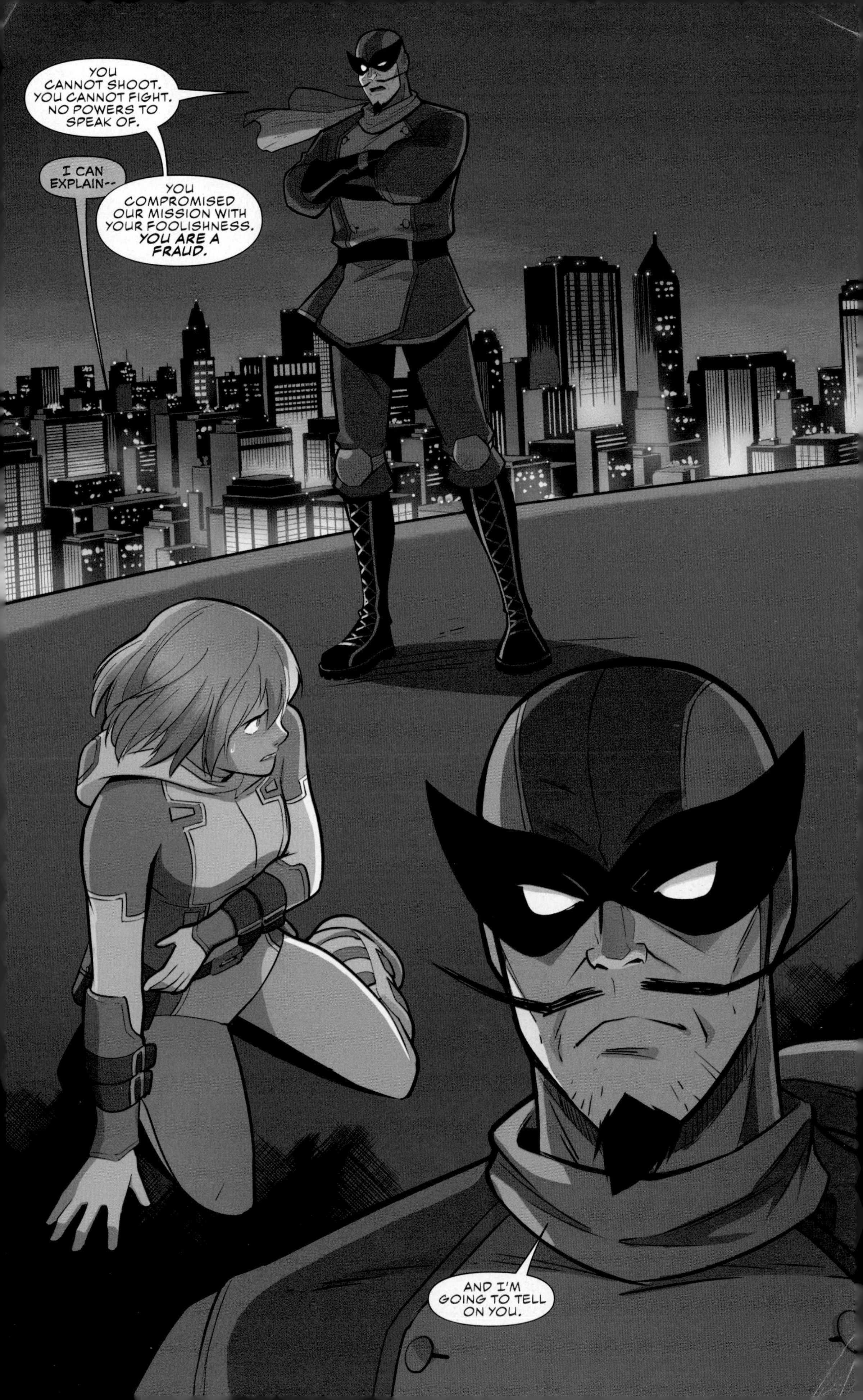
YOU CANNOT SHOOT. YOU CANNOT FIGHT. NO POWERS TO SPEAK OF.
I CAN EXPLAIN--
YOU COMPROMISED OUR MISSION WITH YOUR FOOLISHNESS. *YOU ARE A FRAUD.*
AND I'M GOING TO TELL ON YOU.

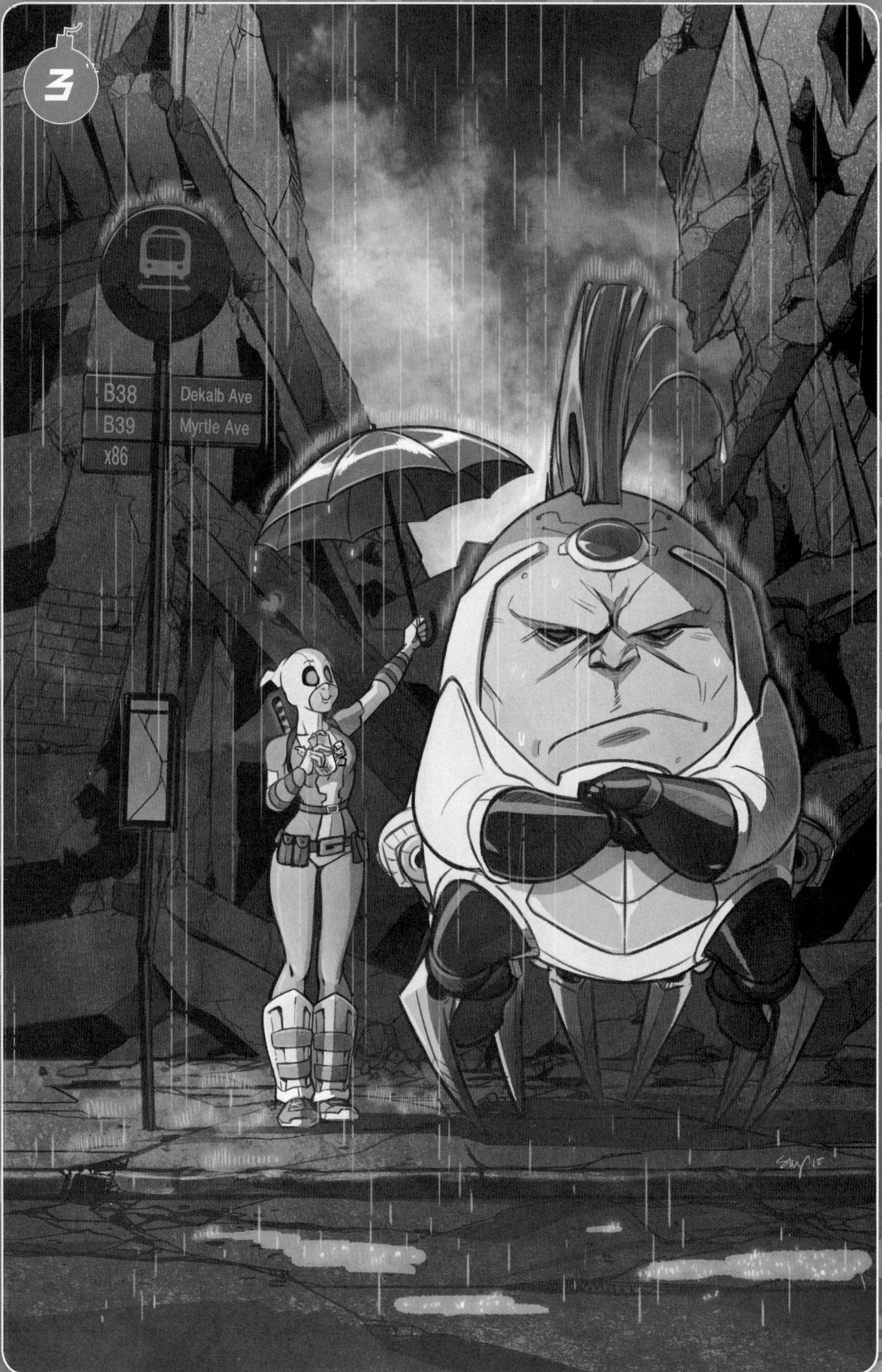
3
B38
Dekalb Ave
B39
Myrtle Ave
x86

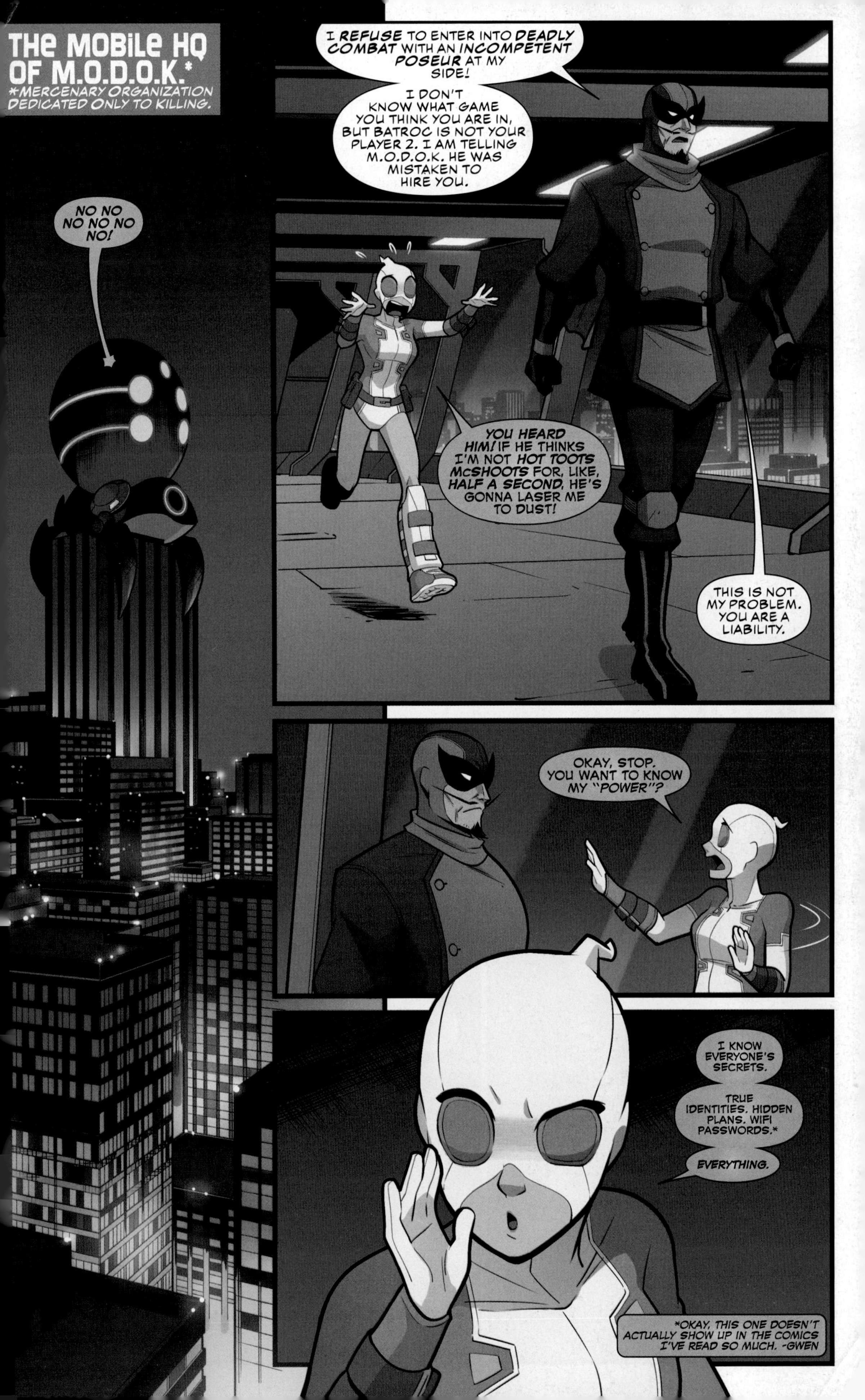
THE MOBILE HQ OF M.O.D.O.K.*
*MERCENARY ORGANIZATION DEDICATED ONLY TO KILLING.
NO NO NO NO NO NO!
I REFUSE TO ENTER INTO DEADLY COMBAT WITH AN INCOMPETENT POSEUR AT MY SIDE!
I DON'T KNOW WHAT GAME YOU THINK YOU ARE IN, BUT BATROC IS NOT YOUR PLAYER 2. I AM TELLING M.O.D.O.K. HE WAS MISTAKEN TO HIRE YOU.
YOU HEARD HIM! IF HE THINKS I'M NOT HOT TOOTS McSHOOTS FOR, LIKE, HALF A SECOND, HE'S GONNA LASER ME TO DUST!
THIS IS NOT MY PROBLEM. YOU ARE A LIABILITY.
OKAY, STOP. YOU WANT TO KNOW MY "POWER"?
I KNOW EVERYONE'S SECRETS.
TRUE IDENTITIES. HIDDEN PLANS. WIFI PASSWORDS.*
EVERYTHING.
*OKAY, THIS ONE DOESN'T ACTUALLY SHOW UP IN THE COMICS I'VE READ SO MUCH. -GWEN

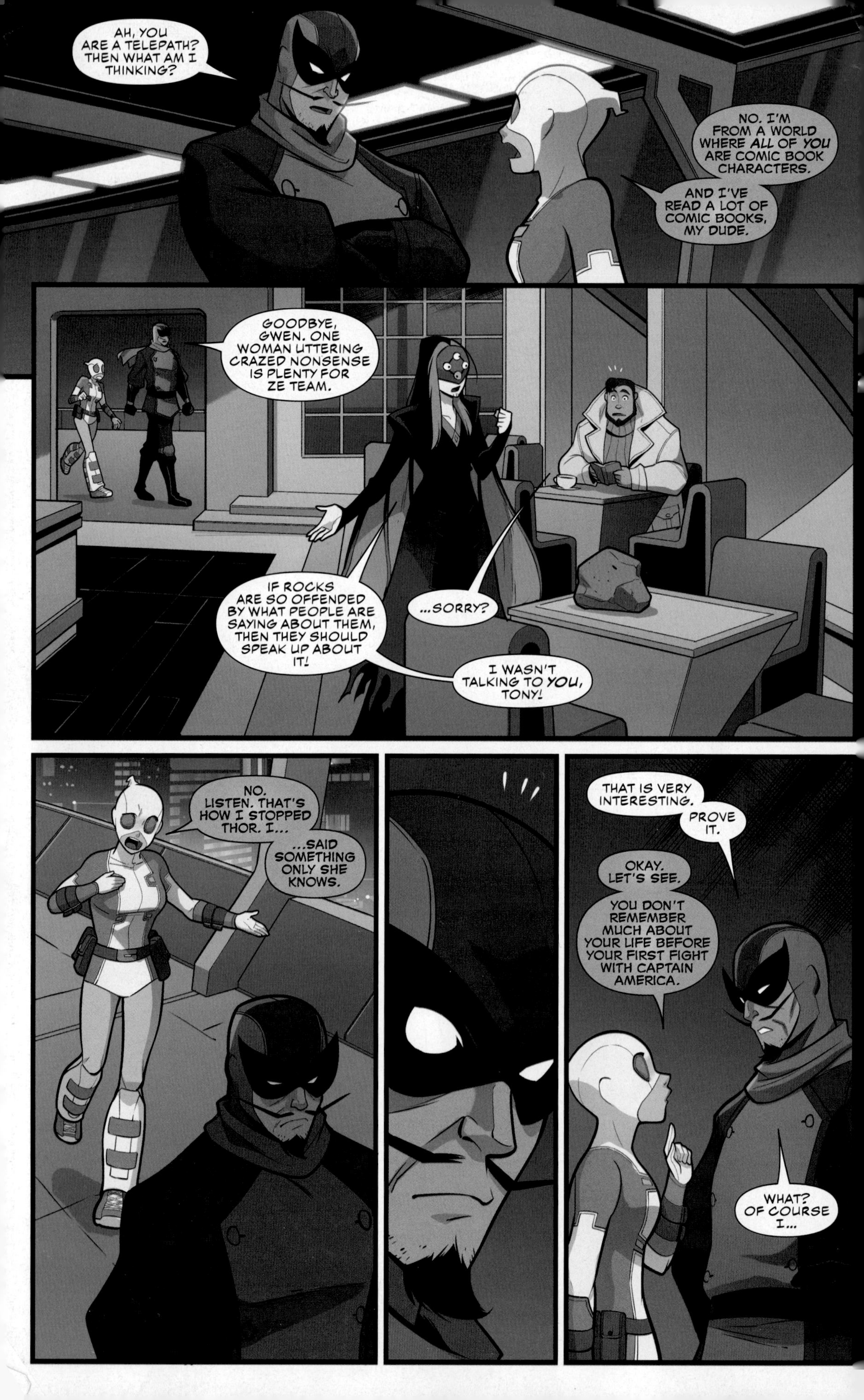
AH, YOU ARE A TELEPATH? THEN WHAT AM I THINKING?
NO. I'M FROM A WORLD WHERE ALL OF YOU ARE COMIC BOOK CHARACTERS.
AND I'VE READ A LOT OF COMIC BOOKS, MY DUDE.
GOODBYE, GWEN. ONE WOMAN UTTERING CRAZED NONSENSE IS PLENTY FOR ZE TEAM.
IF ROCKS ARE SO OFFENDED BY WHAT PEOPLE ARE SAYING ABOUT THEM, THEN THEY SHOULD SPEAK UP ABOUT IT!
...SORRY?
I WASN'T TALKING TO YOU, TONY!
NO. LISTEN. THAT'S HOW I STOPPED THOR. I...
...SAID SOMETHING ONLY SHE KNOWS.
THAT IS VERY INTERESTING.
PROVE IT.
OKAY. LET'S SEE.
YOU DON'T REMEMBER MUCH ABOUT YOUR LIFE BEFORE YOUR FIRST FIGHT WITH CAPTAIN AMERICA.
WHAT? OF COURSE I...

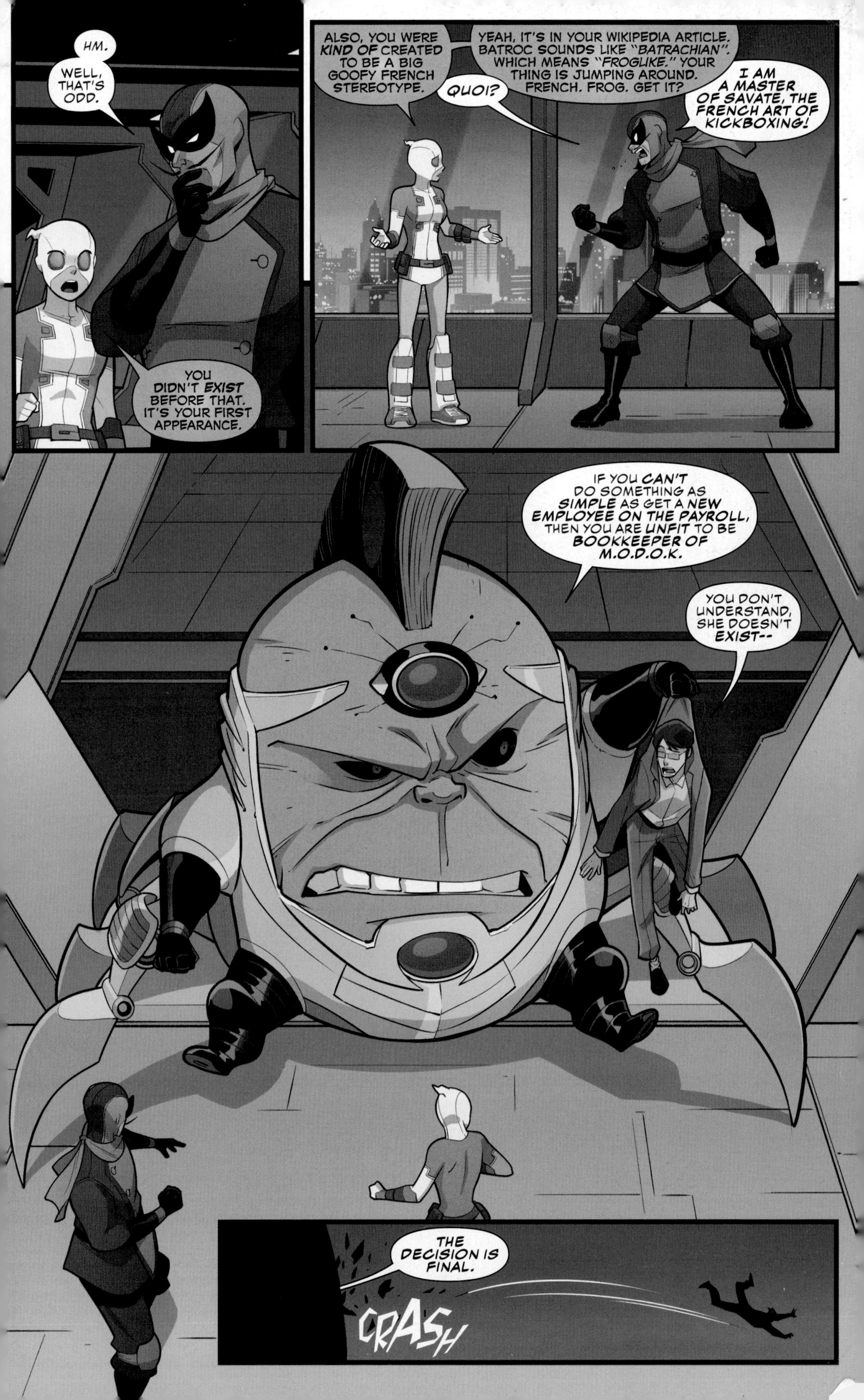
HM.
WELL, THAT'S ODD.
YOU DIDN'T EXIST BEFORE THAT. IT'S YOUR FIRST APPEARANCE.
ALSO, YOU WERE KIND OF CREATED TO BE A BIG GOOFY FRENCH STEREOTYPE.
QUOI?
YEAH, IT'S IN YOUR WIKIPEDIA ARTICLE. BATROC SOUNDS LIKE "BATRACHIAN", WHICH MEANS "FROGLIKE." YOUR THING IS JUMPING AROUND. FRENCH. FROG. GET IT?
I AM A MASTER OF SAVATE, THE FRENCH ART OF KICKBOXING!
IF YOU CAN'T DO SOMETHING AS SIMPLE AS GET A NEW EMPLOYEE ON THE PAYROLL, THEN YOU ARE UNFIT TO BE BOOKKEEPER OF M.O.D.O.K.
YOU DON'T UNDERSTAND, SHE DOESN'T EXIST--
THE DECISION IS FINAL.
CRASH

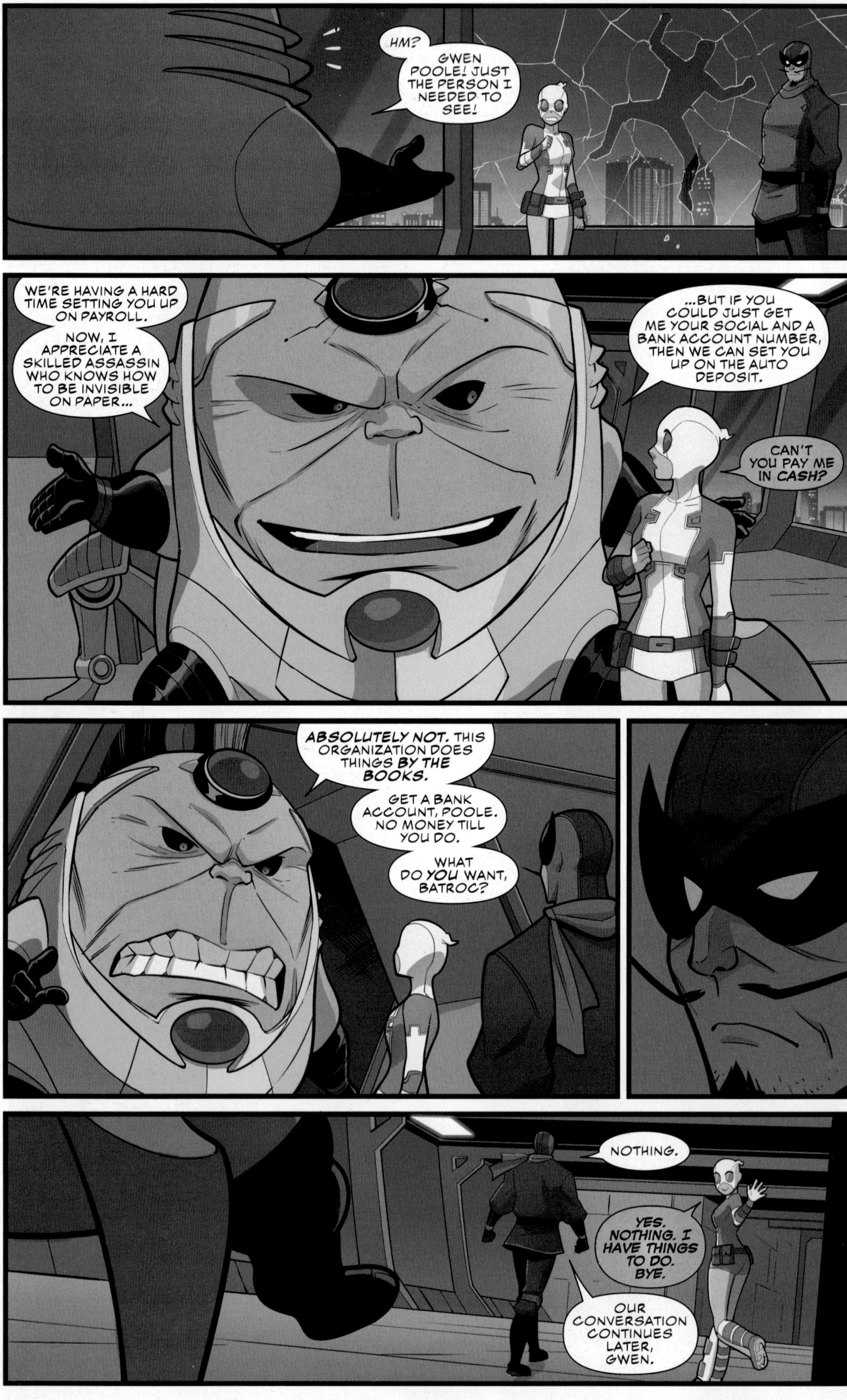
HM?
GWEN POOLE! JUST THE PERSON I NEEDED TO SEE!
WE'RE HAVING A HARD TIME SETTING YOU UP ON PAYROLL.
NOW, I APPRECIATE A SKILLED ASSASSIN WHO KNOWS HOW TO BE INVISIBLE ON PAPER...
...BUT IF YOU COULD JUST GET ME YOUR SOCIAL AND A BANK ACCOUNT NUMBER, THEN WE CAN SET YOU UP ON THE AUTO DEPOSIT.
CAN'T YOU PAY ME IN CASH?
ABSOLUTELY NOT. THIS ORGANIZATION DOES THINGS BY THE BOOKS.
GET A BANK ACCOUNT, POOLE. NO MONEY TILL YOU DO.
WHAT DO YOU WANT, BATROC?
NOTHING.
YES. NOTHING. I HAVE THINGS TO DO. BYE.
OUR CONVERSATION CONTINUES LATER, GWEN.

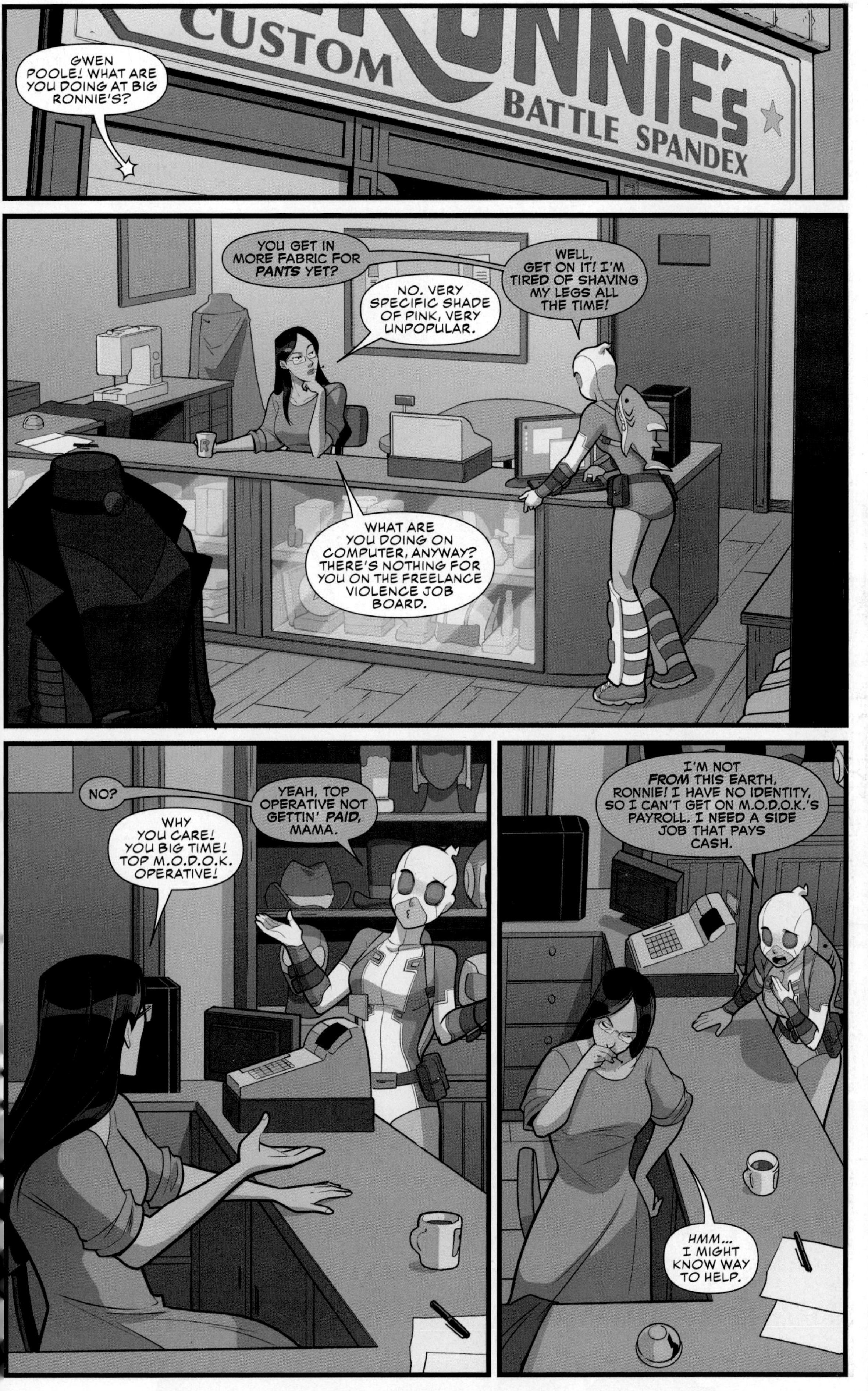

RONNIE'S
CUSTOM
BATTLE SPANDEX
GWEN POOLE! WHAT ARE YOU DOING AT BIG RONNIE'S?
YOU GET IN MORE FABRIC FOR PANTS YET?
NO. VERY SPECIFIC SHADE OF PINK, VERY UNPOPULAR.
WELL, GET ON IT! I'M TIRED OF SHAVING MY LEGS ALL THE TIME!
WHAT ARE YOU DOING ON COMPUTER, ANYWAY? THERE'S NOTHING FOR YOU ON THE FREELANCE VIOLENCE JOB BOARD.
NO?
WHY YOU CARE! YOU BIG TIME! TOP M.O.D.O.K. OPERATIVE!
YEAH, TOP OPERATIVE NOT GETTIN' PAID, MAMA.
I'M NOT FROM THIS EARTH, RONNIE! I HAVE NO IDENTITY, SO I CAN'T GET ON M.O.D.O.K.'S PAYROLL. I NEED A SIDE JOB THAT PAYS CASH.
HMM... I MIGHT KNOW WAY TO HELP.

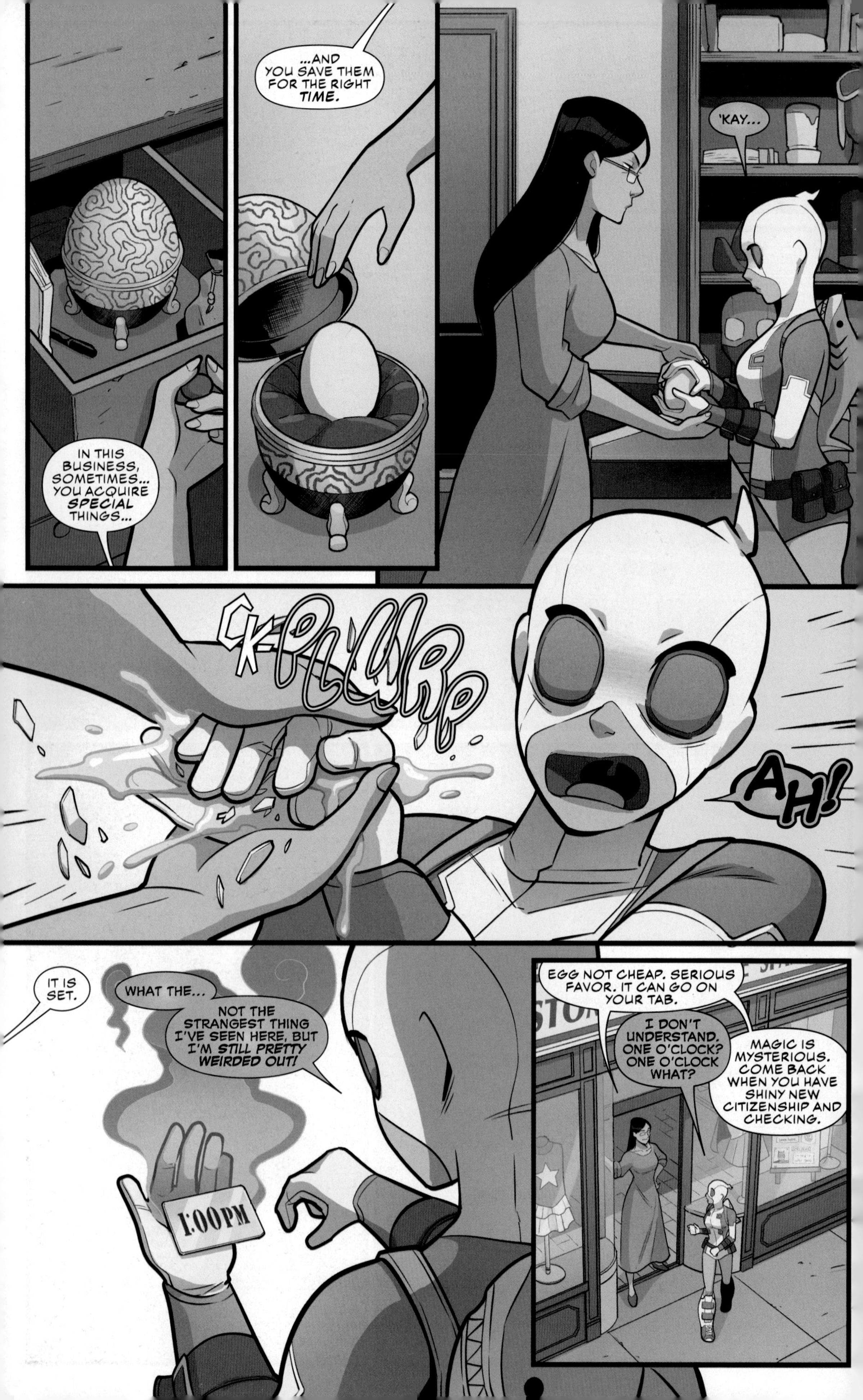
IN THIS BUSINESS, SOMETIMES... YOU ACQUIRE SPECIAL THINGS...
...AND YOU SAVE THEM FOR THE RIGHT TIME.
'KAY...
CK-PLLURP
AH!
IT IS SET.
WHAT THE...
NOT THE STRANGEST THING I'VE SEEN HERE, BUT I'M STILL PRETTY WEIRDED OUT!
1:00PM
EGG NOT CHEAP. SERIOUS FAVOR. IT CAN GO ON YOUR TAB.
I DON'T UNDERSTAND. ONE O'CLOCK? ONE O'CLOCK WHAT?
MAGIC IS MYSTERIOUS. COME BACK WHEN YOU HAVE SHINY NEW CITIZENSHIP AND CHECKING.

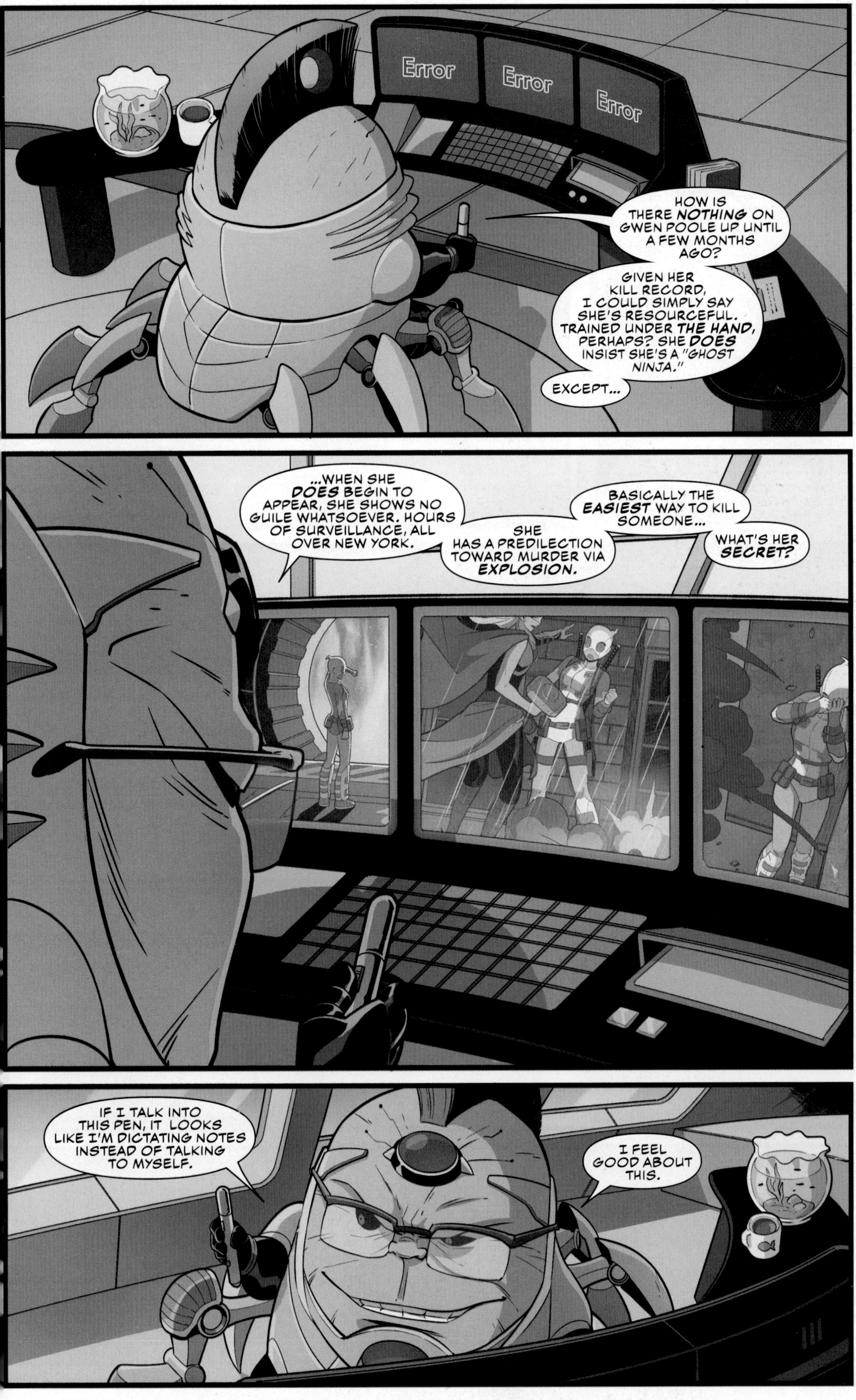
Error
Error
Error
HOW IS THERE NOTHING ON GWEN POOLE UP UNTIL A FEW MONTHS AGO?
GIVEN HER KILL RECORD, I COULD SIMPLY SAY SHE'S RESOURCEFUL. TRAINED UNDER THE HAND, PERHAPS? SHE DOES INSIST SHE'S A "GHOST NINJA."
EXCEPT...
...WHEN SHE DOES BEGIN TO APPEAR, SHE SHOWS NO GUILE WHATSOEVER. HOURS OF SURVEILLANCE, ALL OVER NEW YORK.
SHE HAS A PREDILECTION TOWARD MURDER VIA EXPLOSION.
BASICALLY THE EASIEST WAY TO KILL SOMEONE...
WHAT'S HER SECRET?
IF I TALK INTO THIS PEN, IT LOOKS LIKE I'M DICTATING NOTES INSTEAD OF TALKING TO MYSELF.
I FEEL GOOD ABOUT THIS.

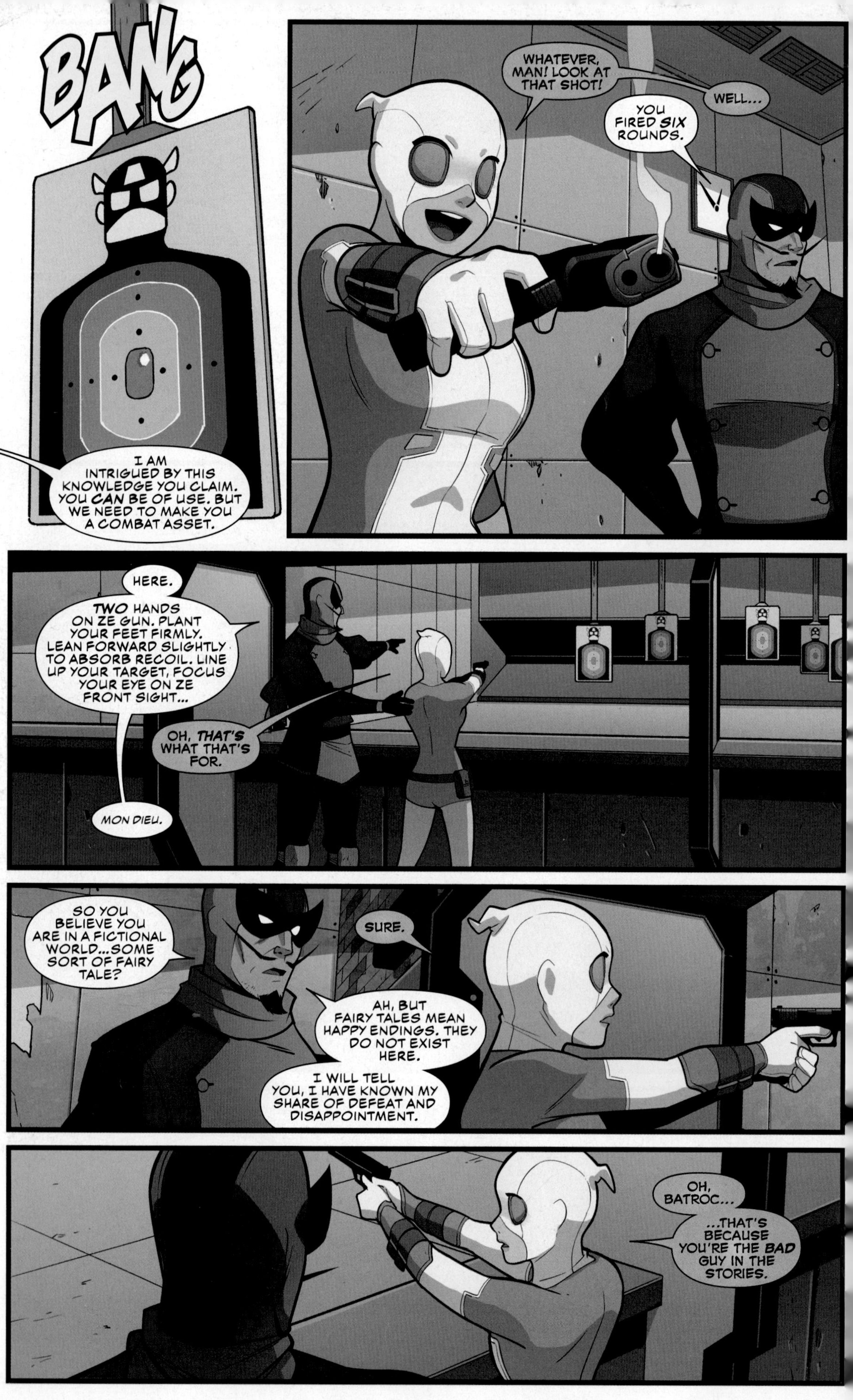
BANG
WHATEVER, MAN! LOOK AT THAT SHOT!
WELL...
YOU FIRED SIX ROUNDS.
I AM INTRIGUED BY THIS KNOWLEDGE YOU CLAIM. YOU CAN BE OF USE. BUT WE NEED TO MAKE YOU A COMBAT ASSET.
HERE.
TWO HANDS ON ZE GUN. PLANT YOUR FEET FIRMLY. LEAN FORWARD SLIGHTLY TO ABSORB RECOIL. LINE UP YOUR TARGET, FOCUS YOUR EYE ON ZE FRONT SIGHT...
OH, THAT'S WHAT THAT'S FOR.
MON DIEU.
SO YOU BELIEVE YOU ARE IN A FICTIONAL WORLD...SOME SORT OF FAIRY TALE?
SURE.
AH, BUT FAIRY TALES MEAN HAPPY ENDINGS. THEY DO NOT EXIST HERE.
I WILL TELL YOU, I HAVE KNOWN MY SHARE OF DEFEAT AND DISAPPOINTMENT.
OH, BATROC...
...THAT'S BECAUSE YOU'RE THE BAD GUY IN THE STORIES.

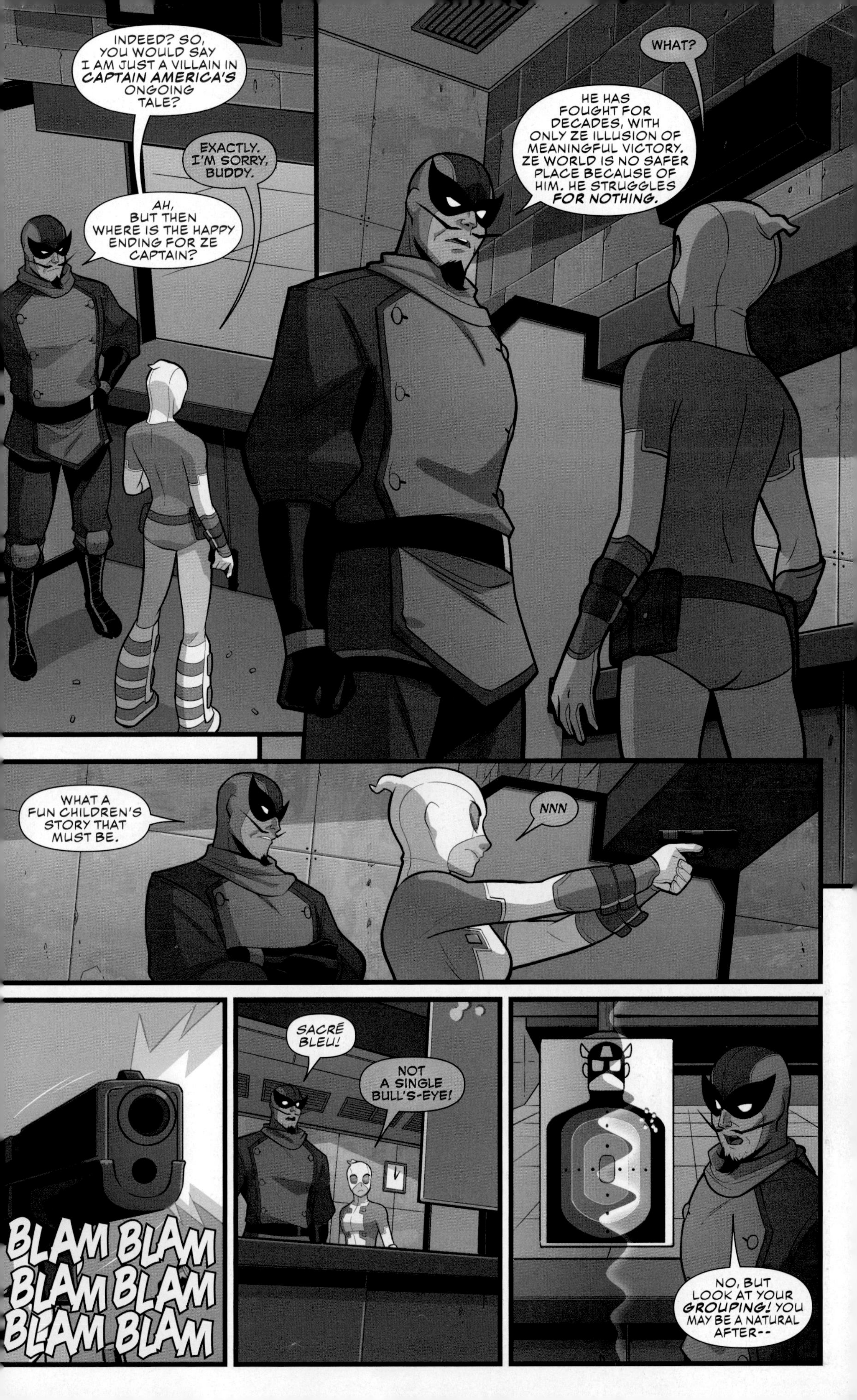
INDEED? SO, YOU WOULD SAY I AM JUST A VILLAIN IN CAPTAIN AMERICA'S ONGOING TALE?
EXACTLY. I'M SORRY, BUDDY.
AH, BUT THEN WHERE IS THE HAPPY ENDING FOR ZE CAPTAIN?
WHAT?
HE HAS FOUGHT FOR DECADES, WITH ONLY ZE ILLUSION OF MEANINGFUL VICTORY. ZE WORLD IS NO SAFER PLACE BECAUSE OF HIM. HE STRUGGLES FOR NOTHING.
WHAT A FUN CHILDREN'S STORY THAT MUST BE.
NNN
BLAM BLAM BLAM BLAM BLAM BLAM
SACRÉ BLEU!
NOT A SINGLE BULL'S-EYE!
NO, BUT LOOK AT YOUR GROUPING! YOU MAY BE A NATURAL AFTER--

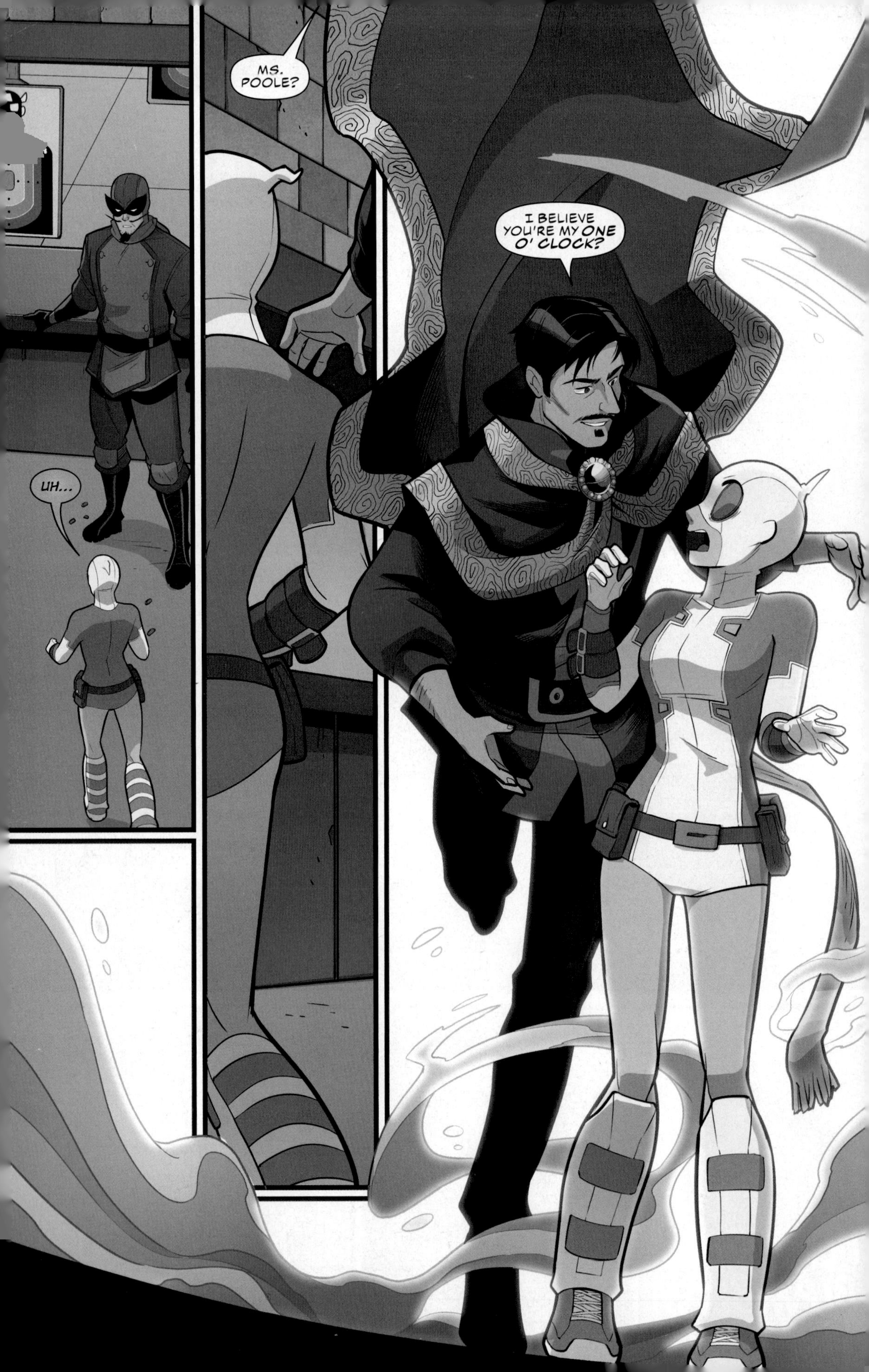
MS. POOLE?
UH...
I BELIEVE YOU'RE MY ONE O' CLOCK?

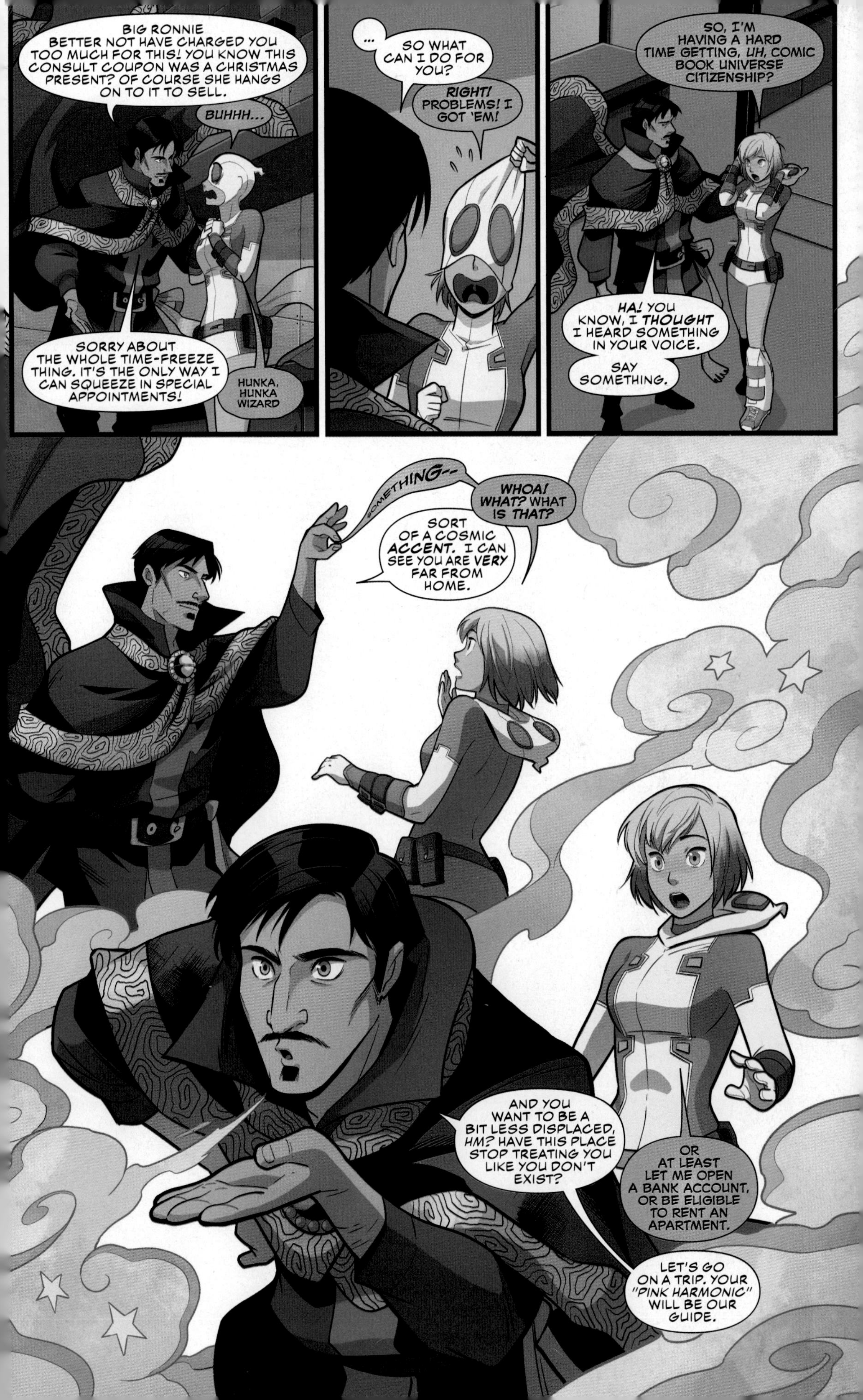
BIG RONNIE BETTER NOT HAVE CHARGED YOU TOO MUCH FOR THIS! YOU KNOW THIS CONSULT COUPON WAS A CHRISTMAS PRESENT? OF COURSE SHE HANGS ON TO IT TO SELL.
BUHHH...
SORRY ABOUT THE WHOLE TIME-FREEZE THING. IT'S THE ONLY WAY I CAN SQUEEZE IN SPECIAL APPOINTMENTS!
HUNKA, HUNKA WIZARD
...
SO WHAT CAN I DO FOR YOU?
RIGHT! PROBLEMS! I GOT 'EM!
SO, I'M HAVING A HARD TIME GETTING, UH, COMIC BOOK UNIVERSE CITIZENSHIP?
HA! YOU KNOW, I THOUGHT I HEARD SOMETHING IN YOUR VOICE.
SAY SOMETHING.
SOMETHING--
WHOA! WHAT? WHAT IS THAT?
SORT OF A COSMIC ACCENT. I CAN SEE YOU ARE VERY FAR FROM HOME.
AND YOU WANT TO BE A BIT LESS DISPLACED, HM? HAVE THIS PLACE STOP TREATING YOU LIKE YOU DON'T EXIST?
OR AT LEAST LET ME OPEN A BANK ACCOUNT, OR BE ELIGIBLE TO RENT AN APARTMENT.
LET'S GO ON A TRIP. YOUR "PINK HARMONIC" WILL BE OUR GUIDE.

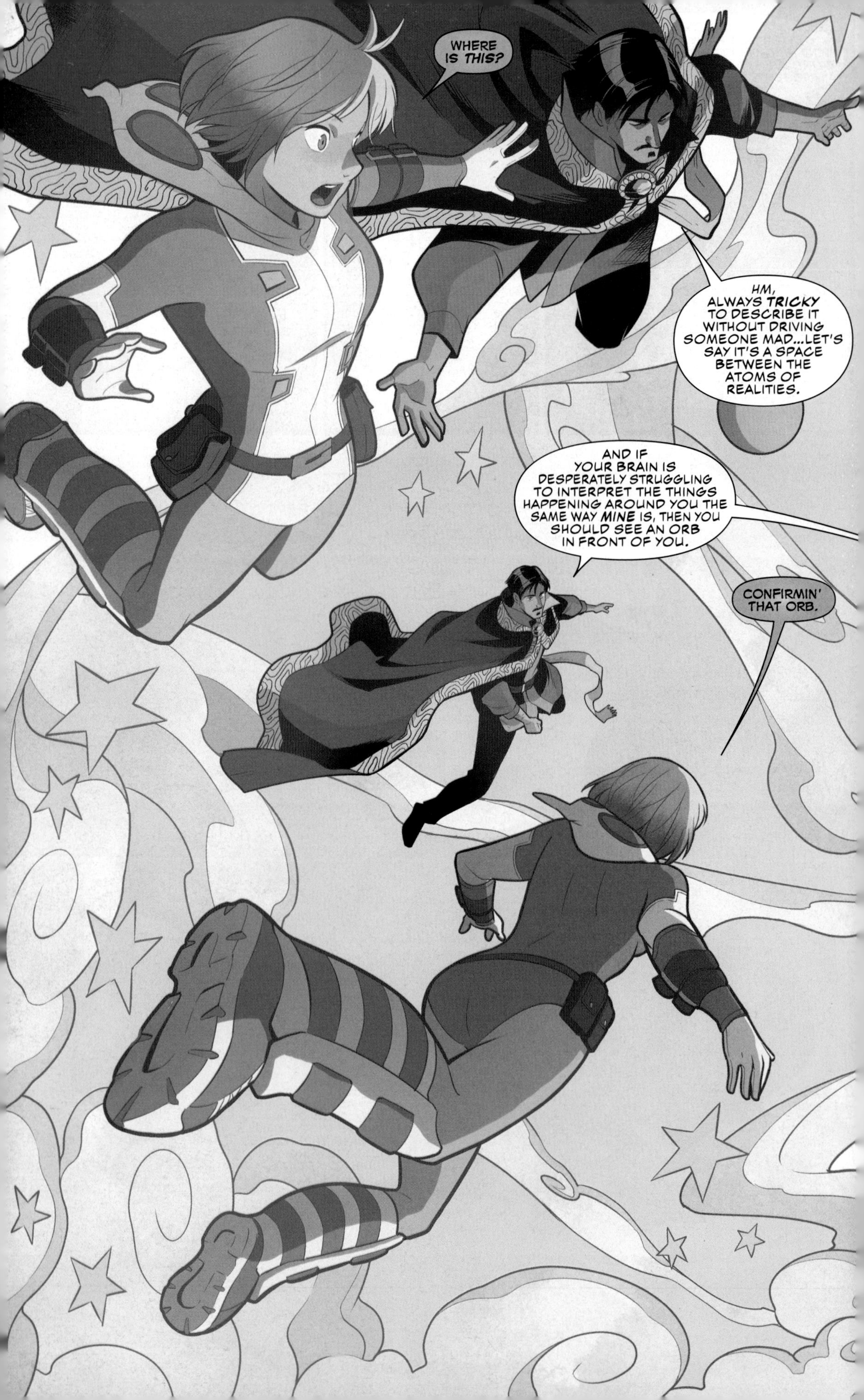
WHERE IS THIS?
HM, ALWAYS TRICKY TO DESCRIBE IT WITHOUT DRIVING SOMEONE MAD...LET'S SAY IT'S A SPACE BETWEEN THE ATOMS OF REALITIES.
AND IF YOUR BRAIN IS DESPERATELY STRUGGLING TO INTERPRET THE THINGS HAPPENING AROUND YOU THE SAME WAY MINE IS, THEN YOU SHOULD SEE AN ORB IN FRONT OF YOU.
CONFIRMIN' THAT ORB.

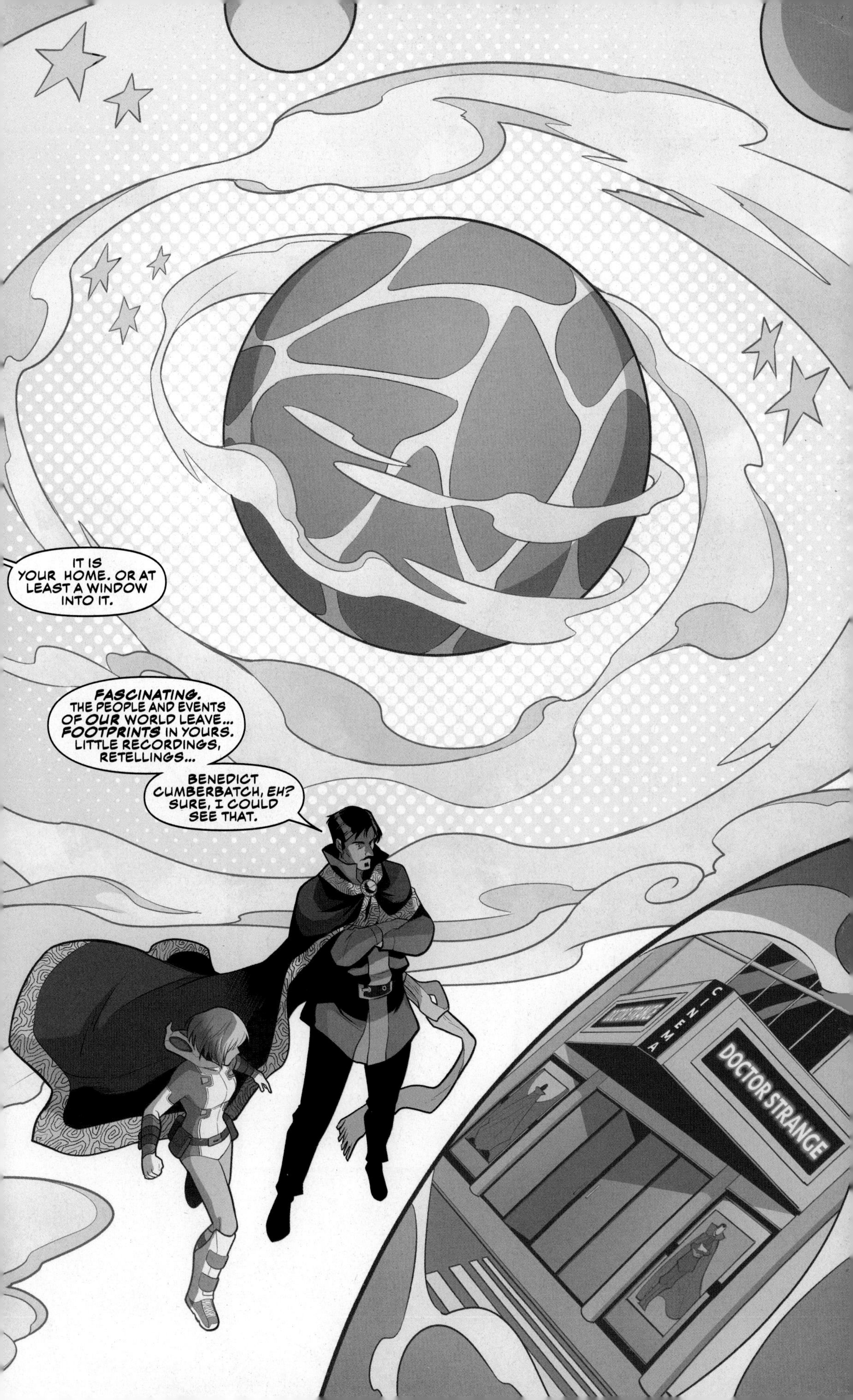
IT IS YOUR HOME. OR AT LEAST A WINDOW INTO IT.
FASCINATING. THE PEOPLE AND EVENTS OF OUR WORLD LEAVE... FOOTPRINTS IN YOURS. LITTLE RECORDINGS, RETELLINGS...
BENEDICT CUMBERBATCH, EH? SURE, I COULD SEE THAT.
CINEMA
DOCTOR STRANGE

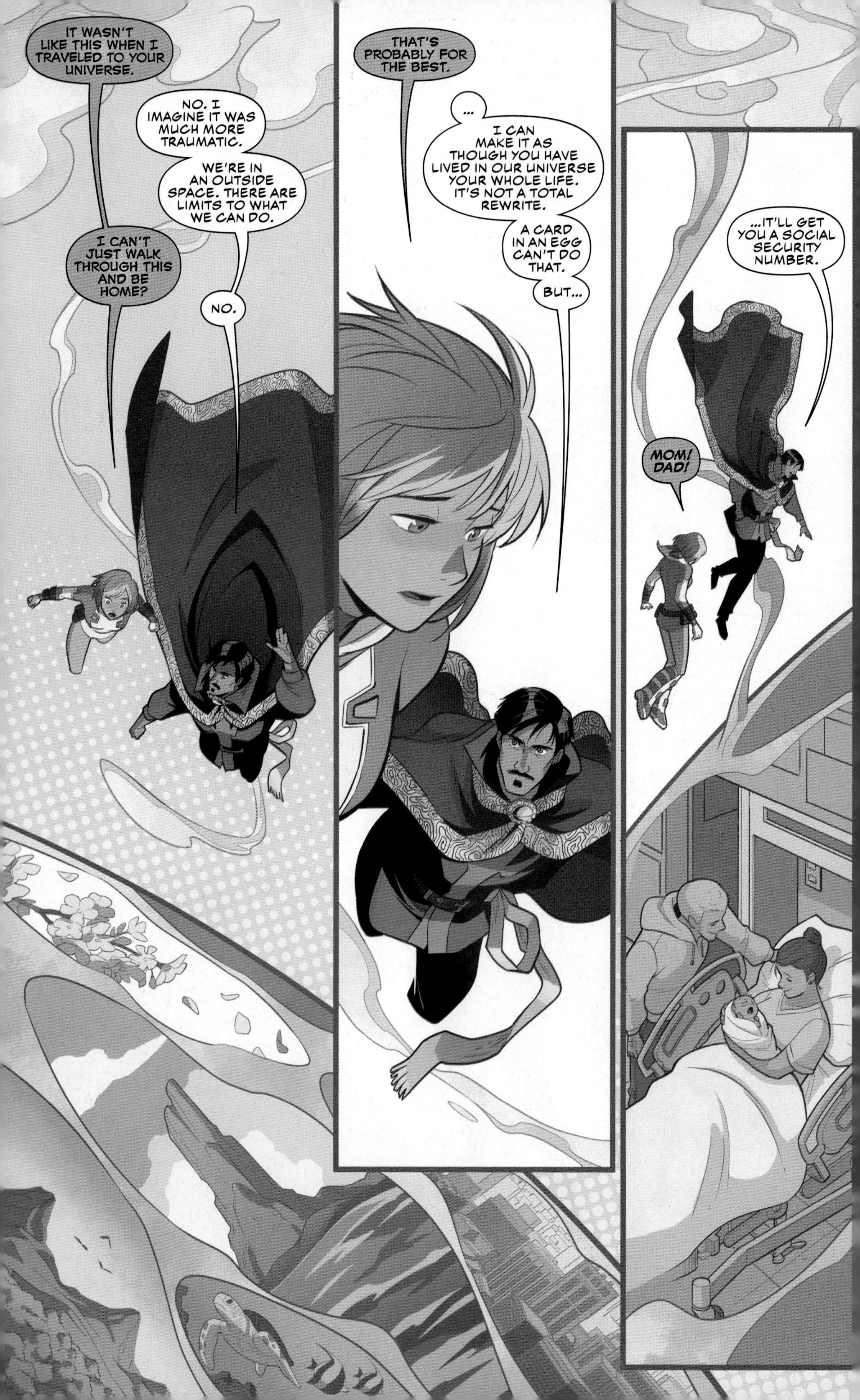
IT WASN'T LIKE THIS WHEN I TRAVELED TO YOUR UNIVERSE.
NO. I IMAGINE IT WAS MUCH MORE TRAUMATIC.
WE'RE IN AN OUTSIDE SPACE. THERE ARE LIMITS TO WHAT WE CAN DO.
I CAN'T JUST WALK THROUGH THIS AND BE HOME?
NO.
THAT'S PROBABLY FOR THE BEST.
...
I CAN MAKE IT AS THOUGH YOU HAVE LIVED IN OUR UNIVERSE YOUR WHOLE LIFE. IT'S NOT A TOTAL REWRITE.
A CARD IN AN EGG CAN'T DO THAT.
BUT...
...IT'LL GET YOU A SOCIAL SECURITY NUMBER.
MOM! DAD!

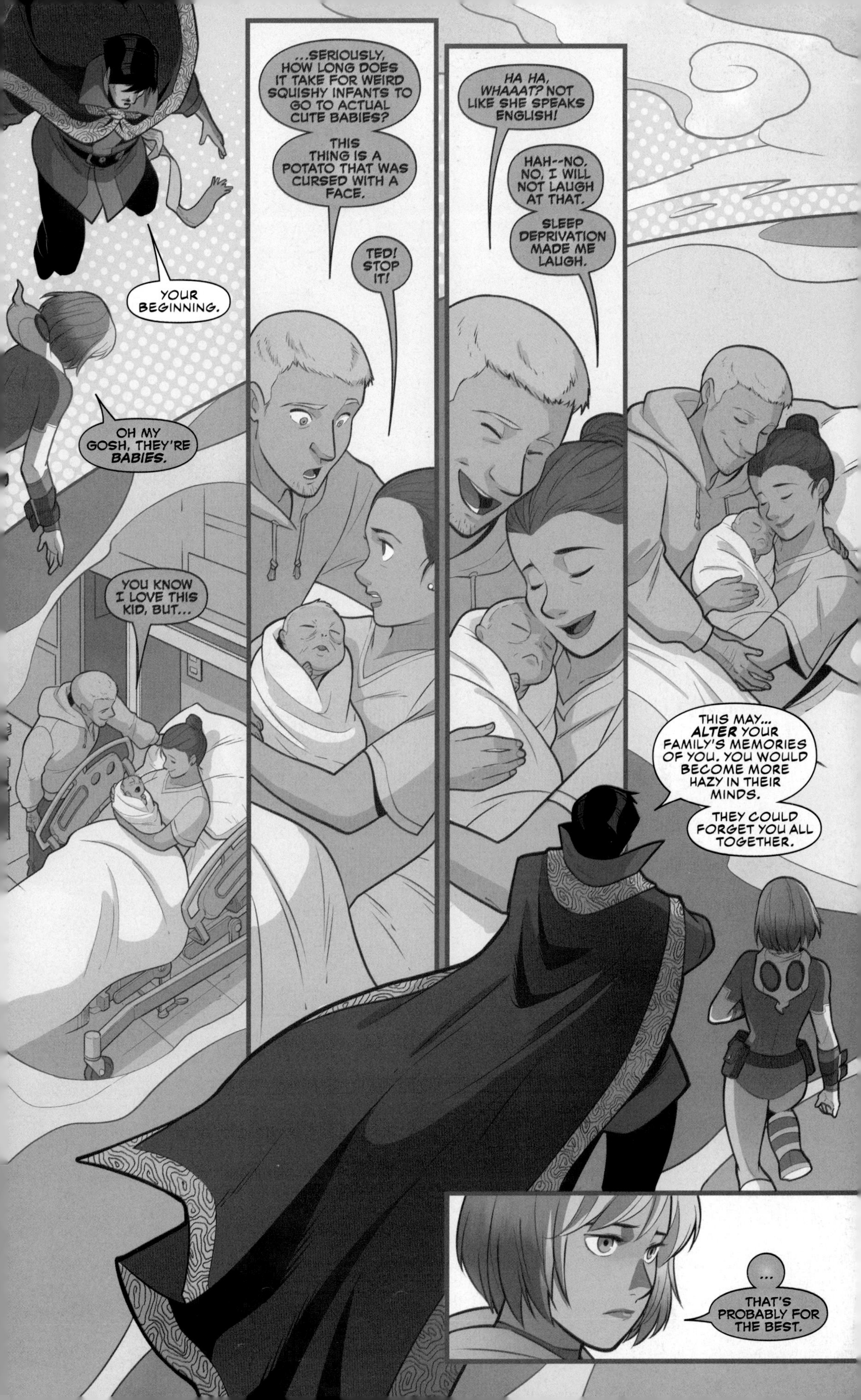
YOUR BEGINNING.
OH MY GOSH, THEY'RE *BABIES.*
YOU KNOW I LOVE THIS KID, BUT...
...SERIOUSLY, HOW LONG DOES IT TAKE FOR WEIRD SQUISHY INFANTS TO GO TO ACTUAL CUTE BABIES?
THIS THING IS A POTATO THAT WAS CURSED WITH A FACE.
TED! STOP IT!
HA HA, WHAAAT? NOT LIKE SHE SPEAKS ENGLISH!
HAH--NO. NO, I WILL NOT LAUGH AT THAT.
SLEEP DEPRIVATION MADE ME LAUGH.
THIS MAY... **ALTER** YOUR FAMILY'S MEMORIES OF YOU. YOU WOULD BECOME MORE HAZY IN THEIR MINDS.
THEY COULD FORGET YOU ALL TOGETHER.
...
THAT'S PROBABLY FOR THE BEST.

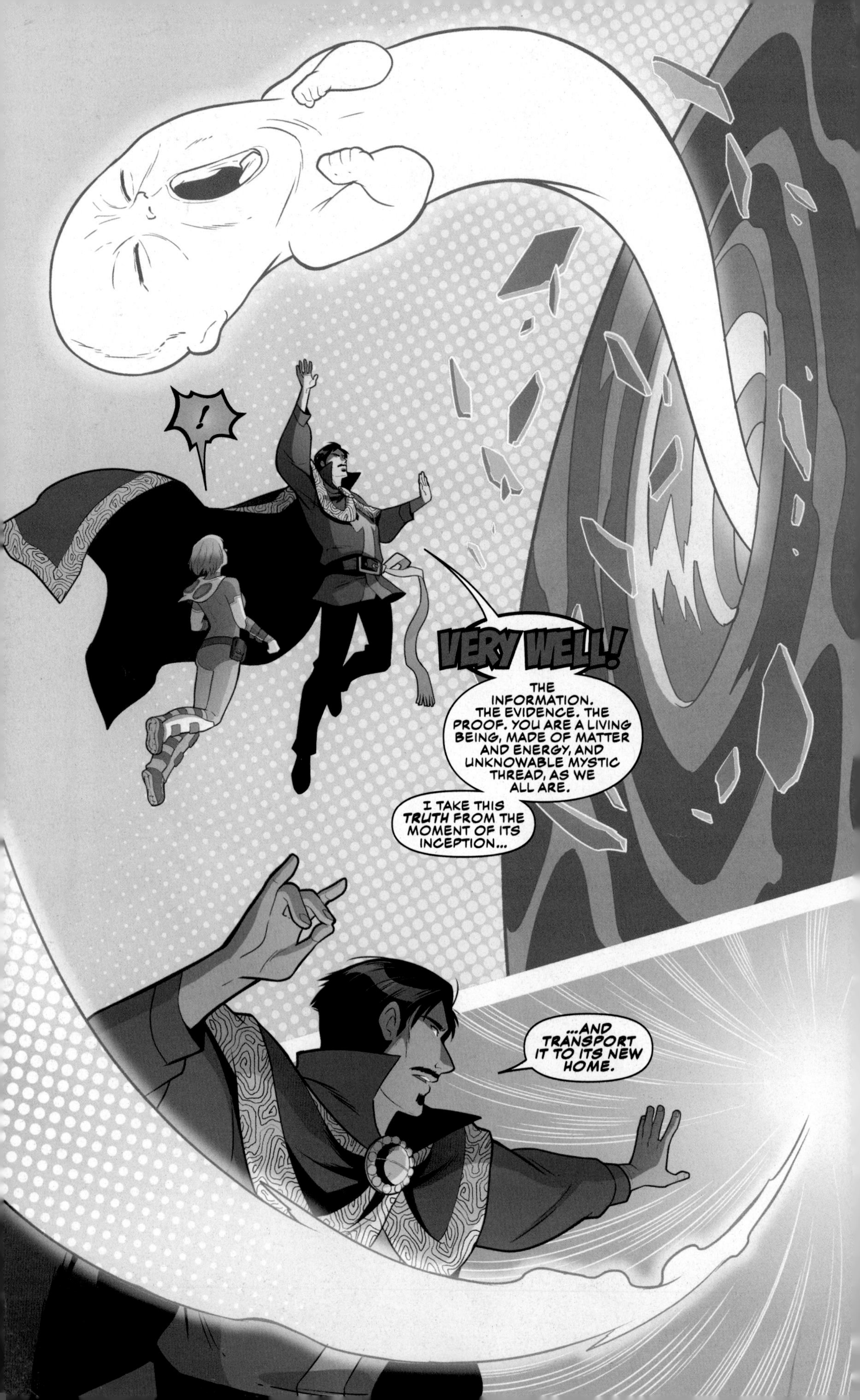
!
VERY WELL!
THE INFORMATION. THE EVIDENCE. THE PROOF. YOU ARE A LIVING BEING, MADE OF MATTER AND ENERGY, AND UNKNOWABLE MYSTIC THREAD, AS WE ALL ARE.
I TAKE THIS *TRUTH* FROM THE MOMENT OF ITS INCEPTION...
...AND *TRANSPORT* IT TO ITS NEW *HOME*.

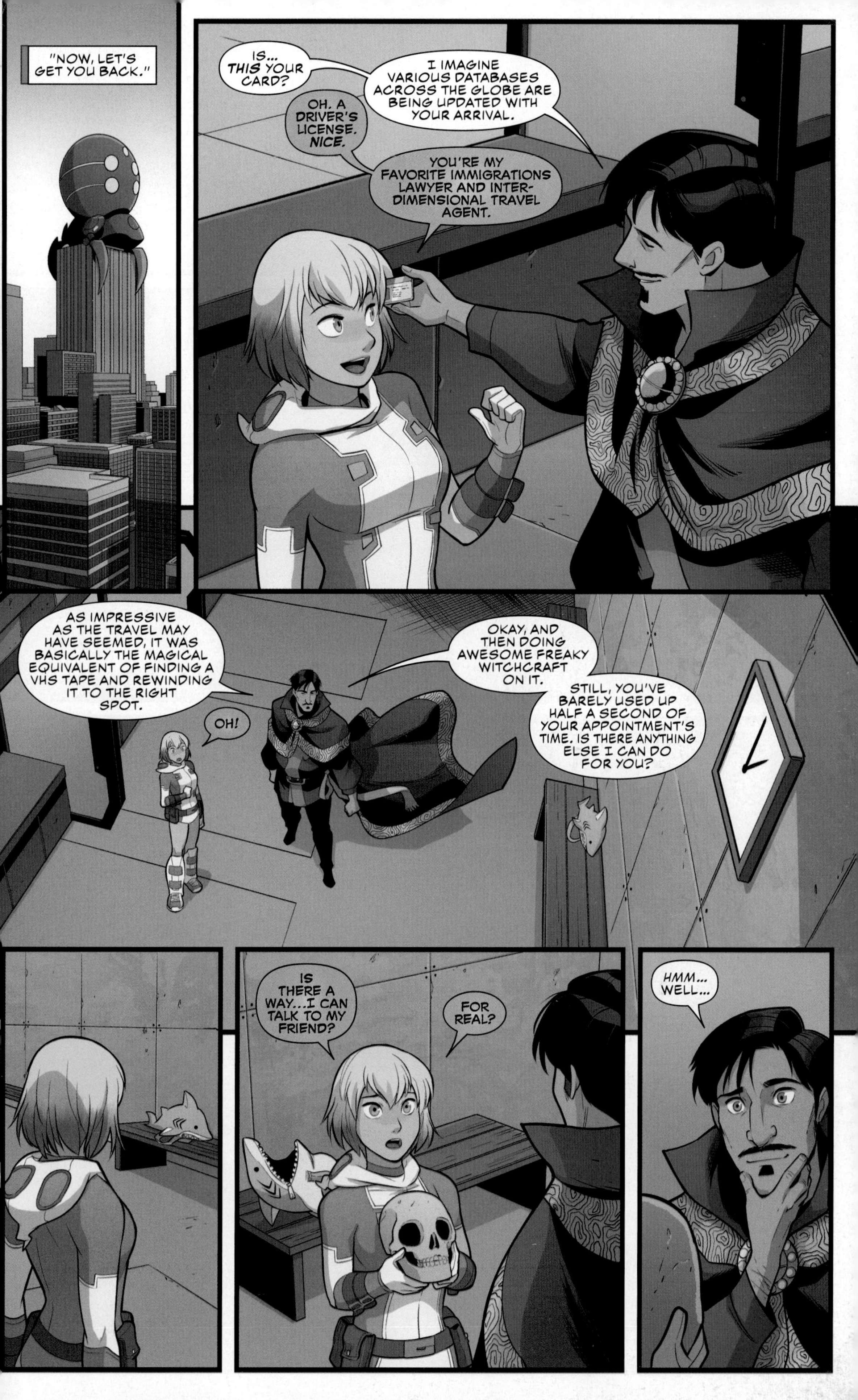
"NOW, LET'S GET YOU BACK."
IS... THIS YOUR CARD?
I IMAGINE VARIOUS DATABASES ACROSS THE GLOBE ARE BEING UPDATED WITH YOUR ARRIVAL.
OH. A DRIVER'S LICENSE. NICE.
YOU'RE MY FAVORITE IMMIGRATIONS LAWYER AND INTER-DIMENSIONAL TRAVEL AGENT.
AS IMPRESSIVE AS THE TRAVEL MAY HAVE SEEMED, IT WAS BASICALLY THE MAGICAL EQUIVALENT OF FINDING A VHS TAPE AND REWINDING IT TO THE RIGHT SPOT.
OH!
OKAY, AND THEN DOING AWESOME FREAKY WITCHCRAFT ON IT.
STILL, YOU'VE BARELY USED UP HALF A SECOND OF YOUR APPOINTMENT'S TIME. IS THERE ANYTHING ELSE I CAN DO FOR YOU?
IS THERE A WAY...I CAN TALK TO MY FRIEND?
FOR REAL?
HMM... WELL...

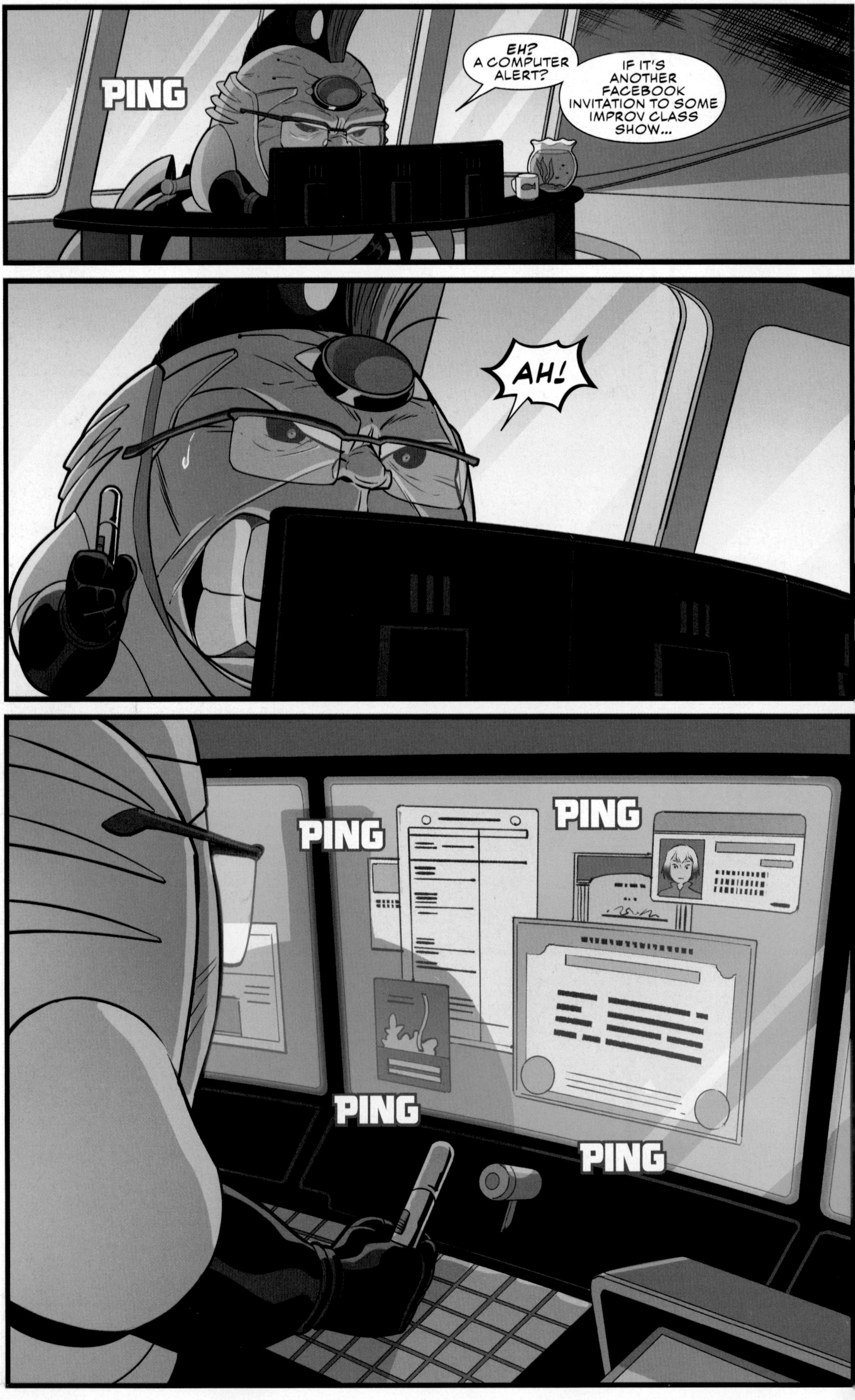
PING
EH? A COMPUTER ALERT?
IF IT'S ANOTHER FACEBOOK INVITATION TO SOME IMPROV CLASS SHOW...
AH!
PING
PING
PING
PING

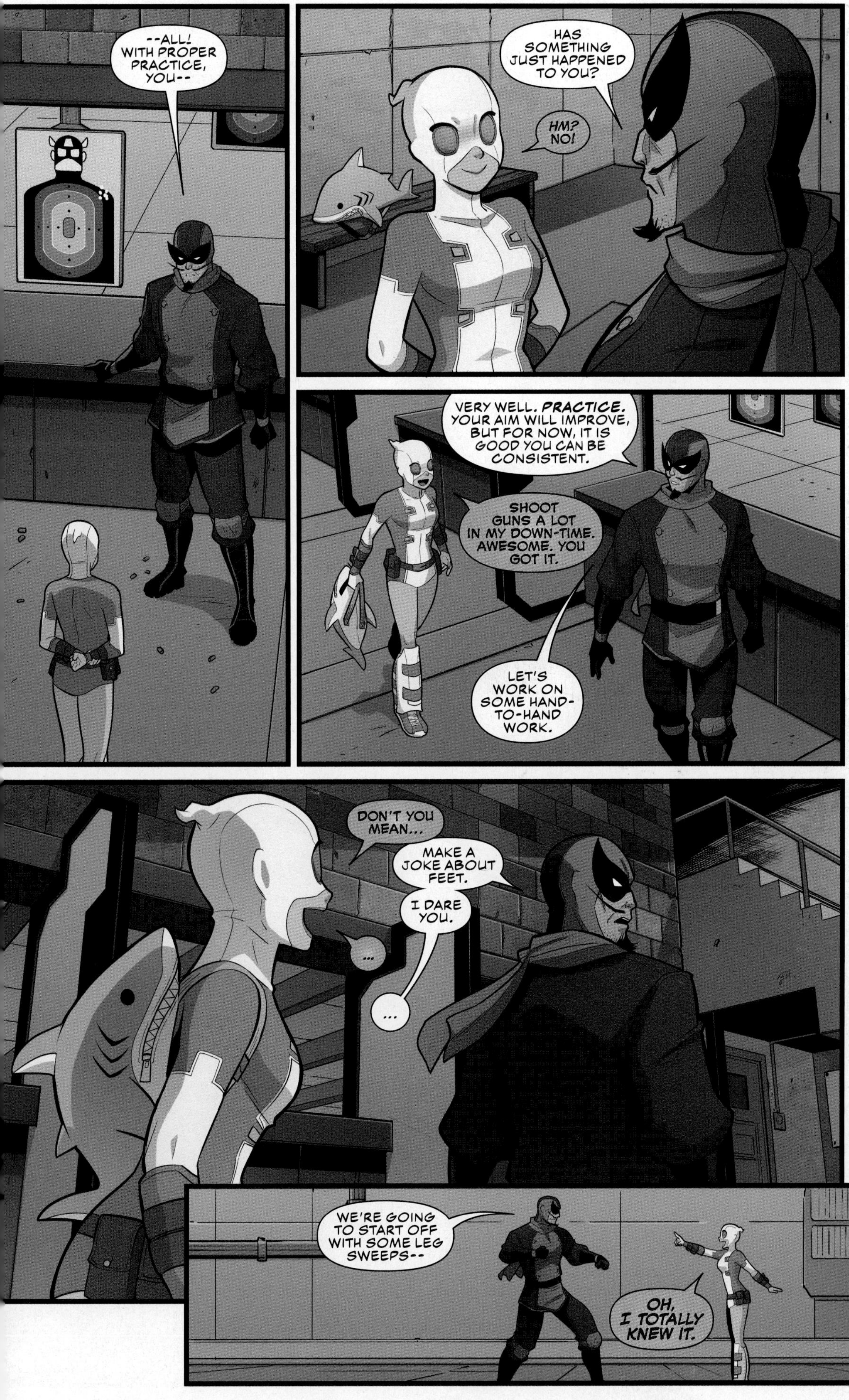
--ALL! WITH PROPER PRACTICE, YOU--
HAS SOMETHING JUST HAPPENED TO YOU?
HM? NO!
VERY WELL. PRACTICE. YOUR AIM WILL IMPROVE, BUT FOR NOW, IT IS GOOD YOU CAN BE CONSISTENT.
SHOOT GUNS A LOT IN MY DOWN-TIME. AWESOME. YOU GOT IT.
LET'S WORK ON SOME HAND-TO-HAND WORK.
DON'T YOU MEAN...
MAKE A JOKE ABOUT FEET.
I DARE YOU.
...
...
WE'RE GOING TO START OFF WITH SOME LEG SWEEPS--
OH, I TOTALLY KNEW IT.

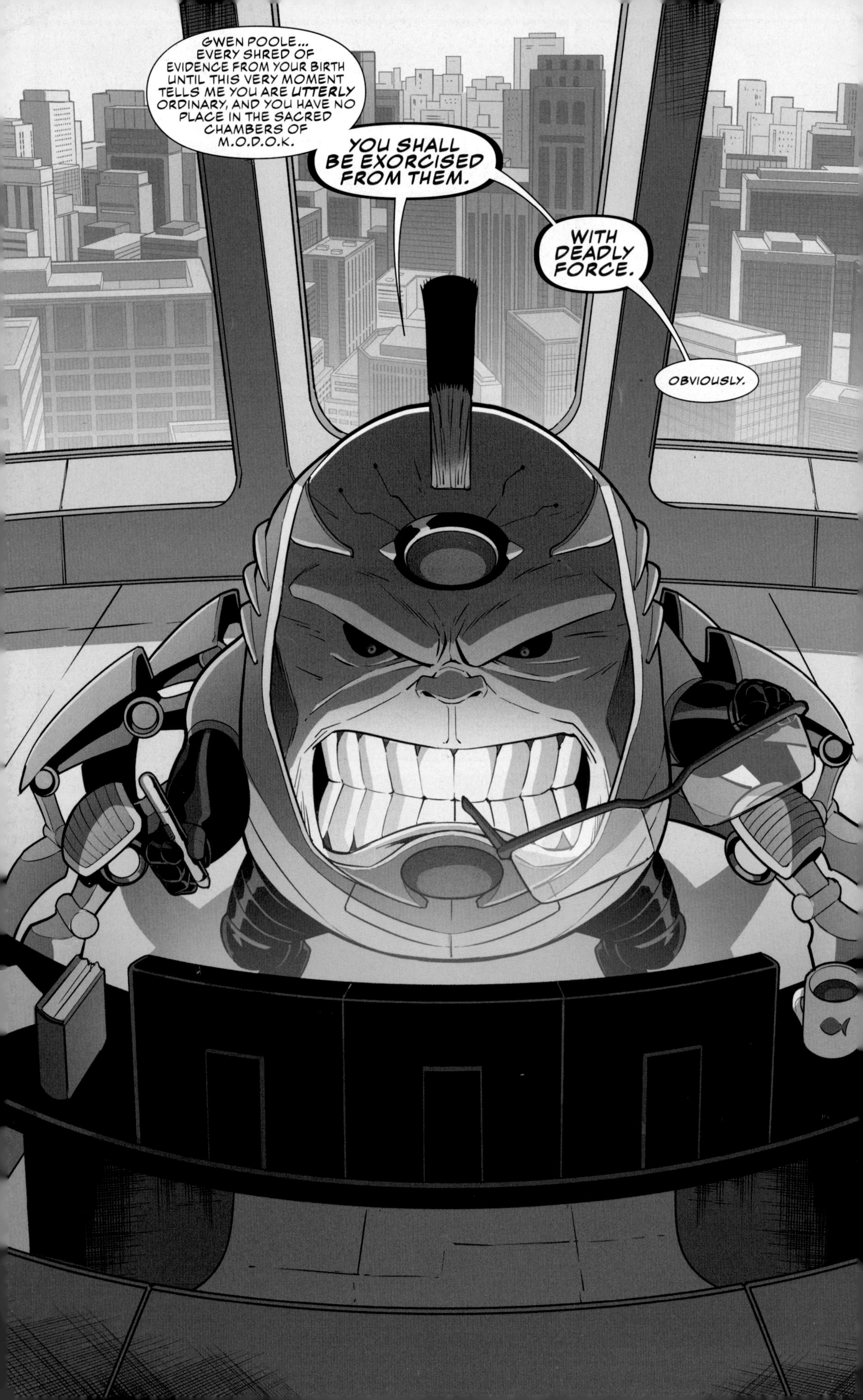
GWEN POOLE... EVERY SHRED OF EVIDENCE FROM YOUR BIRTH UNTIL THIS VERY MOMENT TELLS ME YOU ARE UTTERLY ORDINARY, AND YOU HAVE NO PLACE IN THE SACRED CHAMBERS OF M.O.D.O.K.
YOU SHALL BE EXORCISED FROM THEM.
WITH DEADLY FORCE.
OBVIOUSLY.

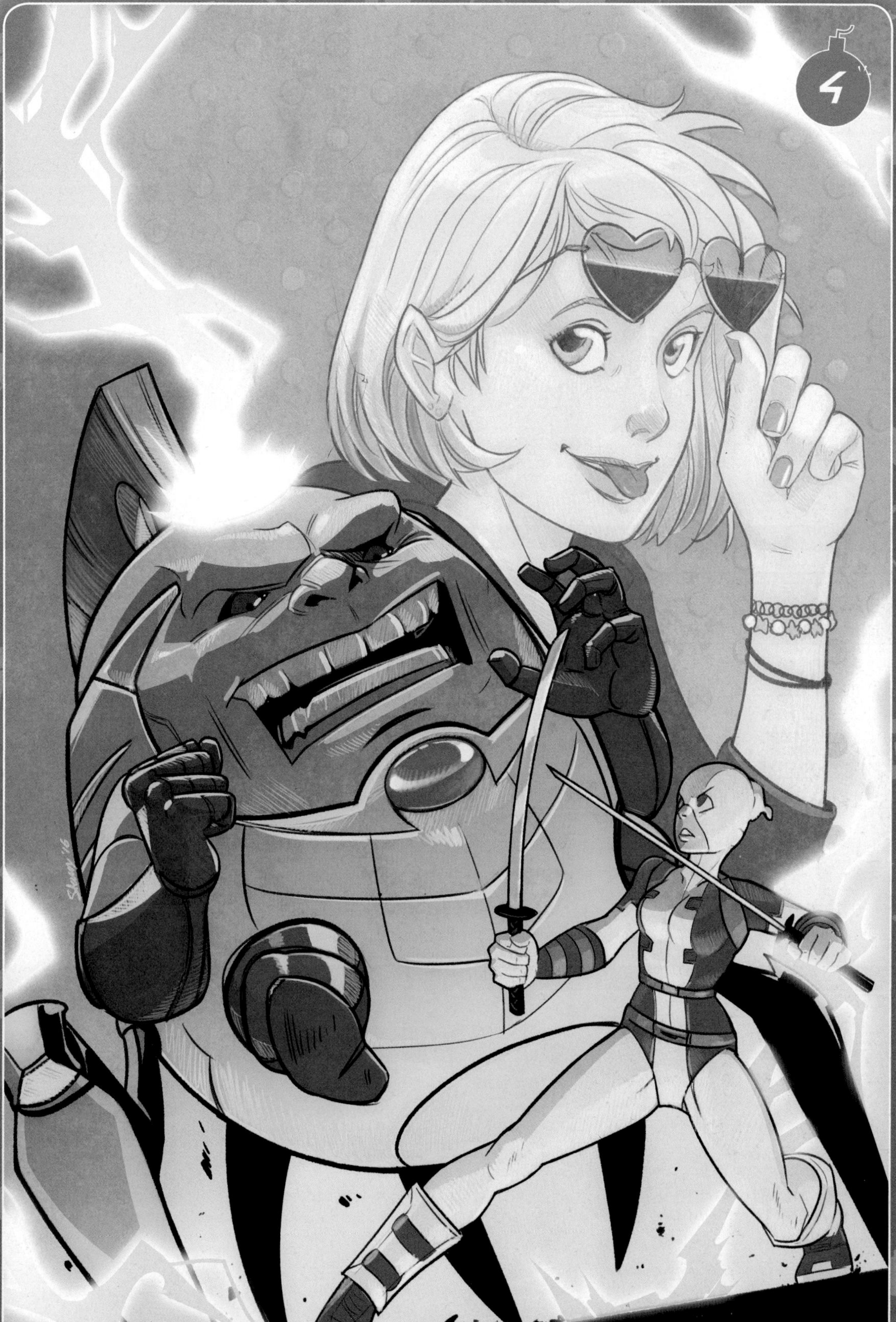

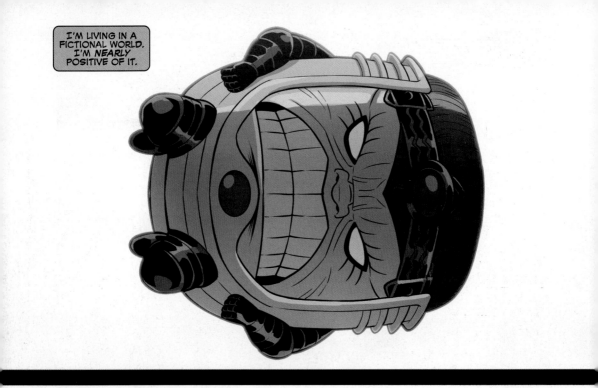

I'M LIVING IN A FICTIONAL WORLD. I'M *NEARLY* POSITIVE OF IT.

HERE, SUPER HEROES AND SUPER VILLAINS FIGHT OVER THE SAME FIVE-ISH THINGS ON A PRETTY REGULAR BASIS:

-POWER
-LOVE
-INFINITY GEMS
-MONEY
-MISCELLANY

IT'S A SCARY PLACE FOR A NORMAL PERSON WITH NO POWERS.

BUT I THINK I'M GETTING THE HANG OF IT

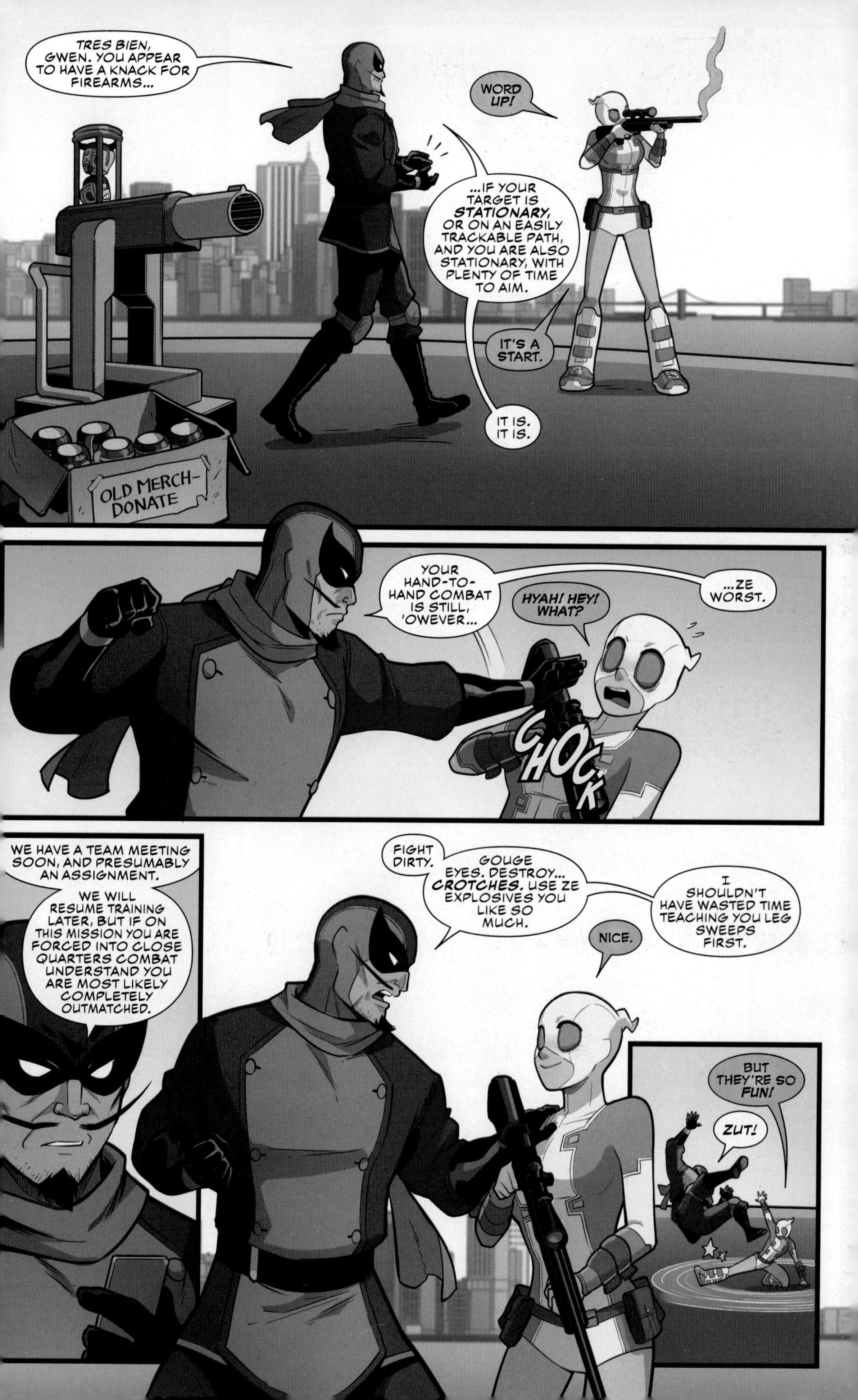
TRES BIEN, GWEN. YOU APPEAR TO HAVE A KNACK FOR FIREARMS...
WORD UP!
...IF YOUR TARGET IS STATIONARY, OR ON AN EASILY TRACKABLE PATH, AND YOU ARE ALSO STATIONARY, WITH PLENTY OF TIME TO AIM.
IT'S A START.
IT IS. IT IS.
OLD MERCH-DONATE
YOUR HAND-TO-HAND COMBAT IS STILL, 'OWEVER...
HYAH! HEY! WHAT?
...ZE WORST.
CHOCK
WE HAVE A TEAM MEETING SOON, AND PRESUMABLY AN ASSIGNMENT.
WE WILL RESUME TRAINING LATER, BUT IF ON THIS MISSION YOU ARE FORCED INTO CLOSE QUARTERS COMBAT UNDERSTAND YOU ARE MOST LIKELY COMPLETELY OUTMATCHED.
FIGHT DIRTY.
GOUGE EYES. DESTROY... CROTCHES. USE ZE EXPLOSIVES YOU LIKE SO MUCH.
NICE.
I SHOULDN'T HAVE WASTED TIME TEACHING YOU LEG SWEEPS FIRST.
BUT THEY'RE SO FUN!
ZUT!

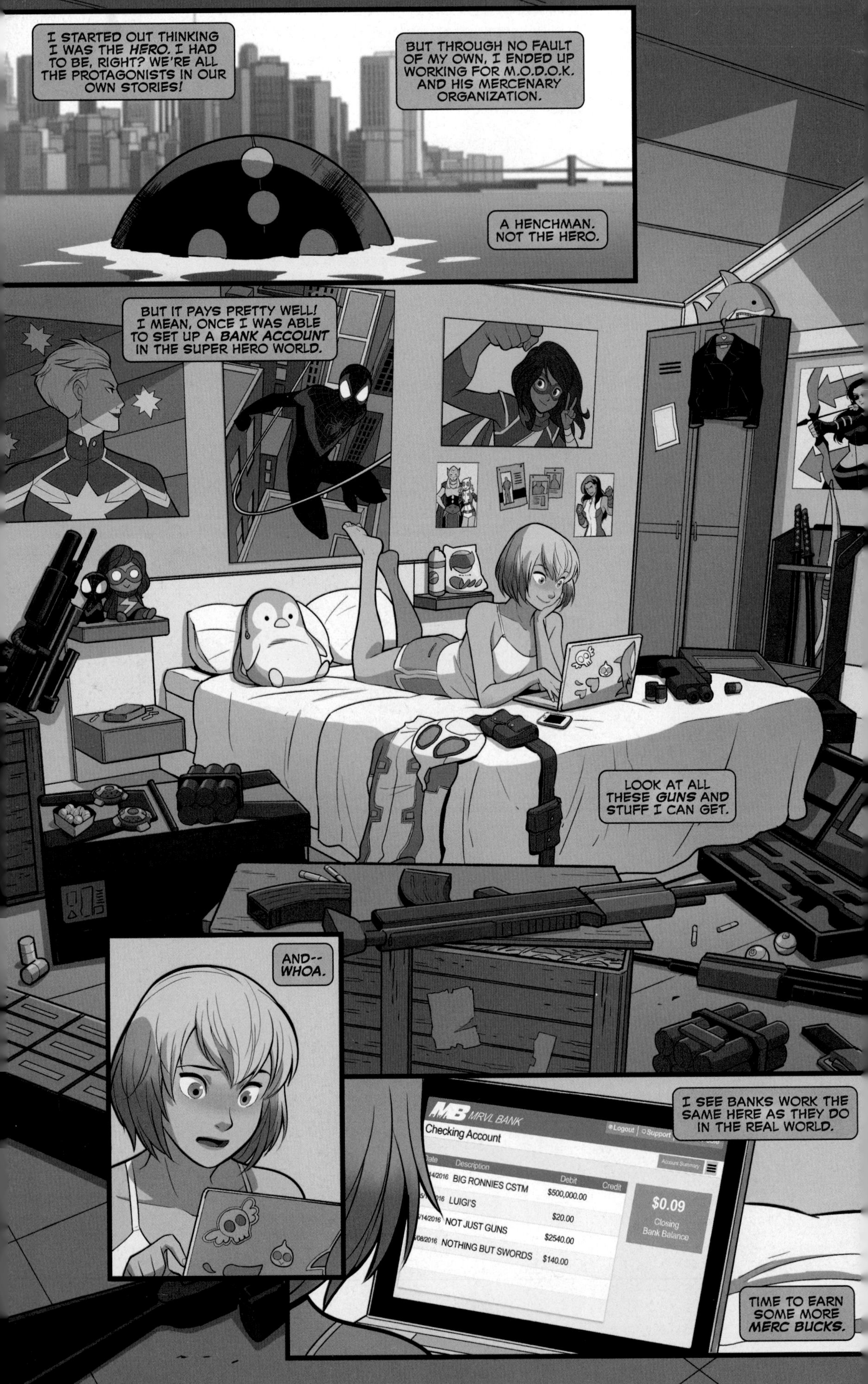
I STARTED OUT THINKING I WAS THE *HERO.* I HAD TO BE, RIGHT? WE'RE ALL THE PROTAGONISTS IN OUR OWN STORIES!
BUT THROUGH NO FAULT OF MY OWN, I ENDED UP WORKING FOR M.O.D.O.K. AND HIS MERCENARY ORGANIZATION.
A HENCHMAN. NOT THE HERO.
BUT IT PAYS PRETTY WELL! I MEAN, ONCE I WAS ABLE TO SET UP A *BANK ACCOUNT* IN THE SUPER HERO WORLD.
LOOK AT ALL THESE *GUNS* AND STUFF I CAN GET.
AND-- WHOA.
MB MRVL BANK
Checking Account
Logout
Support
Description
Debit
Credit
Account Summary
BIG RONNIES CSTM $500,000.00
LUIGI'S $20.00
NOT JUST GUNS $2540.00
NOTHING BUT SWORDS $140.00
$0.09
Closing Bank Balance
I SEE BANKS WORK THE SAME HERE AS THEY DO IN THE REAL WORLD.
TIME TO EARN SOME MORE *MERC BUCKS.*

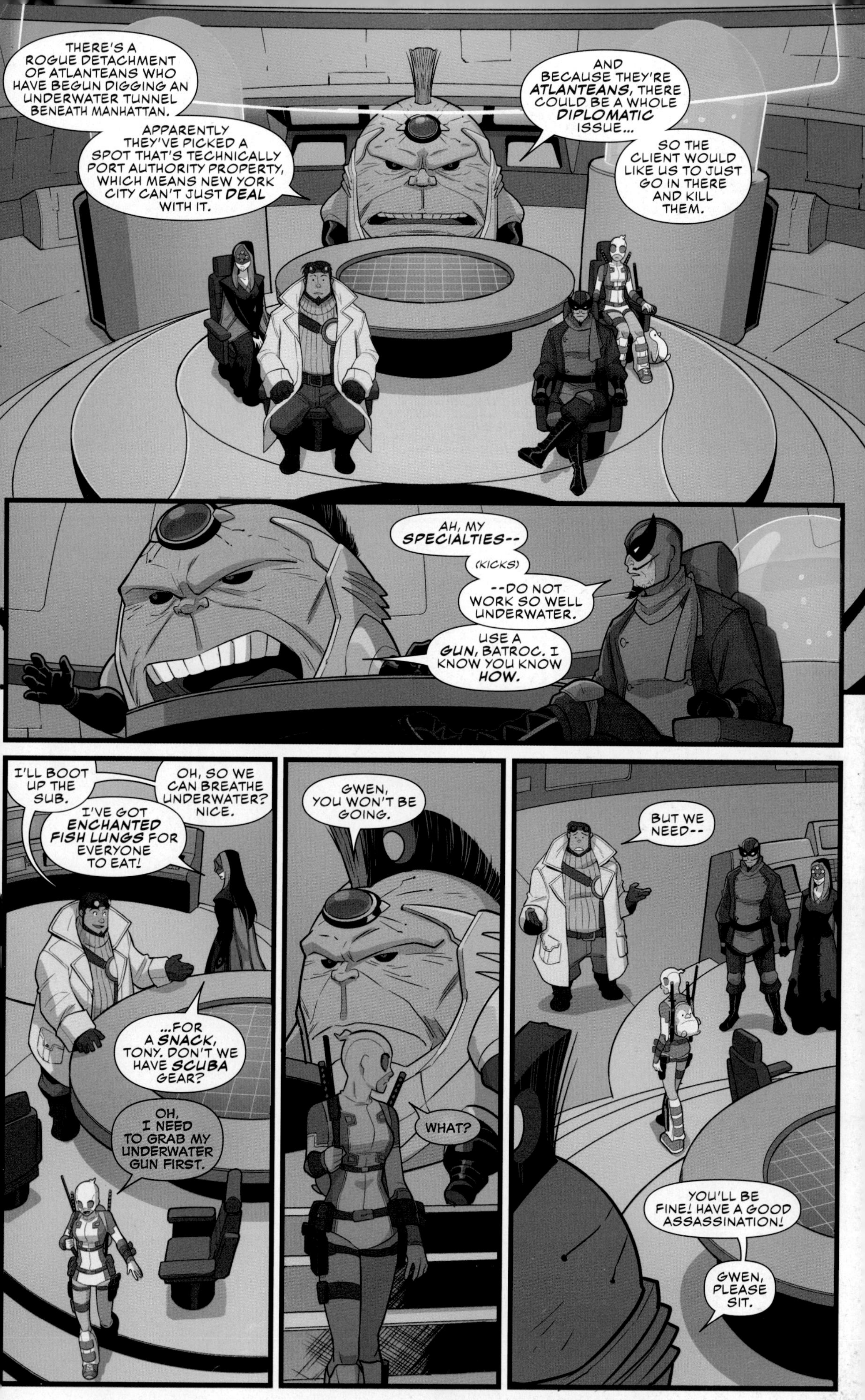
THERE'S A ROGUE DETACHMENT OF ATLANTEANS WHO HAVE BEGUN DIGGING AN UNDERWATER TUNNEL BENEATH MANHATTAN.
APPARENTLY THEY'VE PICKED A SPOT THAT'S TECHNICALLY PORT AUTHORITY PROPERTY, WHICH MEANS NEW YORK CITY CAN'T JUST DEAL WITH IT.
AND BECAUSE THEY'RE ATLANTEANS, THERE COULD BE A WHOLE DIPLOMATIC ISSUE...
SO THE CLIENT WOULD LIKE US TO JUST GO IN THERE AND KILL THEM.
AH, MY SPECIALTIES--
(KICKS)
--DO NOT WORK SO WELL UNDERWATER.
USE A GUN, BATROC. I KNOW YOU KNOW HOW.
I'LL BOOT UP THE SUB.
OH, SO WE CAN BREATHE UNDERWATER? NICE.
I'VE GOT ENCHANTED FISH LUNGS FOR EVERYONE TO EAT!
...FOR A SNACK, TONY. DON'T WE HAVE SCUBA GEAR?
OH, I NEED TO GRAB MY UNDERWATER GUN FIRST.
GWEN, YOU WON'T BE GOING.
WHAT?
BUT WE NEED--
YOU'LL BE FINE! HAVE A GOOD ASSASSINATION!
GWEN, PLEASE SIT.

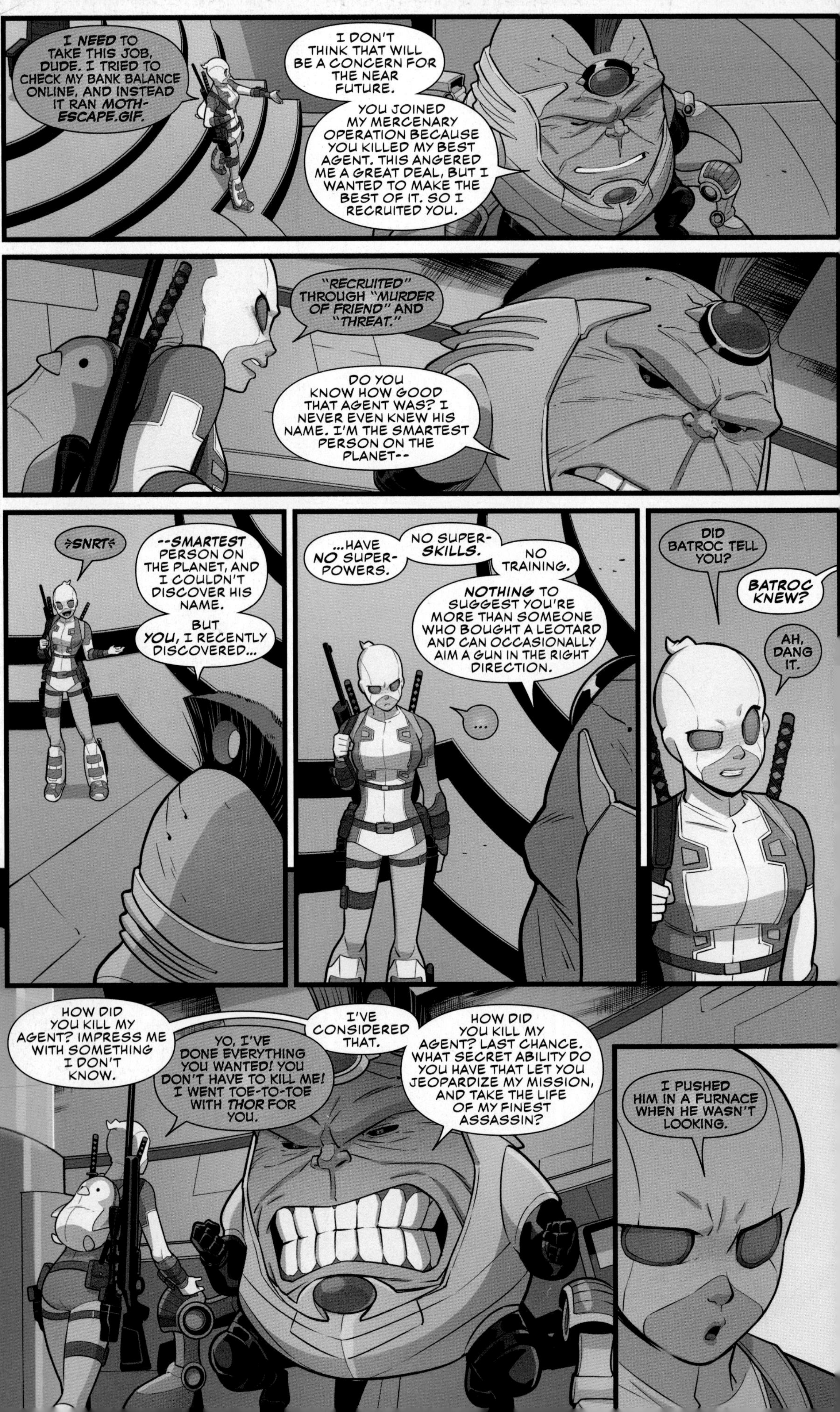
I NEED TO TAKE THIS JOB, DUDE. I TRIED TO CHECK MY BANK BALANCE ONLINE, AND INSTEAD IT RAN MOTH-ESCAPE.GIF.
I DON'T THINK THAT WILL BE A CONCERN FOR THE NEAR FUTURE.
YOU JOINED MY MERCENARY OPERATION BECAUSE YOU KILLED MY BEST AGENT. THIS ANGERED ME A GREAT DEAL, BUT I WANTED TO MAKE THE BEST OF IT. SO I RECRUITED YOU.
"RECRUITED" THROUGH "MURDER OF FRIEND" AND "THREAT."
DO YOU KNOW HOW GOOD THAT AGENT WAS? I NEVER EVEN KNEW HIS NAME. I'M THE SMARTEST PERSON ON THE PLANET--
SNRT
--SMARTEST PERSON ON THE PLANET, AND I COULDN'T DISCOVER HIS NAME.
BUT YOU, I RECENTLY DISCOVERED...
...HAVE NO SUPER-POWERS.
NO SUPER-SKILLS.
NO TRAINING.
NOTHING TO SUGGEST YOU'RE MORE THAN SOMEONE WHO BOUGHT A LEOTARD AND CAN OCCASIONALLY AIM A GUN IN THE RIGHT DIRECTION.
...
DID BATROC TELL YOU?
BATROC KNEW?
AH, DANG IT.
HOW DID YOU KILL MY AGENT? IMPRESS ME WITH SOMETHING I DON'T KNOW.
YO, I'VE DONE EVERYTHING YOU WANTED! YOU DON'T HAVE TO KILL ME! I WENT TOE-TO-TOE WITH THOR FOR YOU.
I'VE CONSIDERED THAT.
HOW DID YOU KILL MY AGENT? LAST CHANCE. WHAT SECRET ABILITY DO YOU HAVE THAT LET YOU JEOPARDIZE MY MISSION, AND TAKE THE LIFE OF MY FINEST ASSASSIN?
I PUSHED HIM IN A FURNACE WHEN HE WASN'T LOOKING.

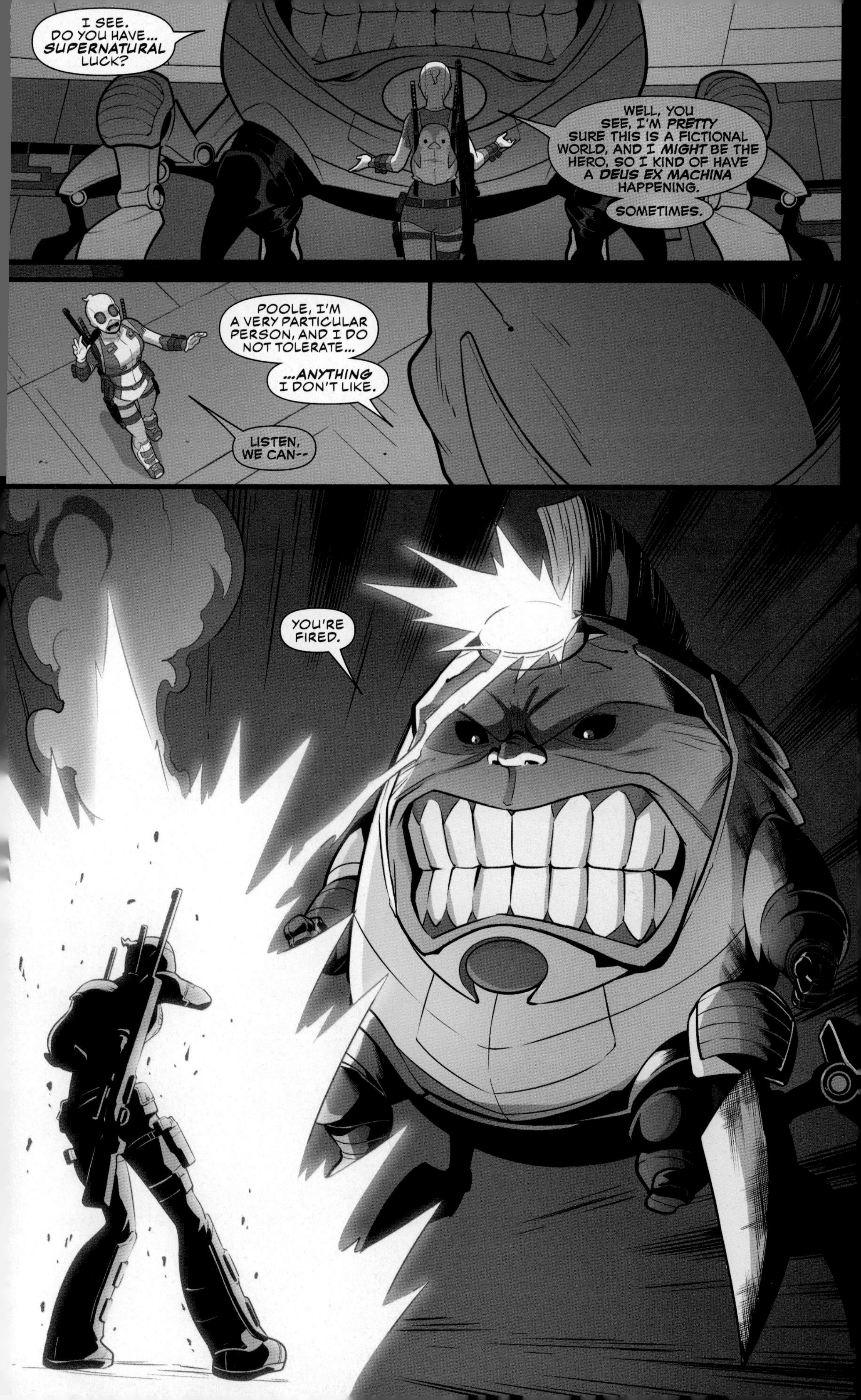
I SEE. DO YOU HAVE... SUPERNATURAL LUCK?
WELL, YOU SEE, I'M PRETTY SURE THIS IS A FICTIONAL WORLD, AND I MIGHT BE THE HERO, SO I KIND OF HAVE A DEUS EX MACHINA HAPPENING.
SOMETIMES.
POOLE, I'M A VERY PARTICULAR PERSON, AND I DO NOT TOLERATE...
...ANYTHING I DON'T LIKE.
LISTEN, WE CAN--
YOU'RE FIRED.

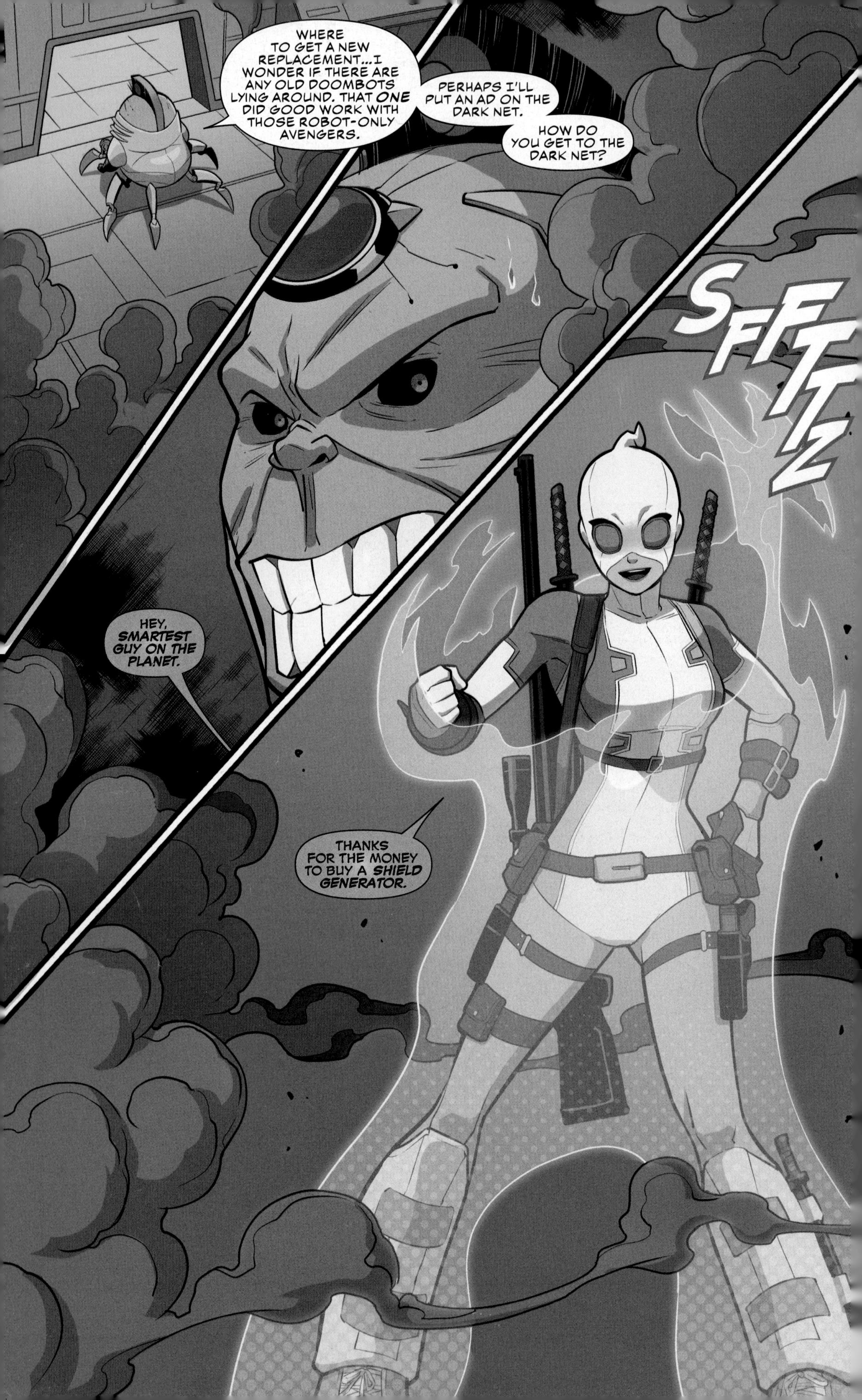
WHERE TO GET A NEW REPLACEMENT...I WONDER IF THERE ARE ANY OLD DOOMBOTS LYING AROUND. THAT ONE DID GOOD WORK WITH THOSE ROBOT-ONLY AVENGERS.
PERHAPS I'LL PUT AN AD ON THE DARK NET.
HOW DO YOU GET TO THE DARK NET?
SFFTTZ
HEY, SMARTEST GUY ON THE PLANET.
THANKS FOR THE MONEY TO BUY A SHIELD GENERATOR.

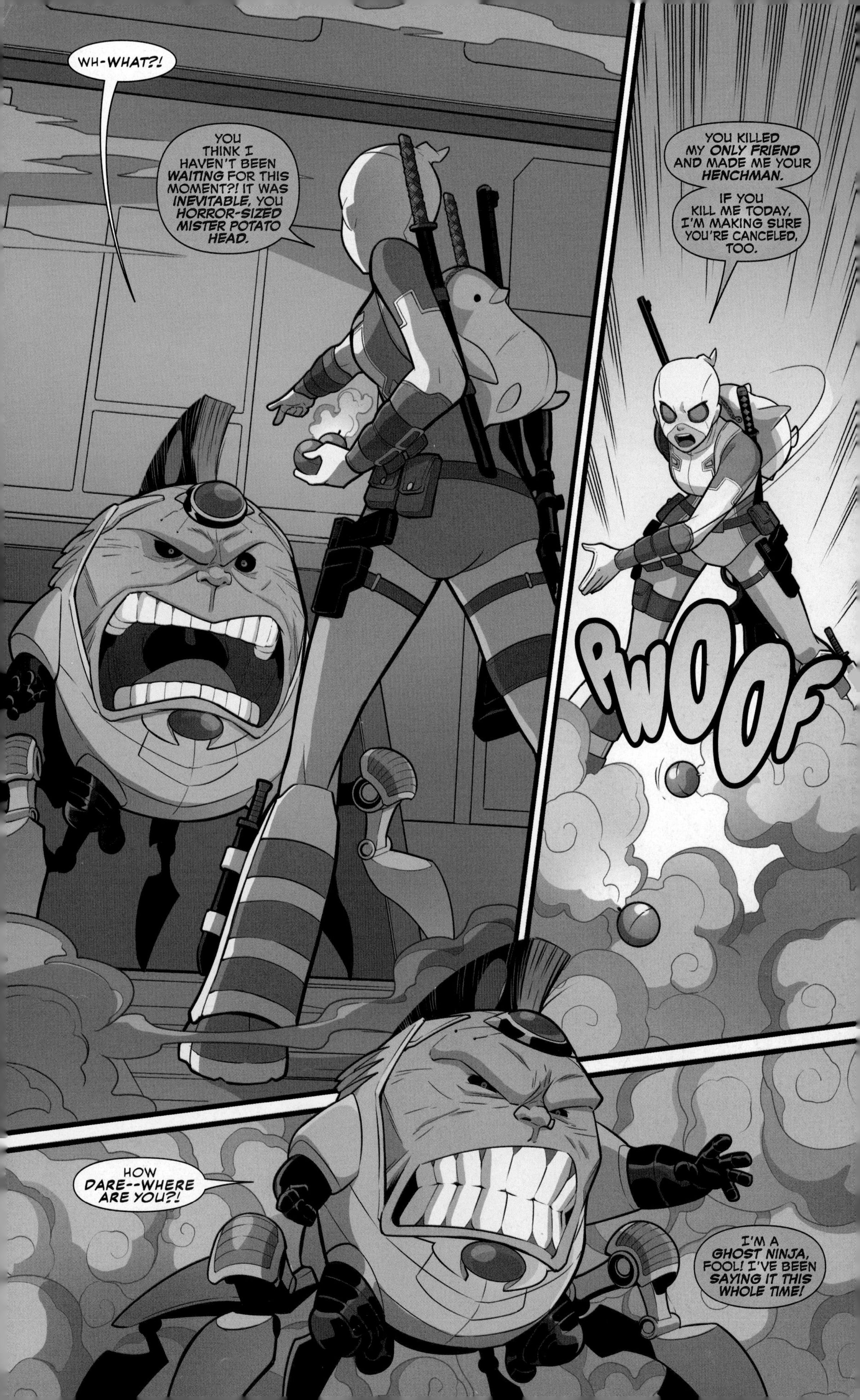
WH-WHAT?!
YOU THINK I HAVEN'T BEEN WAITING FOR THIS MOMENT?! IT WAS INEVITABLE, YOU HORROR-SIZED MISTER POTATO HEAD.
YOU KILLED MY ONLY FRIEND AND MADE ME YOUR HENCHMAN.
IF YOU KILL ME TODAY, I'M MAKING SURE YOU'RE CANCELED, TOO.
PWOOF
HOW DARE--WHERE ARE YOU?!
I'M A GHOST NINJA, FOOL! I'VE BEEN SAYING IT THIS WHOLE TIME!

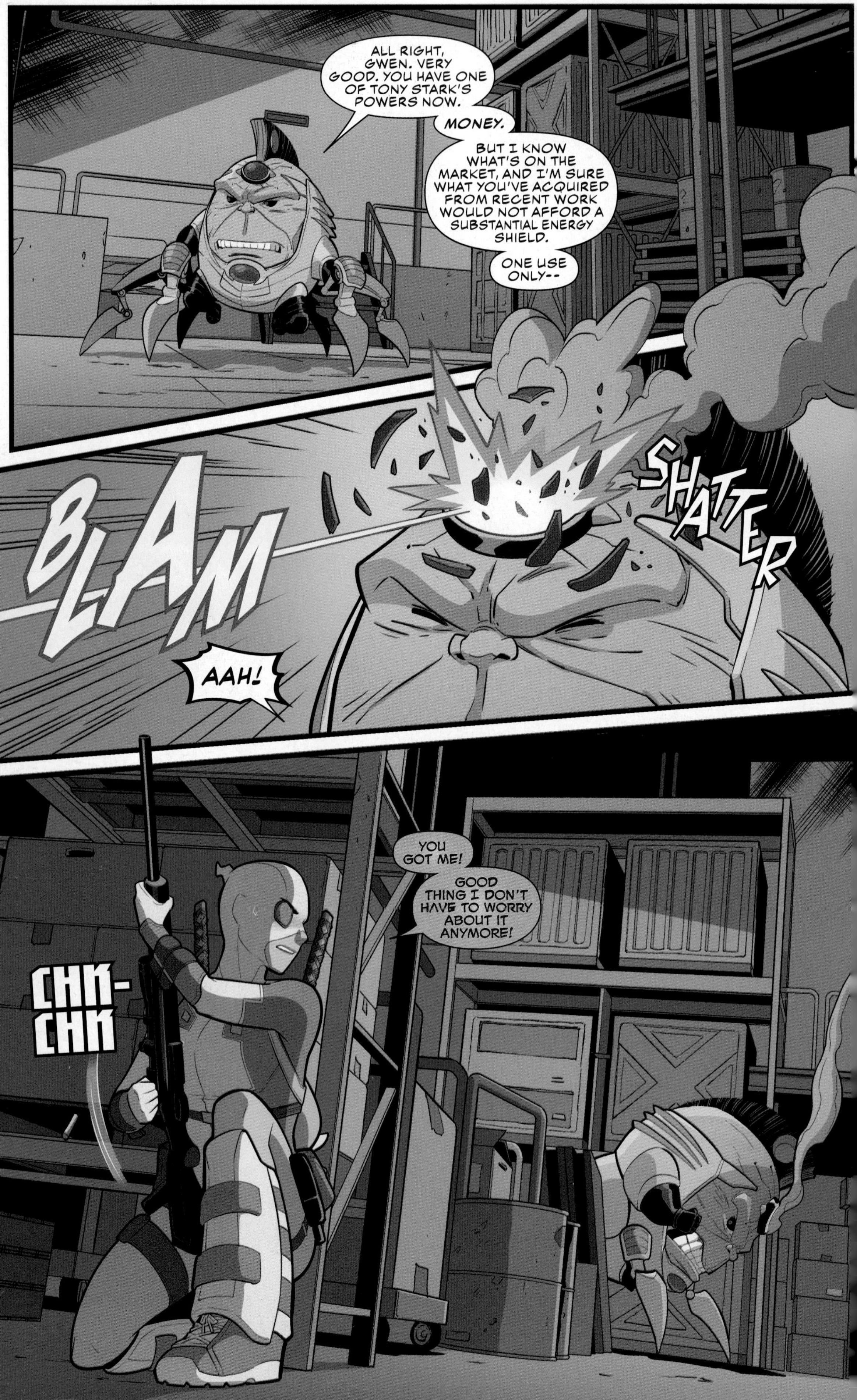
ALL RIGHT, GWEN. VERY GOOD. YOU HAVE ONE OF TONY STARK'S POWERS NOW.
MONEY.
BUT I KNOW WHAT'S ON THE MARKET, AND I'M SURE WHAT YOU'VE ACQUIRED FROM RECENT WORK WOULD NOT AFFORD A SUBSTANTIAL ENERGY SHIELD.
ONE USE ONLY--
BLAM
SHATTER
AAH!
CHK-CHK
YOU GOT ME!
GOOD THING I DON'T HAVE TO WORRY ABOUT IT ANYMORE!

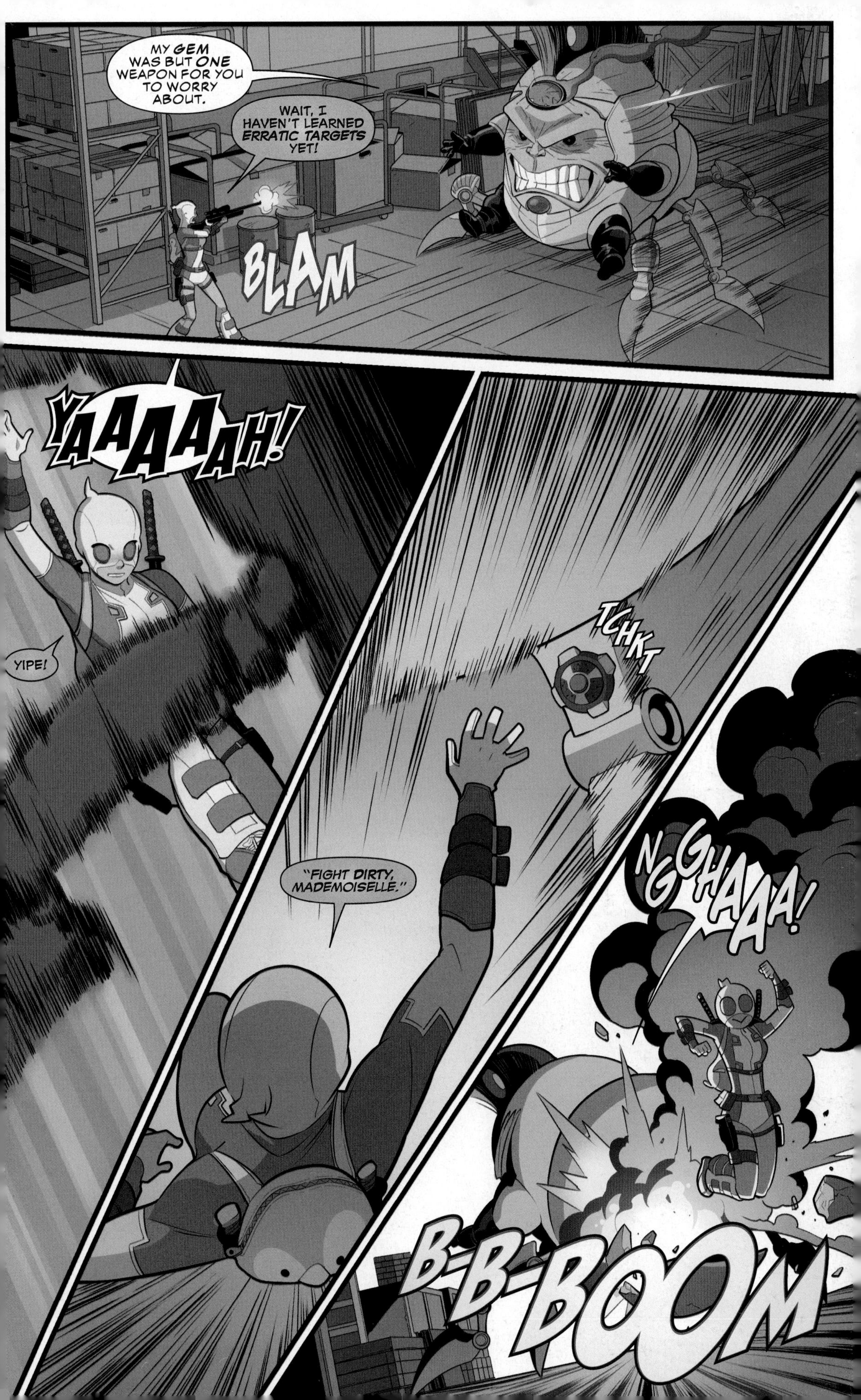

MY GEM WAS BUT ONE WEAPON FOR YOU TO WORRY ABOUT.
WAIT, I HAVEN'T LEARNED ERRATIC TARGETS YET!
BLAM
YAAAAAH!
YIPE!
TCHKT
"FIGHT DIRTY, MADEMOISELLE."
NGGHAAAA!
B-B-BOOM

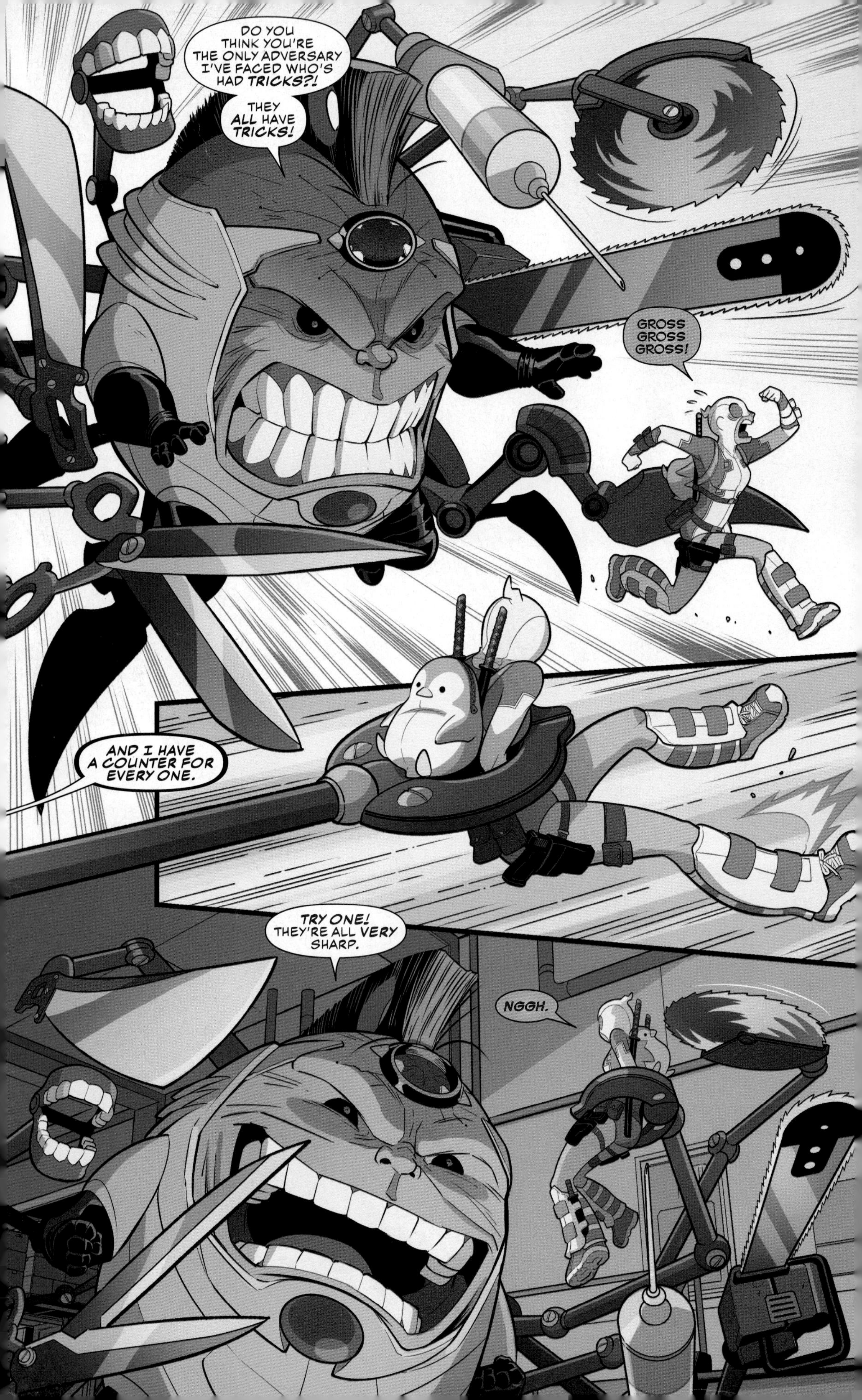
DO YOU THINK YOU'RE THE ONLY ADVERSARY I'VE FACED WHO'S HAD TRICKS?!
THEY ALL HAVE TRICKS!
GROSS GROSS GROSS!
AND I HAVE A COUNTER FOR EVERY ONE.
TRY ONE! THEY'RE ALL VERY SHARP.
NGGH.

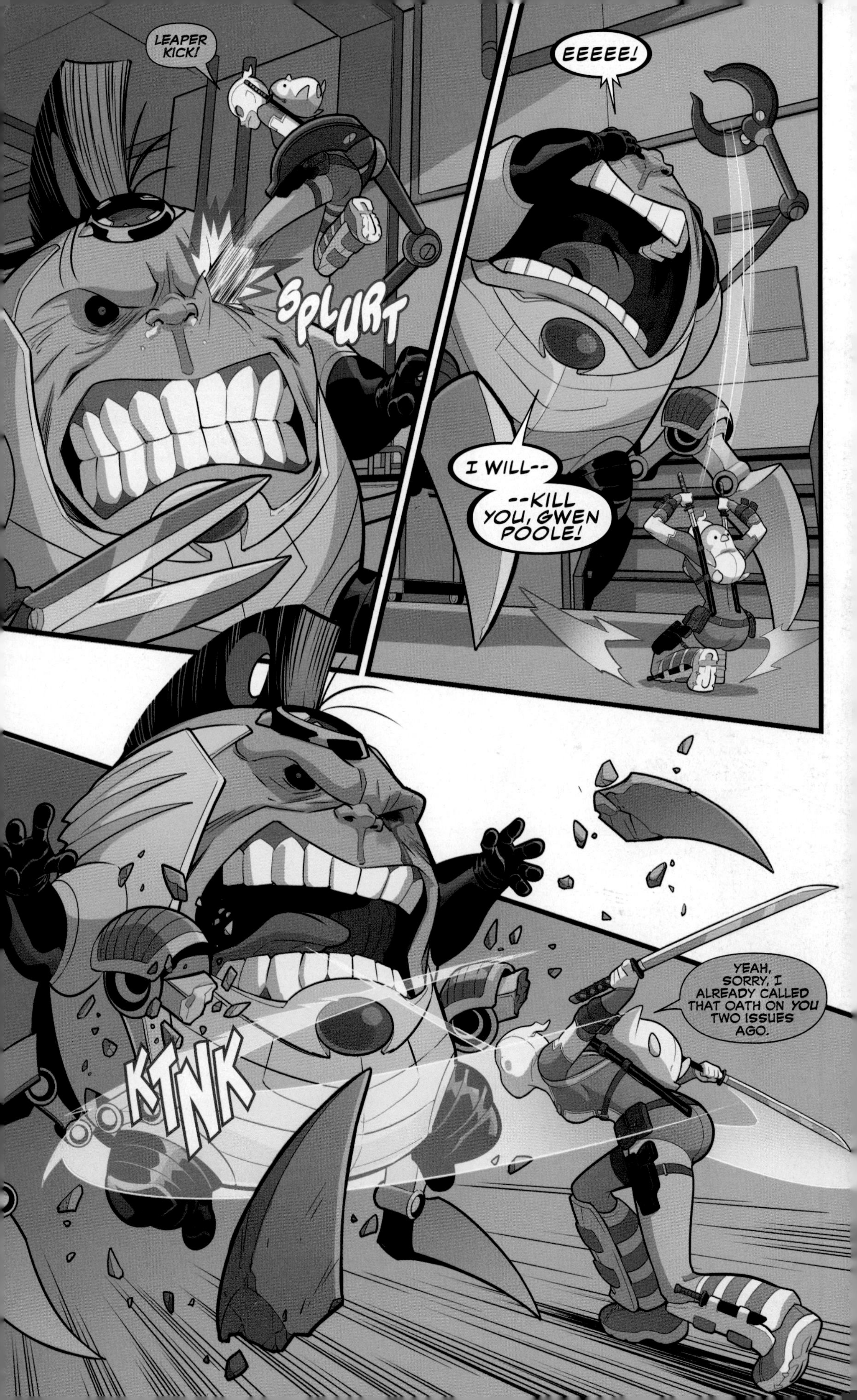
LEAPER KICK!
SPLURT
EEEEE!
I WILL--
--KILL YOU, GWEN POOLE!
YEAH, SORRY, I ALREADY CALLED THAT OATH ON YOU TWO ISSUES AGO.
KTNK

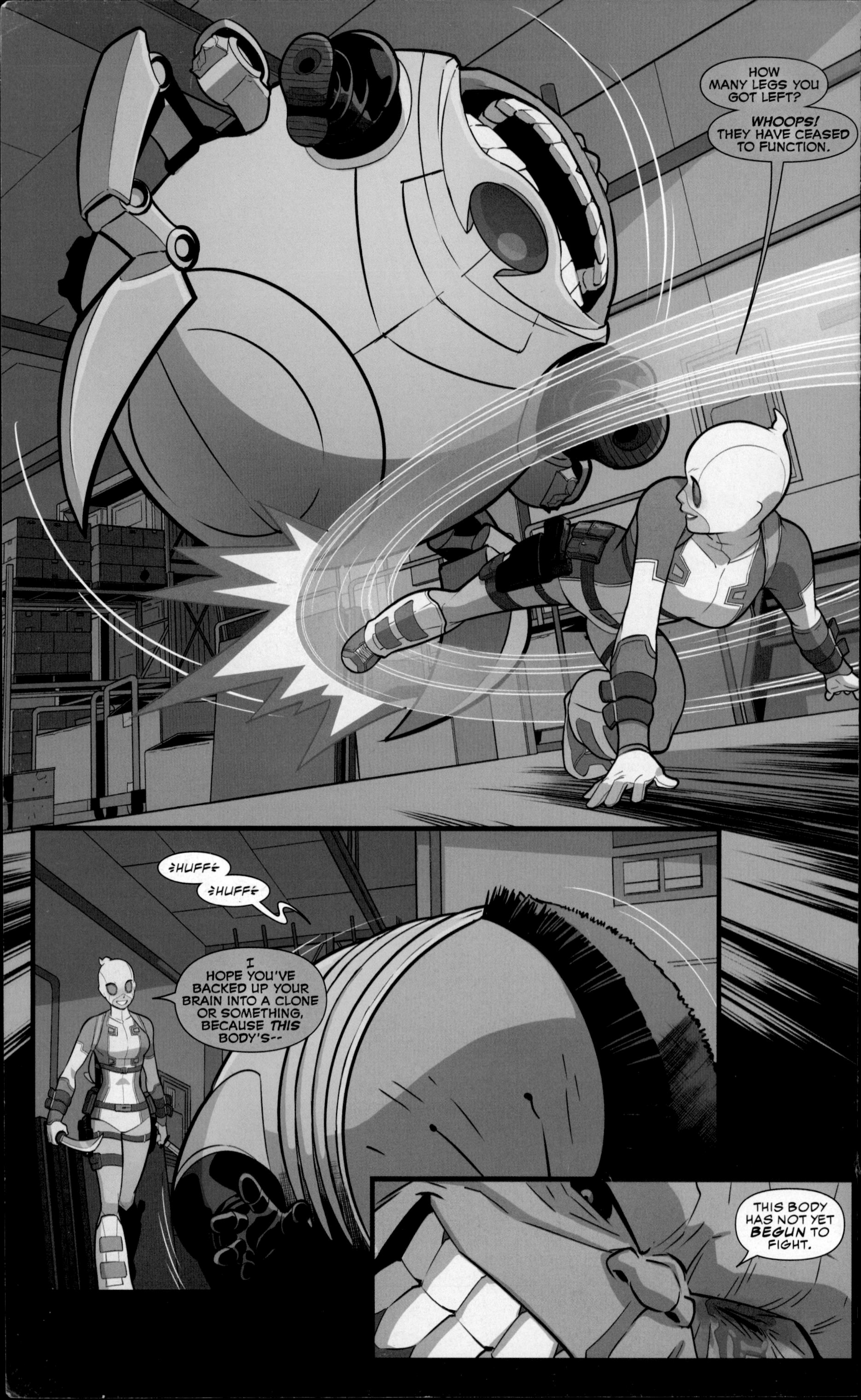
HOW MANY LEGS YOU GOT LEFT?
WHOOPS! THEY HAVE CEASED TO FUNCTION.
=HUFF=
=HUFF=
I HOPE YOU'VE BACKED UP YOUR BRAIN INTO A CLONE OR SOMETHING, BECAUSE THIS BODY'S--
THIS BODY HAS NOT YET BEGUN TO FIGHT.

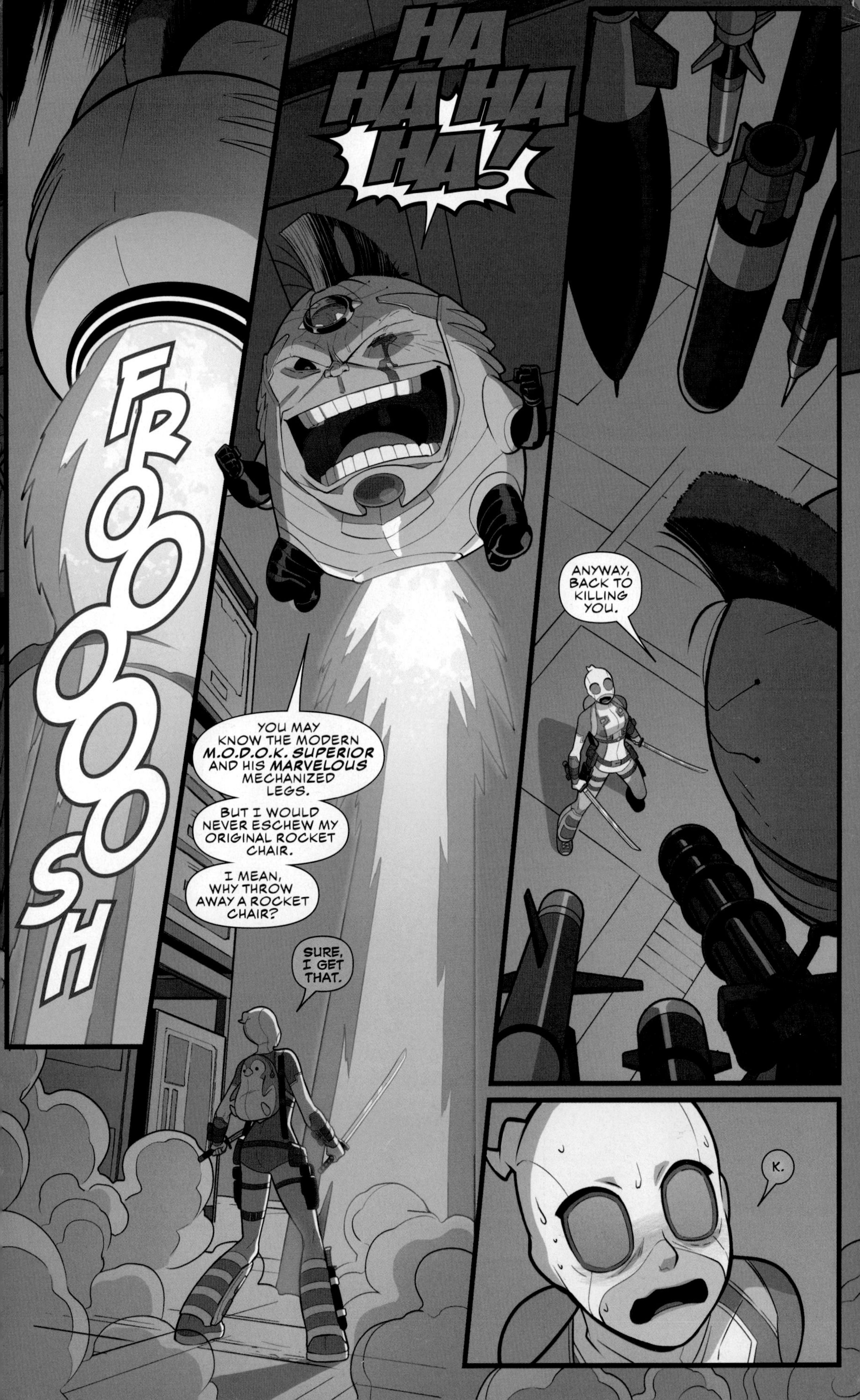

HA HA HA HA HA!
FROOOOOOSH
YOU MAY KNOW THE MODERN M.O.D.O.K. SUPERIOR AND HIS MARVELOUS MECHANIZED LEGS.
BUT I WOULD NEVER ESCHEW MY ORIGINAL ROCKET CHAIR.
I MEAN, WHY THROW AWAY A ROCKET CHAIR?
SURE, I GET THAT.
ANYWAY, BACK TO KILLING YOU.
K.

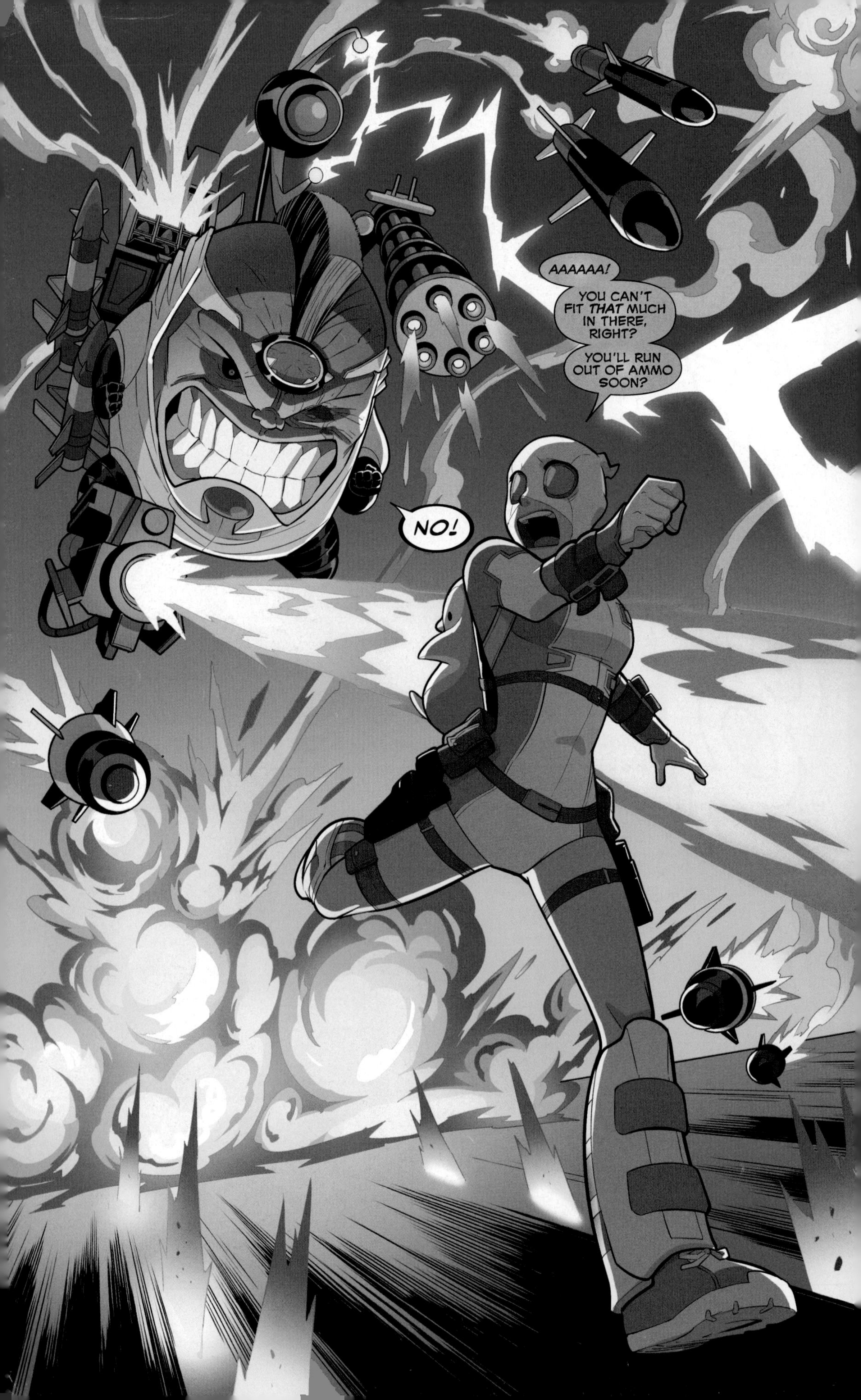
AAAAAA!
YOU CAN'T FIT *THAT* MUCH IN THERE, RIGHT?
YOU'LL RUN OUT OF AMMO SOON?
NO!

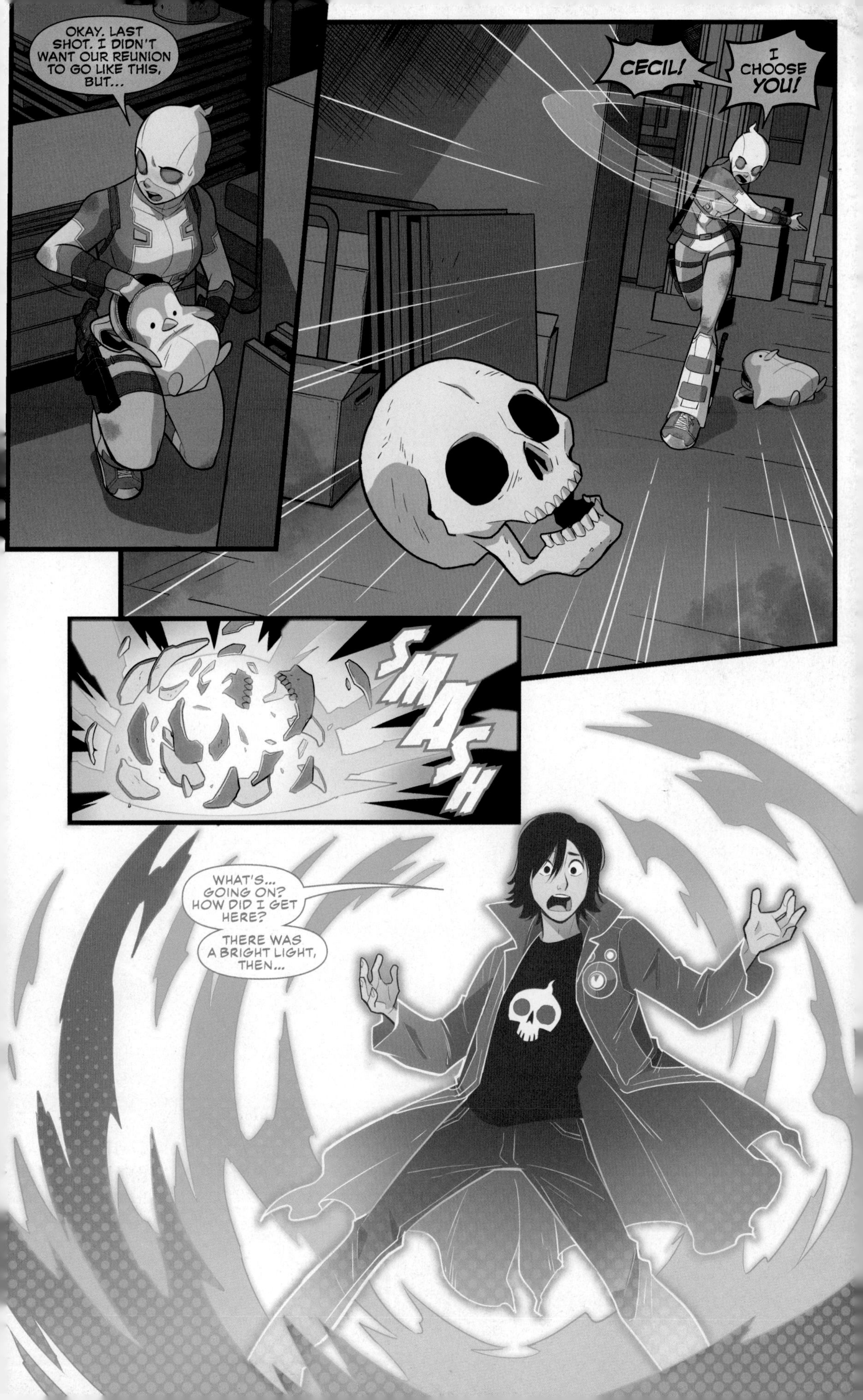
OKAY. LAST SHOT. I DIDN'T WANT OUR REUNION TO GO LIKE THIS, BUT...
CECIL!
I CHOOSE YOU!
SMASH
WHAT'S... GOING ON? HOW DID I GET HERE?
THERE WAS A BRIGHT LIGHT, THEN...

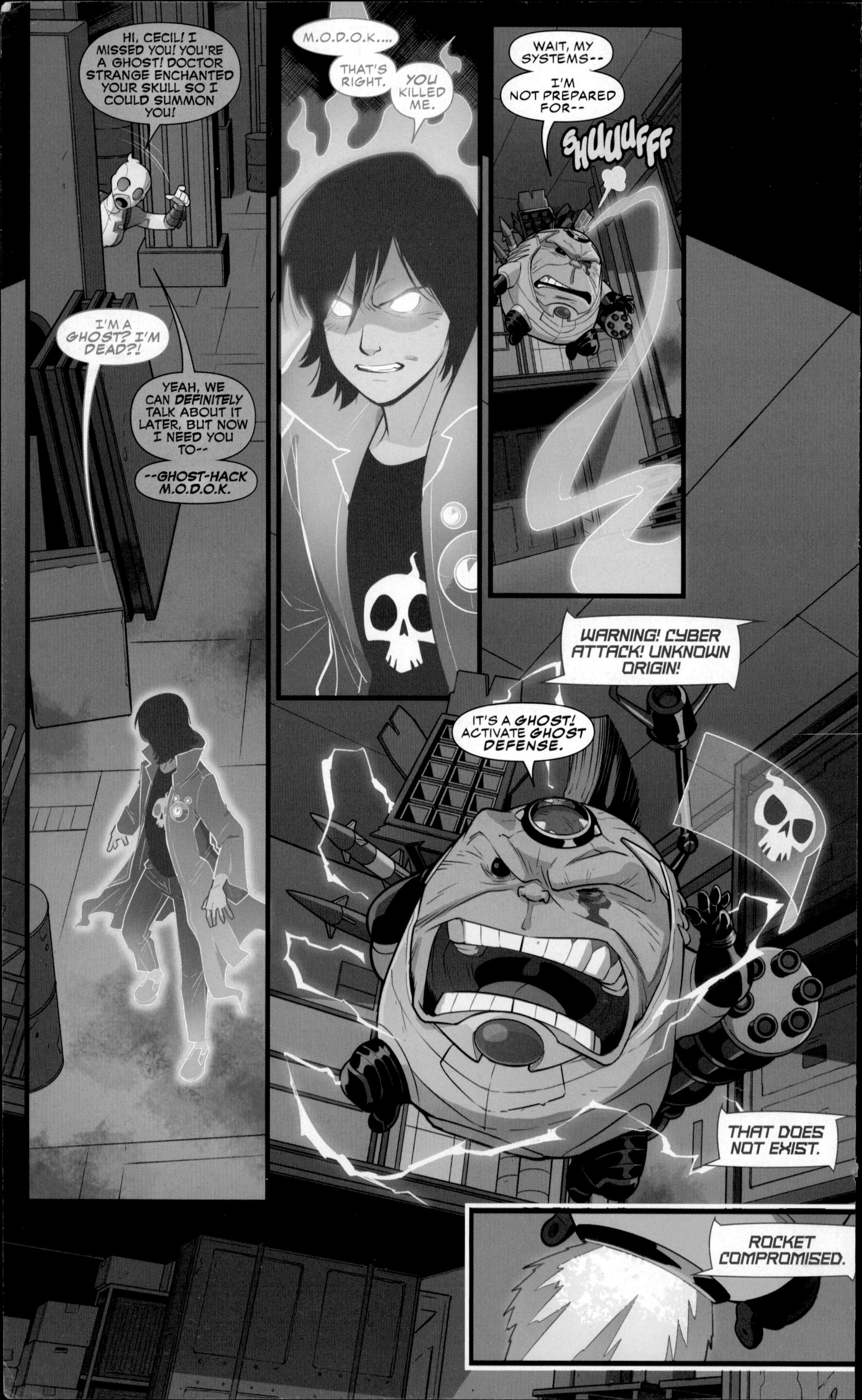
HI, CECIL! I MISSED YOU! YOU'RE A GHOST! DOCTOR STRANGE ENCHANTED YOUR SKULL SO I COULD SUMMON YOU!
I'M A GHOST? I'M DEAD?!
YEAH, WE CAN DEFINITELY TALK ABOUT IT LATER, BUT NOW I NEED YOU TO--
--GHOST-HACK M.O.D.O.K.
M.O.D.O.K....
THAT'S RIGHT.
YOU KILLED ME.
WAIT, MY SYSTEMS--
I'M NOT PREPARED FOR--
SHUUUFFF
WARNING! CYBER ATTACK! UNKNOWN ORIGIN!
IT'S A GHOST! ACTIVATE GHOST DEFENSE.
THAT DOES NOT EXIST.
ROCKET COMPROMISED.

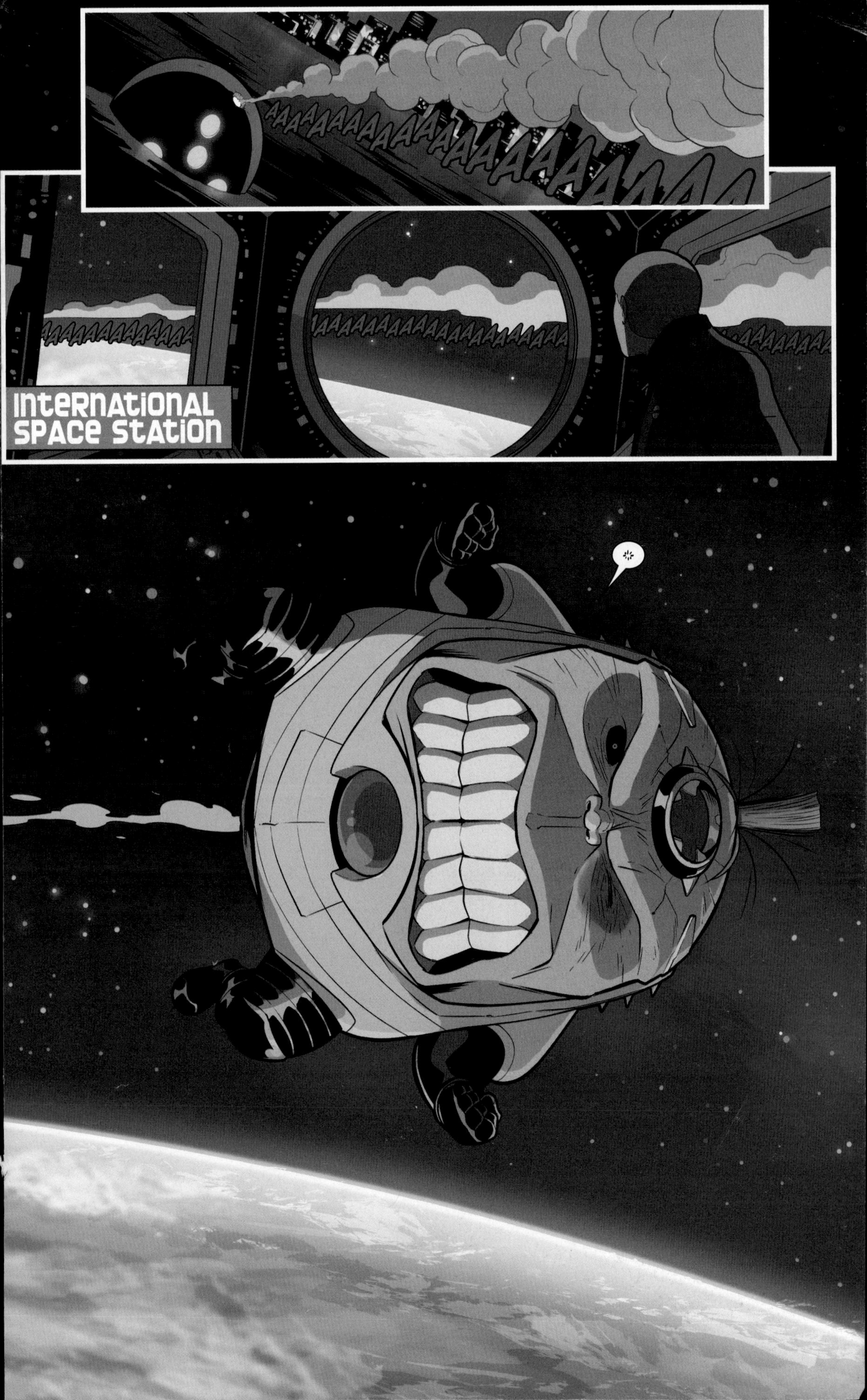
AAAAAAAAAAAAAAAAAAAAAAAA
INTERNATIONAL SPACE STATION
AAAAAAAAAAAAAA
AAAAAAAAAAAAAAAAAAAAAAA
AAAAAAAAAAA

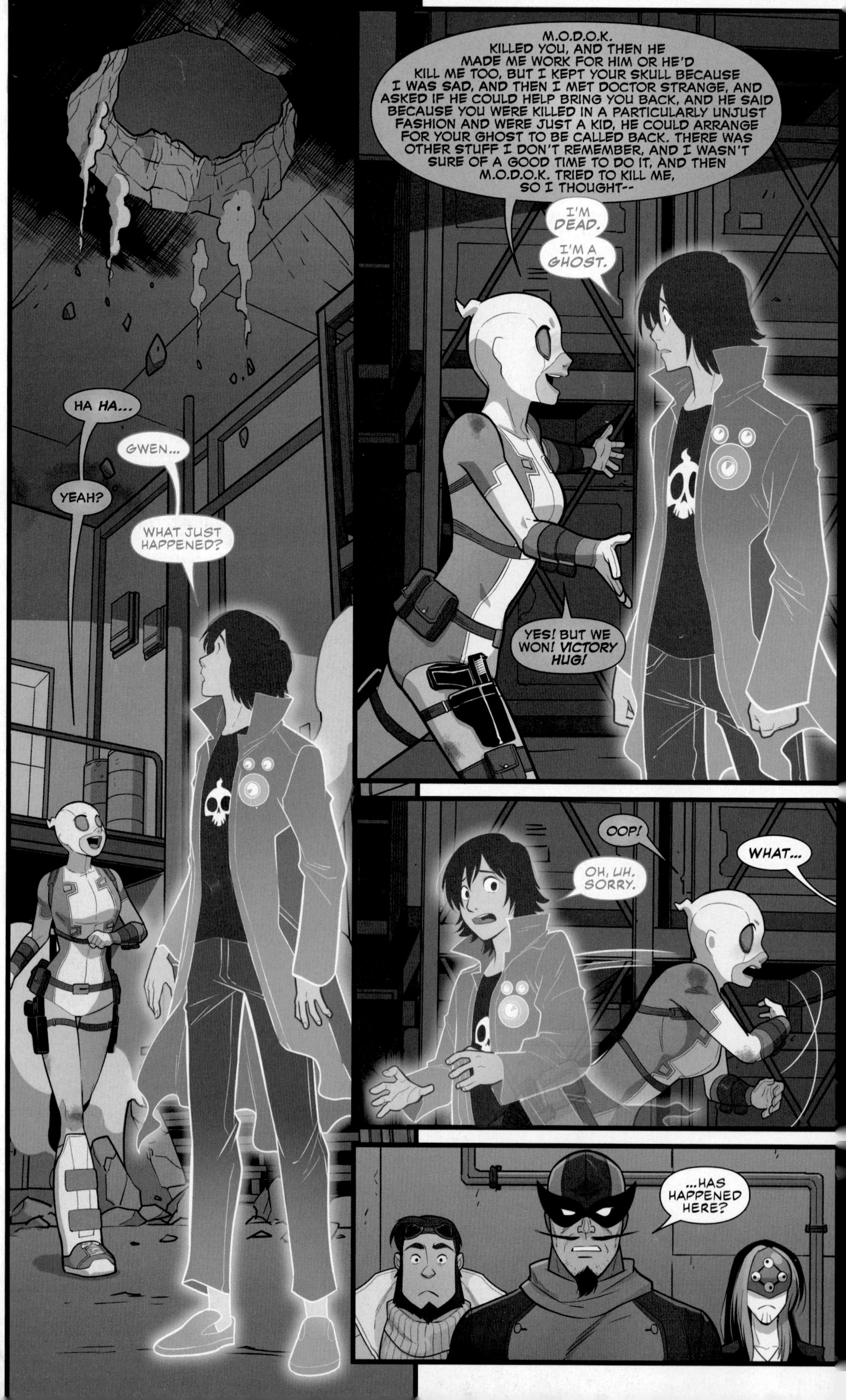
HA HA...
YEAH?
GWEN...
WHAT JUST HAPPENED?
M.O.D.O.K. KILLED YOU, AND THEN HE MADE ME WORK FOR HIM OR HE'D KILL ME TOO, BUT I KEPT YOUR SKULL BECAUSE I WAS SAD, AND THEN I MET DOCTOR STRANGE, AND ASKED IF HE COULD HELP BRING YOU BACK, AND HE SAID BECAUSE YOU WERE KILLED IN A PARTICULARLY UNJUST FASHION AND WERE JUST A KID, HE COULD ARRANGE FOR YOUR GHOST TO BE CALLED BACK. THERE WAS OTHER STUFF I DON'T REMEMBER, AND I WASN'T SURE OF A GOOD TIME TO DO IT, AND THEN M.O.D.O.K. TRIED TO KILL ME, SO I THOUGHT--
I'M DEAD.
I'M A GHOST.
YES! BUT WE WON! VICTORY HUG!
OOP!
OH, UH. SORRY.
WHAT...
...HAS HAPPENED HERE?

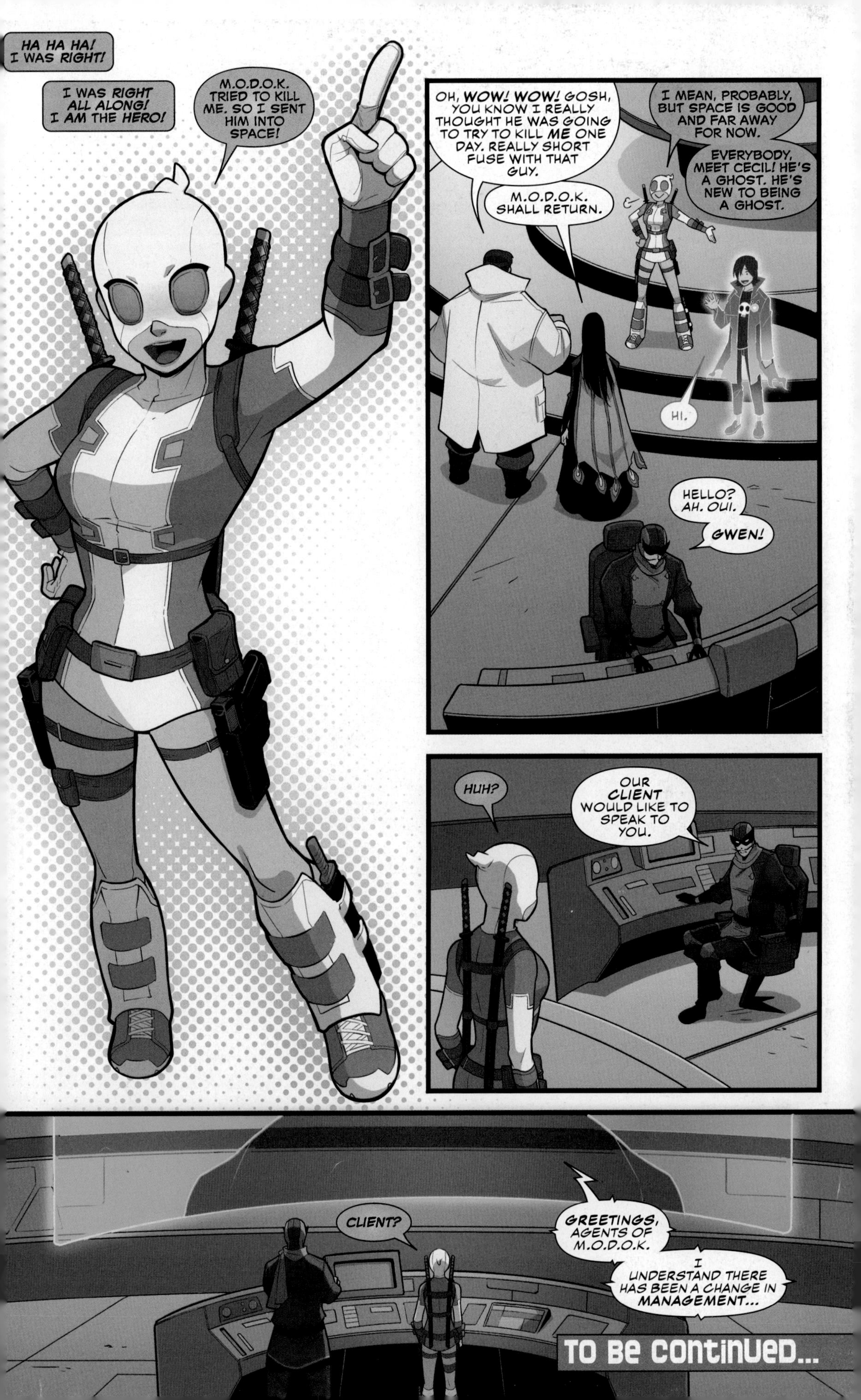
HA HA HA! I WAS RIGHT!
I WAS RIGHT ALL ALONG! I AM THE HERO!
M.O.D.O.K. TRIED TO KILL ME. SO I SENT HIM INTO SPACE!
OH, WOW! WOW! GOSH, YOU KNOW I REALLY THOUGHT HE WAS GOING TO TRY TO KILL ME ONE DAY. REALLY SHORT FUSE WITH THAT GUY.
M.O.D.O.K. SHALL RETURN.
I MEAN, PROBABLY, BUT SPACE IS GOOD AND FAR AWAY FOR NOW.
EVERYBODY, MEET CECIL! HE'S A GHOST. HE'S NEW TO BEING A GHOST.
HI.
HELLO? AH. OUI.
GWEN!
HUH?
OUR CLIENT WOULD LIKE TO SPEAK TO YOU.
CLIENT?
GREETINGS, AGENTS OF M.O.D.O.K.
I UNDERSTAND THERE HAS BEEN A CHANGE IN MANAGEMENT...
TO BE CONTINUED...

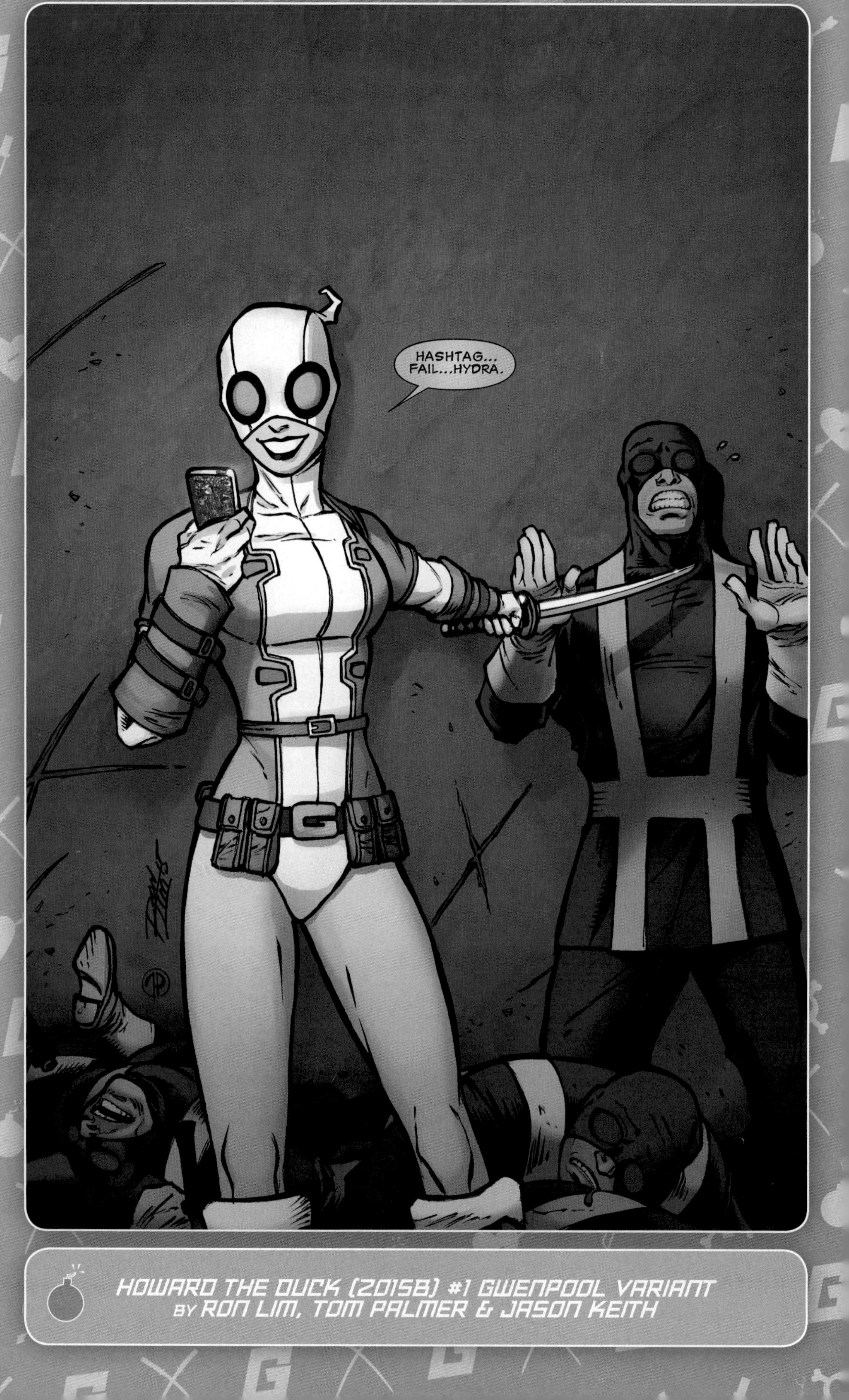
HASHTAG...
FAIL...HYDRA.

HOWARD THE DUCK (2015B) #1 GWENPOOL VARIANT
BY RON LIM, TOM PALMER & JASON KEITH

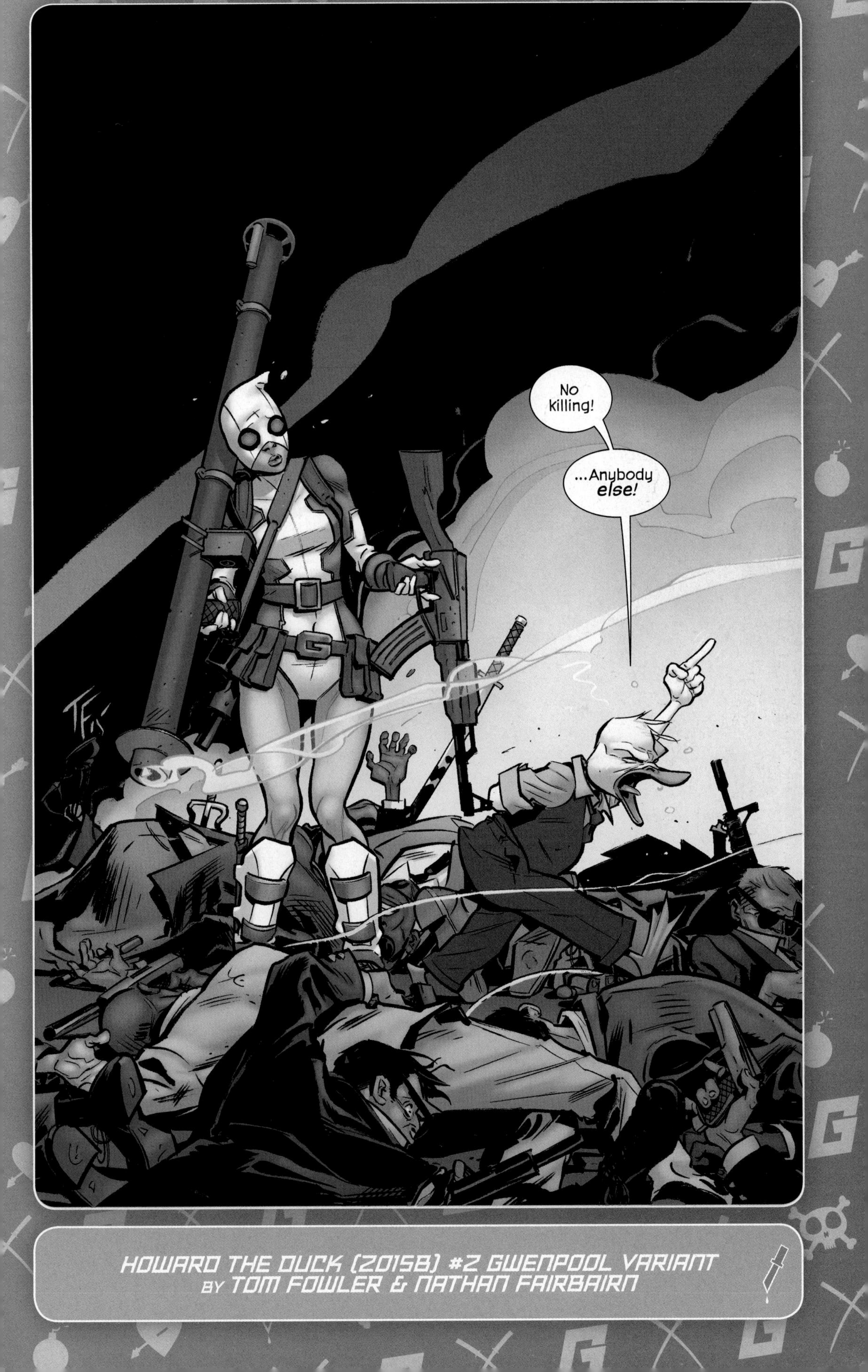

No killing!
...Anybody else!


HOWARD THE DUCK (2015B) #2 GWENPOOL VARIANT
BY TOM FOWLER & NATHAN FAIRBAIRN

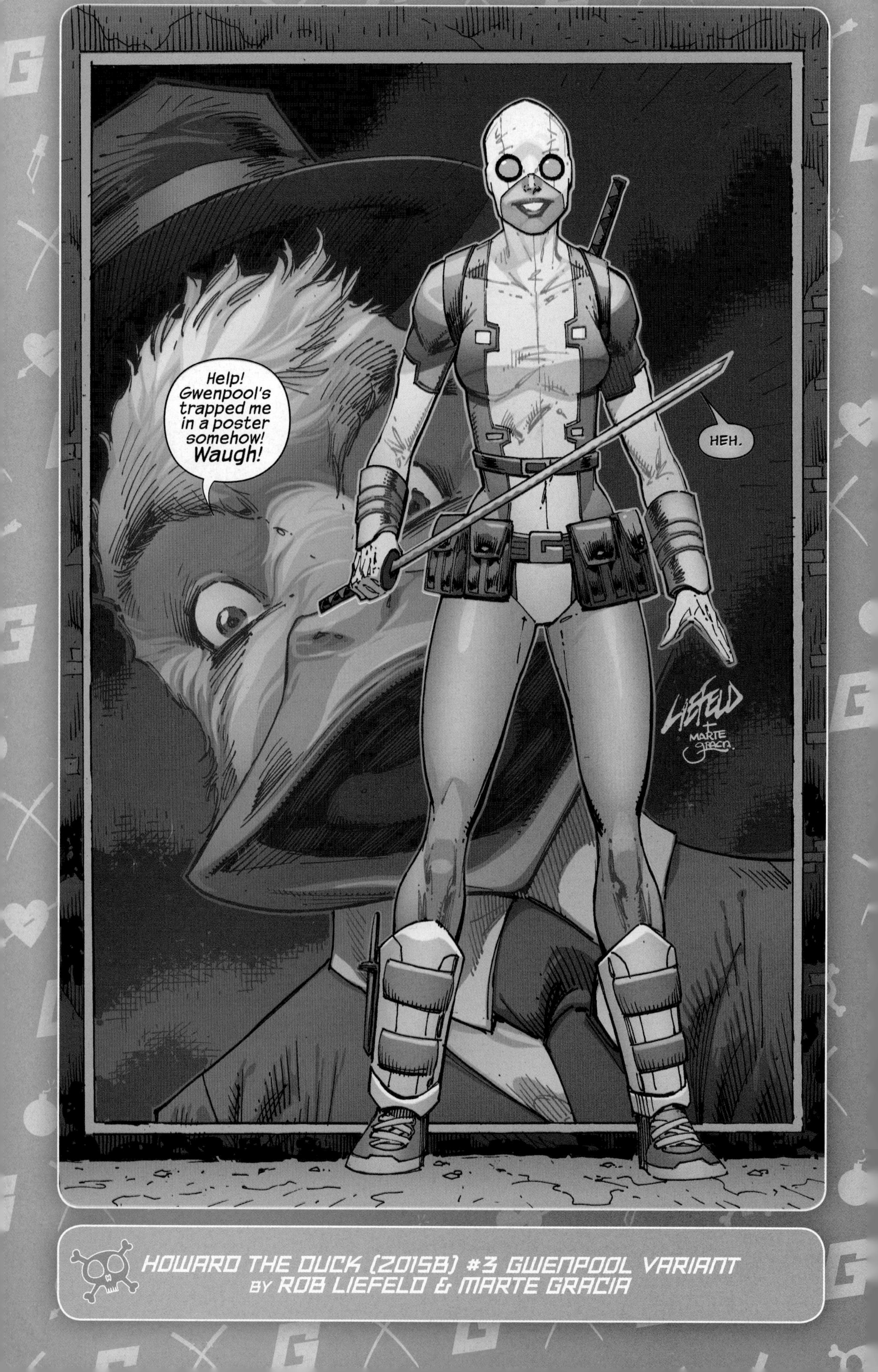
Help! Gwenpool's trapped me in a poster somehow! Waugh!
HEH.

HOWARD THE DUCK (2015B) #3 GWENPOOL VARIANT
BY ROB LIEFELD & MARTE GRACIA

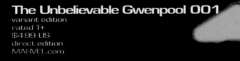

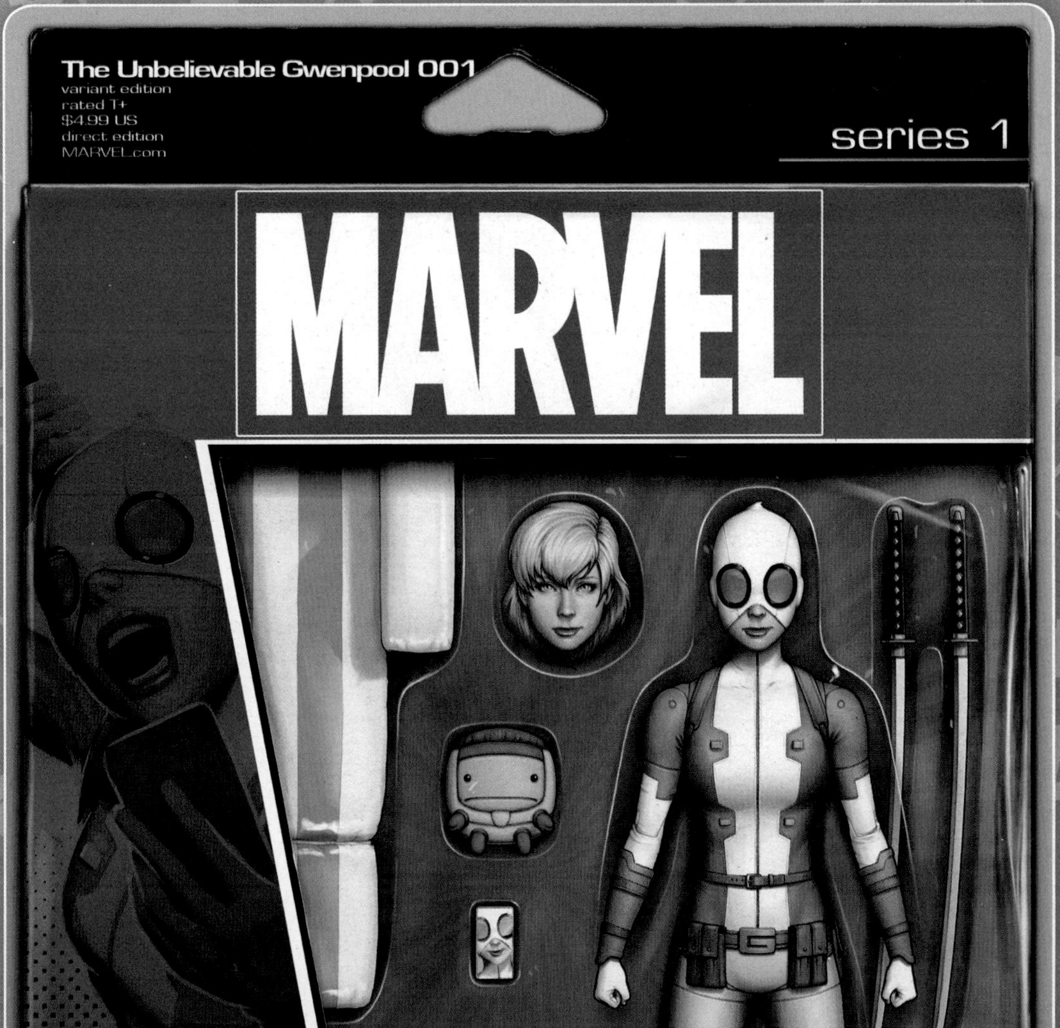

The Unbelievable Gwenpool 001
variant edition
rated T+
$4.99 US
direct edition
MARVEL.com
series 1
MARVEL
THE UNBELIEVABLE
GWENPOOL
GWENPOOL
no, seriously, i'm unbelievable

THE UNBELIEVABLE GWENPOOL #1 ACTION FIGURE VARIANT
BY JOHN TYLER CHRISTOPER

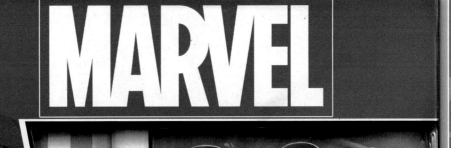

THE UNBELIEVABLE GWENPOOL #1 VARIANT
BY FRANCISCO HERRERA & FERNANDA RIZO

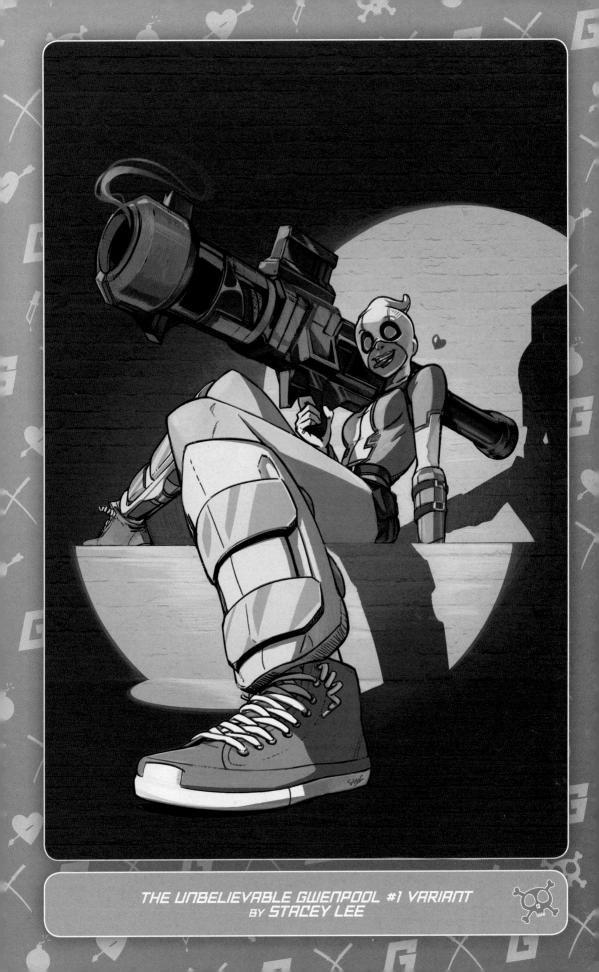

THE UNBELIEVABLE GWENPOOL #1 VARIANT
BY STACEY LEE

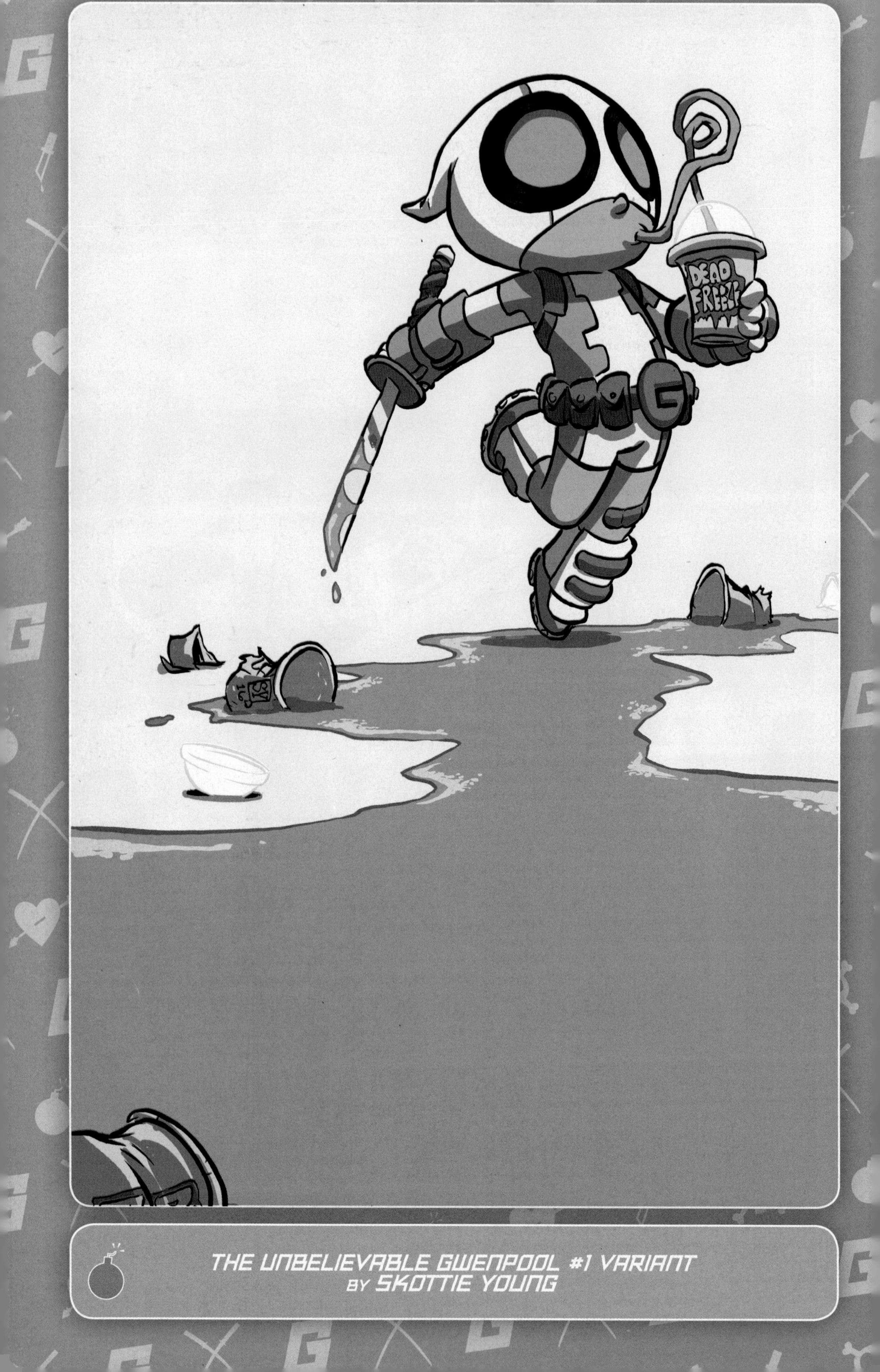
DEAD FREEZE

THE UNBELIEVABLE GWENPOOL #1 VARIANT
BY SKOTTIE YOUNG

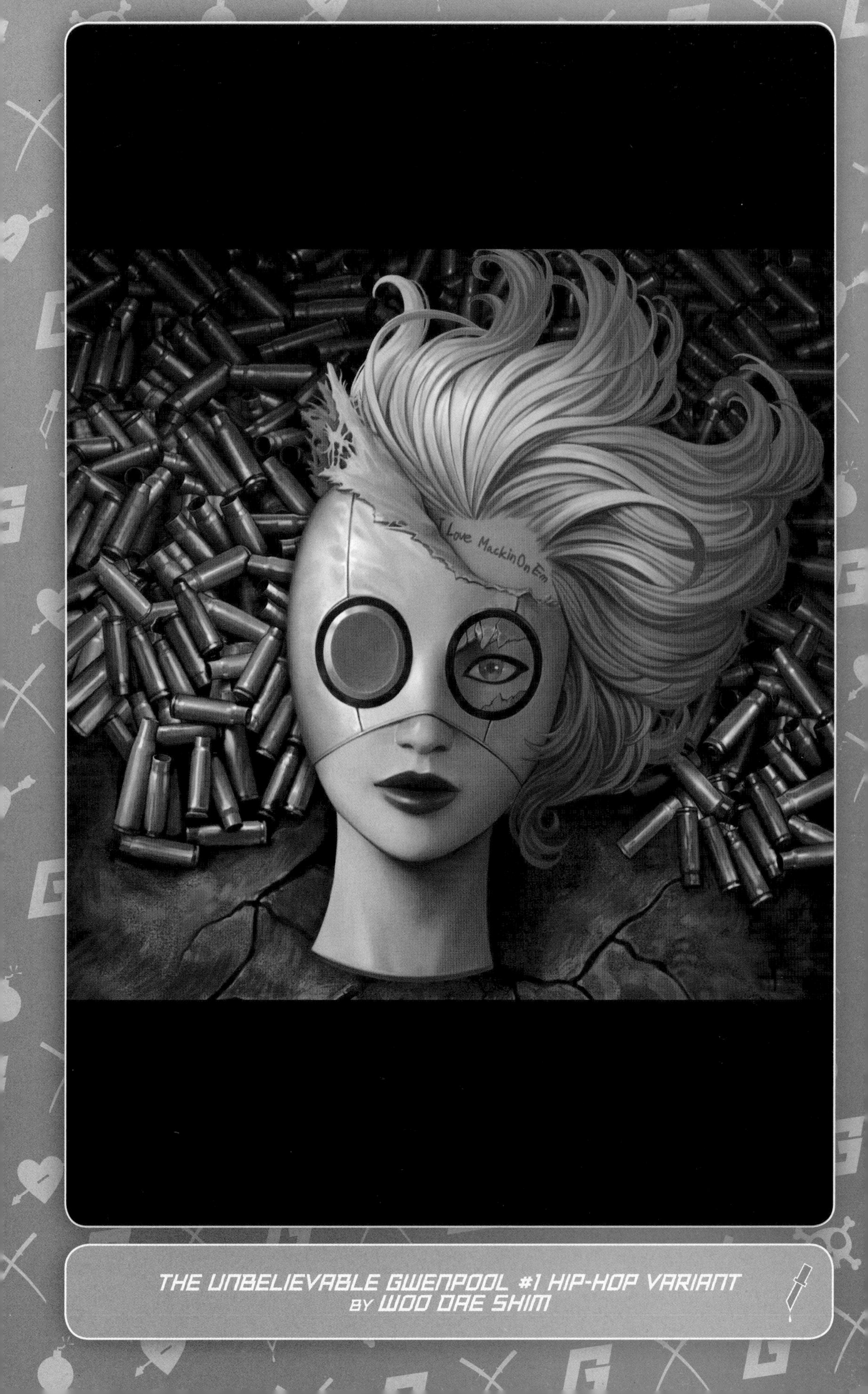
I Love MackinOnEm

THE UNBELIEVABLE GWENPOOL #1 HIP-HOP VARIANT
BY WOO DAE SHIM

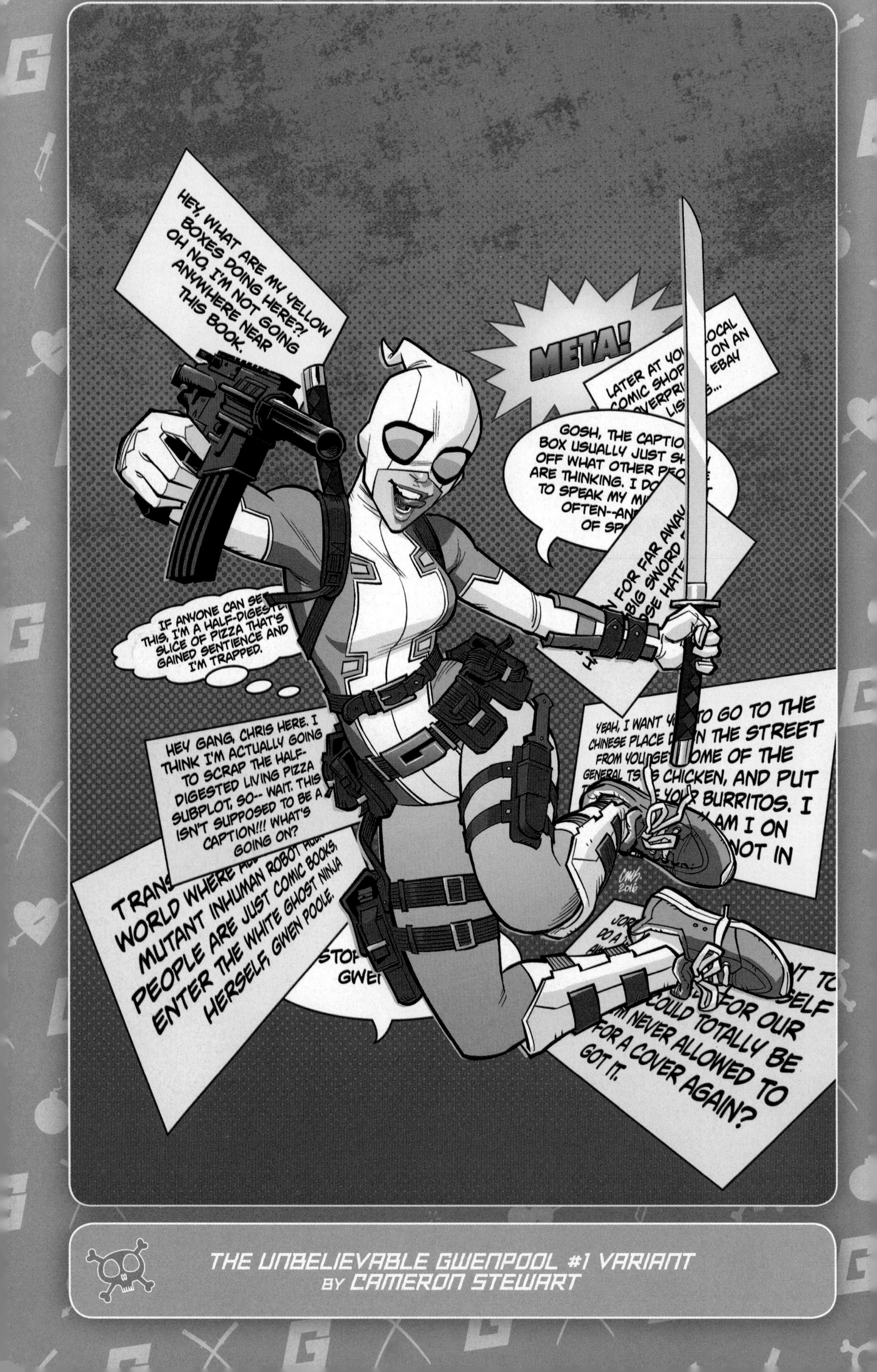
HEY, WHAT ARE MY YELLOW BOXES DOING HERE?! OH NO, I'M NOT GOING ANYWHERE NEAR THIS BOOK.
META!
LATER AT YO... COMIC SHOP... ON AN ... EBAY
GOSH, THE CAPTIO... BOX USUALLY JUST S... OFF WHAT OTHER PEO... ARE THINKING.
... FOR FAR AWAY ... BIG SWORD ...
IF ANYONE CAN SE... THIS, I'M A HALF-DIGESTE... SLICE OF PIZZA THAT'S GAINED SENTIENCE AND I'M TRAPPED.
HEY GANG, CHRIS HERE. I THINK I'M ACTUALLY GOING TO SCRAP THE HALF-DIGESTED LIVING PIZZA SUBPLOT, SO-- WAIT. THIS ISN'T SUPPOSED TO BE A CAPTION!!! WHAT'S GOING ON?
YEAH, I WANT ... TO GO TO THE CHINESE PLACE ... THE STREET FROM YOU... GENERAL TS... CHICKEN, AND PUT ... YOUR BURRITOS. I ... AM I ON ... NOT IN
TRANS... WORLD WHERE ... MUTANT INHUMAN ROBOT ... PEOPLE ARE JUST COMIC BOOKS. ENTER THE WHITE GHOST NINJA HERSELF, GWEN POOLE.
STOP ... GWEN
... FOR OUR ... COULD TOTALLY BE ... NEVER ALLOWED TO ... FOR A COVER AGAIN? GOT IT.

*THE UNBELIEVABLE GWENPOOL #1 VARIANT*
*BY CAMERON STEWART*

THE UNBELIEVABLE GWENPOOL #2 HIP-HOP VARIANT
BY REILLY BROWN & JIM CHARALAMPIDIS

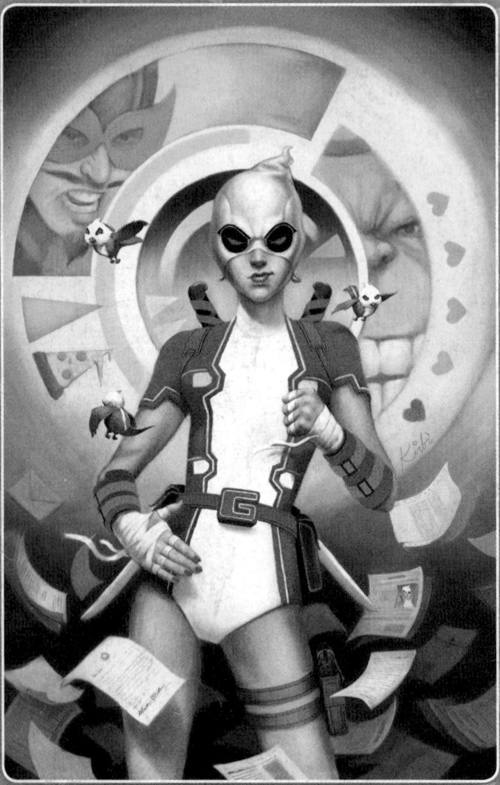

THE UNBELIEVABLE GWENPOOL #3
VARIANT BY KIRBI FAGAN

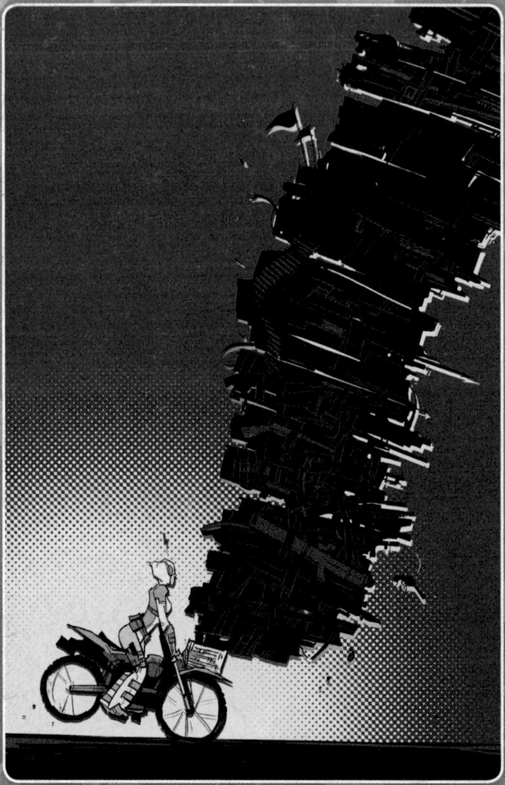

THE UNBELIEVABLE GWENPOOL #4
VARIANT BY ANNIE WU

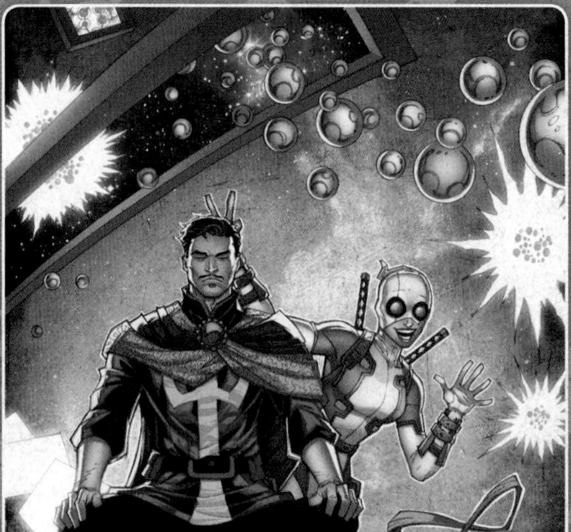

THE UNBELIEVABLE GWENPOOL #4
VARIANT BY RON LIM & ISRAEL SILVA

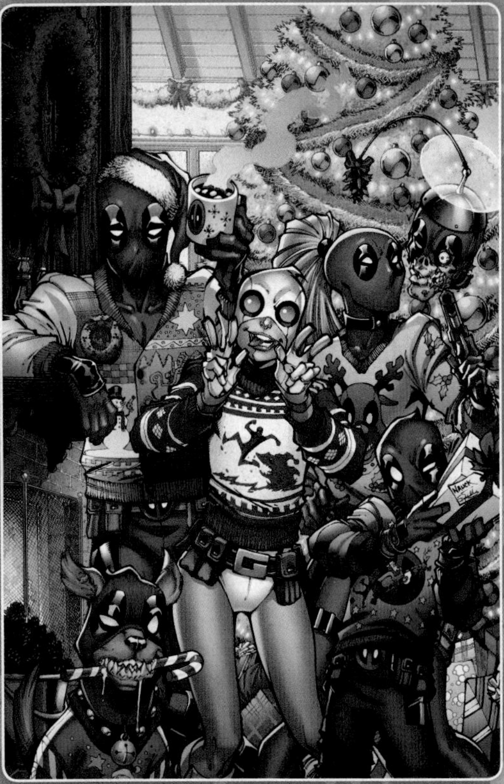

*GWENPOOL SPECIAL #1 VARIANT*
*BY TODD NAUCK*
*& RACHELLE ROSENBERG*

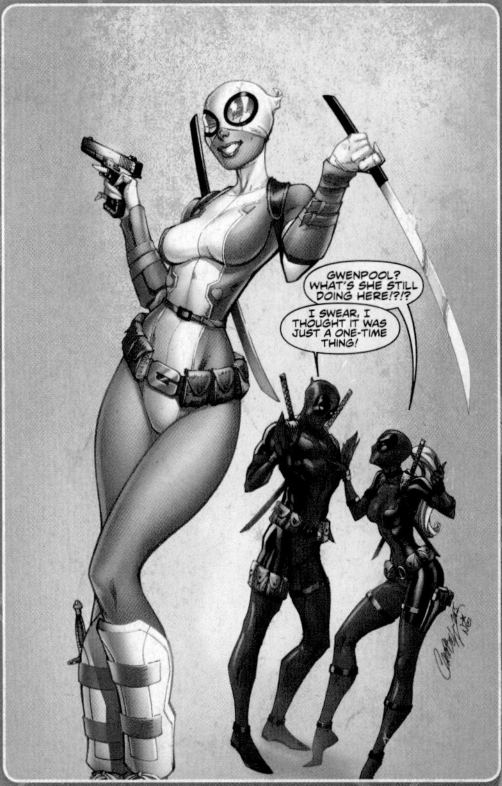
GWENPOOL? WHAT'S SHE STILL DOING HERE!?!?
I SWEAR, I THOUGHT IT WAS JUST A ONE-TIME THING!

*GWENPOOL SPECIAL #1 VARIANT*
*BY J. SCOTT CAMPBELL*
*& NEI RUFFINO*

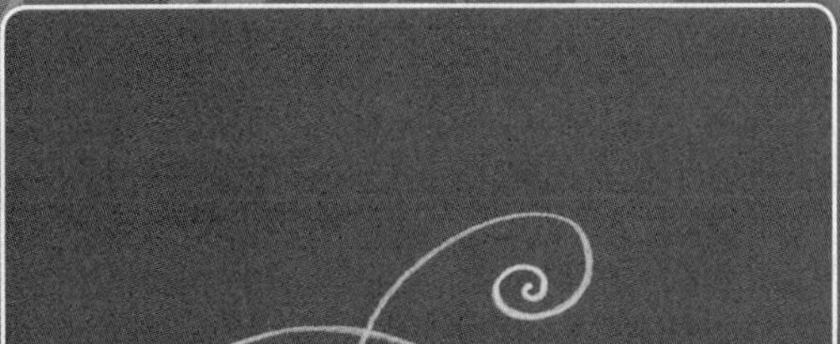

*GWENPOOL SPECIAL #1 VARIANT*
*BY PASQUAL FERRY*
*& DAVE McCAIG*

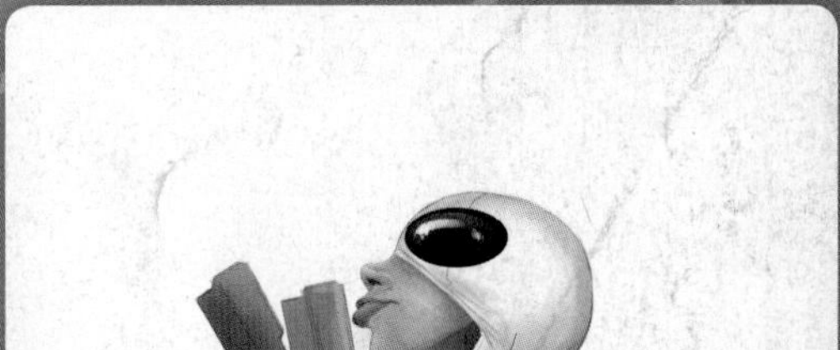

*GWENPOOL SPECIAL #1 VARIANT*
*BY ROBBI RODRIGUEZ*

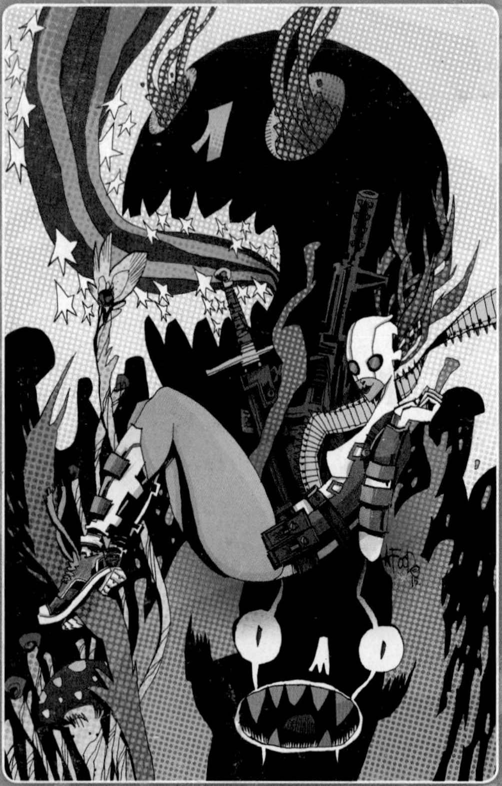

GWENPOOL SPECIAL #1 VARIANT
BY JIM MAHFOOD

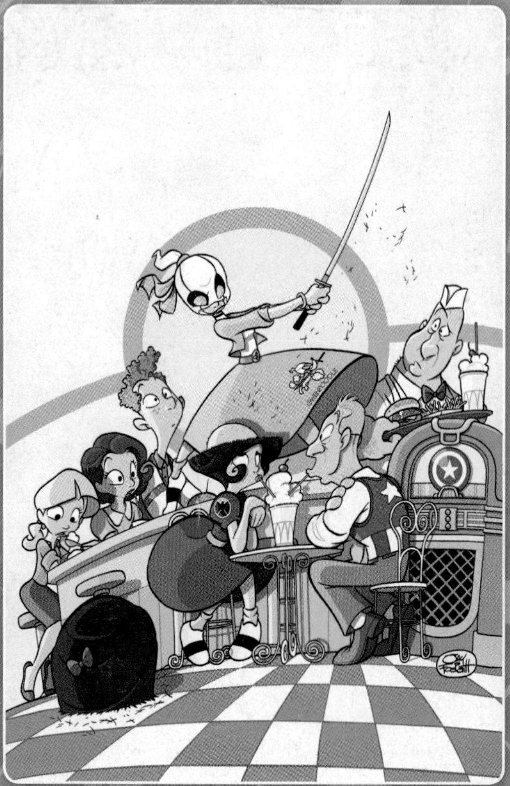

AVENGERS STANDOFF: ASSAULT ON PLEASANT HILL ALPHA #1 GWENPOOL PARTY VARIANT
BY JAY FOSGITT

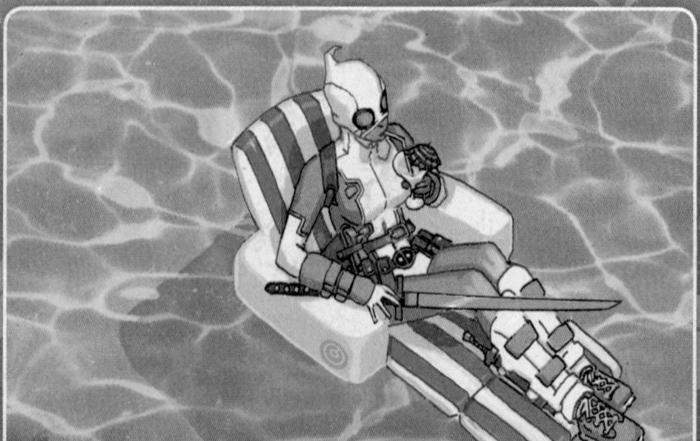

DEADPOOL'S SECRET SECRET WARS #2 GWENPOOL VARIANT
BY CHRIS BACHALO

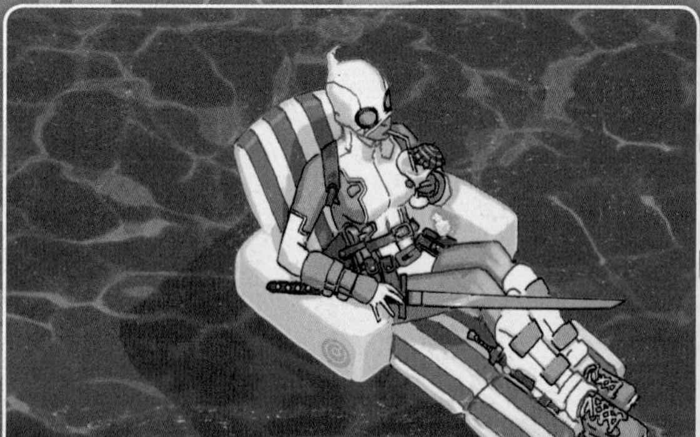

THE UNBELIEVABLE GWENPOOL #0 VARIANT
BY CHRIS BACHALO